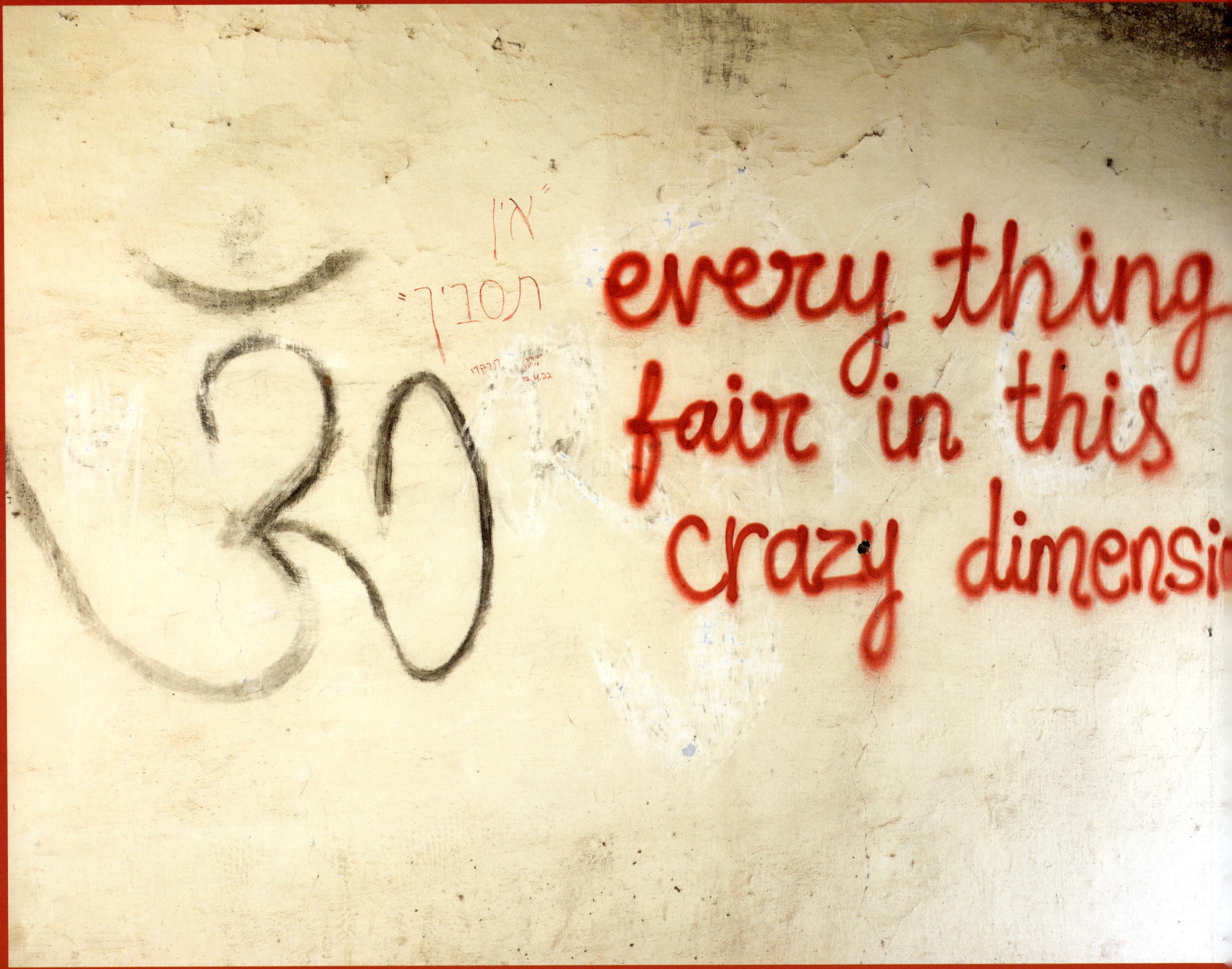

every thing
fair in this
crazy dimensi

"אין"
"חסר"
הרקדו
17.4.22

DAVID ZURICK

HIPPIE INDIA

DREAMERS AND SEEKERS IN THE LAND OF NIRVANA

FOREWORD BY PICO IYER

goff
BOOKS

PREFATORY NOTE

It was 1975. I was sitting in a back-alley café in Istanbul on my way to India, drinking a cup of strong Turkish coffee and reading a book, when a disheveled-looking couple entered the building and took seats at a nearby table. They showed me a stapled typescript with a pale blue cardboard cover, a guide to help travelers navigate the journey from Europe to Australia. The 94-page pamphlet was entitled "Across Asia on the Cheap."

It was the first volume in what was to become the eponymous *Lonely Planet* guidebook series. At the time, a growing number of young westerners were traveling to Asia in search of adventure and life experiences. I was one of them. Not a few of us were also engaged in a spiritual inquiry. We followed a circuitous route that led from Amsterdam to Kathmandu. Over time, the overland journey became known as the Hippie Trail. It was as much a way of being as a traveler's path across Asia.

Prominent among its stopovers were a handful of destinations in India—Pushkar in the Thar Desert, the Hampi ruins, Rishikesh on the banks of the Ganges, Goa on the Arabian Sea coast, and the Parvati Valley located in the Himalayan mountains. Fifty years on and these places continue to attract counterculture visitors from around the world. While the old Hippie Trail across Iran and Afghanistan no longer exists, having succumbed to war and revolution, the kind of traveling it fostered back in the 1970s continues to inspire young sojourners in India today.

But that's not the whole story. Several generations of Indians have grown up in these places since they first appeared on the Hippie Trail, and just as travelers from the West have absorbed experiences and material culture, even wisdom, from their Indian hosts, so, too, have many of the local residents learned a thing or two from their hippie guests. An intermingling has occurred, in which ideas and lifeways are exchanged as freely as costumes, music, and hairstyles. People's lives are transformed on both sides of the cultural divide, places change, and the gap between East and West is narrowed.

These remarkable settings and the free-spirited people who visit or reside in them—Westerners and Indians, alike—are the subjects of this book.

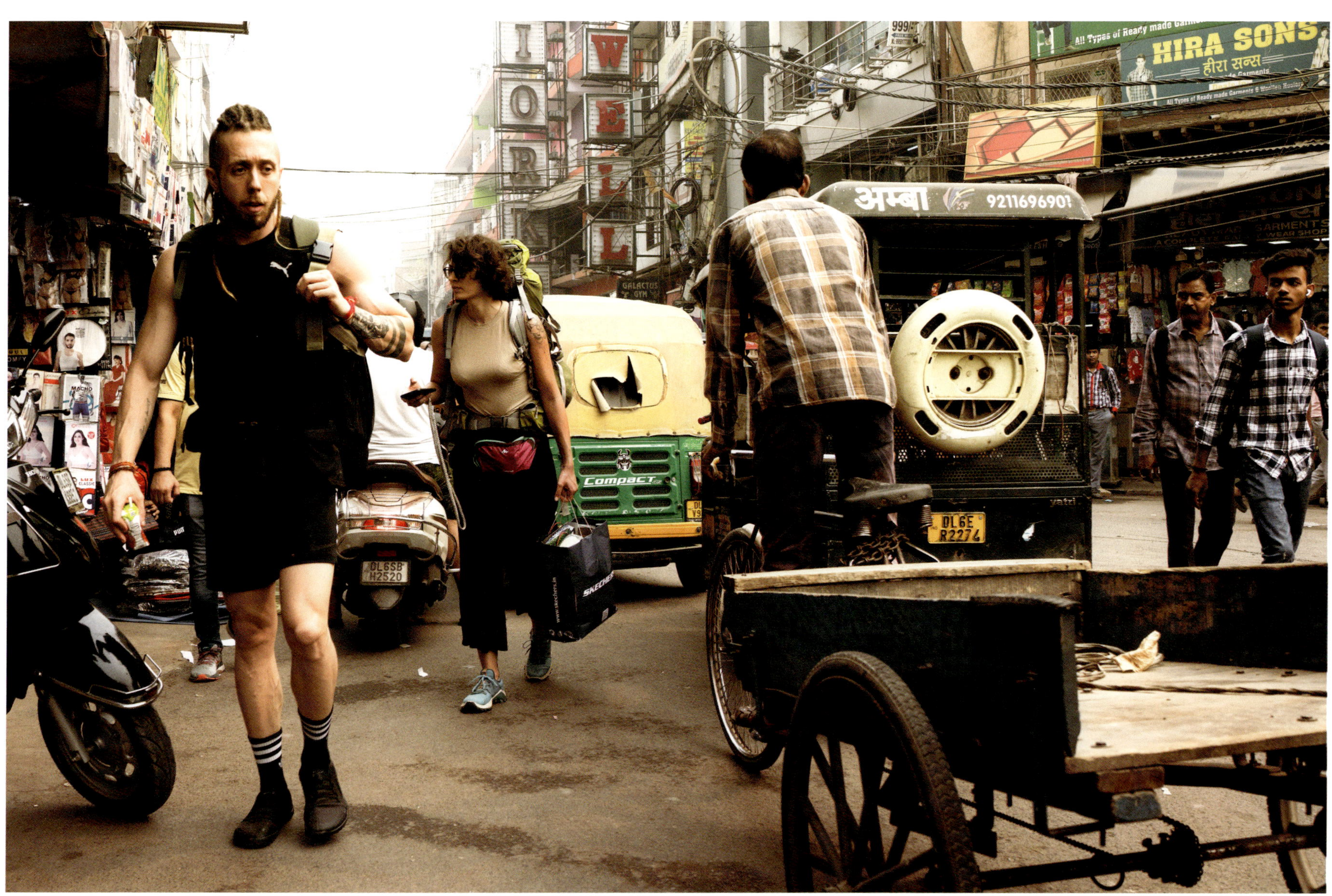

HIRA SONS
हीरा सन्स
अम्बा 9211696901
CompacT
DL6SB
H2520
DL6E
R2274
GALACTUS
GYM

O you temples fairer than lilies, pour'd over by the rising sun!
O you fables, spurning the known, eluding the hold of the unknown,
mounting to heaven!

—Walt Whitman, from A Passage to India

CONTENTS

THE LONG STRANGE TRIP

BY PICO IYER

One of the few regrets I have in life, as I pass through my sixties, is that I was born just a few years too late to partake of the transformative revolutions of the Summer of Love as it first spread across the world. The Magic Bus, the Pudding Shop in Istanbul, Chicken Street in Afghanistan: I inhaled such names, passed down in an oral tradition everywhere from Santa Cruz to Lhasa, and felt like someone sorting through the broken bottles and debris of a global party on the morning after.

But the beauty of the Hippie Trail, as suggested by David Zurick's fond and aromatic photographs, is that its legacy lives on, and not just in the older folks among us, but in all the places that it made new and old. Anyone who has savored chai in the backstreets of Varanasi, or sat on a rooftop in Manali discussing Herman Hesse, anyone who has made her way to one of the ashrams still encircling Rishikesh or been handed down his father's (or grandfather's) Grateful Dead tie-dyed t-shirt, originally swapped for a transistor radio in a truck somewhere along the Khyber Pass, knows that the truest things never die.

By the time I made it to Pushkar, in 1985, the fumes around the tribal scene were not so different from the ones recorded here; McDonald's and gleaming shopping malls may have come to India, but anyone who arrives there tomorrow will find the same intensity, warmth, overwhelming explosion of color and mystery, and chatter that her great-aunt saw in 1975. Indeed, even someone who has never left Santa Monica or Frankfurt may realize, as she heads from her yoga studio to the local Tibetan restaurant and then relaxes over that new translation of Rumi, that the '60s weren't just a flash of lightning, but really threw open the doors to a constant cultural and spiritual traffic between East and West that continues, often deepens, to this day.

I write this in a Californian small town filled with dharma centers and Ayurveda clinics, where blonde young women are as often as not called Ananda and Maya; my editors at *Time* magazine knew all about karma and Nirvana long before they put yoga on their cover. The Hippie Trail marked the planetary explosion of a revolution that changed the assumptions of us all, from Bondi Beach to Oslo; my cousins in India started thinking that maybe Big Sur or Woodstock were places worthy of a pilgrimage, even as others of us made the trek to Hampi and Kasol.

The images in this book speak for traditions now as entrenched as many of the nomad circuits and festival gatherings of old: I run into Tony and Maureen Wheeler on many continents and the books they initiated remain my Bibles everywhere from Antarctica to Zanzibar; the barter economy that came to light among harem pants and Kashmiri scarves is now a universal reality as people share apartments, couches, rides. In truth, as is mentioned in the text, *sadhus* and travelers along the gypsy trail so merge in their ashes and dreadlocks that often it becomes impossible to separate East from West.

The first time I made it to Goa was 2018, fifty years after the Summer of Love, but as my Japanese wife and I sought out her yoga teacher from Dharamsala near Arambol Beach, we came across women from Scandinavia doing sun salutations on the sand while an almost-naked Frenchman was standing on his head. One earnest soul was seated cross-legged on the beach, deep in a worn copy of *Siddhartha*, and a young woman was pushing a pram past the Forgotten Land Café (with The Last Monk store next door).

To make the trip from Hippie Island to the Chill-Out Café with David Zurick, to encounter travelers from Kathmandu and Russia (a long way from the oligarchs who fill Goa's five-star hotels at Christmas), is not just to awaken memories, but to see how we live right now. The Beatles Ashram may be peeling, but it's a magnet for every new generation of seekers. Places with their origins in ancient Indian mythology are home these days to a more recent kind of myth-making that mingles New Age trends with old-soul truths. Jimi Hendrix gazes right at you in the Buddha Café. It's hard not to feel that this book is an evocative record of our future as much as of a savory, and powerfully enduring, past.

Pico Iyer is the author of 16 books, translated into 23 languages, including *Video Night in Kathmandu*, *The Open Road*, *The Art of Stillness* and, most recently, *The Half Known Life*.

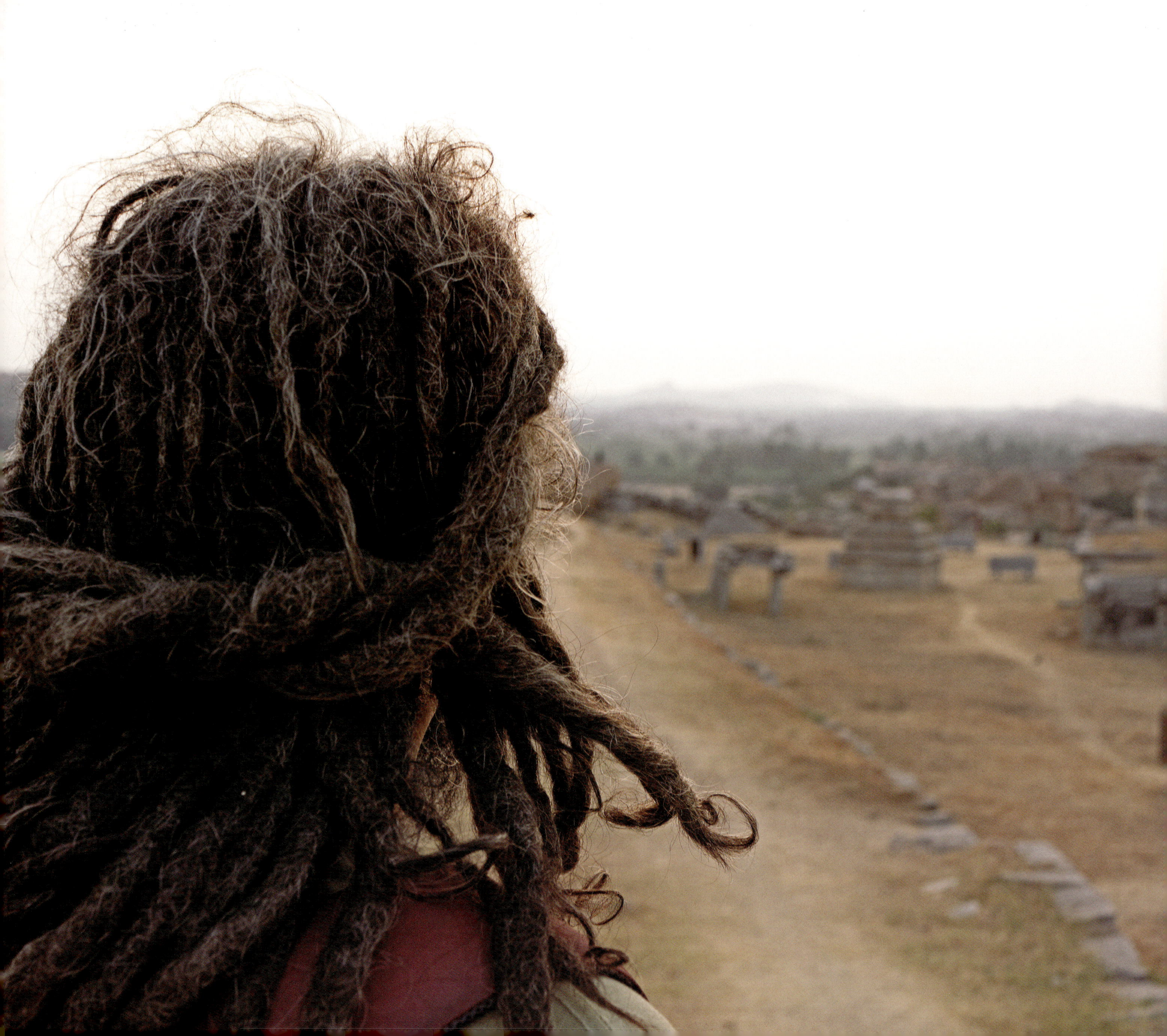

HAMPI

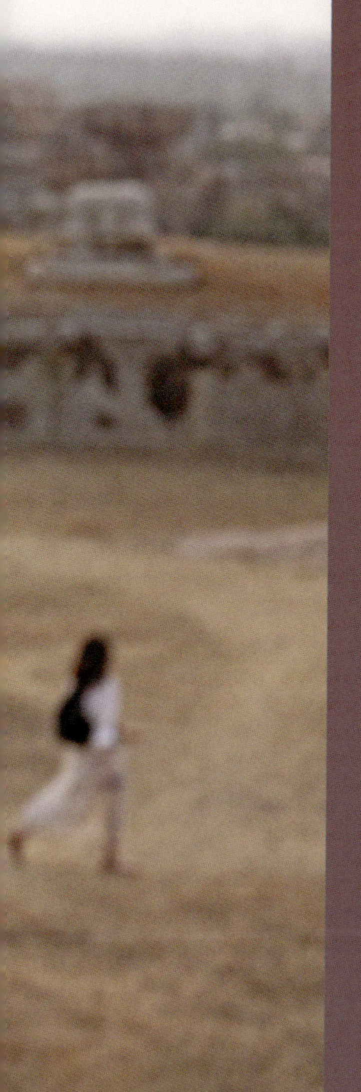

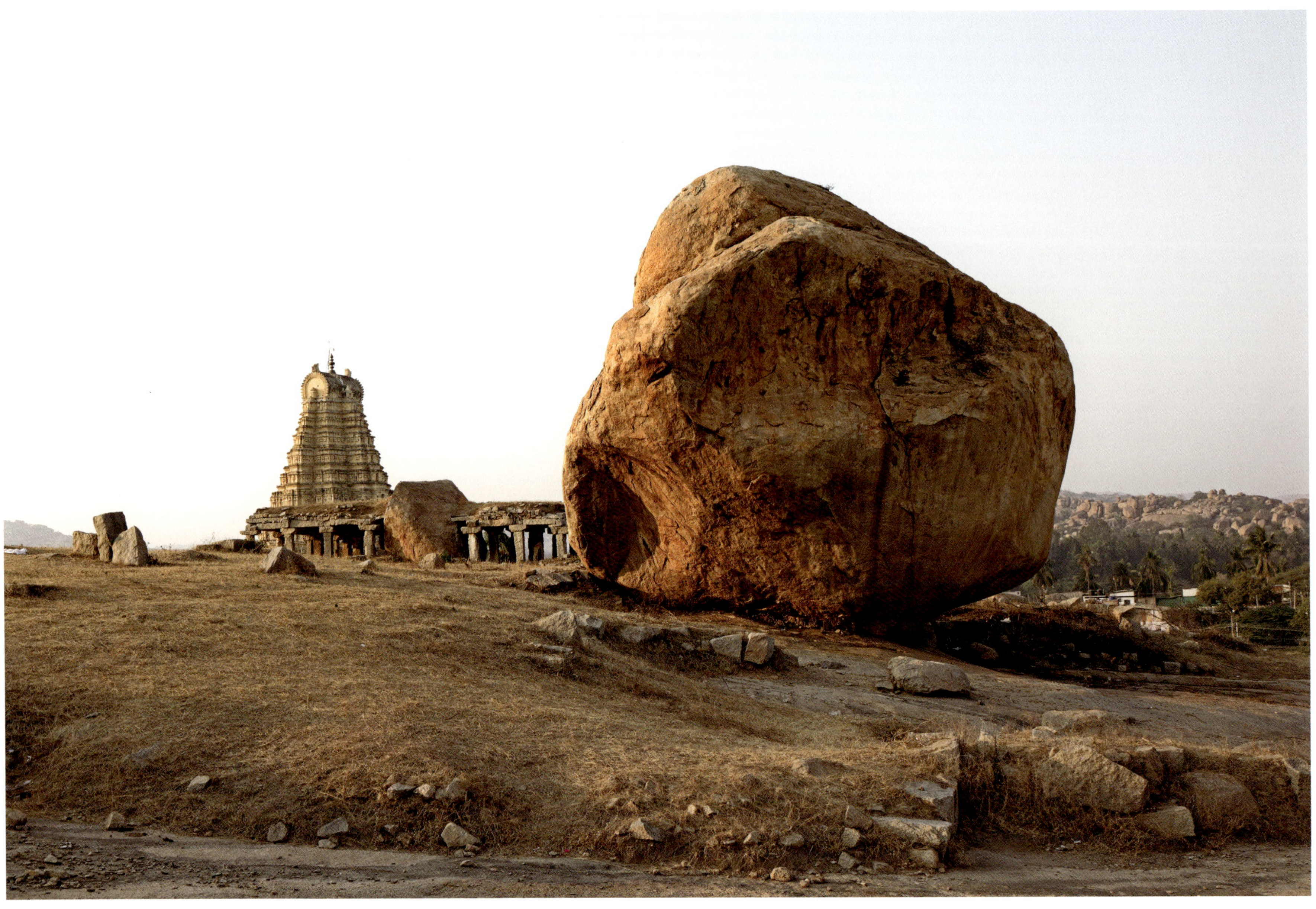

I'd known about Hampi for decades. It's been on the India hippie circuit since the early 1970s. But for one reason or another, I never had a chance to visit until recently.

I found out that it's not an easy place to reach. There is no nearby airport, and no direct trains either. An overnight bus plies the bad roads from Goa or Bangalore, but I was told not to expect to get any sleep on it. The bus went only as far as the district town of Hospet, so from there I had to arrange a local country bus or a rickshaw to take me the rest of the way.

The landscape took on a surreal feel when I got close to Hampi. The terrain began to roll in long seismic waves capped by rocky ledges. Slow-moving streams appeared in the valleys. Huge, rust-colored boulders sat like billiard balls on the ridges above the rice paddies and palm groves. How had they gotten there? The enormous rocks looked ready to fall from their perches in the slightest breeze. The air was clear of pollution and dust. The sky was robin's-egg blue.

Hampi's most arresting features, though, were its ruins. Over sixteen hundred ancient monuments lay scattered across the landscape: carved chariots, deity statues, elephant stables, foundations, religious platforms, audience halls, markets, public baths, Hindu and Jain temples, and mosques. Many date back millennia to when Hampi was an important religious site and the seat of royalty. Others are remnants of the Vijayanagar Empire, India's great 14th-century civilization. Taken together, the architectural ruins denote the spatial boundaries of one of the world's earliest city-states.

The glory days of Hampi ended abruptly in the mid-16th century when it was pillaged, looted, and burned by Muslim invaders from the north. Its infrastructure was destroyed and rulers beheaded. Commoners fled. The intruders didn't stay long and in due course Hampi was abandoned. Overgrown by the encroaching tropical forest, the site was forgotten and ignored until the mid-19th century when British archaeologists began documenting the ruins.

In 1986, Hampi was declared a UNESCO world heritage site. By that time, it was well-known in the hippie travel circles, not only because of its majestic history and the beauty and tranquility of its landscape, but also for the easy and gracious manner in which local people accepted their nonconformist visitors from the western world.

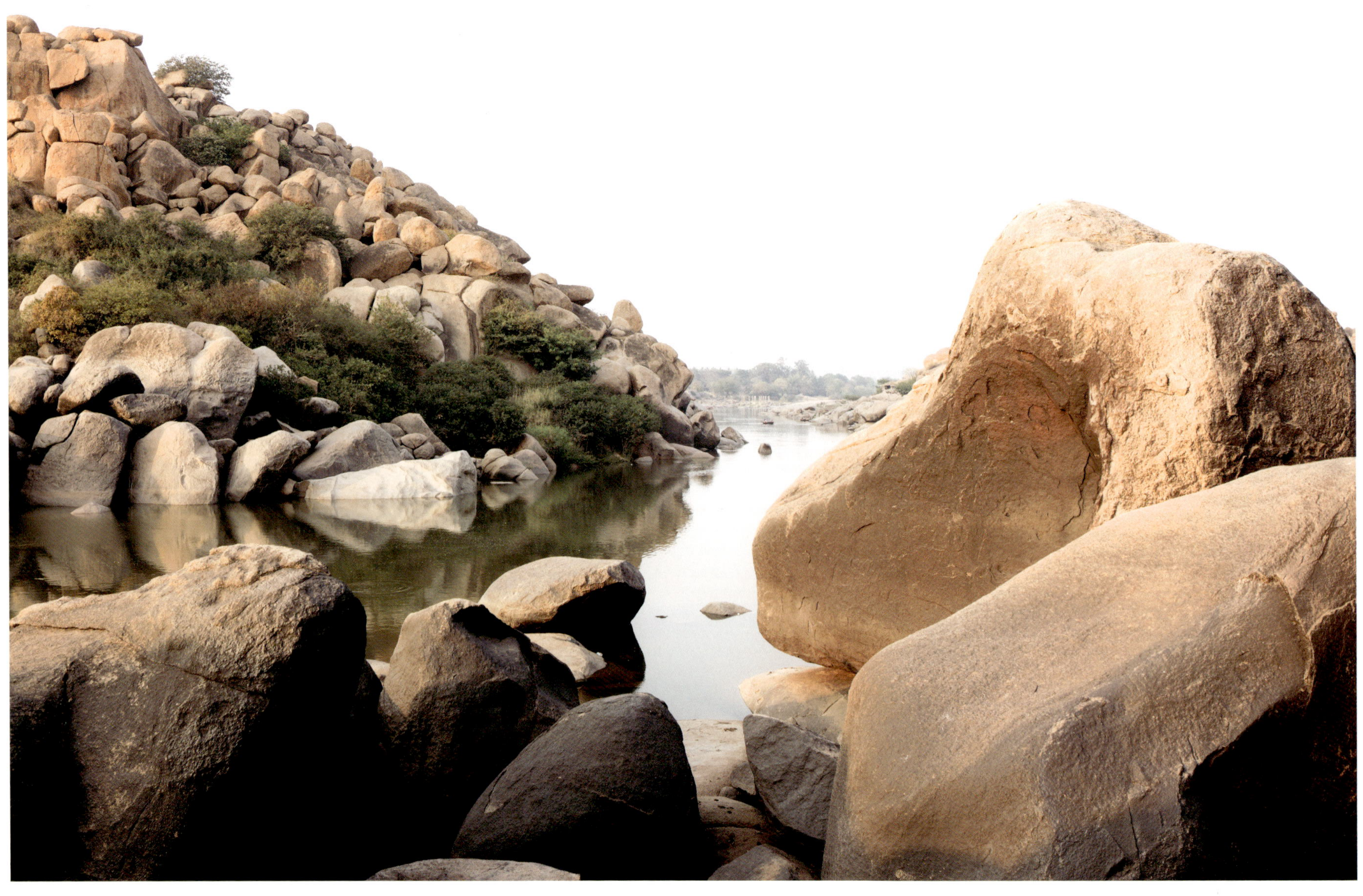

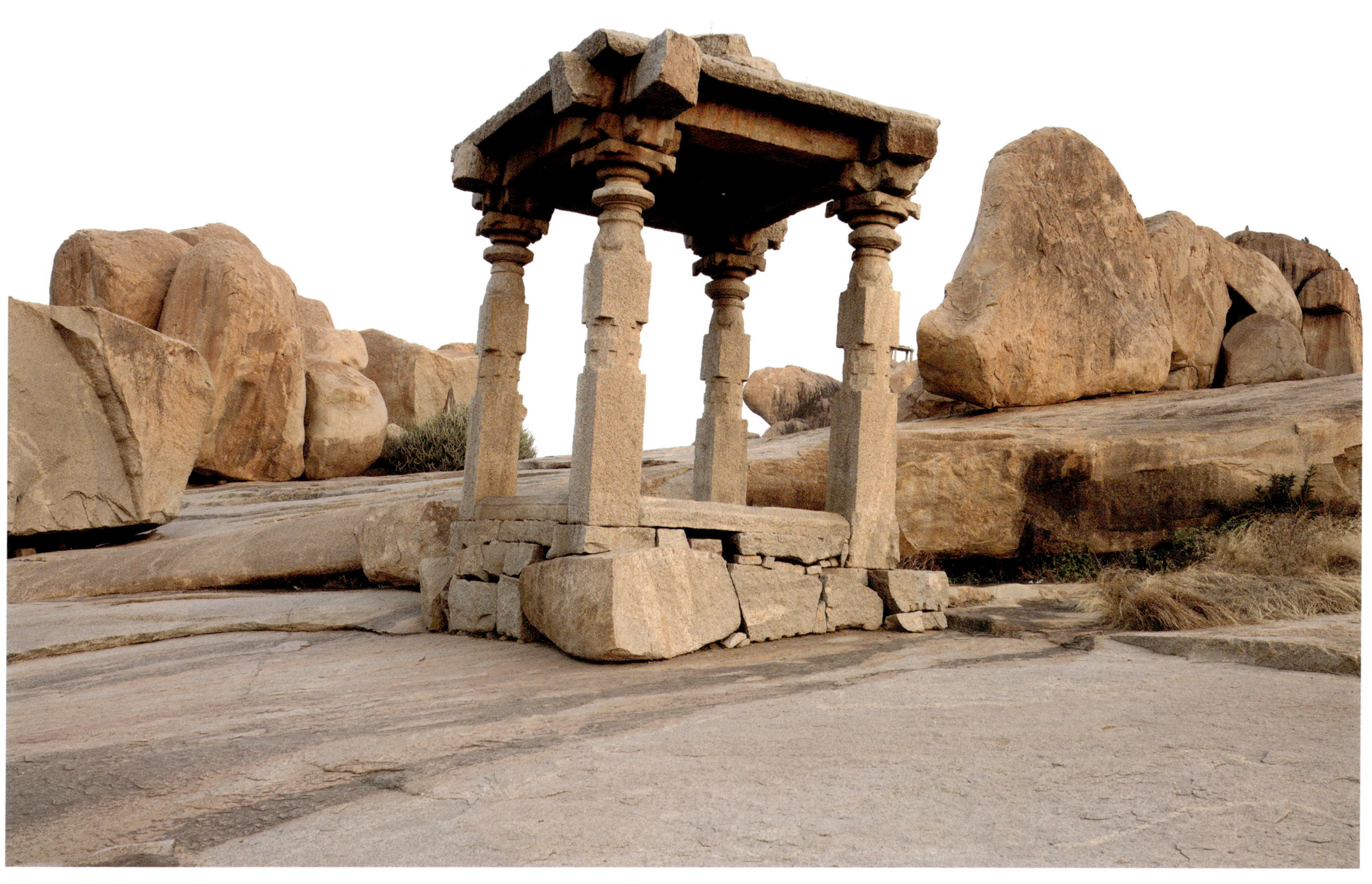

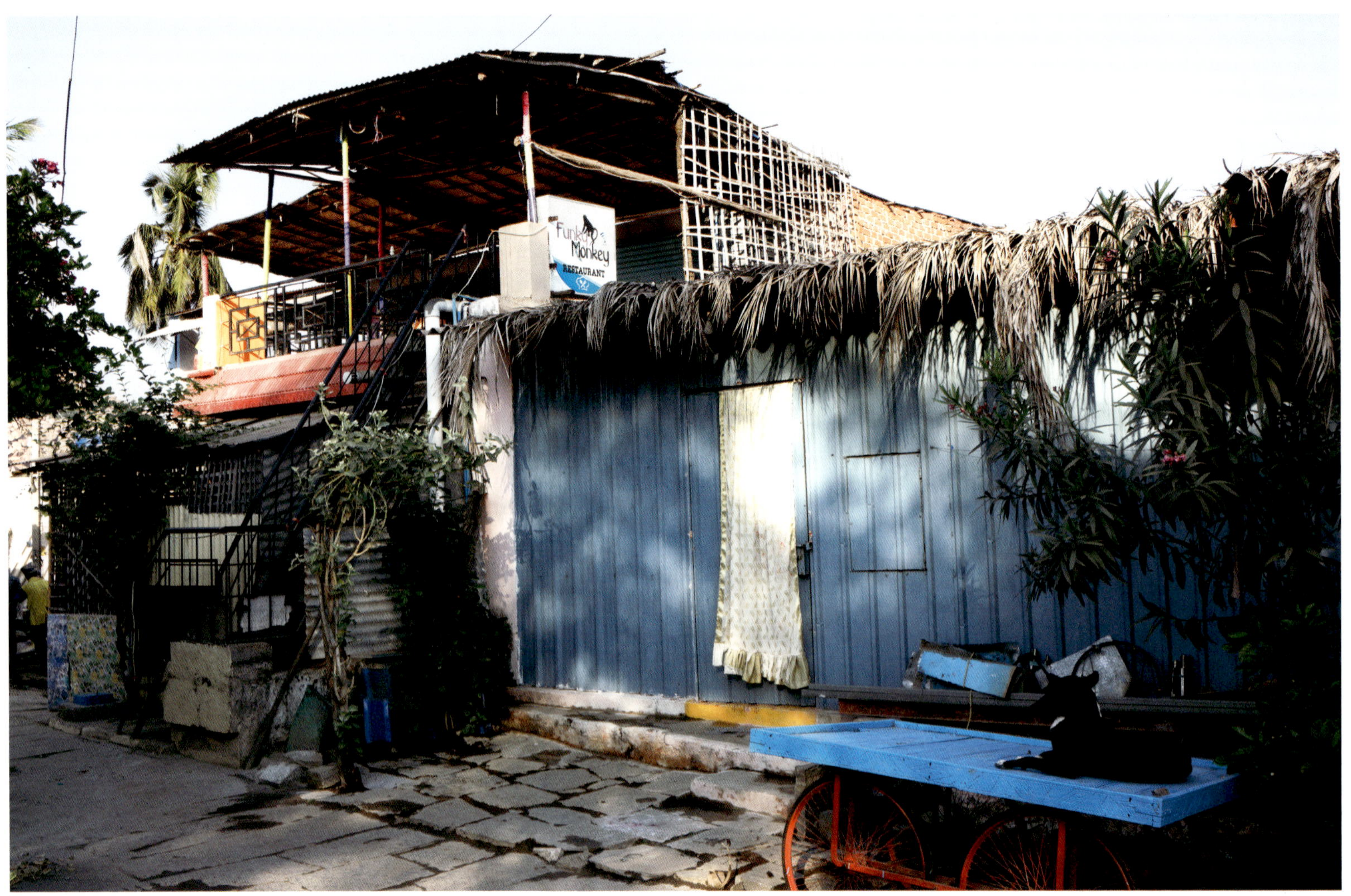

ABOVE: Funky Monkey café.

OPPOSITE: My initial entry into Hampi was through the main bazaar, located in what is known as the "Sacred Center" of the archaeological zone. It looked to me to be anything but sacred. The place was bursting at the seams with thatch-roofed cafés, hostels, homestays, food stalls, and handicraft shops. Hand-painted signboards announced the Mango Tree hostel, Shanti Guesthouse, Golden Beach homestay, Boulder's Resort, and numerous other tourism services: money exchanges, zip lines, Wi-Fi connections. The ubiquitous advertisements blocked the view of the surrounding monuments and the natural landscape. The alleyways of the bazaar bustled with people, for the most part travelers in shorts and tee shirts or wearing dreadlocks and the native kurtas. It was a lively, colorful, and friendly looking scene.

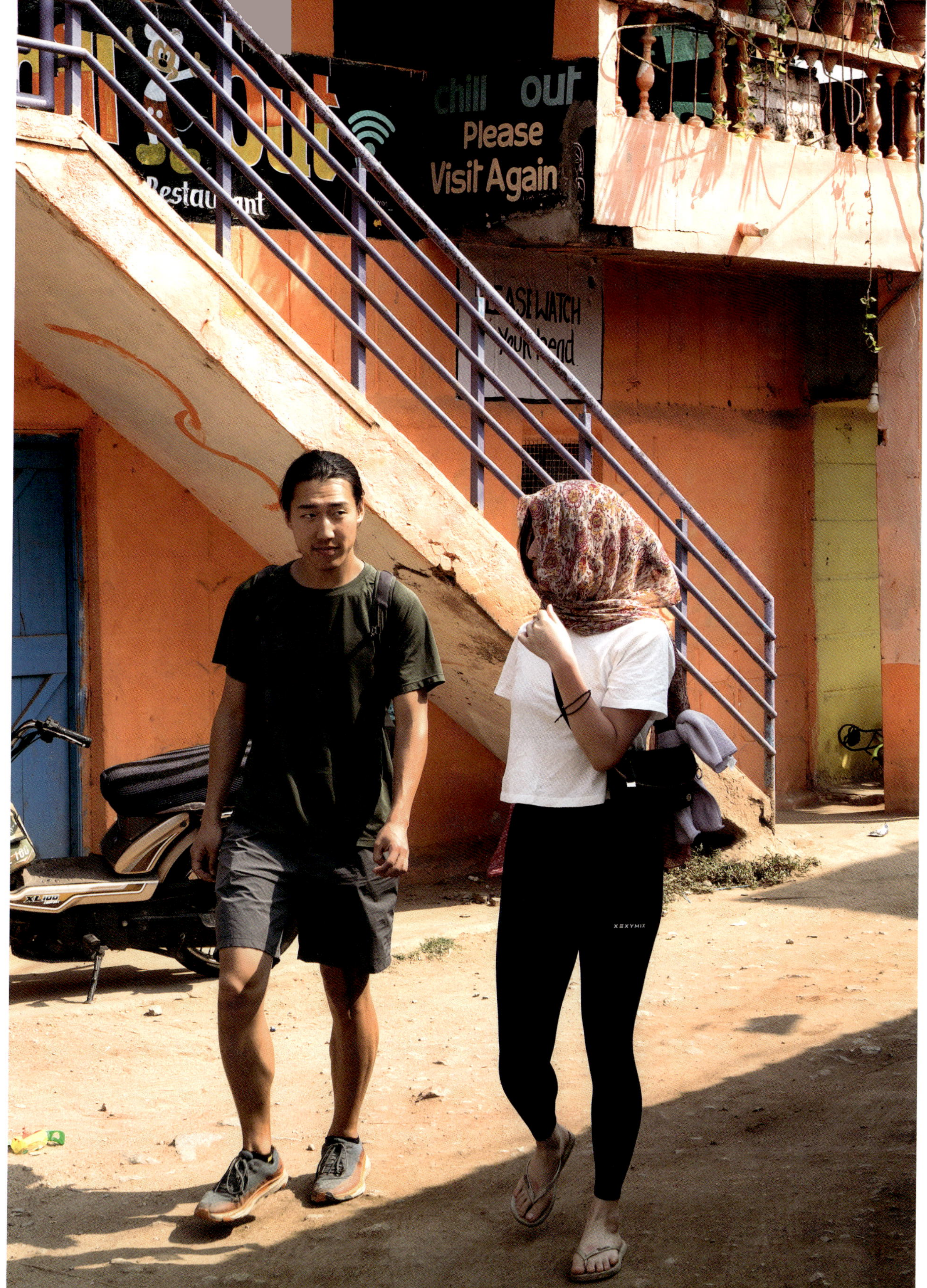
chill out
chill out
Please
Visit Again
Restaurant

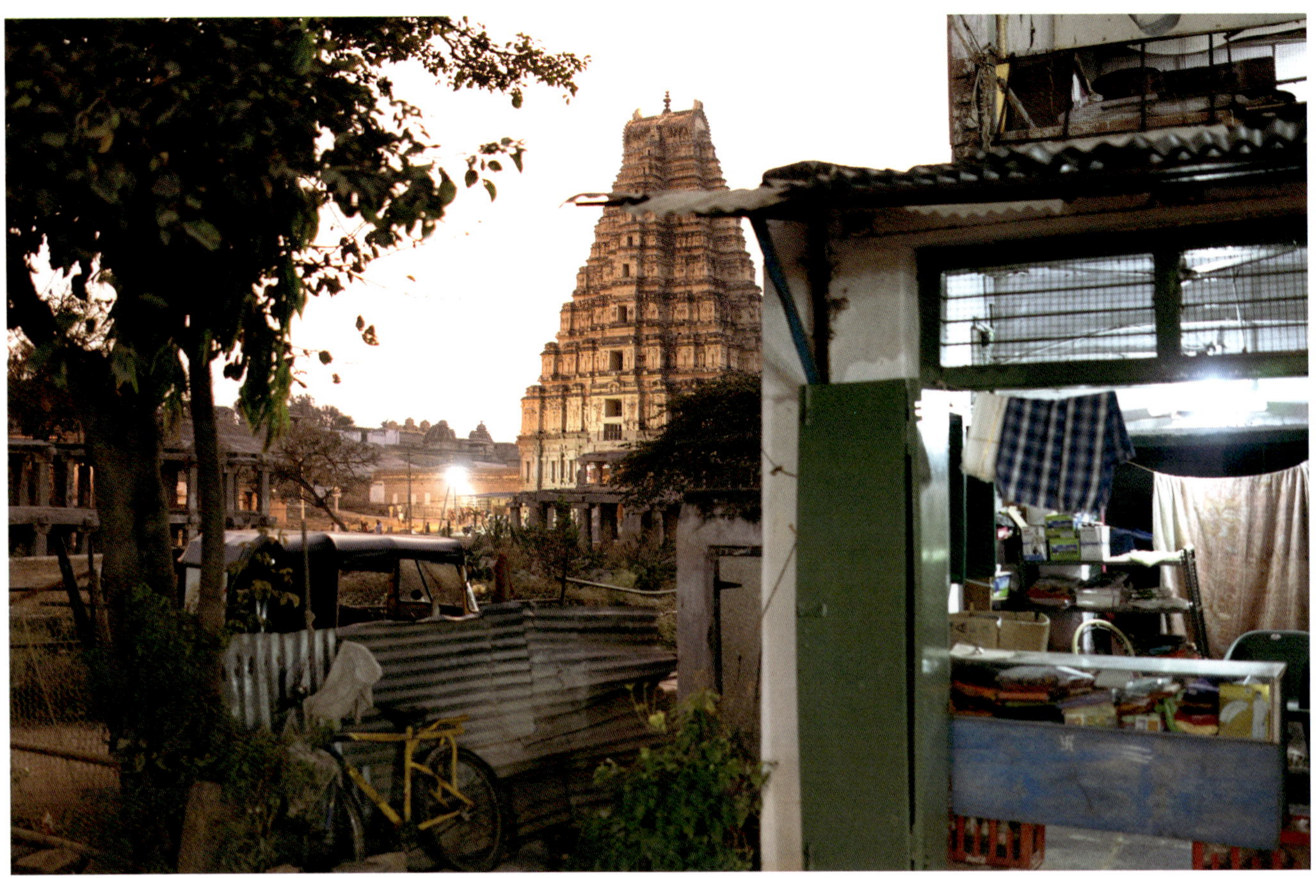

ABOVE: Overlooking the Hampi bazaar is the 600-year-old Virupaksha Temple, which stands 50 meters high. The soaring edifice makes an incongruous site when viewed against the foreground of a busy tourism economy. At prayer times, though, when devotional music emanating from its assembly hall drowns out the noise of commerce, the temple anchors the bazaar in an older time and place. OPPOSITE: Hampi's main bazaar.

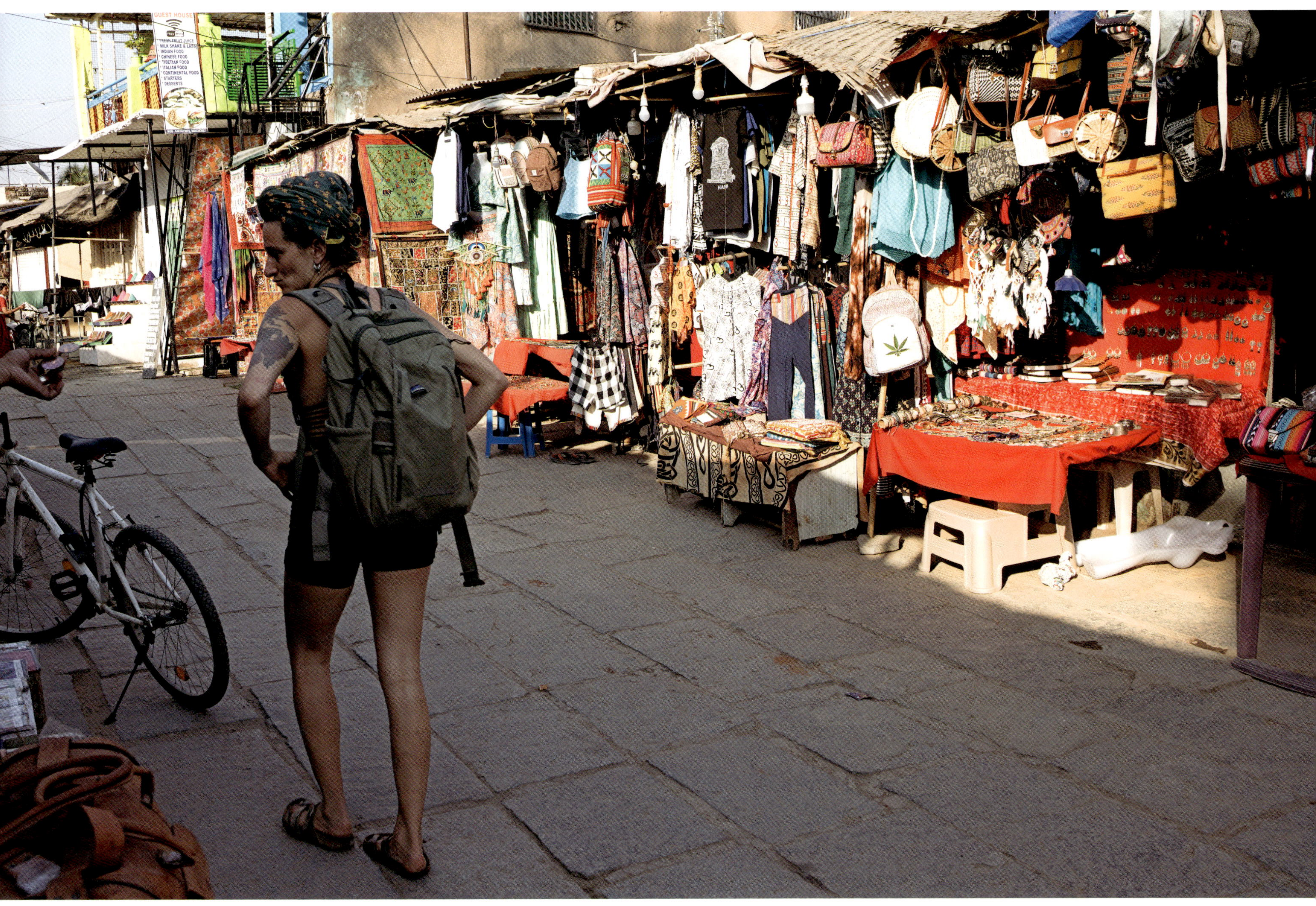

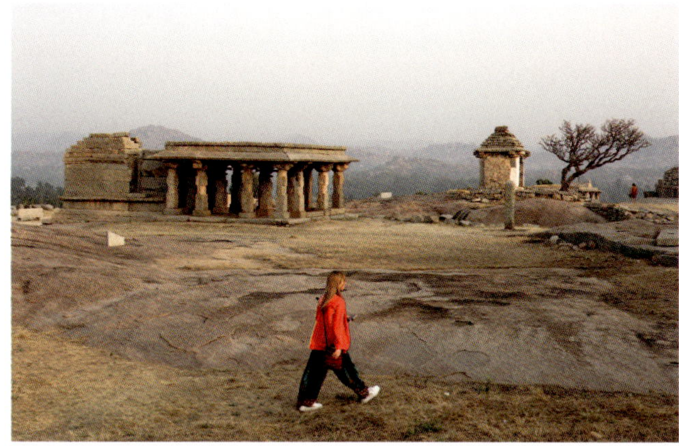

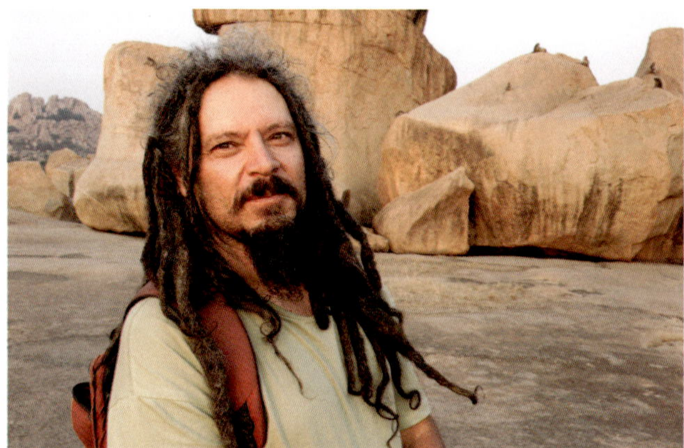

THIS PAGE: Overlooking the main bazaar in Hampi is Hemakuta Hill, where Lord Shiva purportedly once reigned. The hilltop is sprinkled with enormous boulders and old temples. At the top of the hill are stone platforms that provide wonderful sunset views. Each evening the hill swarms with young travelers who climb up from the bazaar to take in the scenery, the peace, and the quiet. Here I met Patrick from New Zealand. He related to me that he'd come to Hampi to "experience the serendipity, the magical occurrences of chance that happen so frequently in India." I thought I knew what he meant; I've been returning to India regularly during the past 50 years for much the same reason.

OPPOSITE: Hemakuta Hill

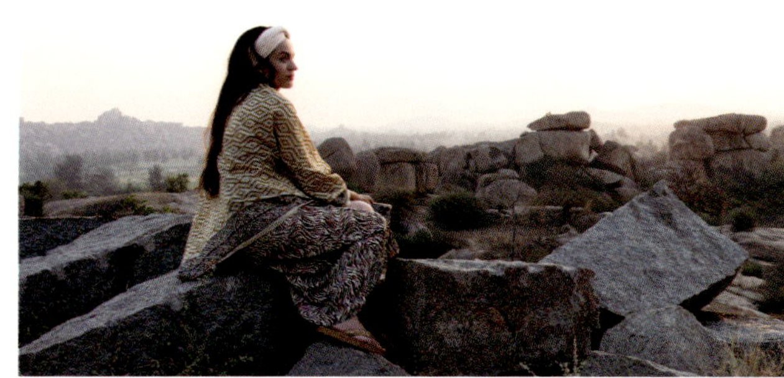

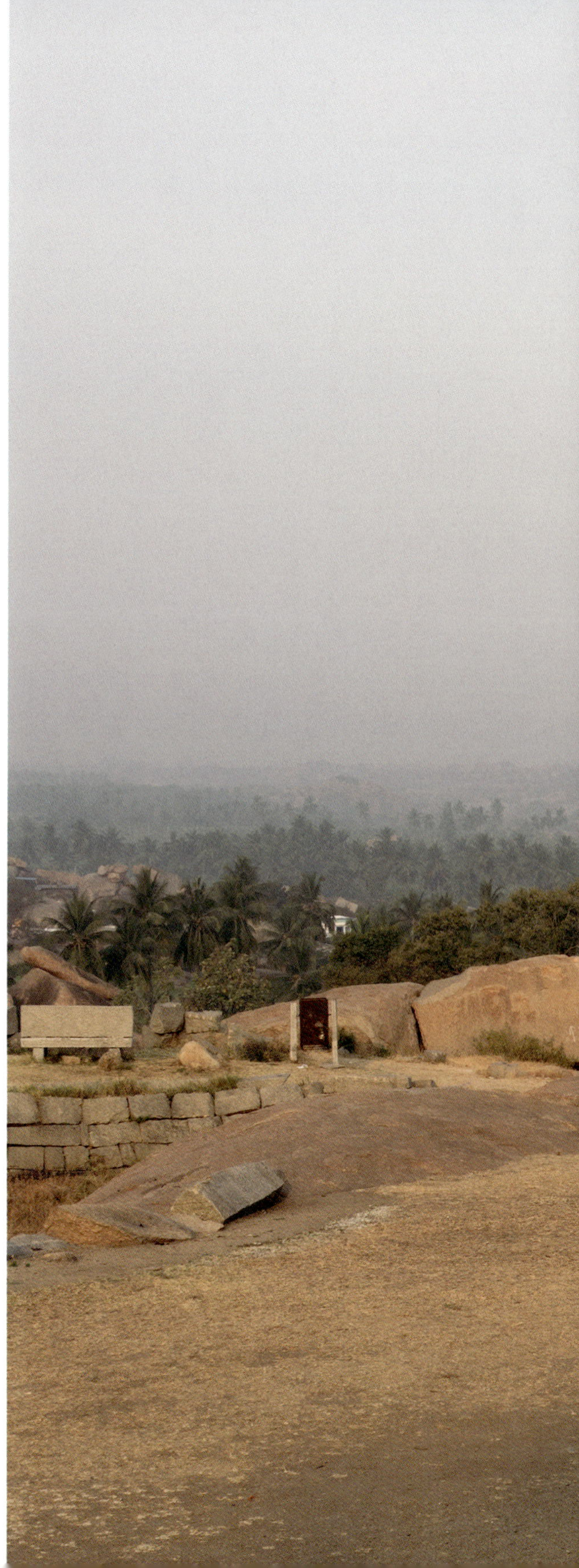

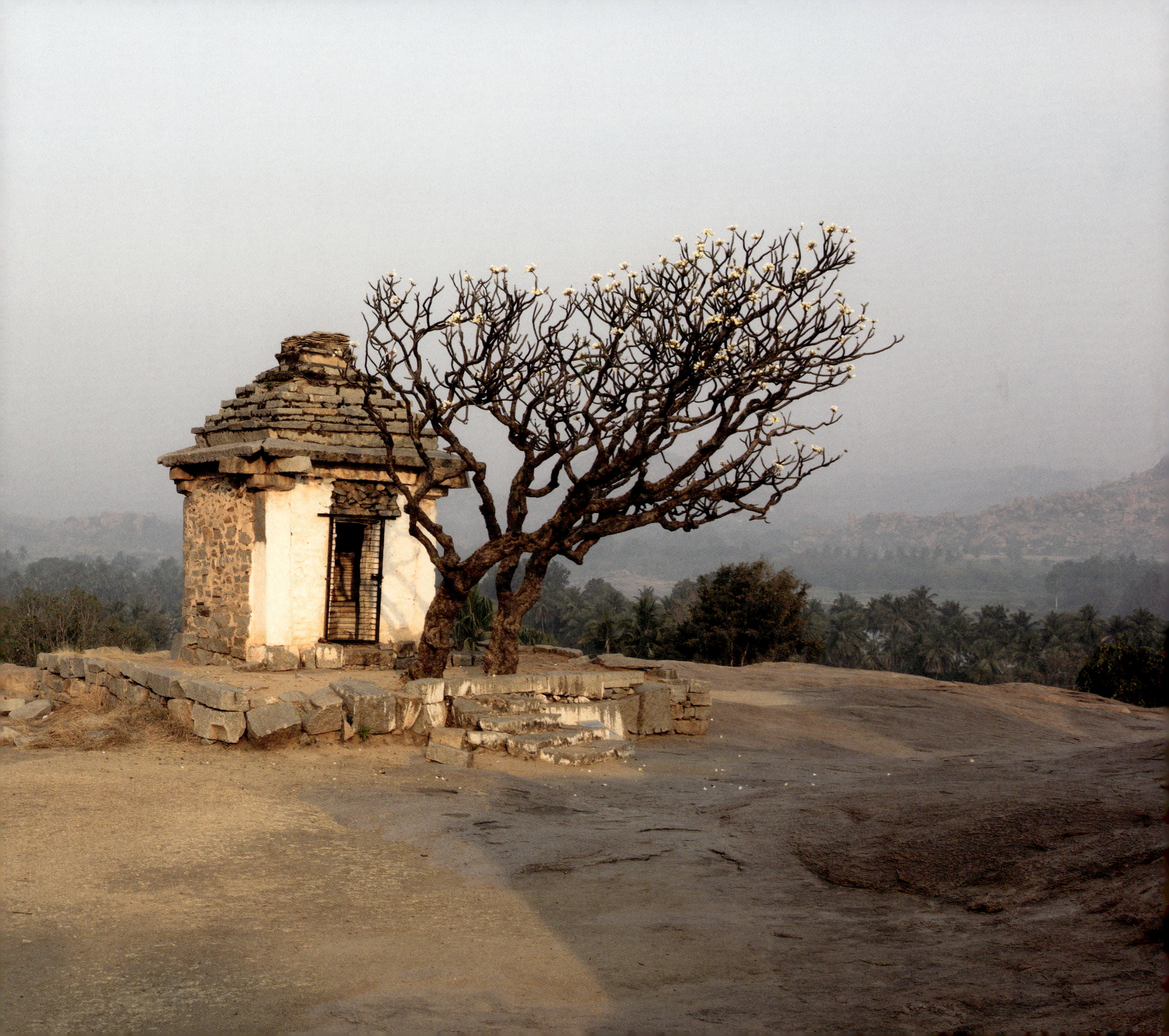

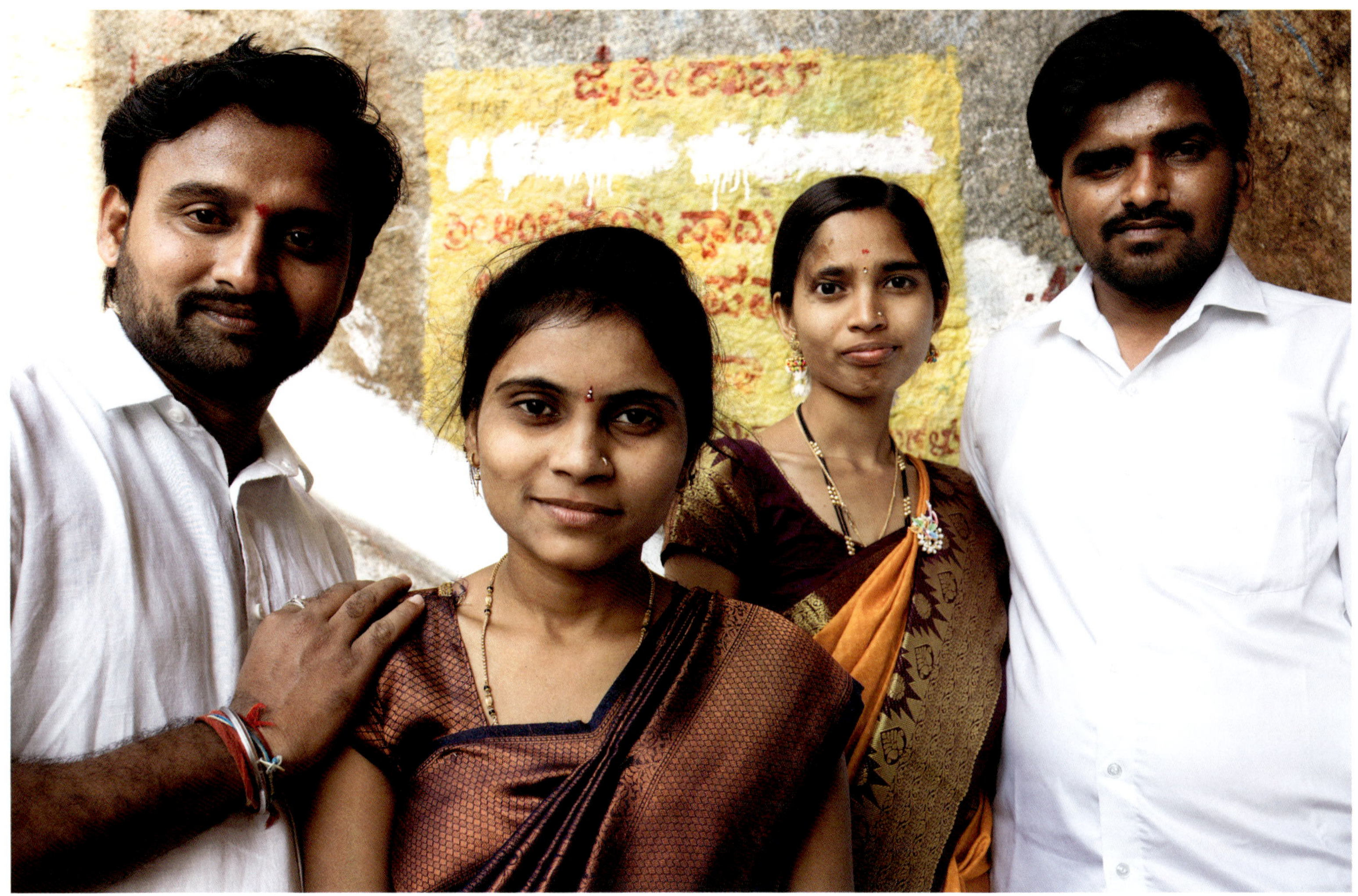

Hampi appears in the *Ramayana* (circa 500 BCE) as the birthplace of the Hindu god Hanuman, who assumes the avatar of a monkey, and for this reason it is known as the Monkey Kingdom. The venerable Hanuman Temple sits atop a bluff above the Anjanadri Hills and the Tungabhadra River. It is one of India's most important religious sites. I met Ravin and Rachina (left side of photo) who were visiting the temple with Rachina's sister Tejaswini and her husband Santosh on the occasion of their first wedding anniversary. They had come to pay homage to Hanuman, who is believed to be the divine source of *shakti* (feminine cosmic energy). Many Western travelers visit the place for its panoramic views and to enjoy the antics of its simian residents, but for the Hindu pilgrims the presence of the monkeys in the temple is the embodiment of God.

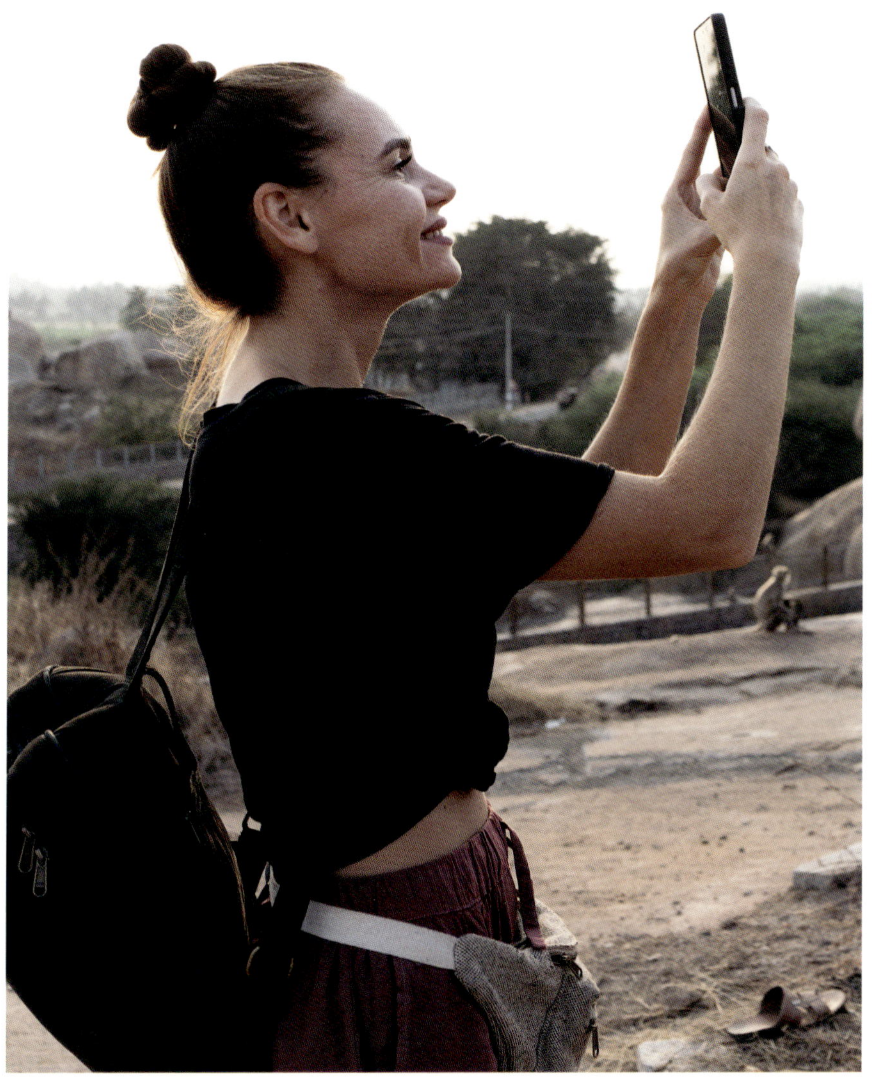

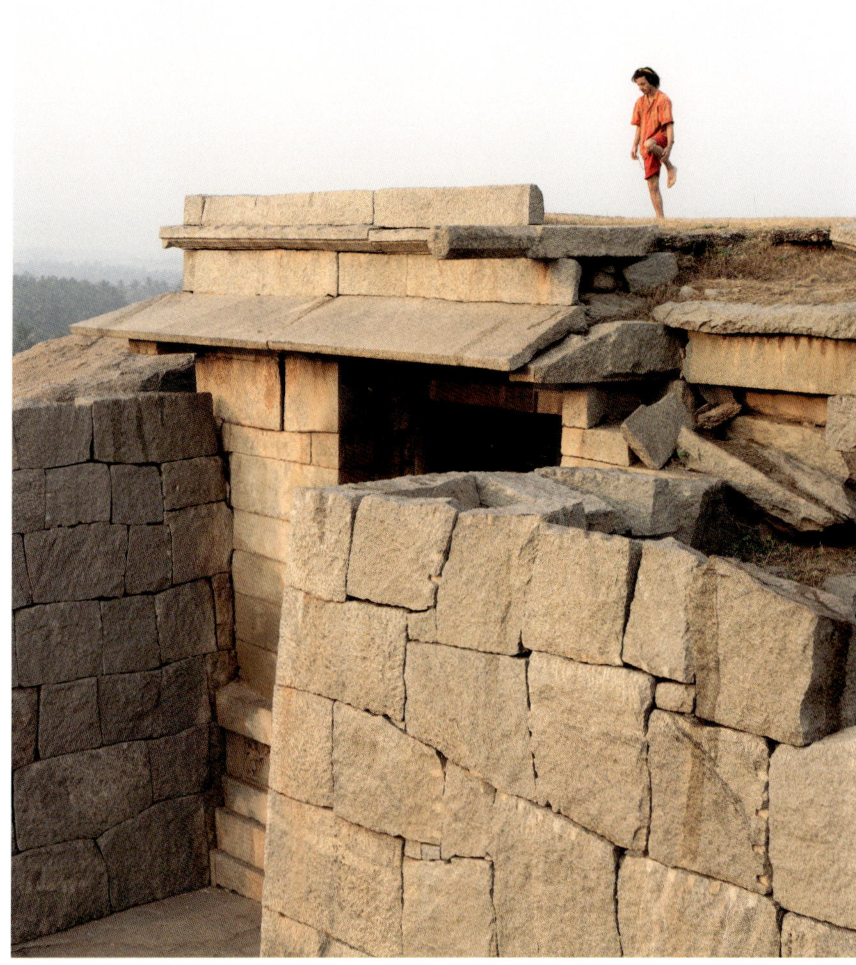

ABOVE LEFT: Selfie
ABOVE RIGHT: Evening meditation

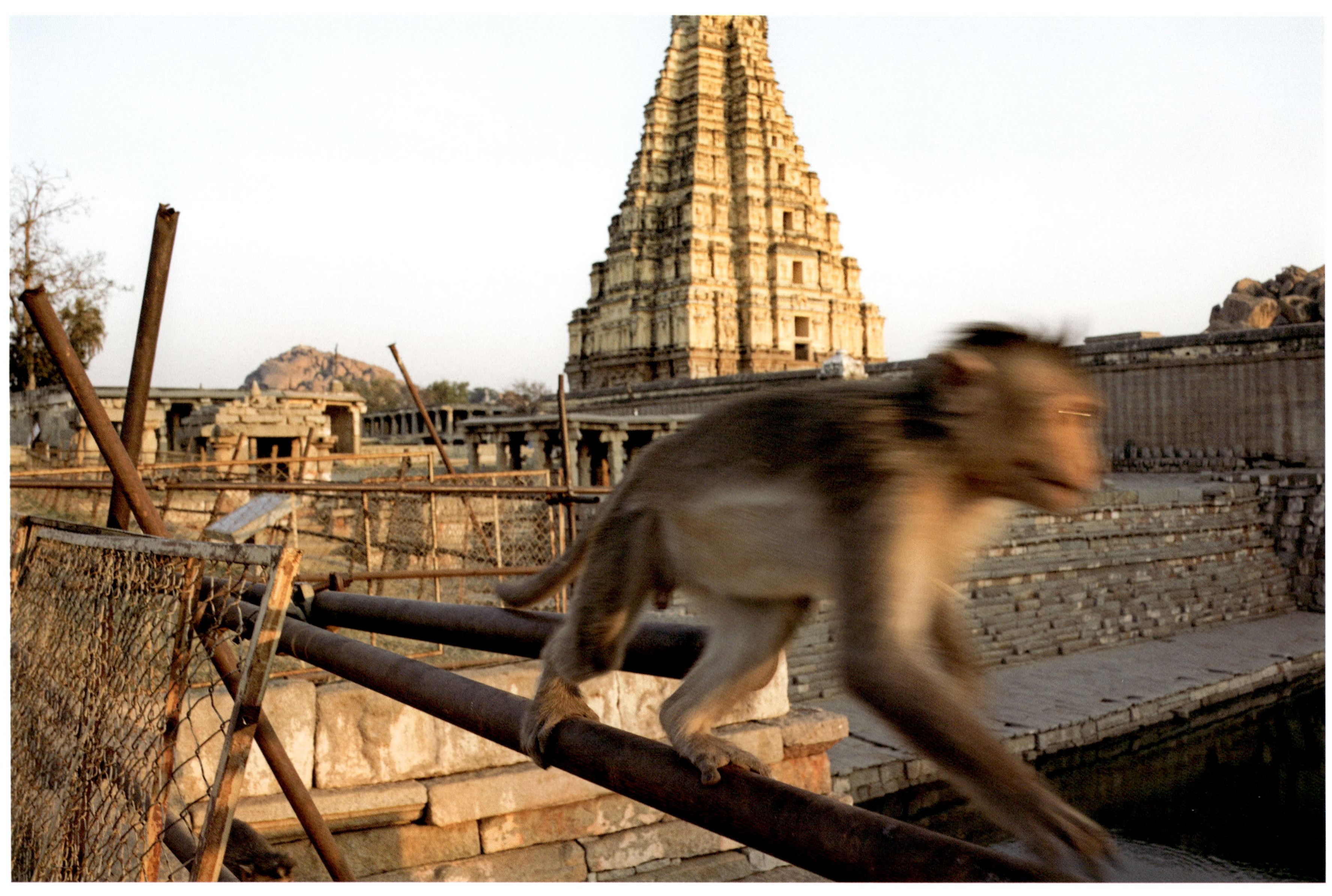

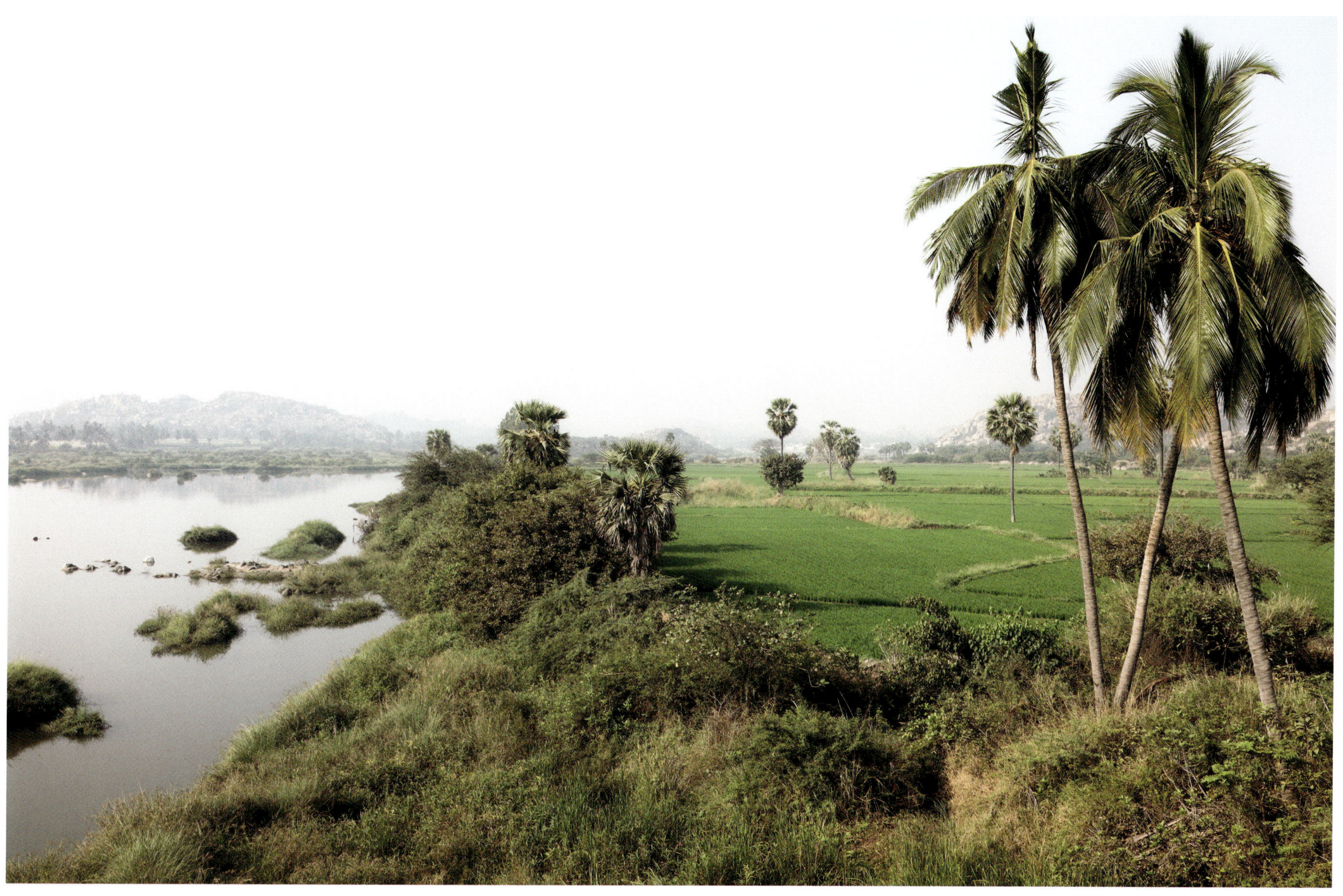

Hippie Island (Virupapur Island)

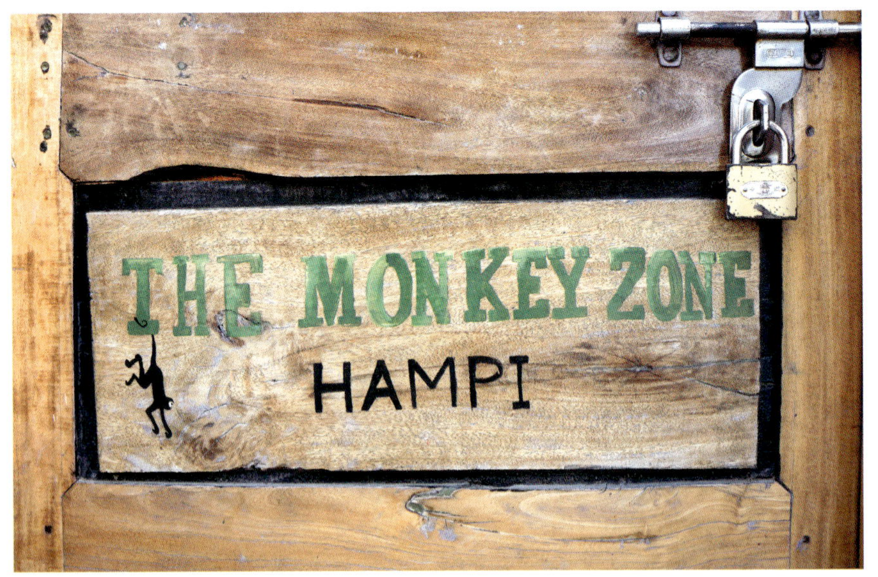

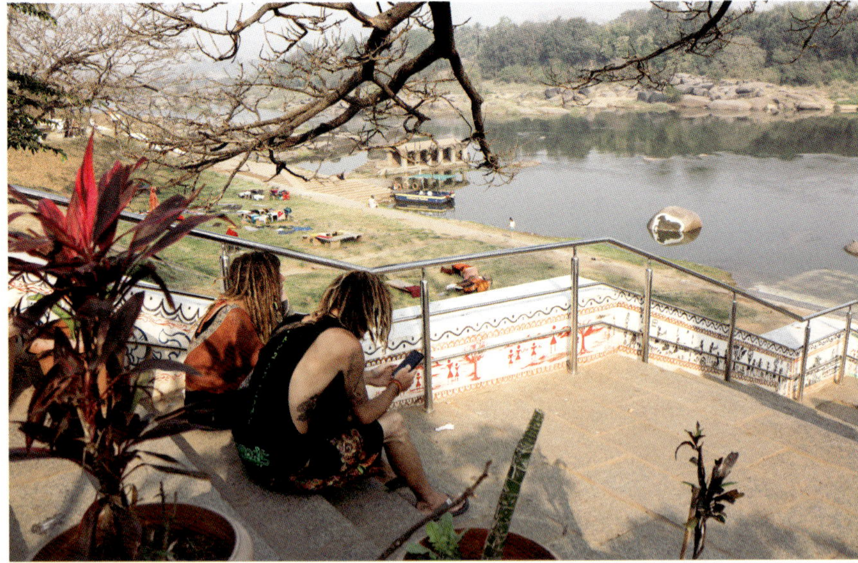

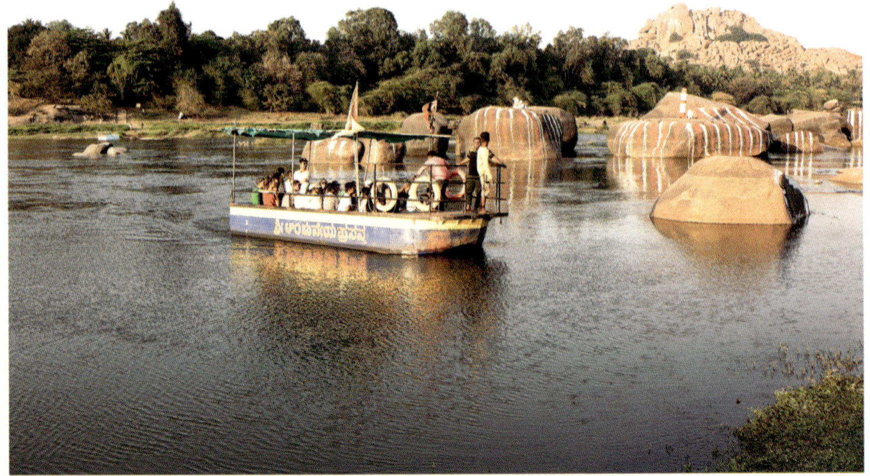

THIS PAGE: I took a ferry across the Tungabhadra River to "Hippie Island" (Virupapur Island). Its laid-back vibe has attracted a backpacking crowd since the early 1970s. Cheap hostels, homestays, cafés, and open-air campgrounds were constructed in the rice fields and surrounding forest to accommodate western travelers. Cannabis was freely consumed. Drum circles and fire-dances went on into the nights. That all ended in 2022, when government officials decreed the infrastructure encroached upon the archeological zone, threatening its World Heritage status. They brought in bulldozers and demolished the tourist facilities. I found the island abandoned. The only visitors I met were those seeking a nostalgic peek into the hippie past—much like myself. Meanwhile, the travelers had scattered to new outposts located farther afield.
OPPOSITE: Ben and Beth (Australia)

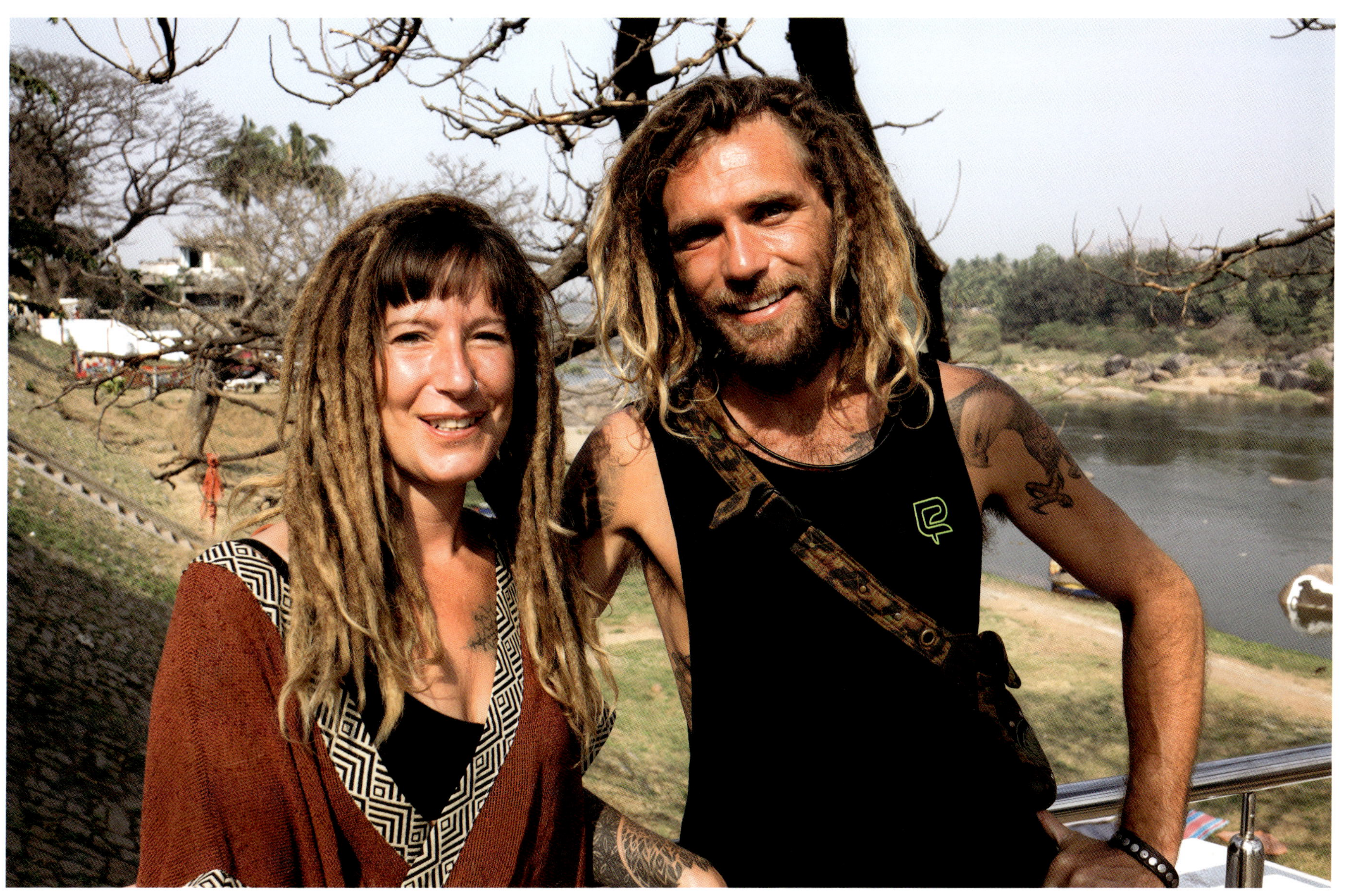

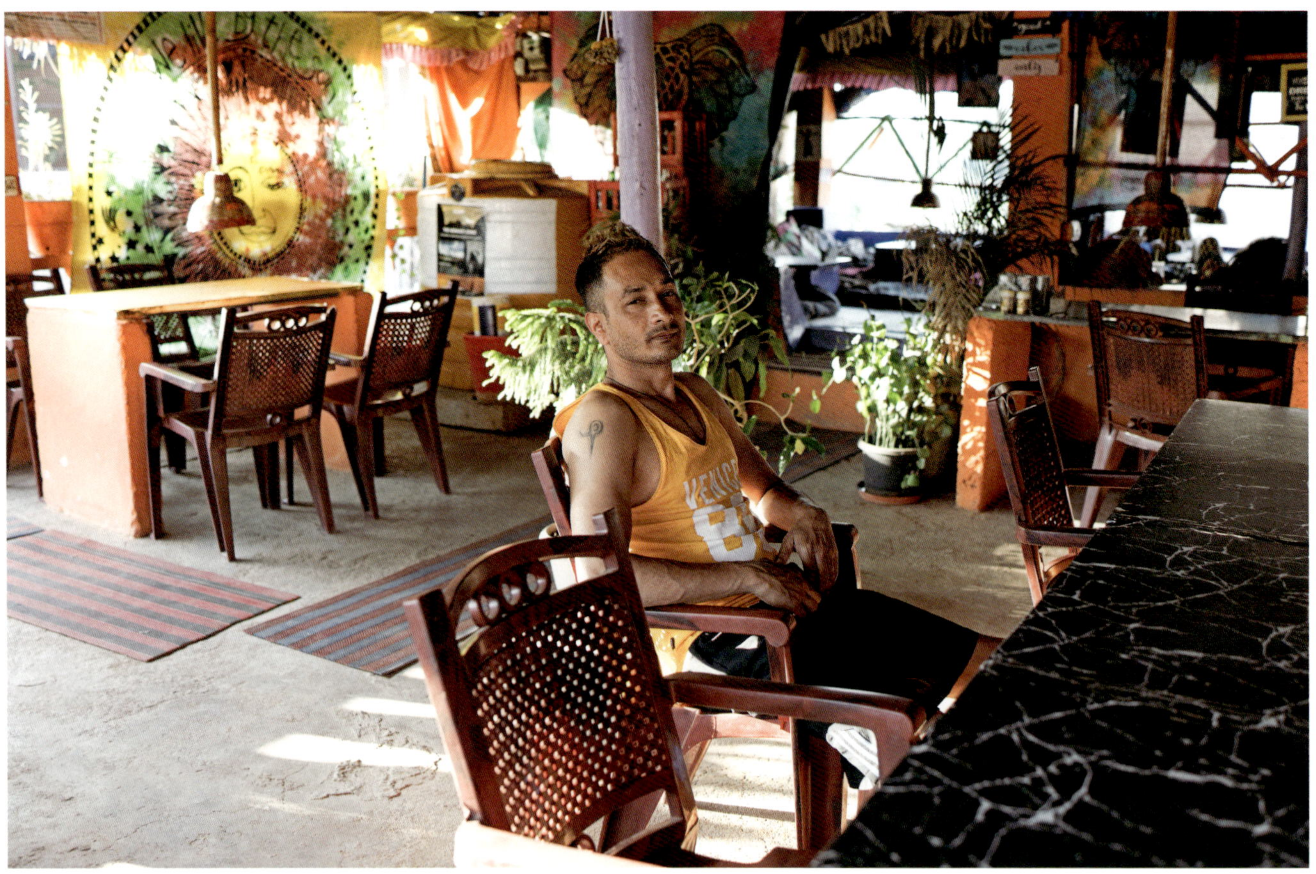

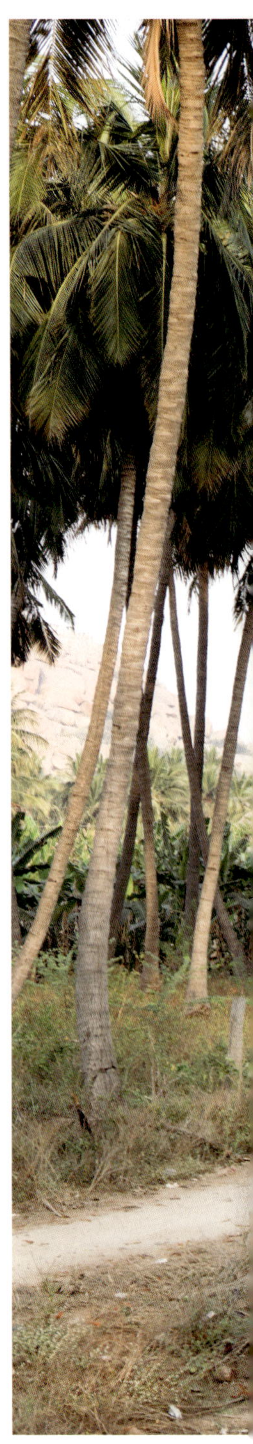

ABOVE: It was mid-afternoon and getting hot, so I popped into the "Chill Out" café for a cold drink. There I met Pamir from Kathmandu. As we chatted, he related to me, "I come down here to India in the winters to escape the cold at home in Nepal. I like the vibe in Hampi." I discovered time and again that counterculture travel is not restricted to persons coming from what I considered to be the "Western World." I met free spirited people hailing from countries located throughout Asia and Latin America. Among other shared attributes, they all expressed a similar desire to escape the conventions of their own societies. The term hippie defies any easy explanation or a place of origin.

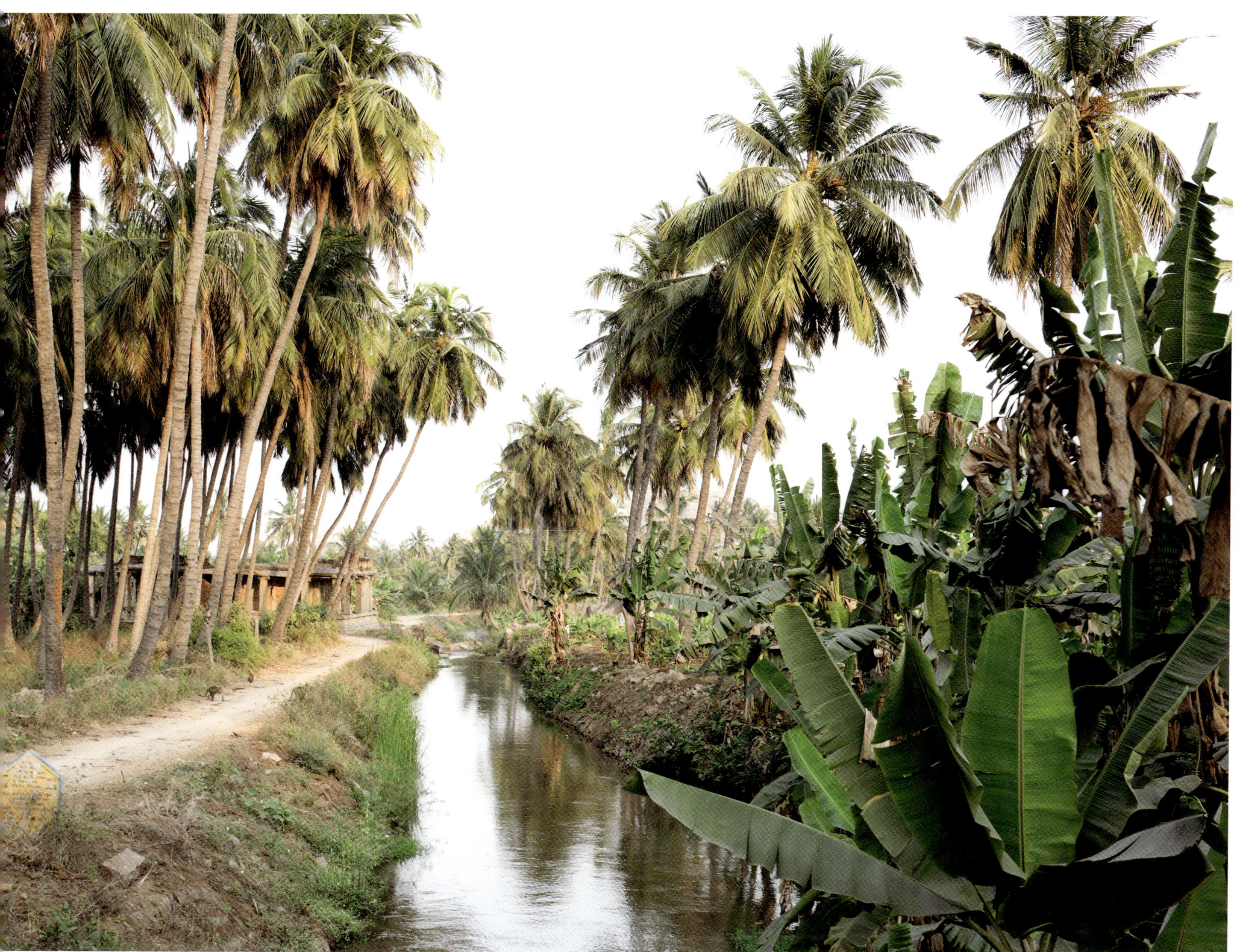

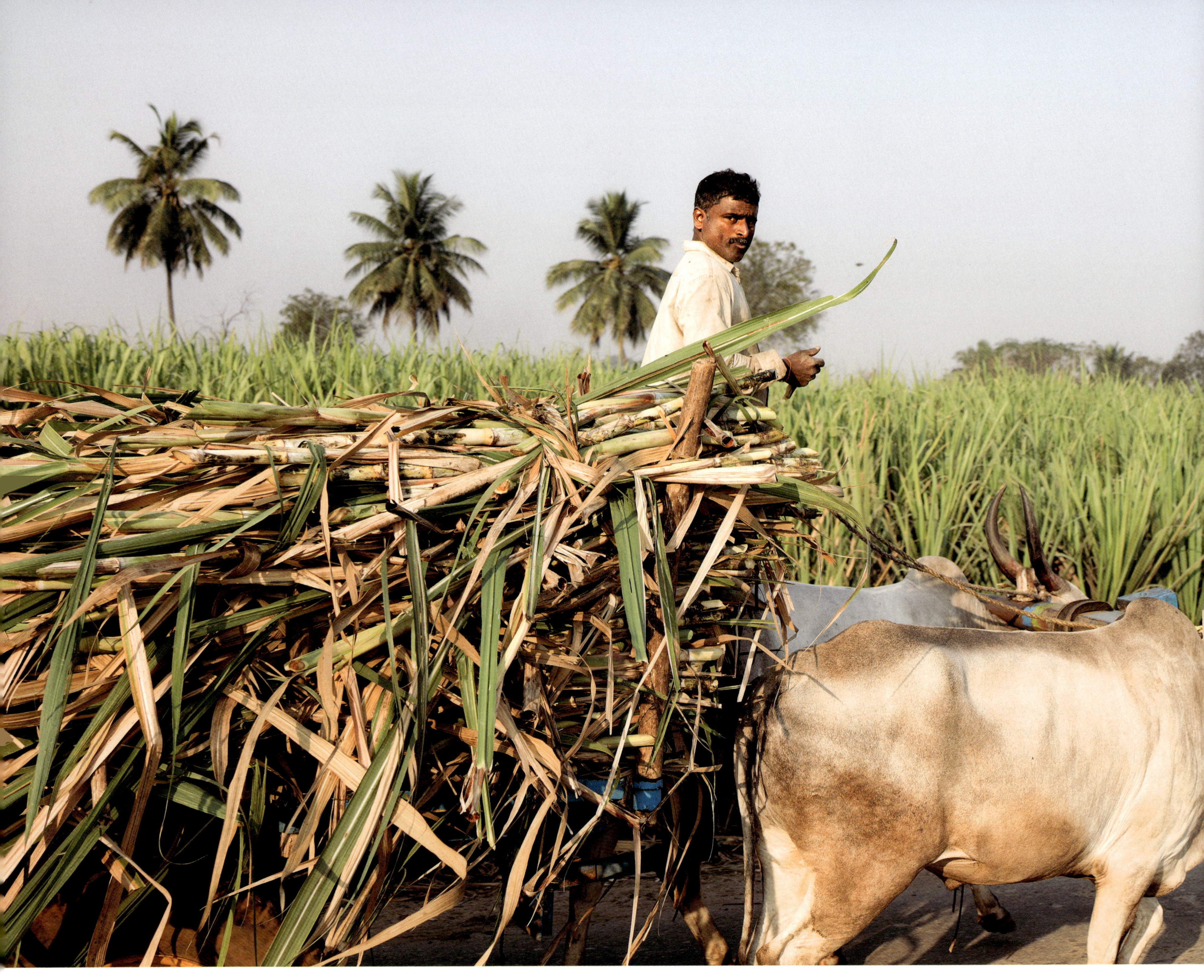

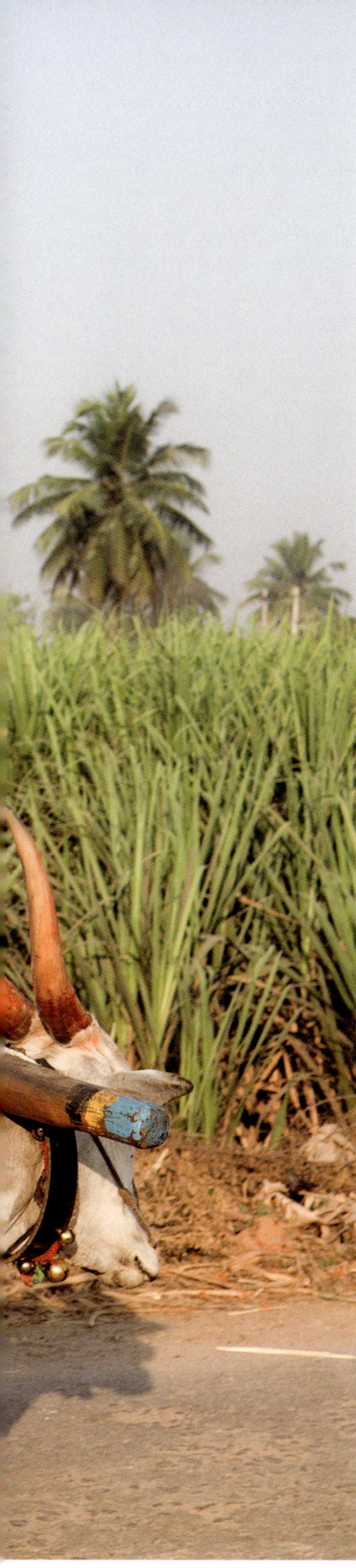

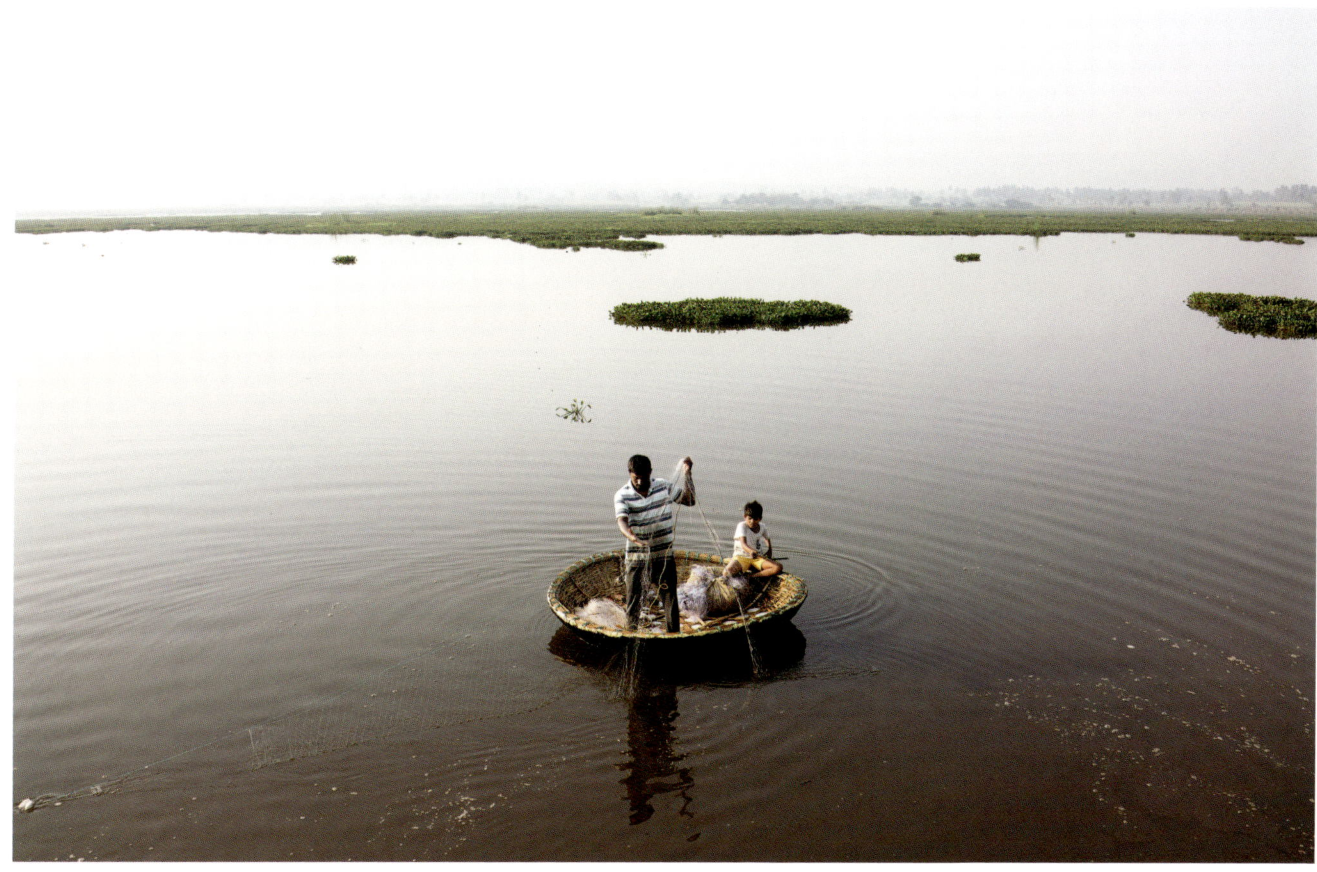

Much of the appeal of Hampi comes from its bucolic character. The countryside is filled with rice paddies, lakes, and sugar cane fields, and it supports a fascinating cast of farmers, fisherfolk, and pilgrims. It's a place where travelers can feel themselves sinking into the local scene. The dirt lanes that connect villages are byways for hippies on bicycles as much as they are for local people traveling on bullock carts. The woven boats called coracles used by fishermen convey tourists across Tungabhadra River to Hippie Island. Travelers help with local chores, including the daily bathing of a temple elephant. In some crazy way, it all fit together in Hampi, to the point where I sometimes found it difficult to distinguish the dreadlocked travelers from the dreadlocked sadhus.

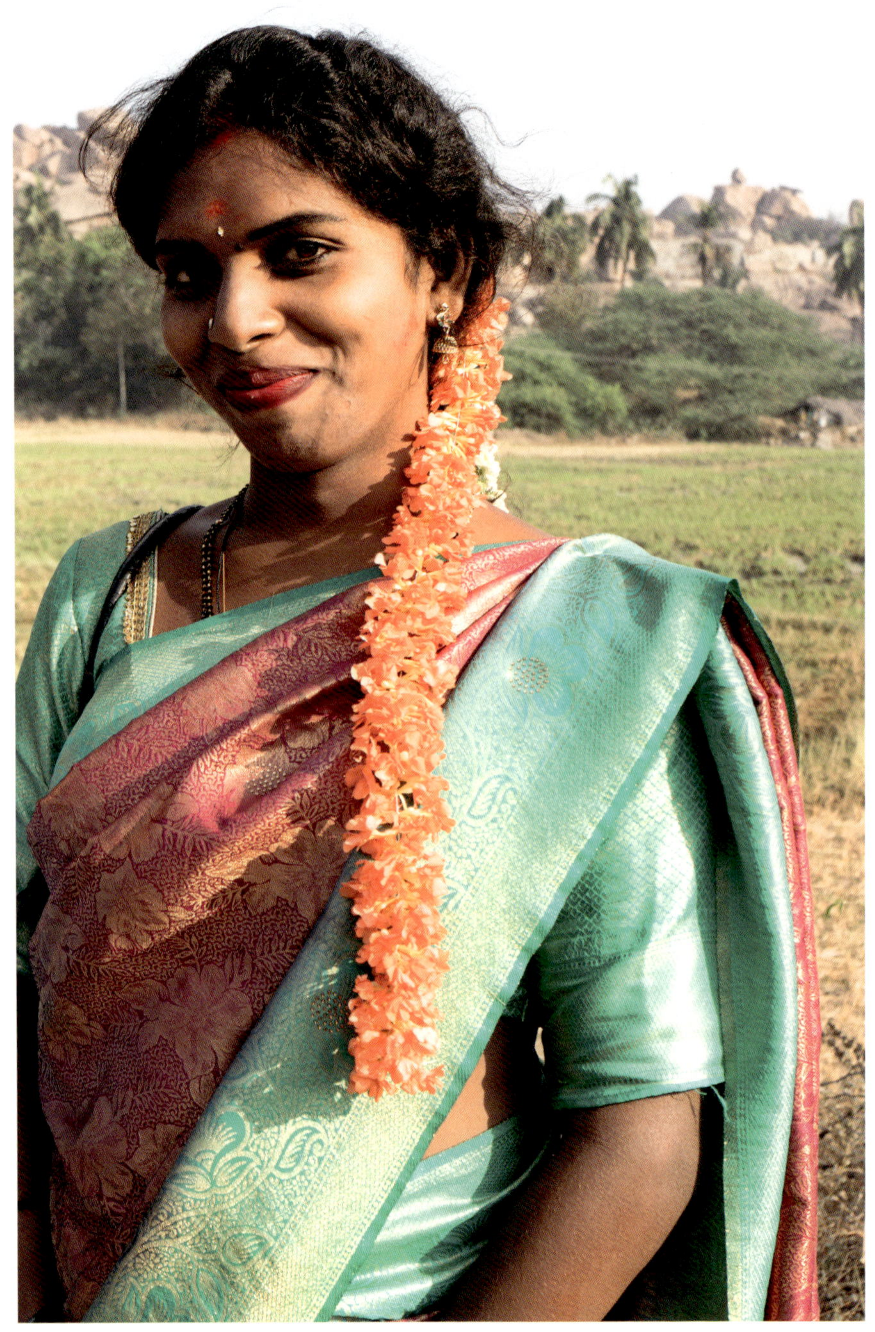

Hijra, transvestite (India)

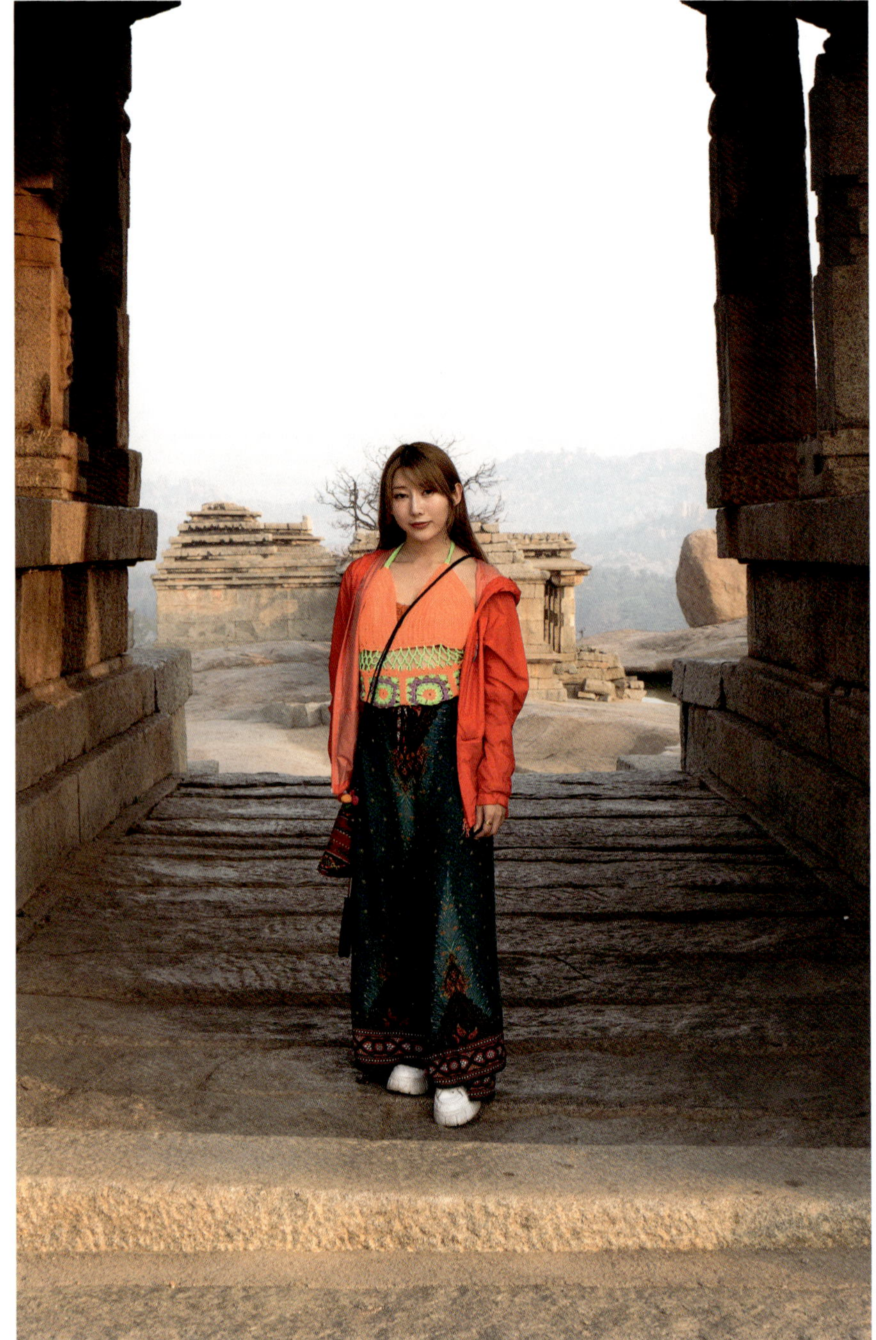

Ran (Japan)

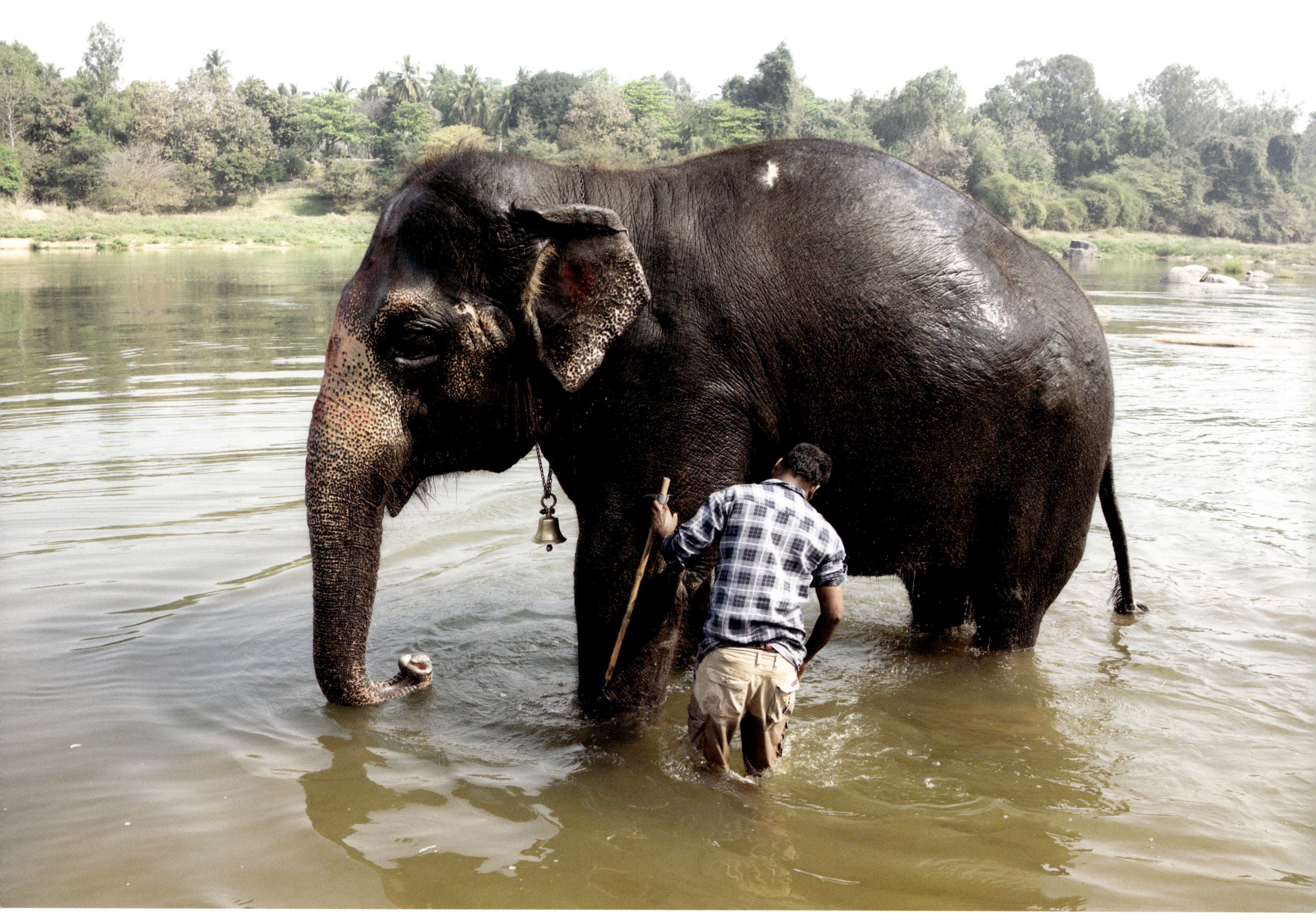

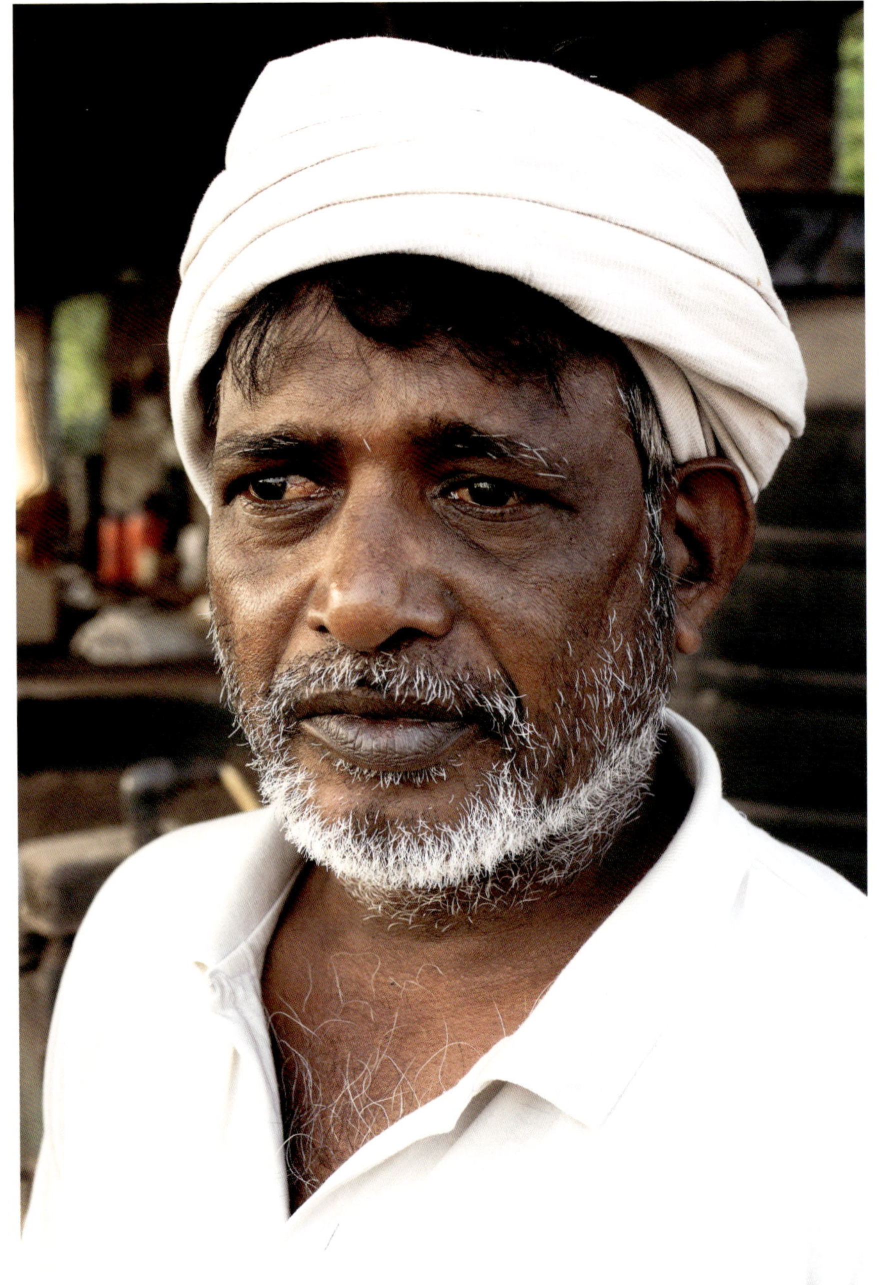

Sugar cane juicer (India)

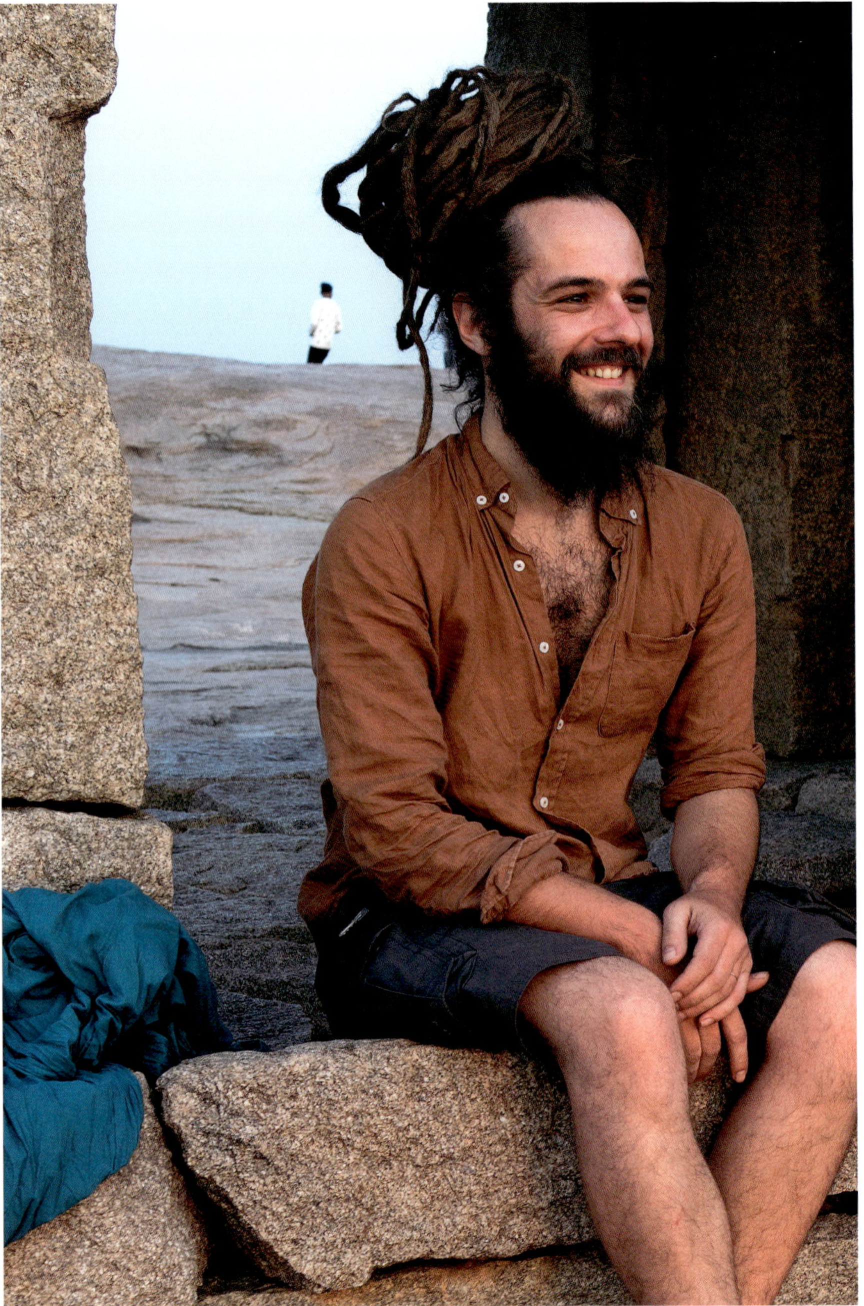

Thibault (France)

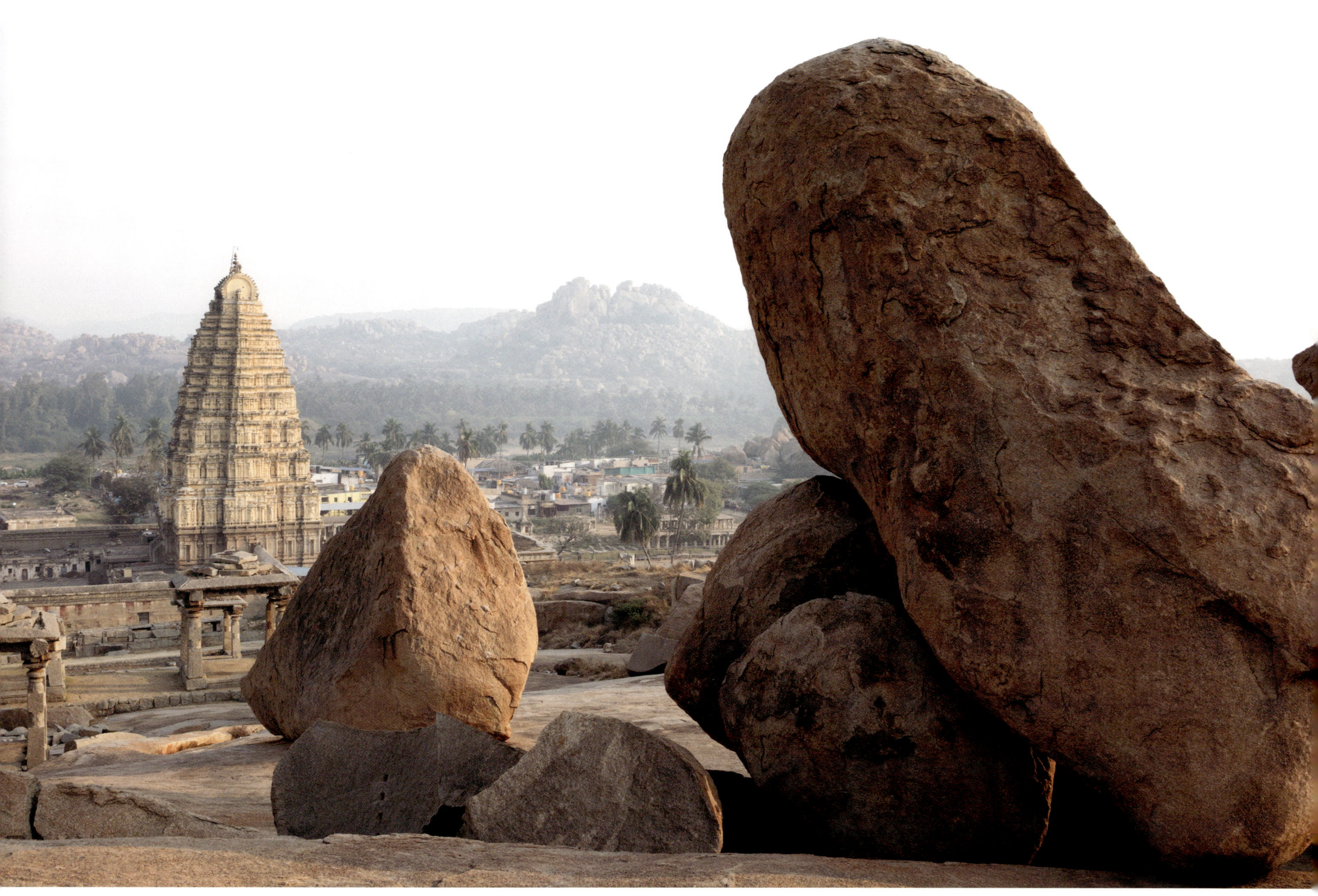

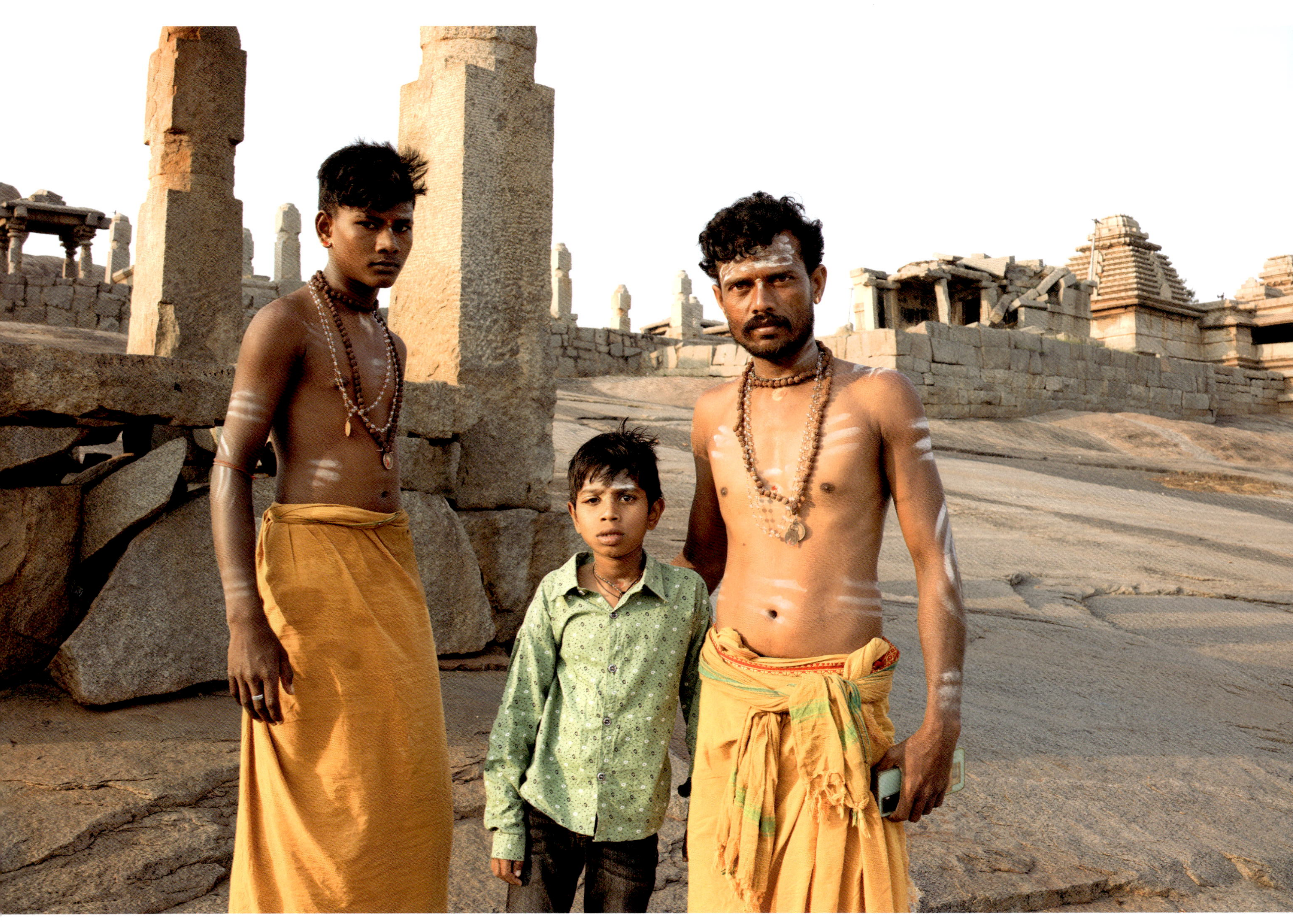

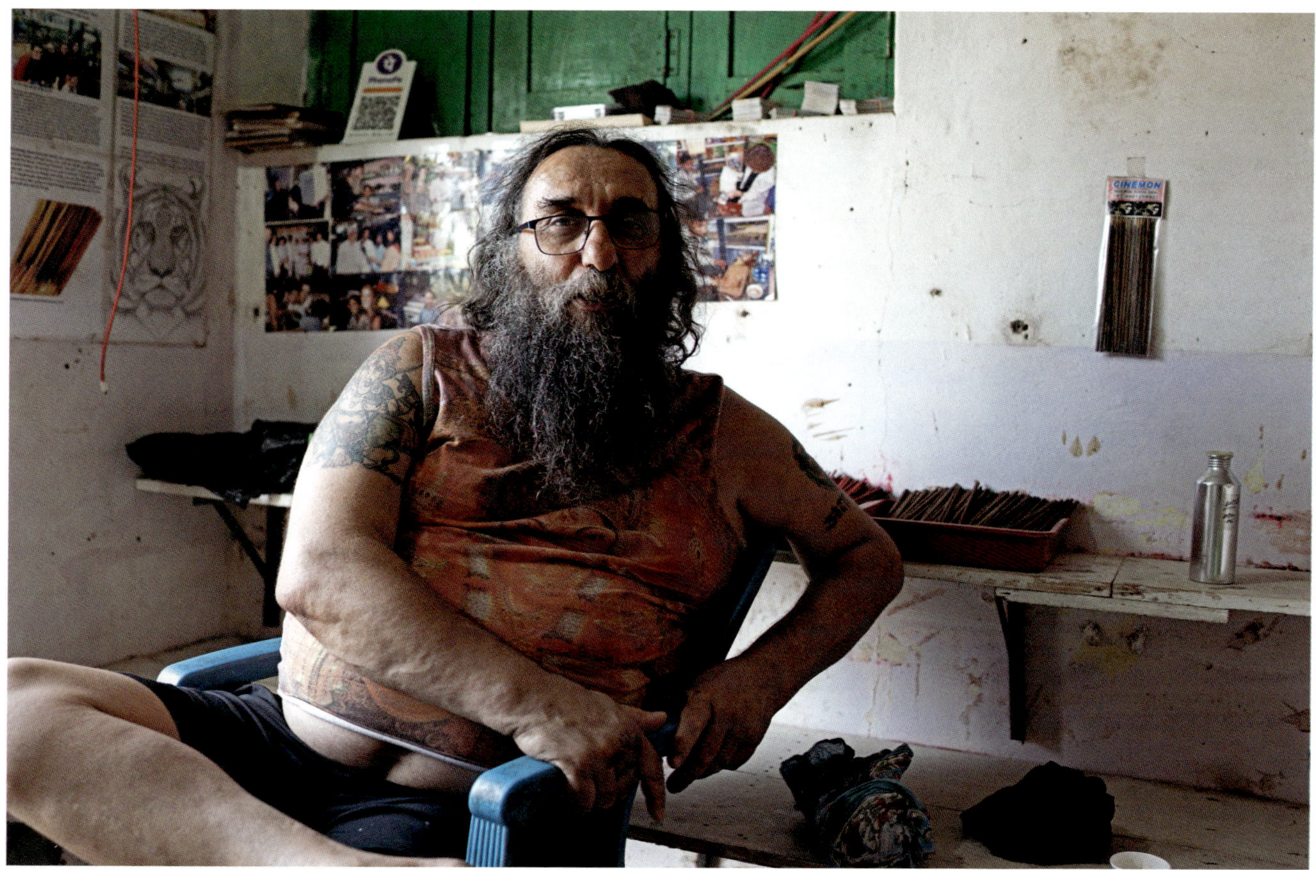

ABOVE: I met Ganesh in an incense shop in the Hampi bazaar. He told me he comes to India "to experience the magic." It's a sentiment I heard expressed time and again by the travelers I met. Ganesh first visited the country in 1979 as one of the last travelers on the Hippie Trail before it succumbed to wars and other geopolitical conflicts, and has been returning regularly to India ever since. To support his travels, he buys incense and essential oils in Hampi to sell in the open markets of France. He said the locals gave him the name Ganesh, "probably because of my belly and nose (laughter)."

OPPOSITE: Vishnu devotees (India)

It was approaching sunset and I was
making photographs at the water tank
behind the Virupaksha Temple when
Stine and Caroline showed up. They
were yoga instructors from Germany.
The pair planned to practice a few
asanas nearby. With the temple in the
background and the soft fading light,
it made for a "picture-perfect" setting.

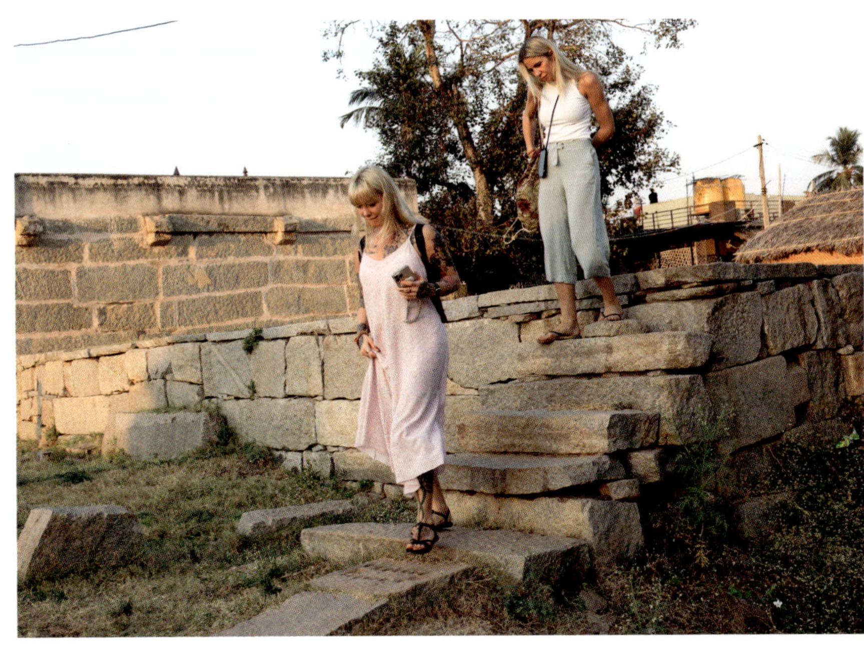

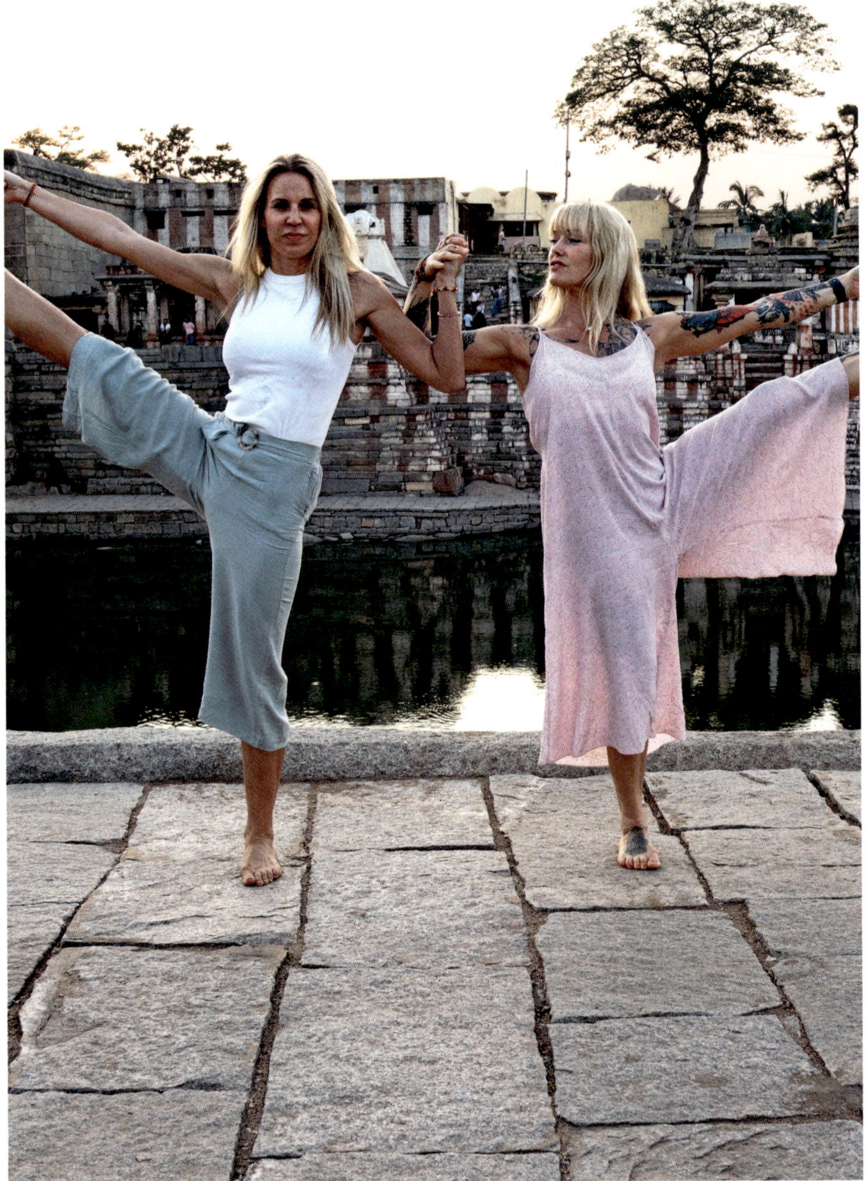

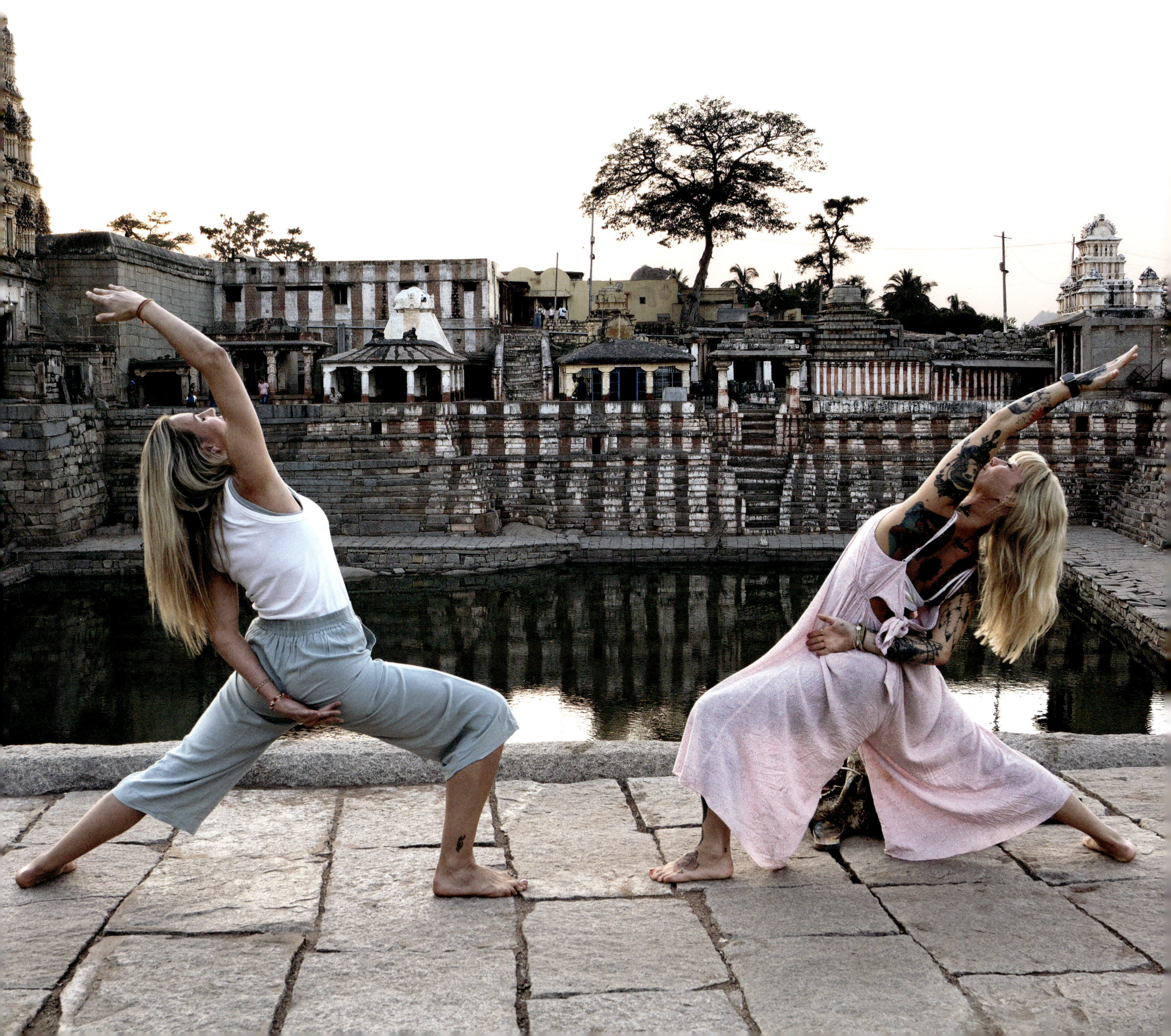

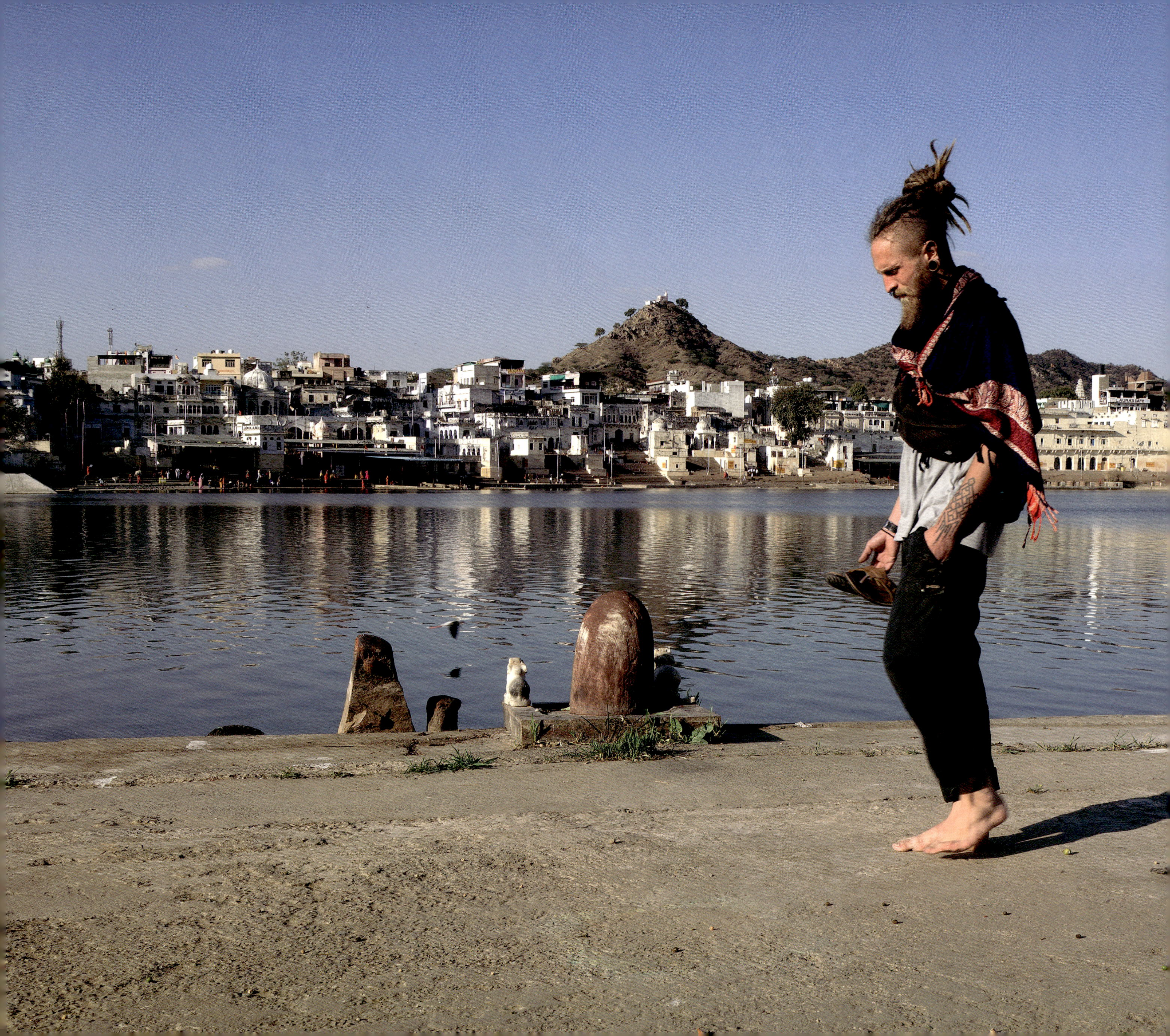

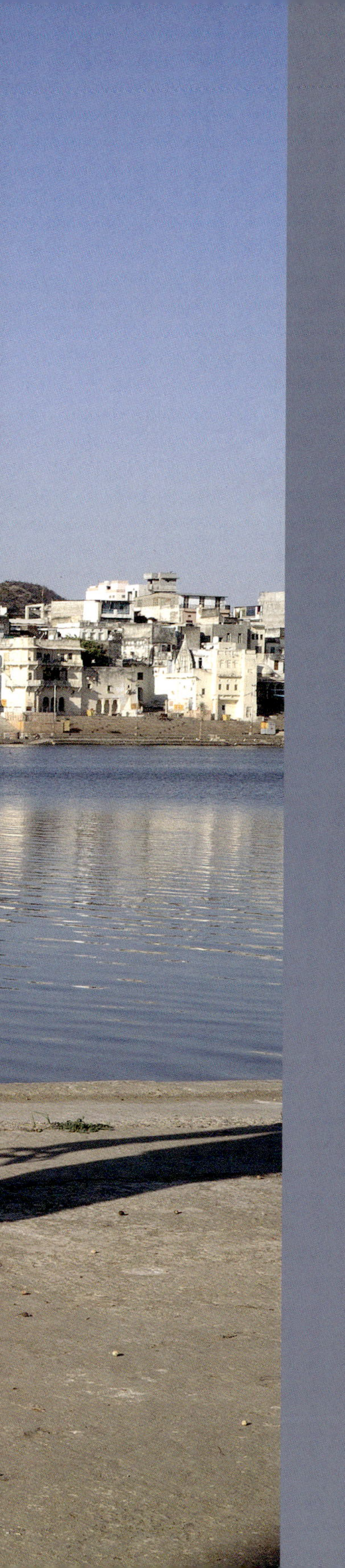

PUSHKAR

I first visited Pushkar years ago, when it was a small scattering of white-washed homes, temples, and guesthouses set around a cobalt blue lake, surrounded by the Thar Desert, and overlooked by the jagged peaks of the Aravalli Range.

On a recent visit I found that not much has changed in terms of its physical appearance. It was a refreshing revelation. For a week or so during the annual camel festival, which is held each year in late October or early November, Pushkar is a riotous affair of livestock sales, nomads in scarlet turbans, folk music and dances, gypsies, dust, hot air balloons, and tour groups, but for the rest of the year it remains a calm and serene place, maintaining, in the words of a young traveler I met, a "chill vibe."

It is hard to say just how old the town is since its origins lie in mythology. Hindu texts going back at least two thousand years make references to Pushkar. And devotees have been making pilgrimages to its temples and lake for at least that long. They come to pray to Lord Brahma, the deity responsible for creating the world and everything in it, and to ritually bath in the holy waters. According to legend, the lake was sanctified when Lord Brahma dropped a lotus flower onto its surface (the word *pushkara* roughly translates from Sanskrit as "blue lotus flower"), and for a few days each year, corresponding to the autumnal full moon, it is believed to be a geophysical manifestation of the celestial deity. To bathe in the Pushkar Lake on those auspicious days is to come as close to God as literally possible.

Counterculture travelers began showing up in Pushkar in the late 1960s, when it first appeared on the Hippie Trail, and soon found themselves blending in with the throngs of other pilgrims flocking to the town. One of the notable daily events in Pushkar is sunset, when people of all persuasions stroll down to the lakeside to watch the sky dissolve into a palette of desert colors—cerulean blue, orange into red, pink, and finally shades of deep purple. The travelers gather at the ghats to play hand drums and dance in beaded harem outfits, to drink chai and smoke, to juggle or hula hoop, or to just quietly sit and gaze at the mesmerizing scene. Sadhus, pilgrims, and the town locals also come to the lake at this time to pray, to chat with one another, or to linger and watch the hippie antics. It's a friendly blend of sacred and secular life, of community, of residents and foreigners, of the past and present. The best place to witness all this has to be the stepped ghats in front of the Sunset Café.

PAGE 40: Pushkar town and lake

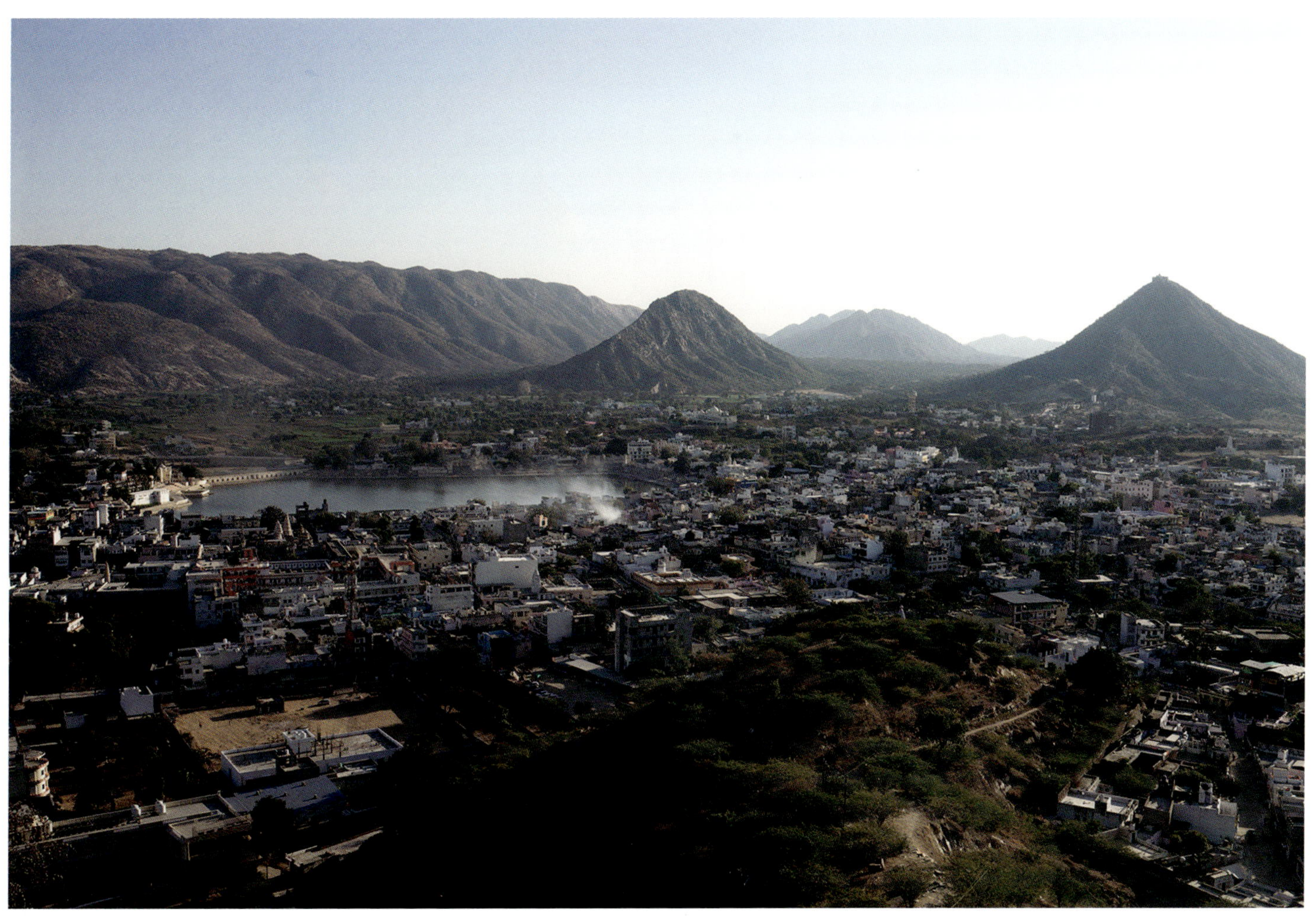

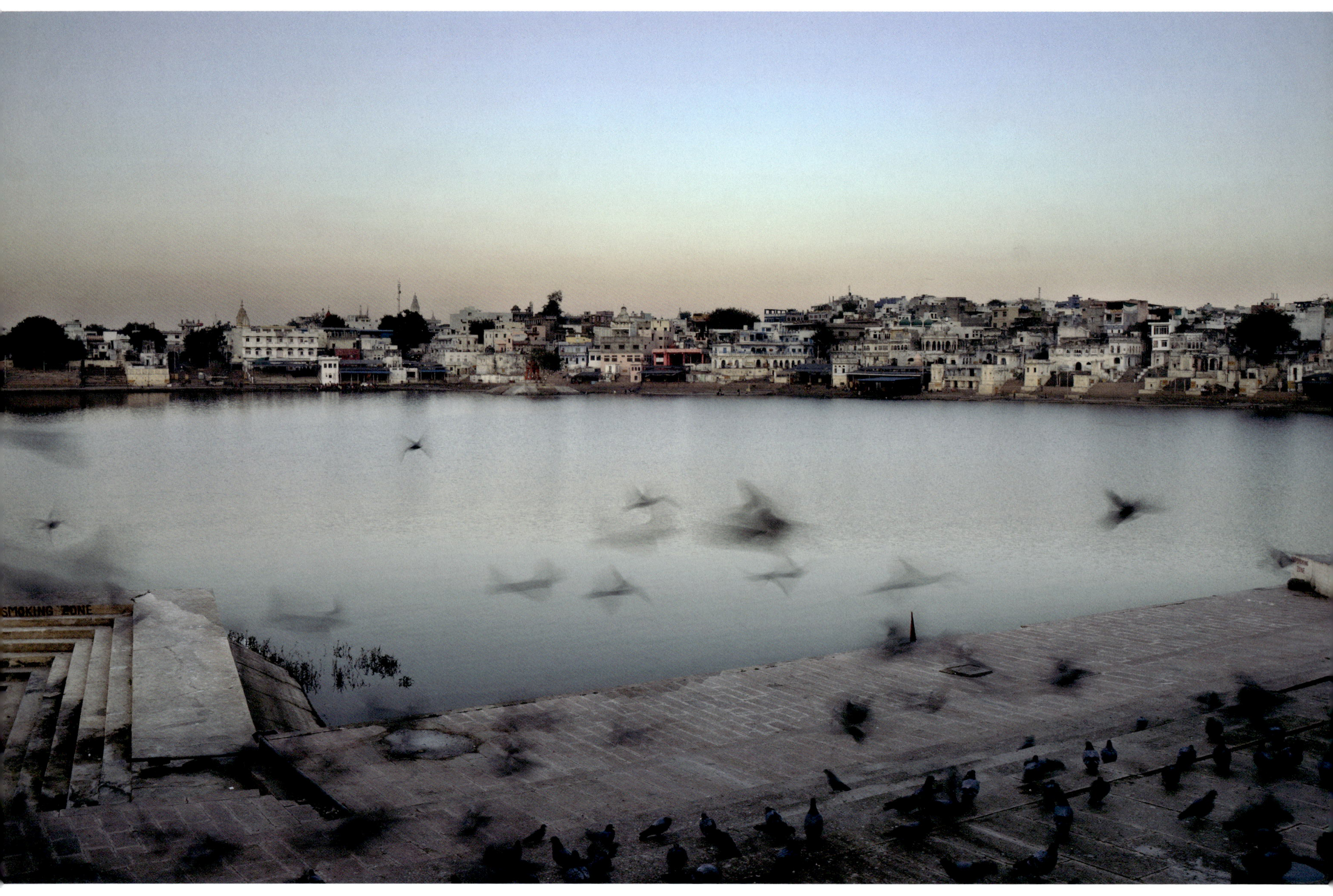
SMOKING ZONE

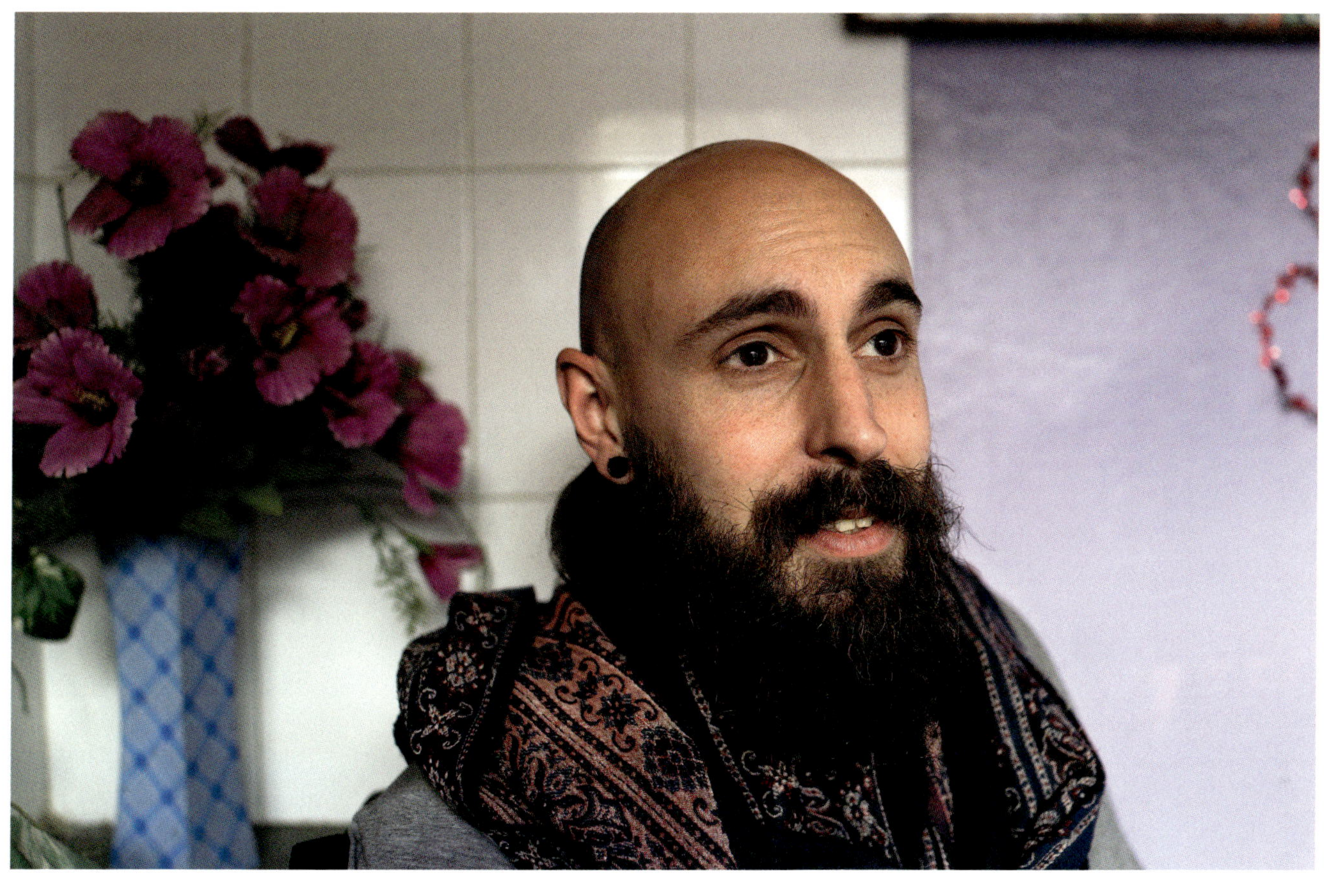

ABOVE: Costa (Germany). A young man smiled and nodded when I entered the "Hare Krishna Café." We began a conversation. Costa told me he'd just spent a month in an ashram and was waiting for his partner, Siri, to return from an outing in the bazaar. He was an engineer in Germany, but his time in India changed all that. "My outlook on life is different now," he admitted.

"When I return to Germany, Siri and I will open a coffee shop and a bookstore specializing in spiritual subjects." I smiled, thinking about his namesake— Costa Coffee, the second largest coffeehouse chain in the world, and wished him well. We never met again, but I sometimes find myself thinking about Costa and wondering whether his plans for a coffee shop and bookstore in Berlin ever came into fruition.

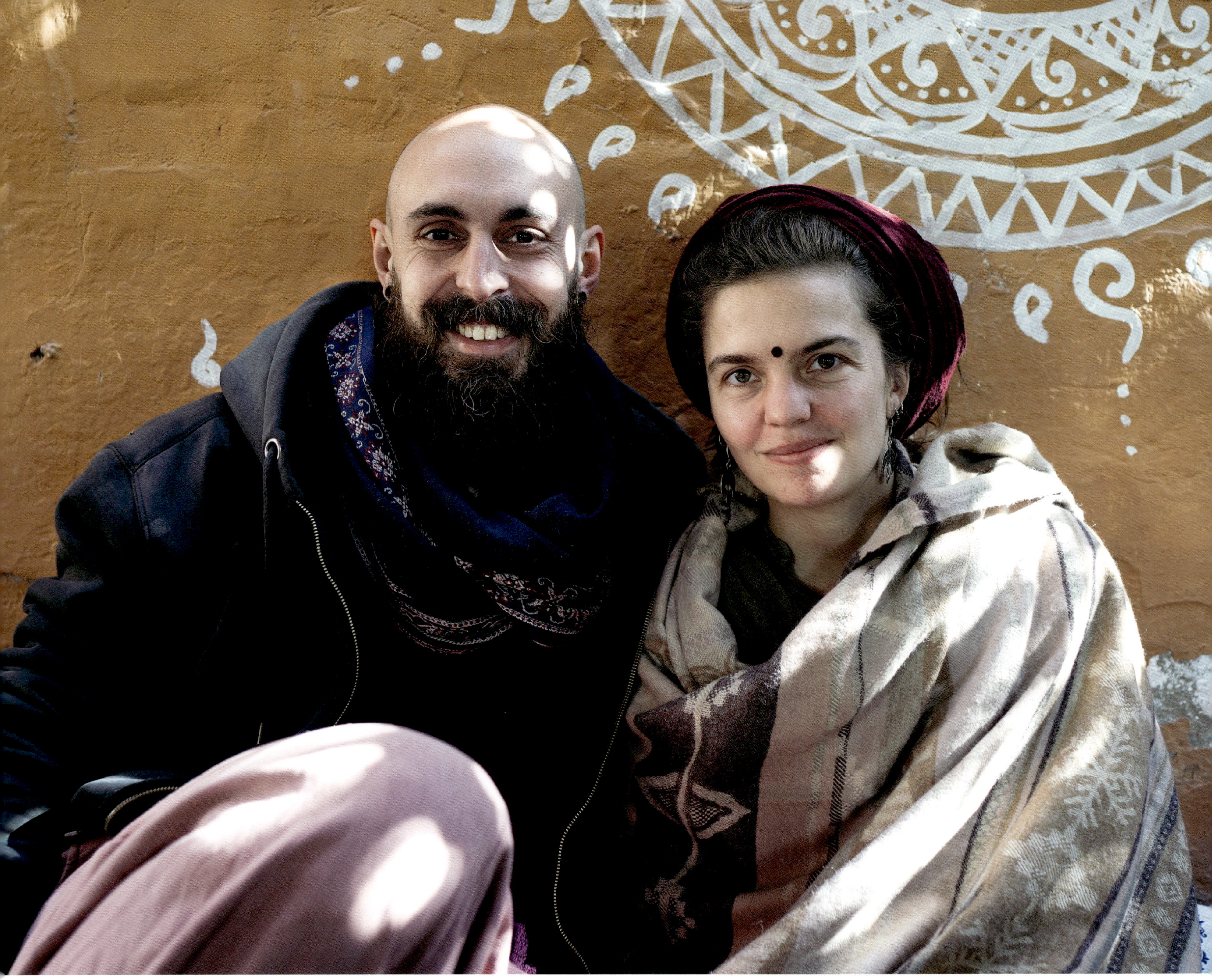

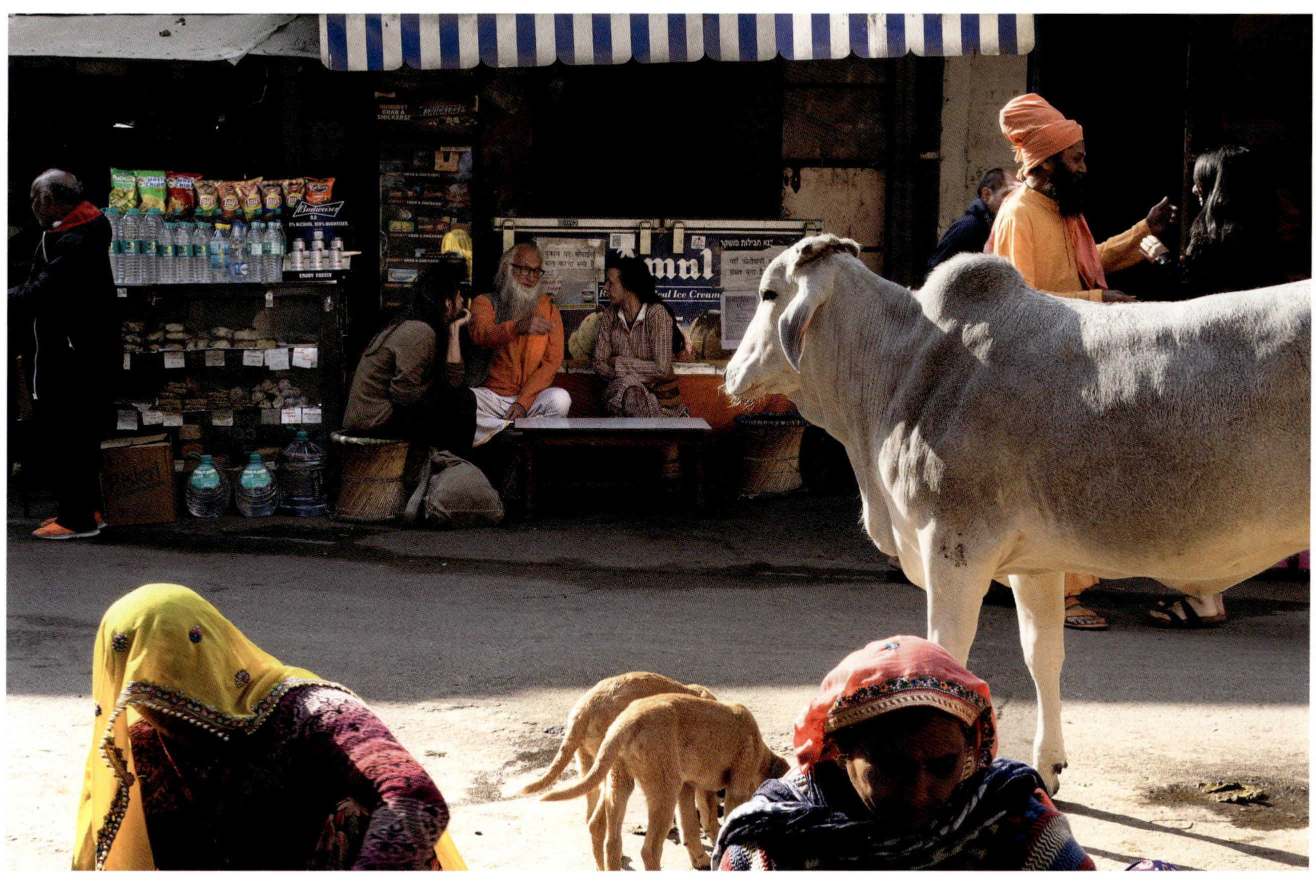

ABOVE: Pushkar's bazaar is the commercial heartbeat of the holy town, where all manner of goods and services are on offer. The intermingling of western travelers, townsfolk, and pilgrims enlivens an already fantastical setting. I lingered at a tea shop to watch the milling crowd and was rewarded with incongruous sights. A European man wearing the saffron and white outfit of a mendicant administered spiritual advice to a pair of young western travelers. A saddhu strolled past. Then a sacred cow. A couple of street dogs fed on thrown-away scraps. Village women sold produce on the roadside. I could have sat there all day.

OPPOSITE: Costa and Siri (Germany)

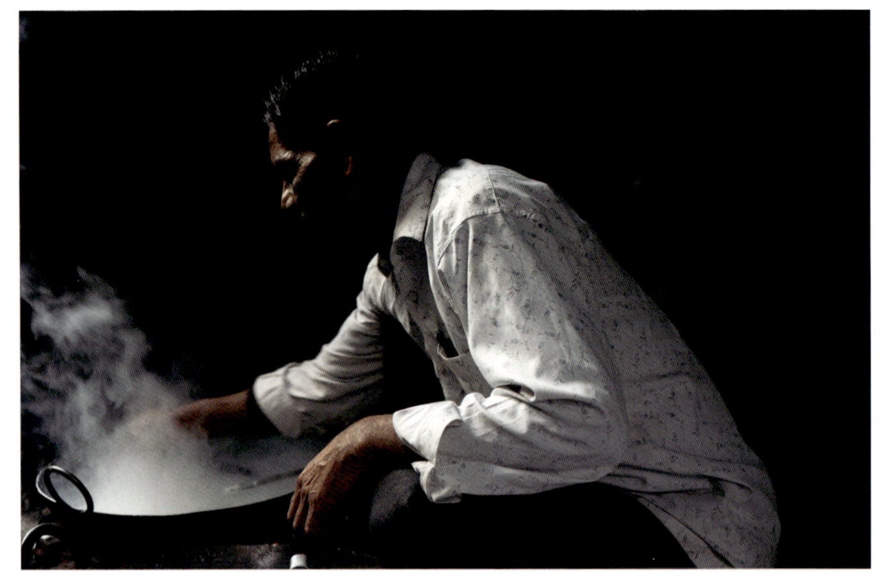
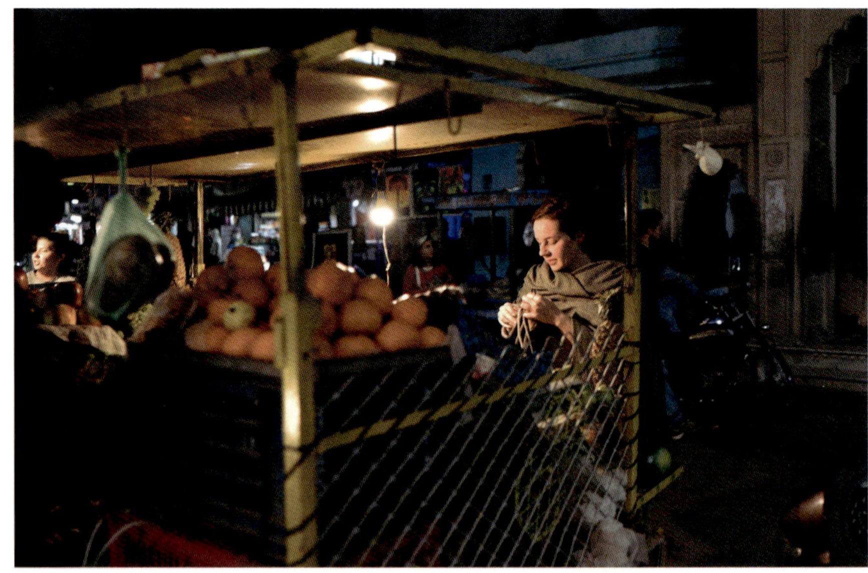
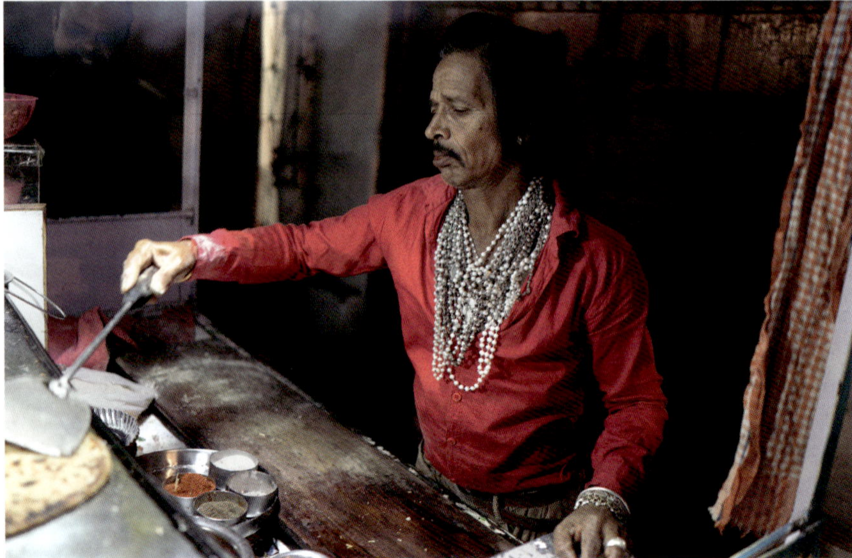
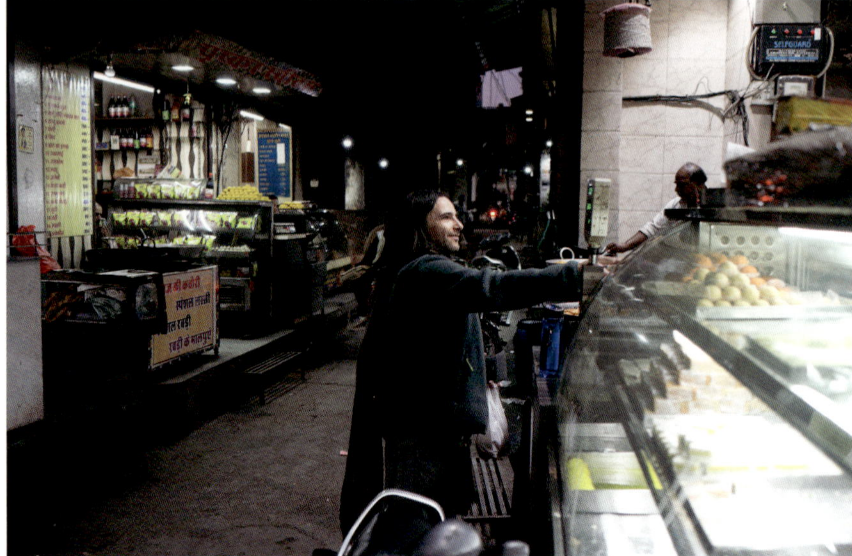

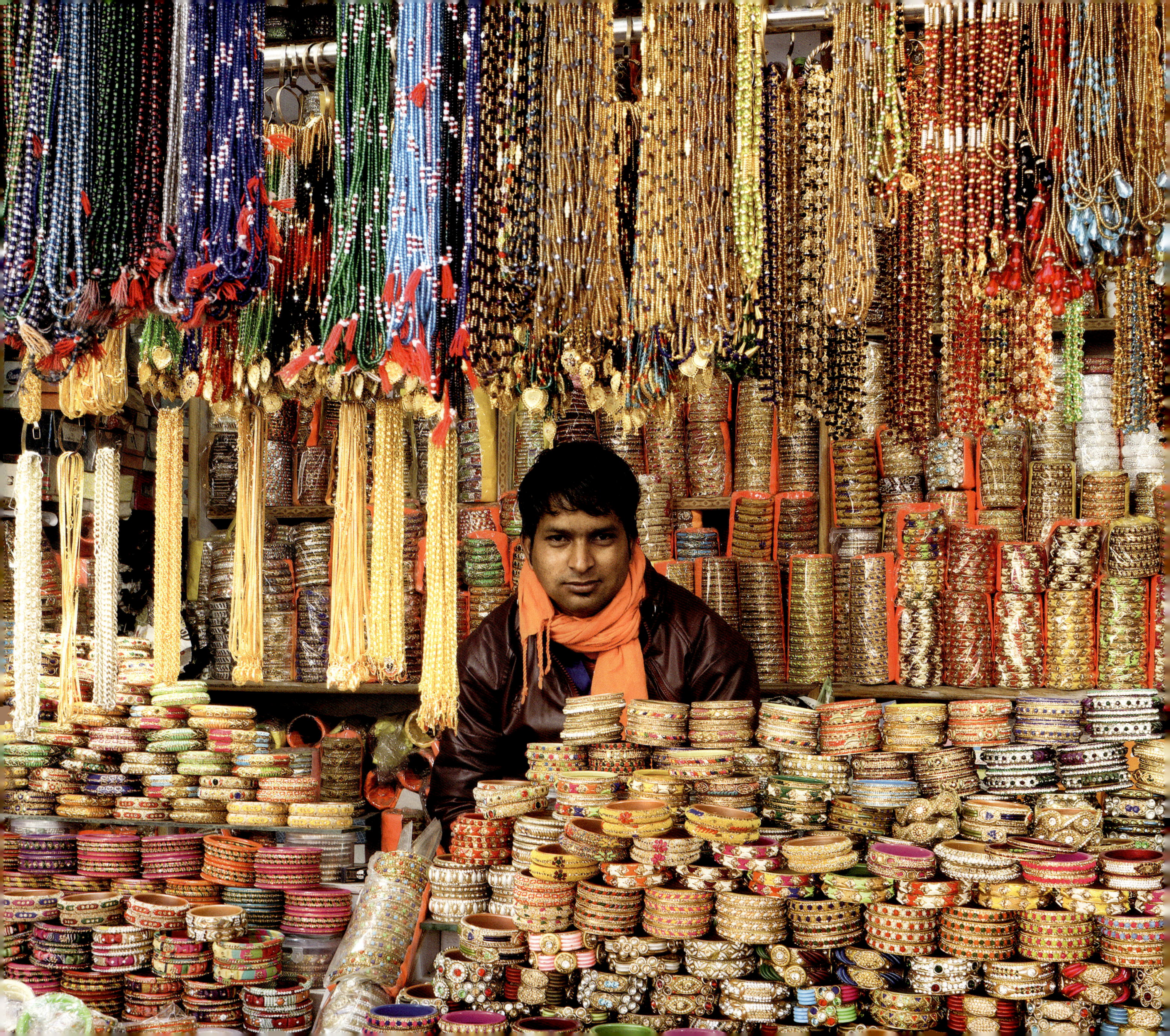

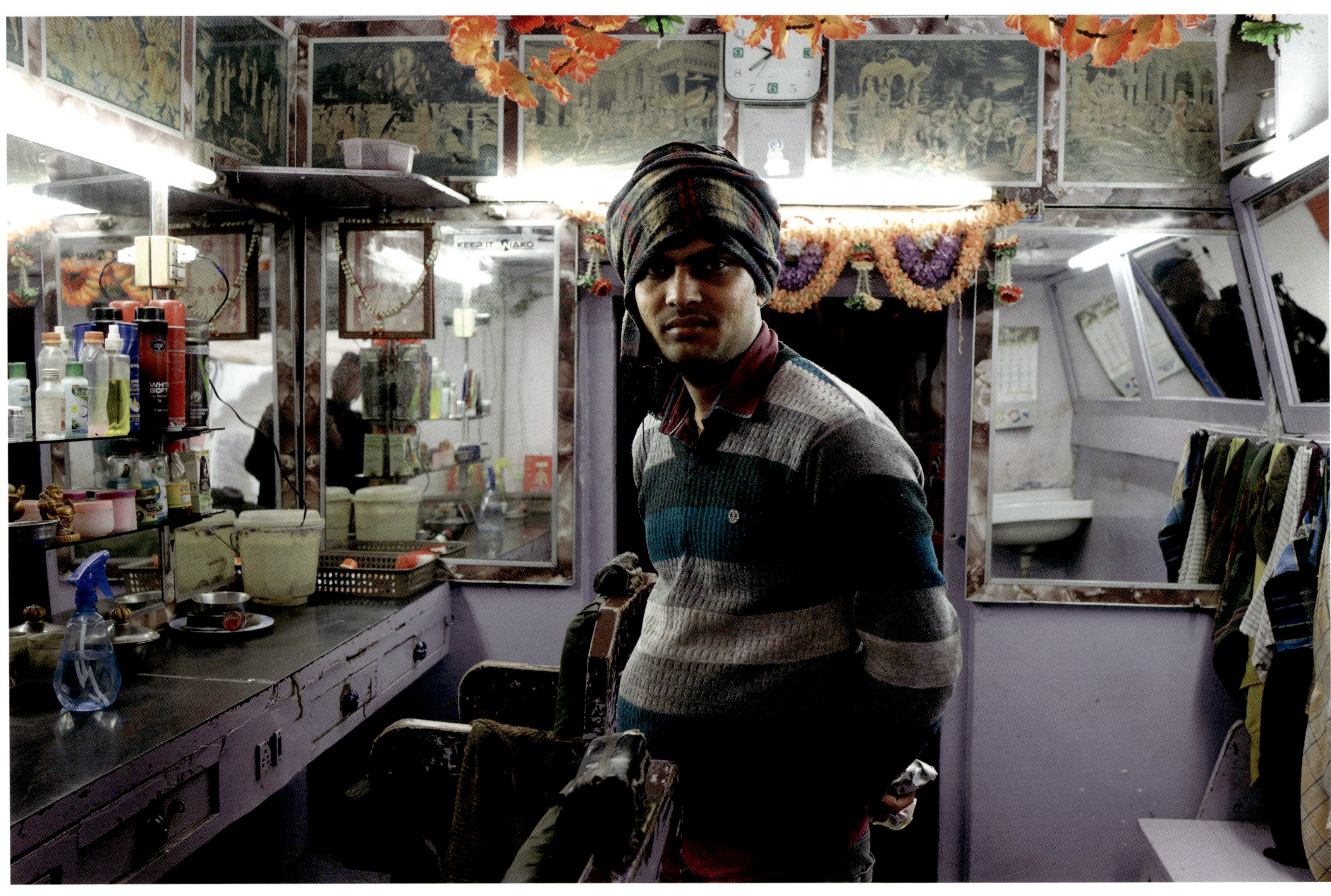

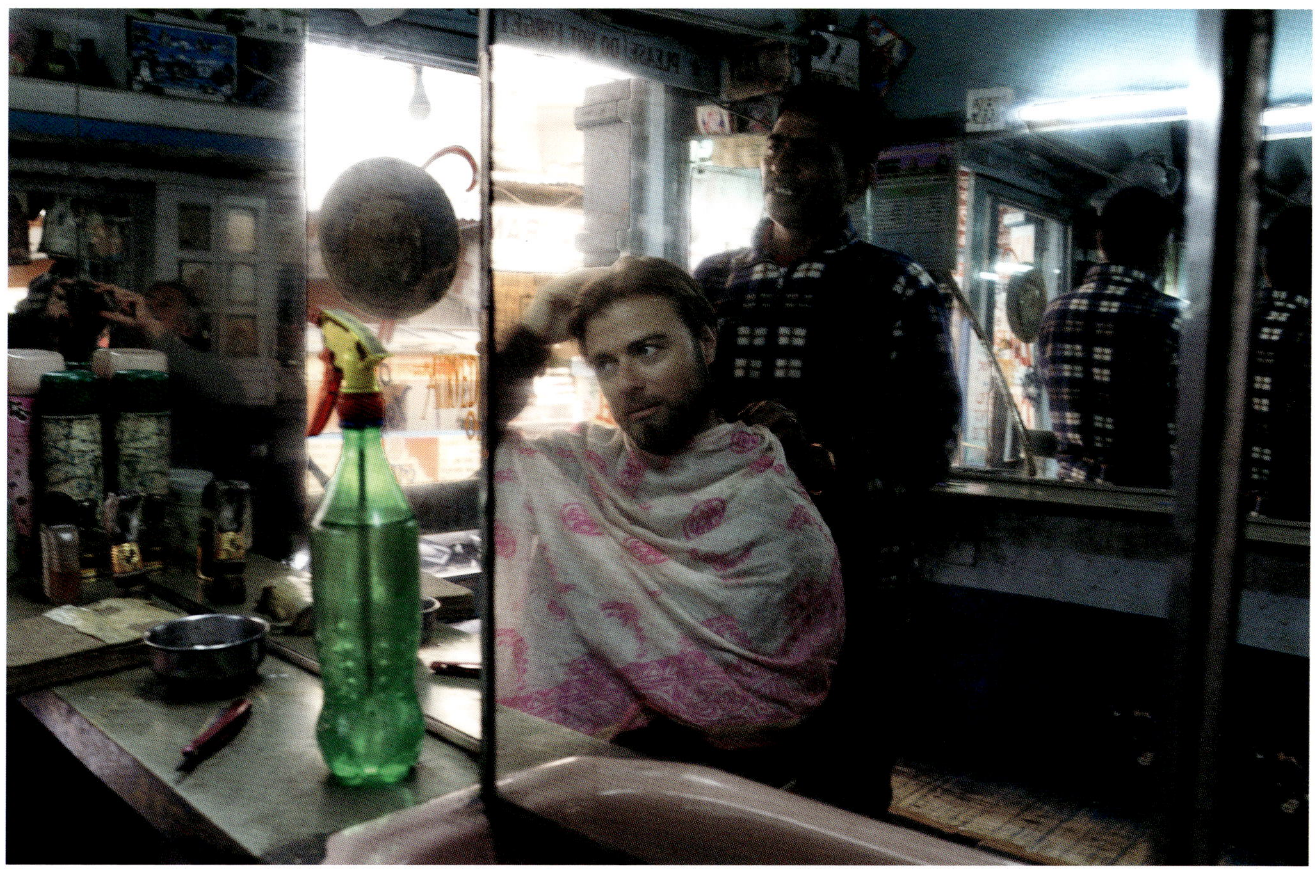

ABOVE: Ethan (Scotland). I visited a barbershop in Pushkar's main bazaar for a morning shave and took a seat in a red chair with cracked vinyl and a broken armrest. A Bollywood song blasted from an old-fashioned radio. A stick of sandalwood incense sent perfumed smoke into the air. It was a tiny space and the only other patron in the shop was Ethan from Scotland. He'd let his hair grow long and was getting it cut. We struck up a conversation. He told me he'd been living for several months in a nearby desert retreat, learning Ayurvedic treatments and practicing yoga. But it was time to go home.

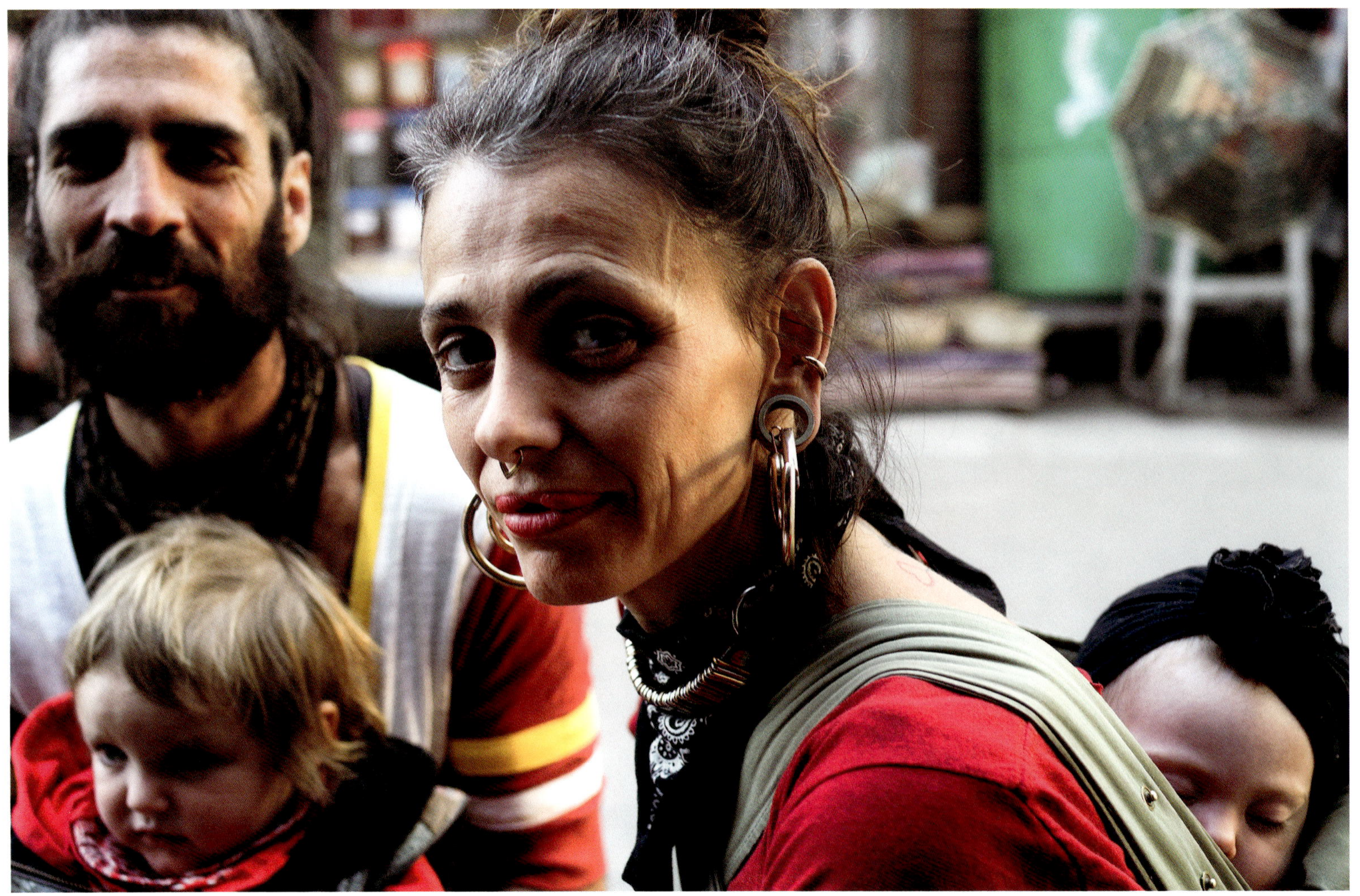

Pinka (Spain) with family: Ato (Argentina), daughter Indiana, and baby Yuma. When Pinka and her family showed up, I mistook them for gypsies. It was an honest mistake. I was in Rajasthan, where the Roma tribes have their geographical origins. The gypsies are sometimes called "The Travelers," an appellation that fit Pinka and her family very well. "We design clothes, have them made here in Pushkar, and sell them in the outdoor markets in Europe," she explained. "We are traveling constantly." After a pause, Pinka continued: "But it is harder now with the children. We are getting tired. We want to buy a small piece of land in Portugal and start an organic farm. I guess we want to settle down after so many years on the road."

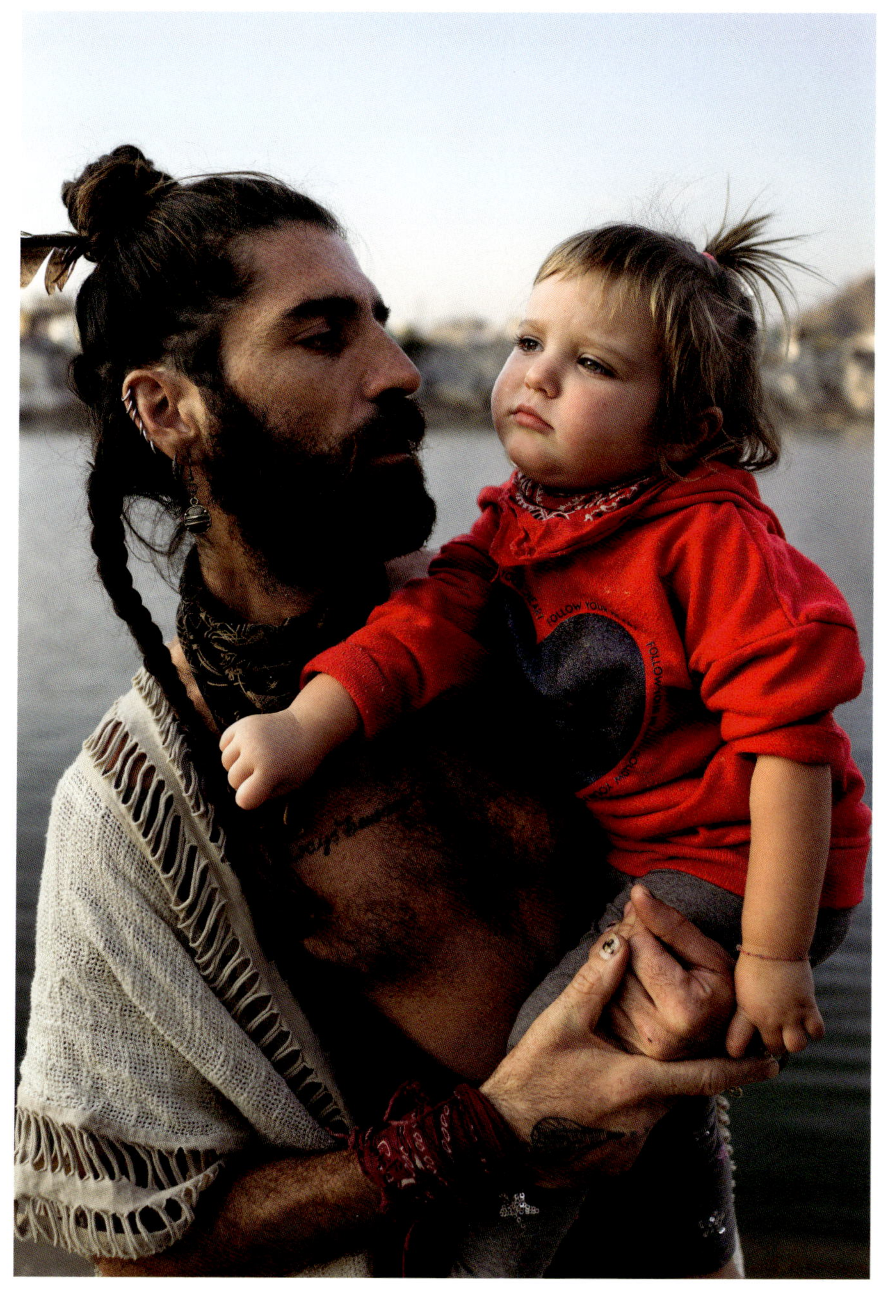
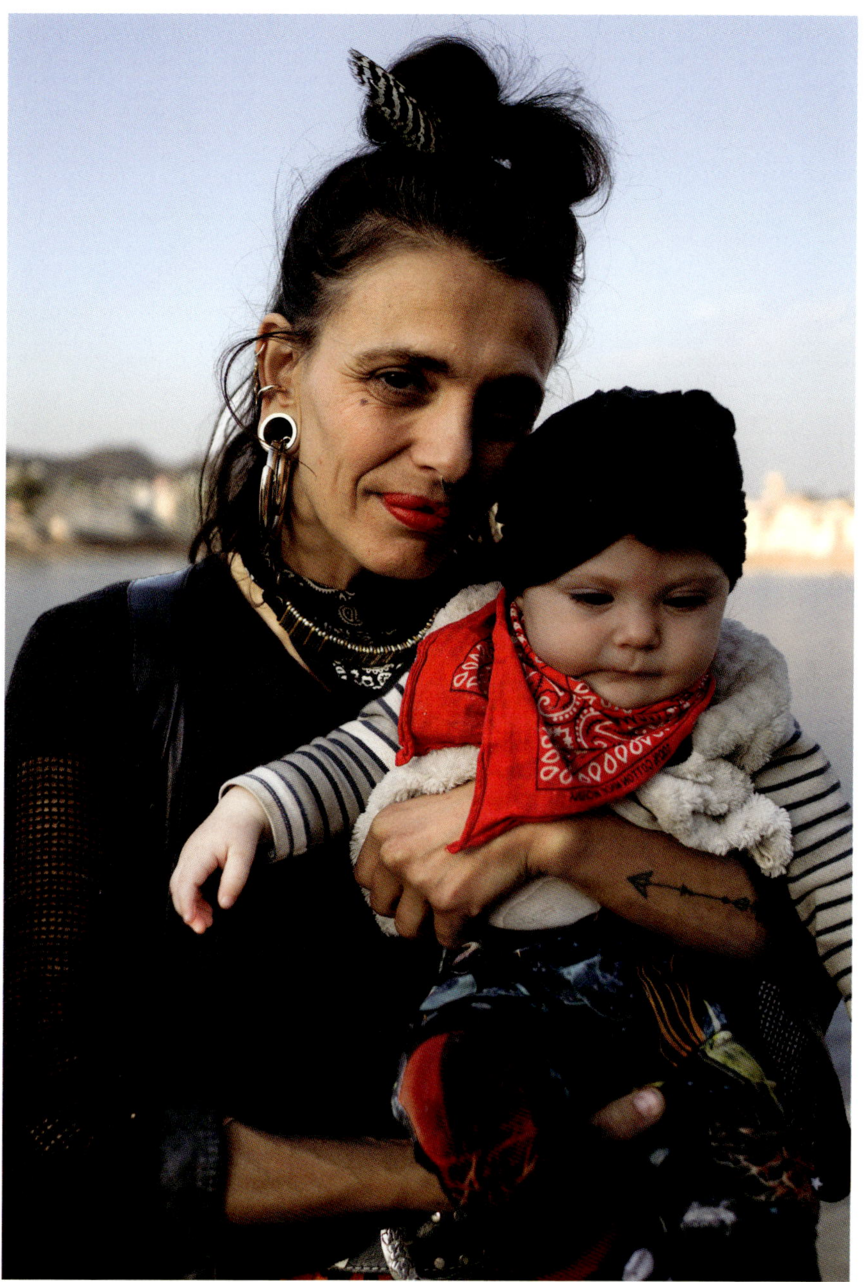

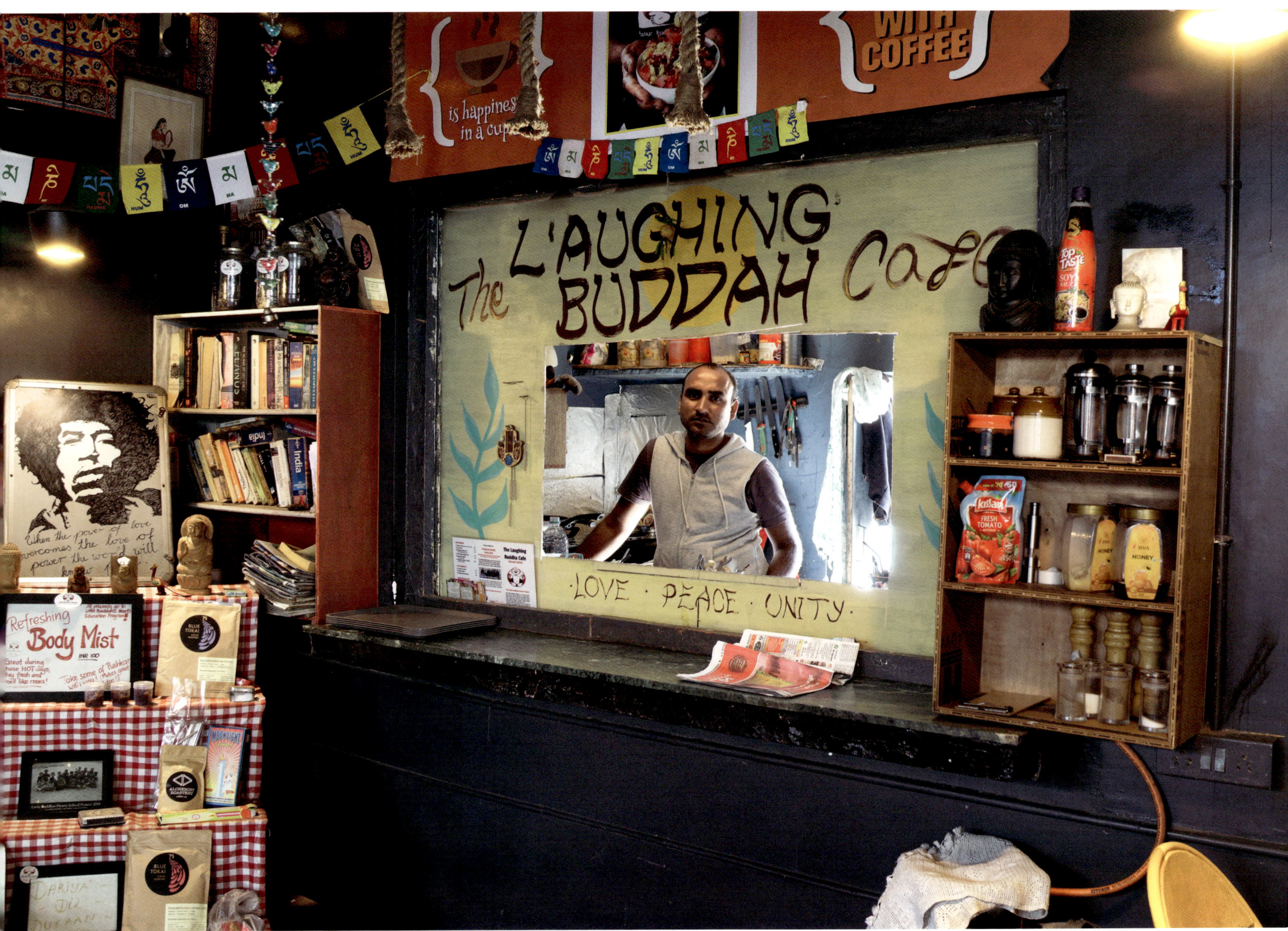
WITH COFFEE
is happiness
in a cup
The L'AUGHING BUDDAH Cafe
LOVE · PEACE · UNITY
Refreshing
Body Mist
INR 100
Great during
those HOT days,
stay fresh and
smell like roses!
Take some of Pushkar
with you! Makes a great
BLUE TOKAI
MOONLIGHT
ALCHEMIST ROASTERS
The Laughing
Buddha Cafe
BLUE TOKAI
DARIYA
DIL
DUKAAN
TOP TASTE
SOY SAUCE
kissan
FRESH TOMATO
HONEY
HONEY

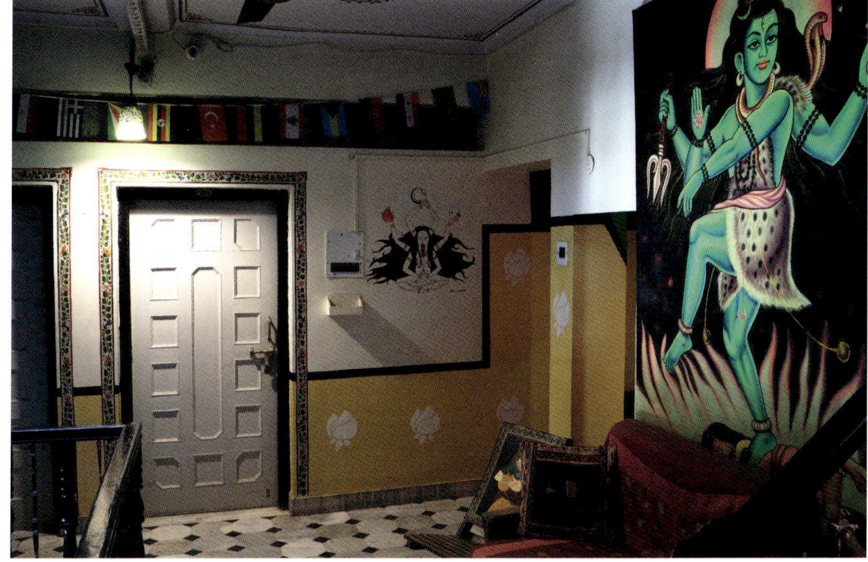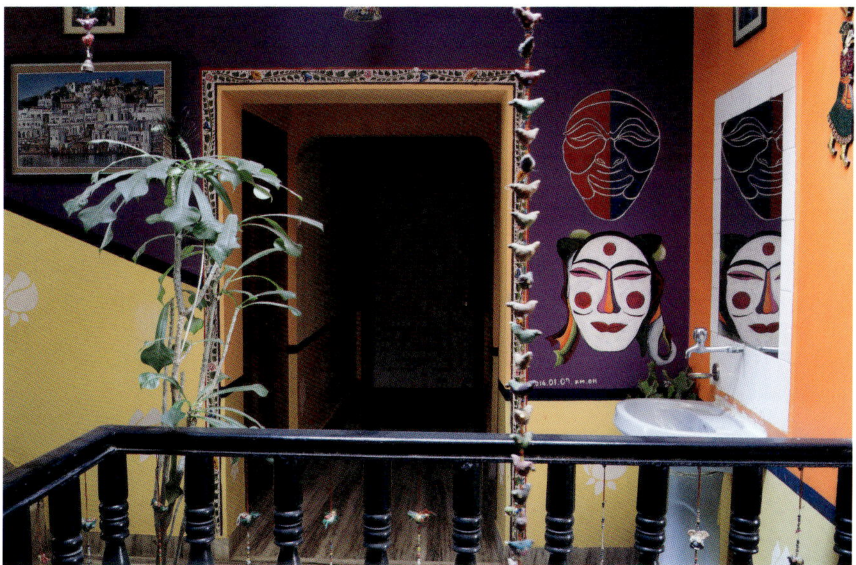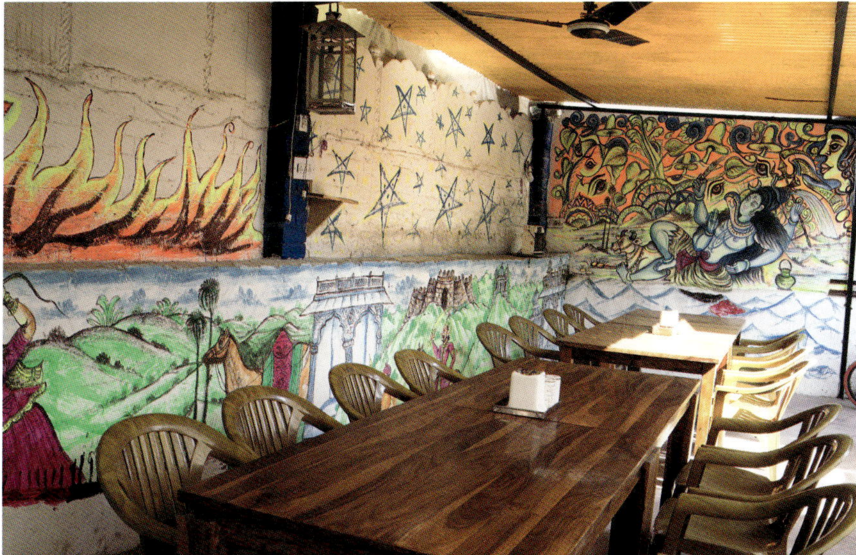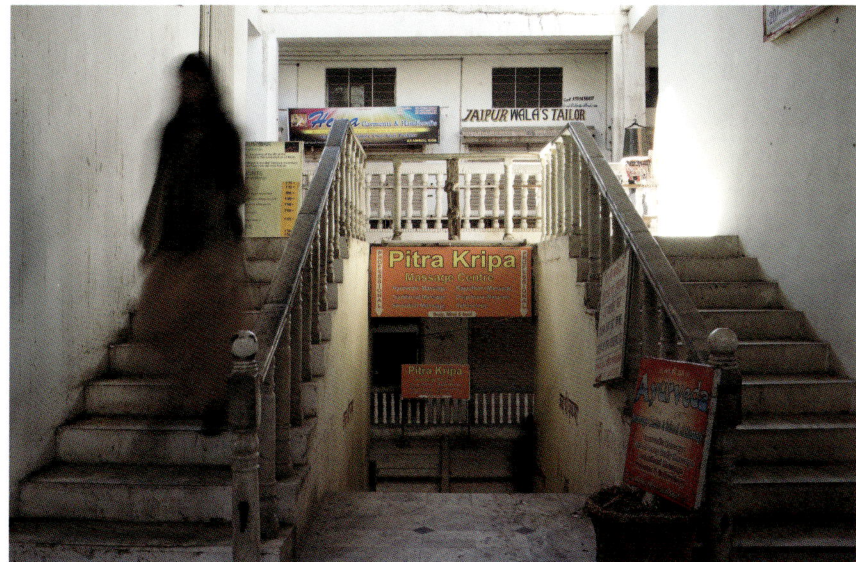

Guesthouses in Pushkar

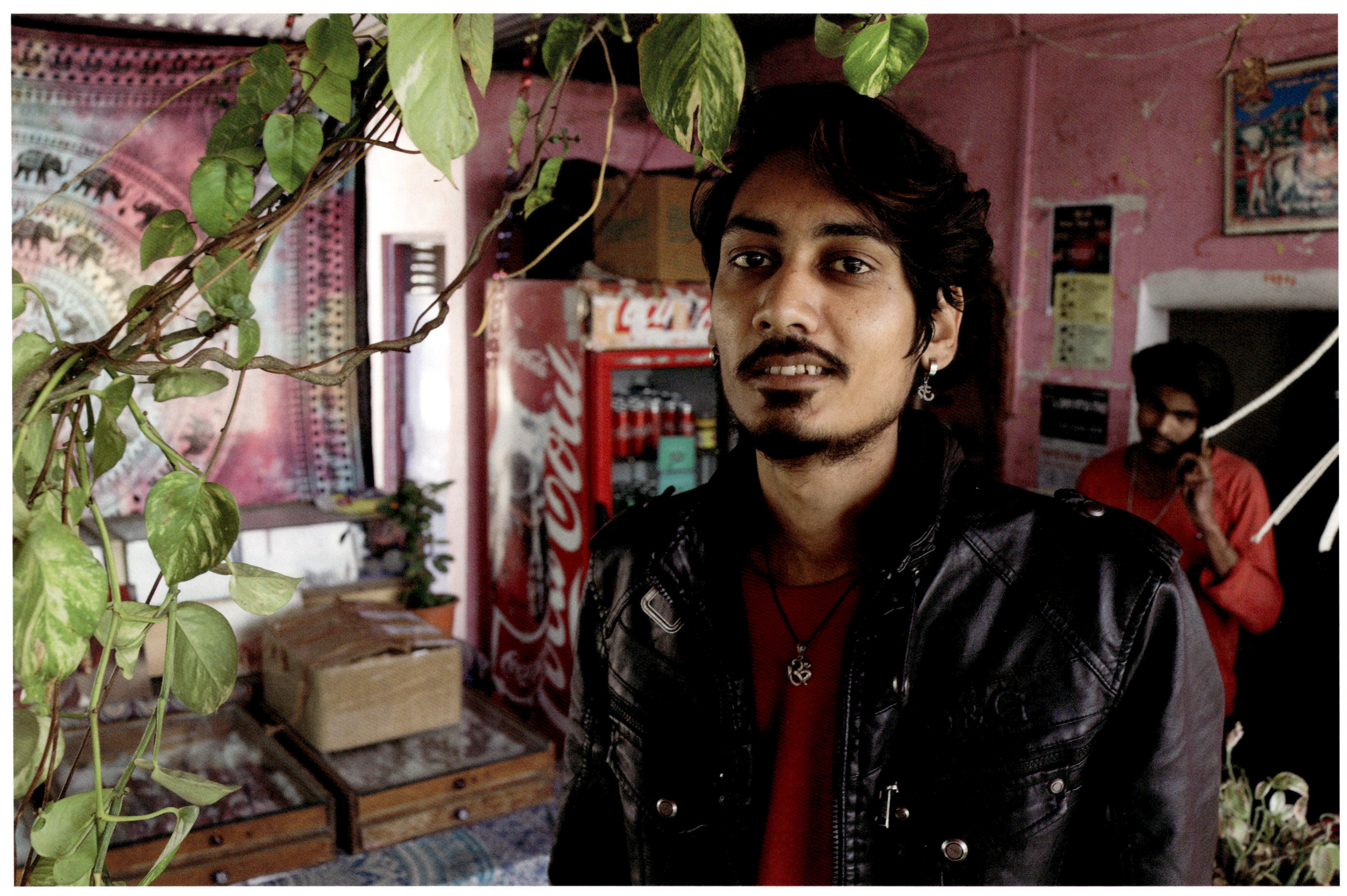

Romi (India), waiter at Raju's Restaurant

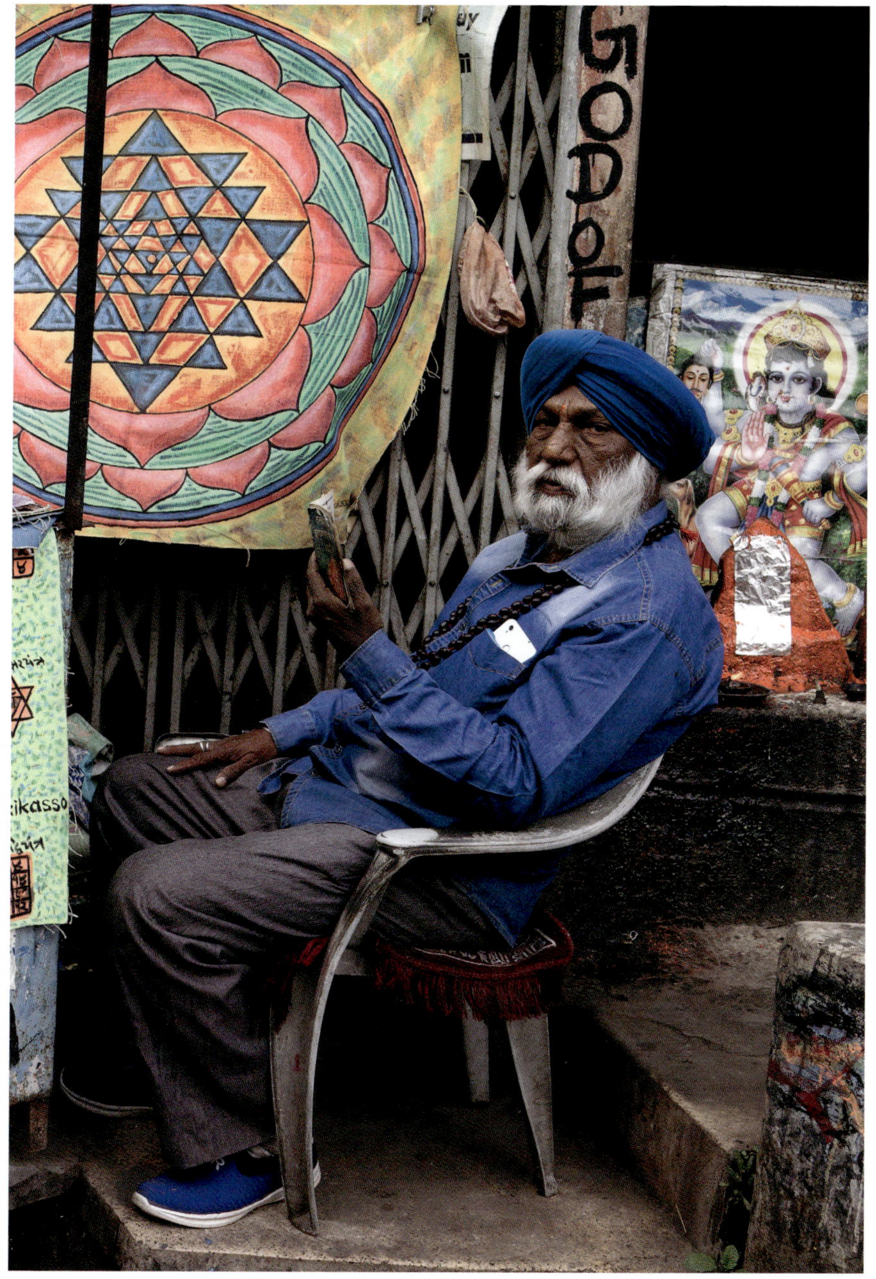

Kishan Singh (India), aka "Kikasso"

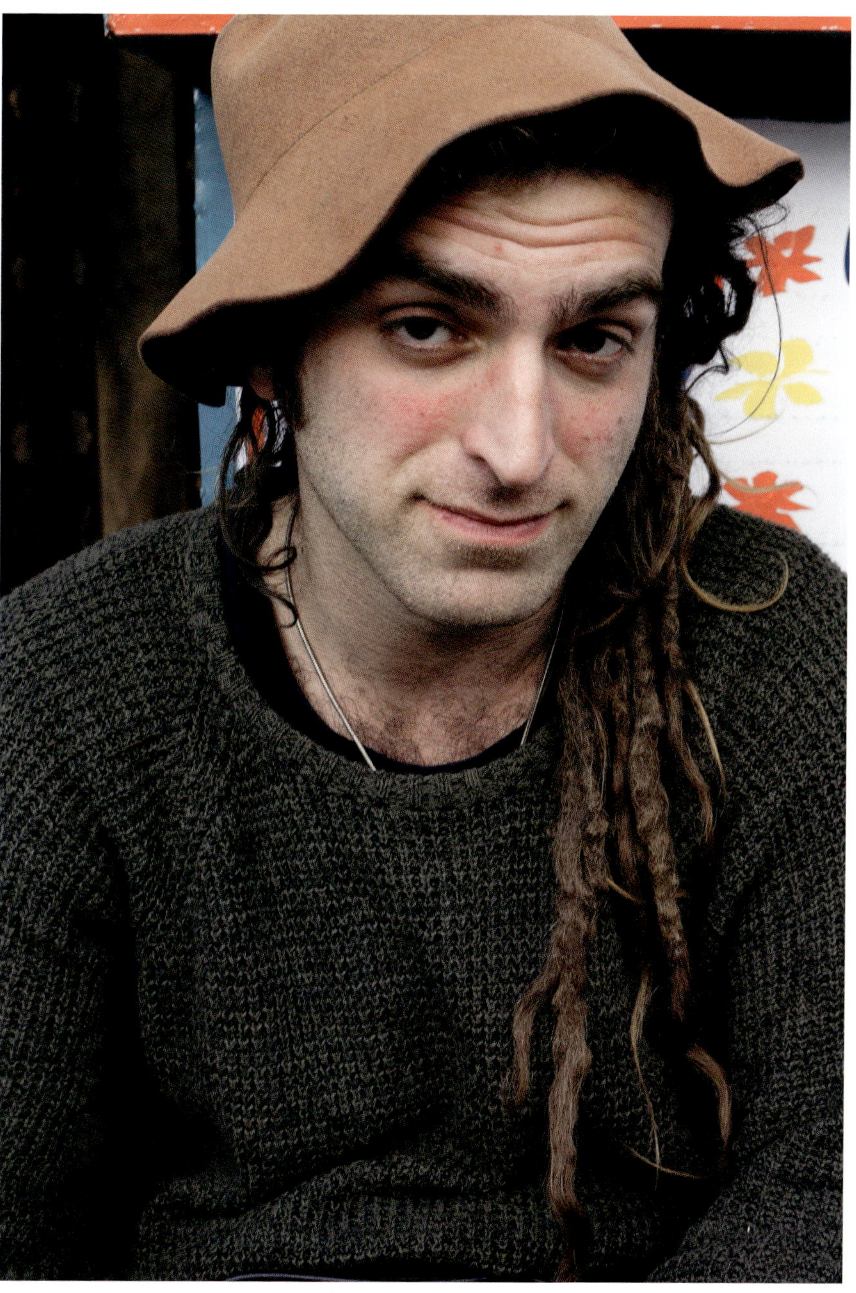

Davide (Italy)

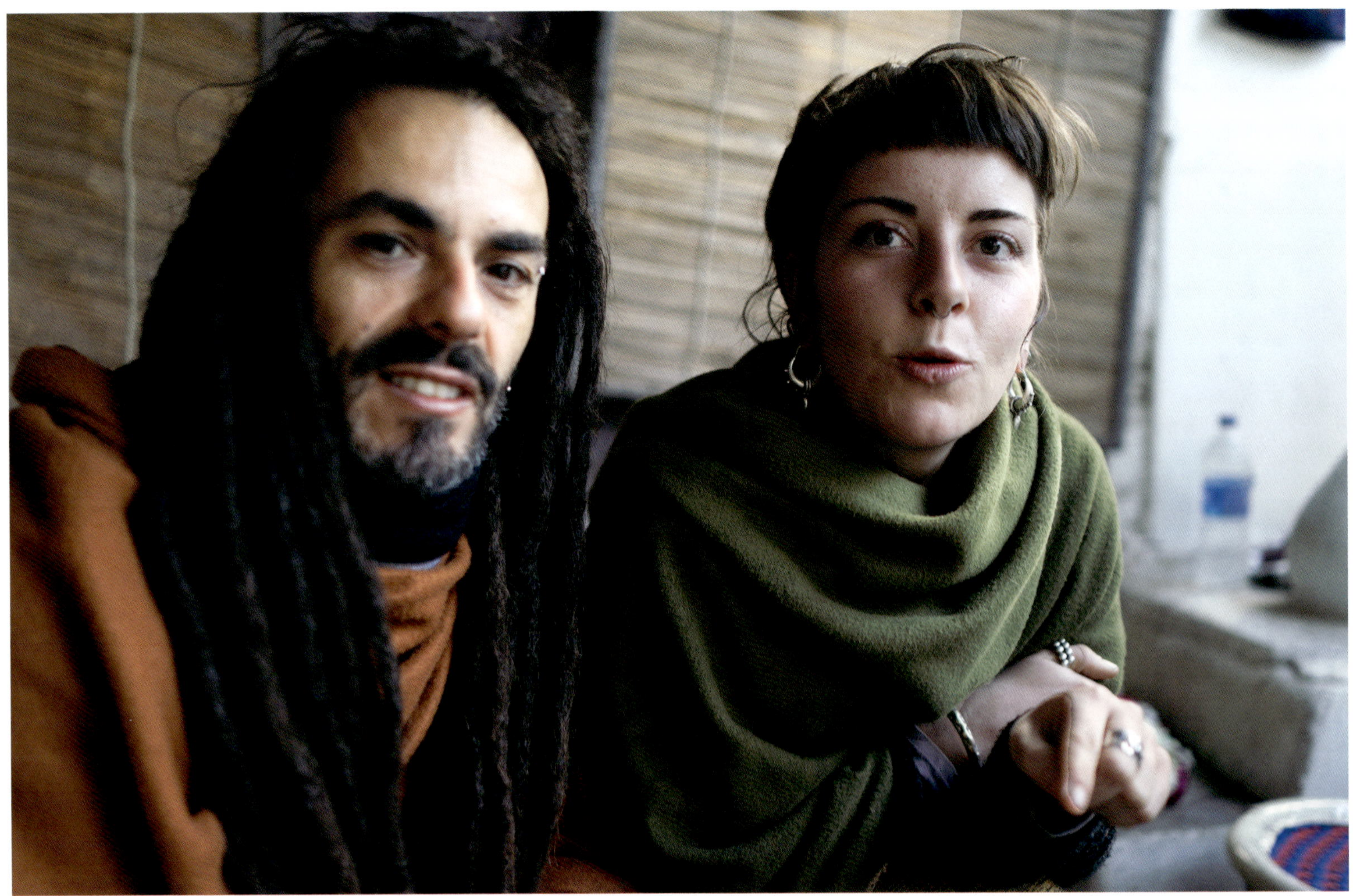

ABOVE: Tiago (Portugal) and Molly (England). One of the joys I gain by visiting places in India that host free spirits from the West are the opportunities it provides to look back on my life and to see myself at a younger age in the travelers I meet. It is a form of time travel for me. When I saw Molly and Tiago making their way through the Pushkar bazaar, all wide-eyed with bright smiles, I was immediately drawn to them. I asked Molly about her motivation to visit India. Her reply: "It is to experience the vivid color of this amazing culture. To witness the kindness of sometimes hectic people. To taste the food. To learn about its history. I guess to experience the magic of India. I will be forever grateful for this journey."

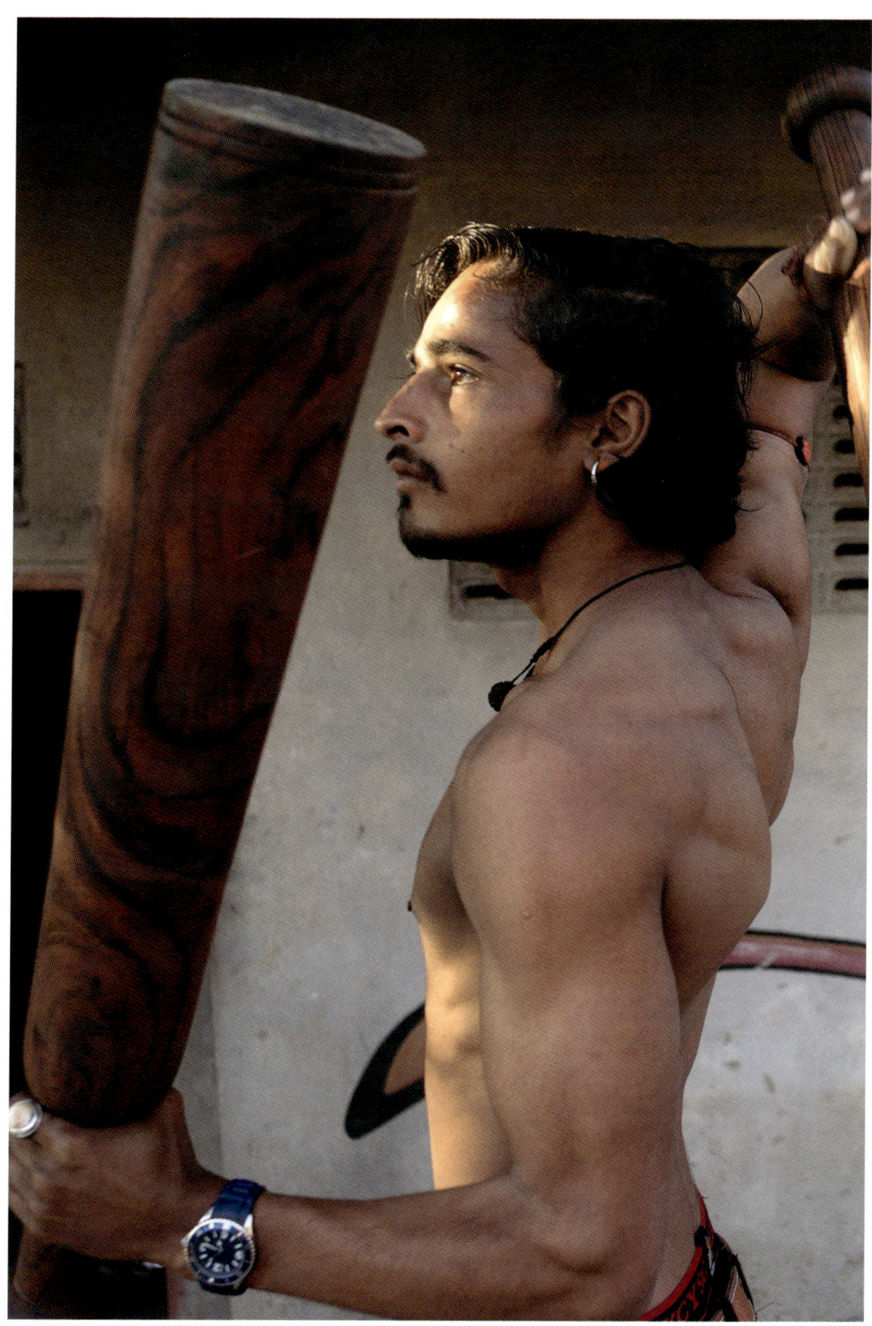

Chandra (India), spiritual guide and Ayurvedic healer

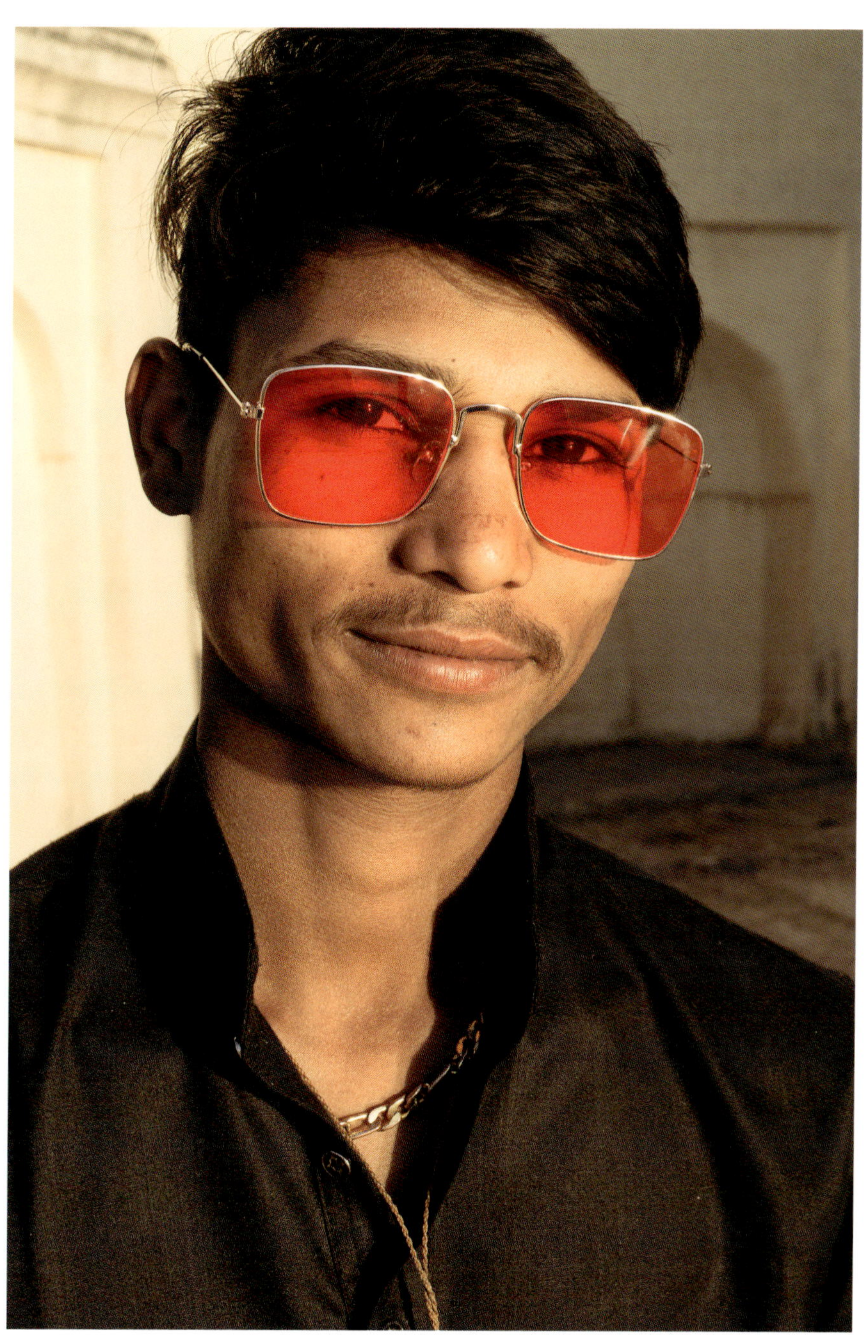

J.P. (India), Gypsy Café owner

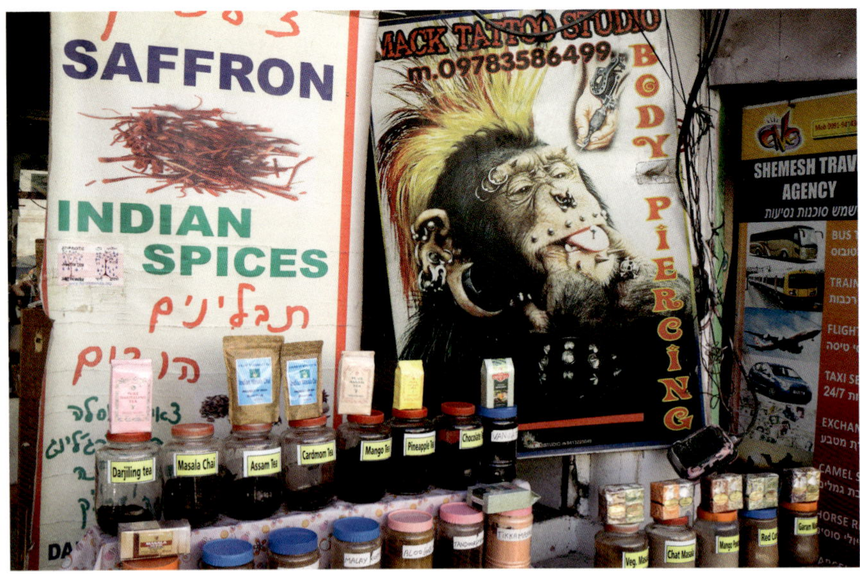

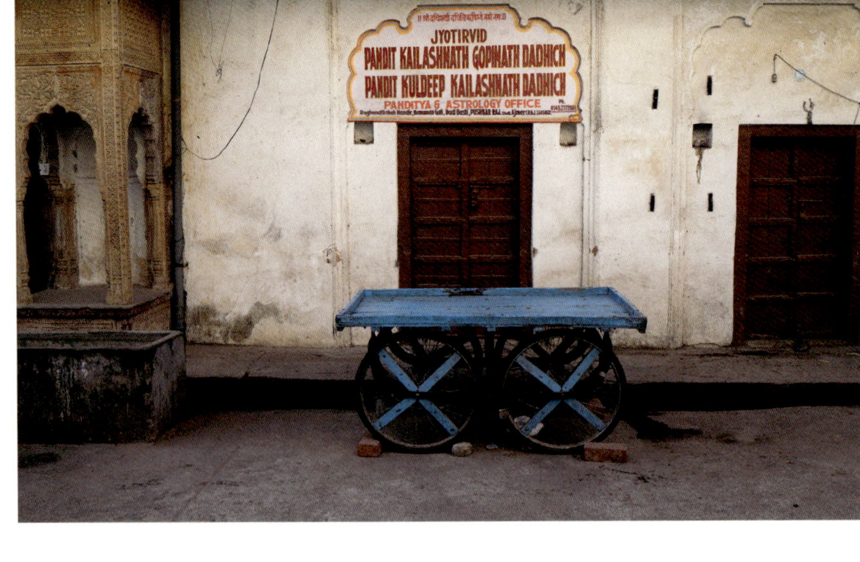

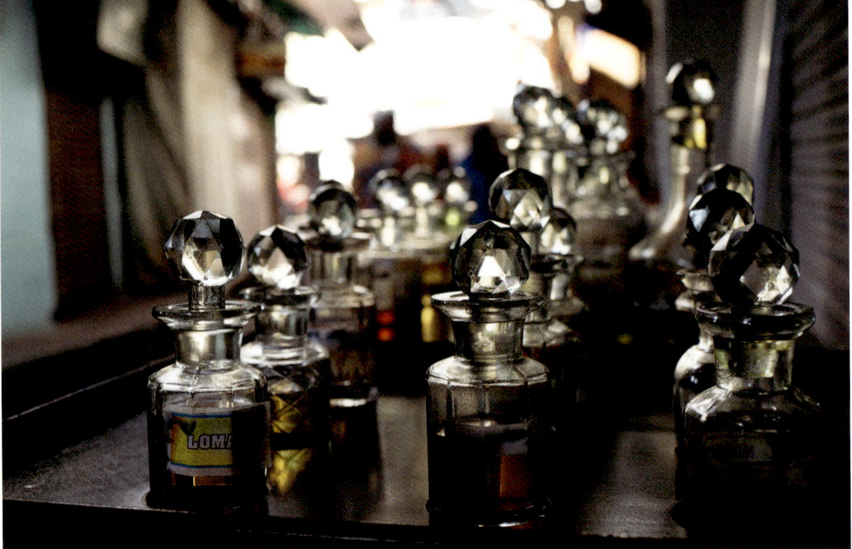

THIS PAGE: Years ago, when I first visited Pushkar, I was struck by the sundry religious articles in the marketplace: rosary beads, incense sticks, wrist bands woven from sacred cotton thread, religious books, brass statuary of gods and goddesses, fresh or dry fruit for altar offerings, coconuts. They reflected the significance of this desert oasis for the visiting Hindu pilgrims.

Nowadays, the puja items in the bazaar are augmented by goods and services directed toward the hippie consumers: tattoos, essential oils, chillums, yoga, healing massages.

I thought it was ironic that Pushkar's New Age products marketed to a Western clientele are not new at all, but originate in the 5,000-year-old Ayurvedic practices of India.

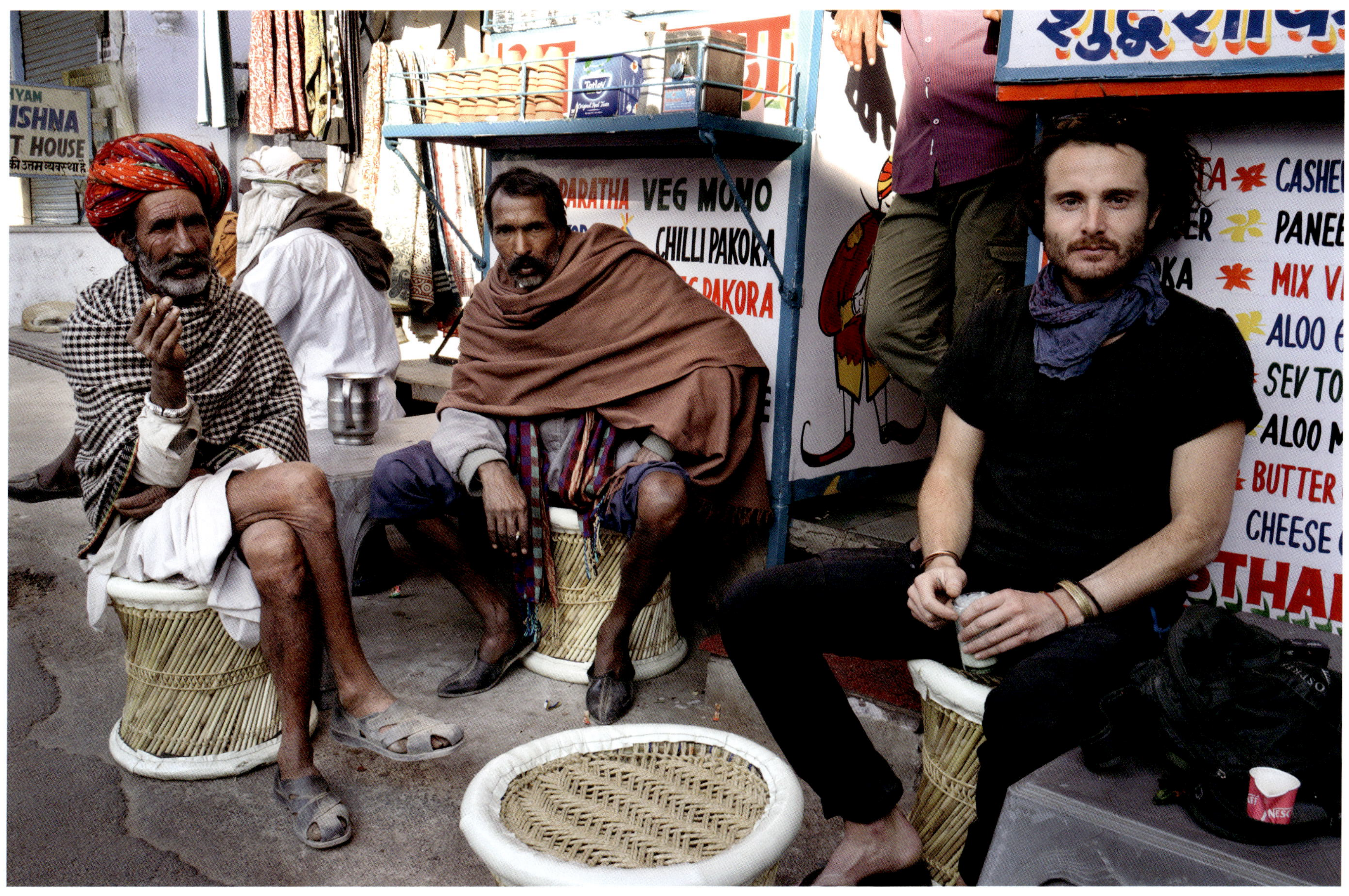

Luca (Italy) has a cup of tea with local
Gujar herdsmen.

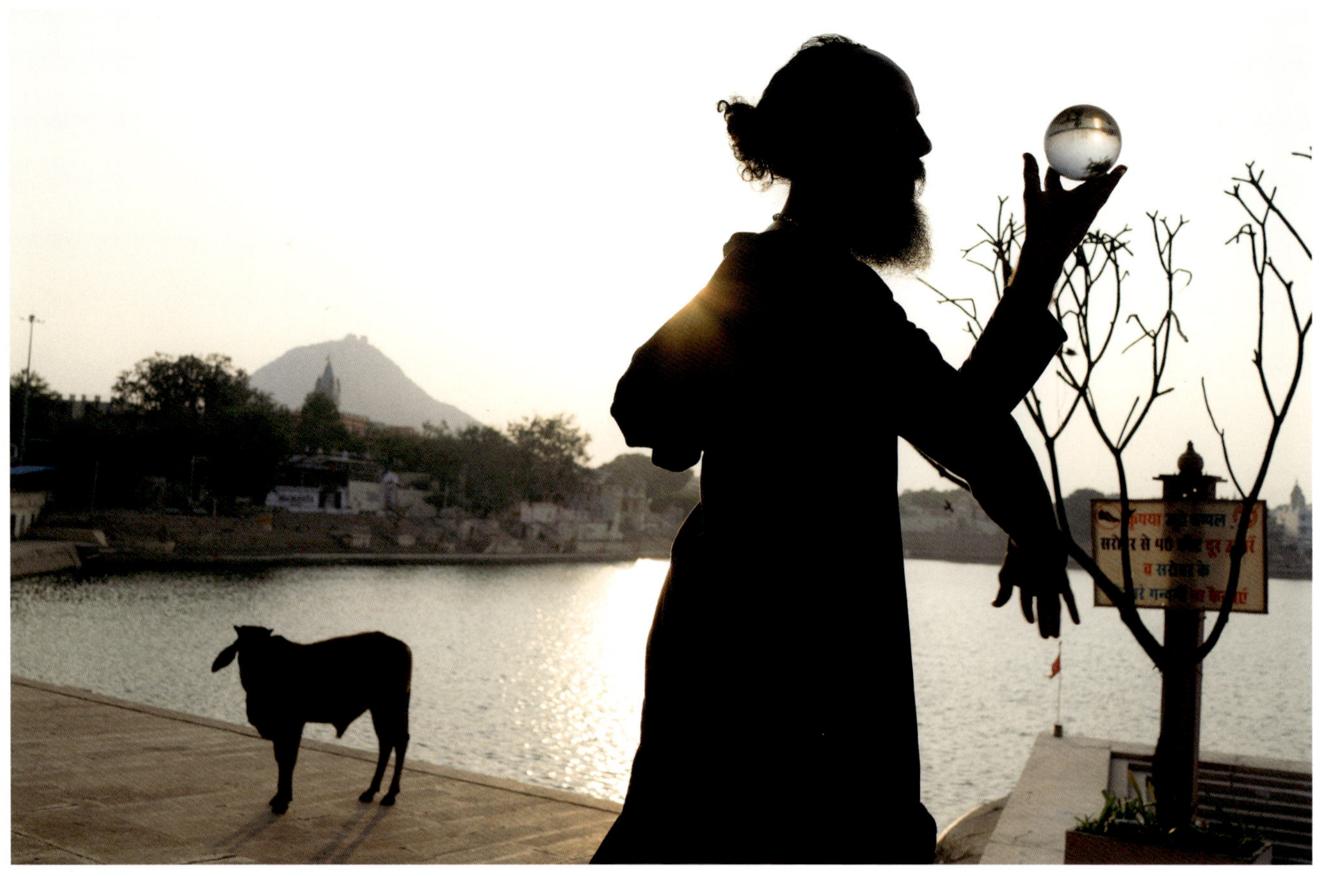

Each evening at sunset a lively stream of people heads to the Jaipur Ghat located in the southeastern corner of Pushkar Lake, to watch the sunset and one another. It's a carnival of sights: jugglers, dancers, Taro card readers, musicians. I met Migu from Italy (upper left corner) who described to me how he learned new skills in Asia—juggling, pantomime, magic— and employed them in Europe, where he performed on the city streets for a living. "I was taught how to use the Fushigi ball in Japan and I practice it daily. It is a moving meditation. I feel myself in the void…full of everything." As I took my leave, he yelled after me: "Big hugs, my friend."

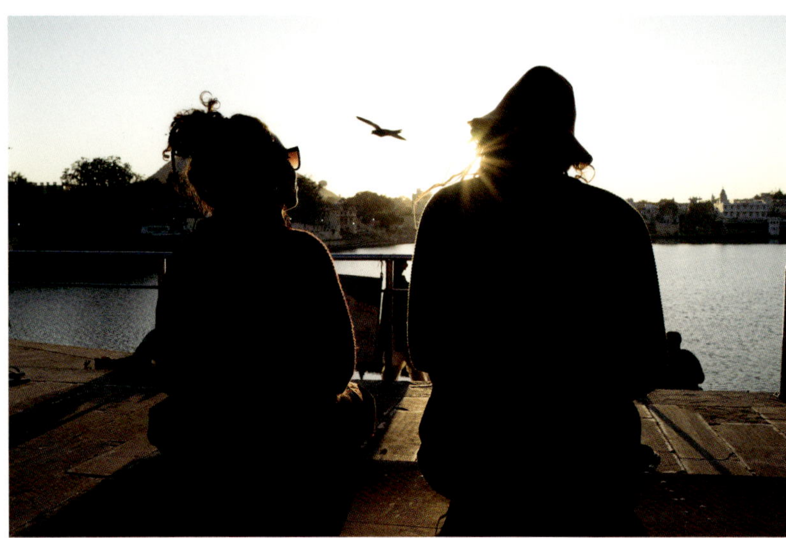

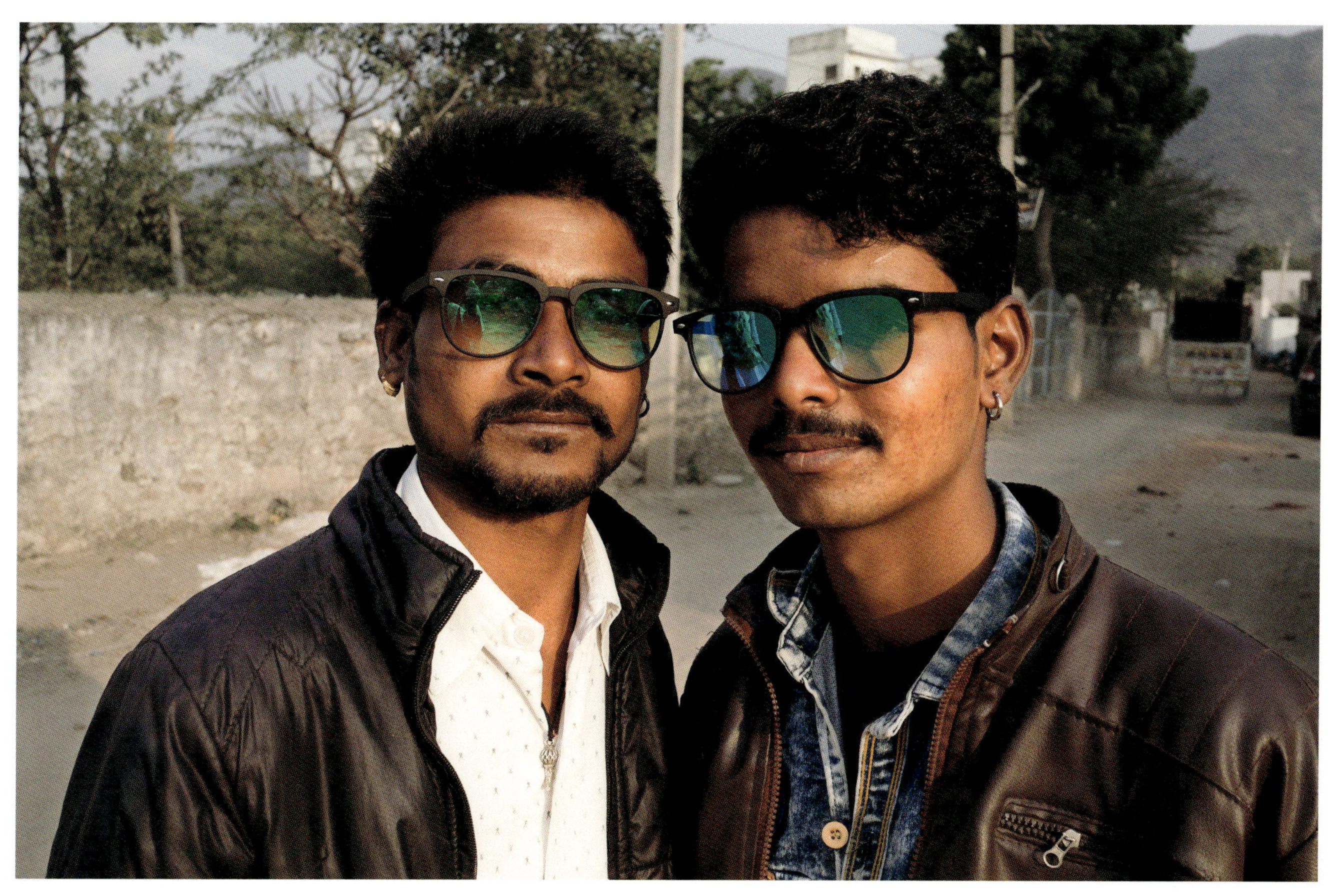

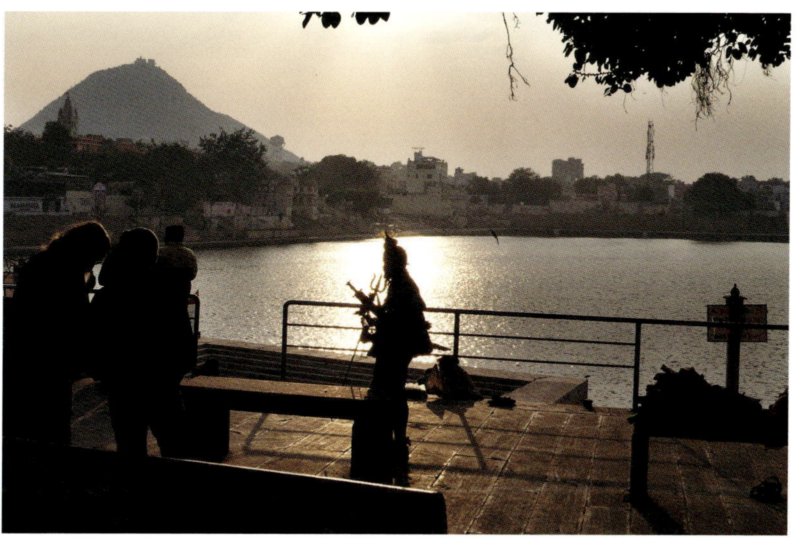

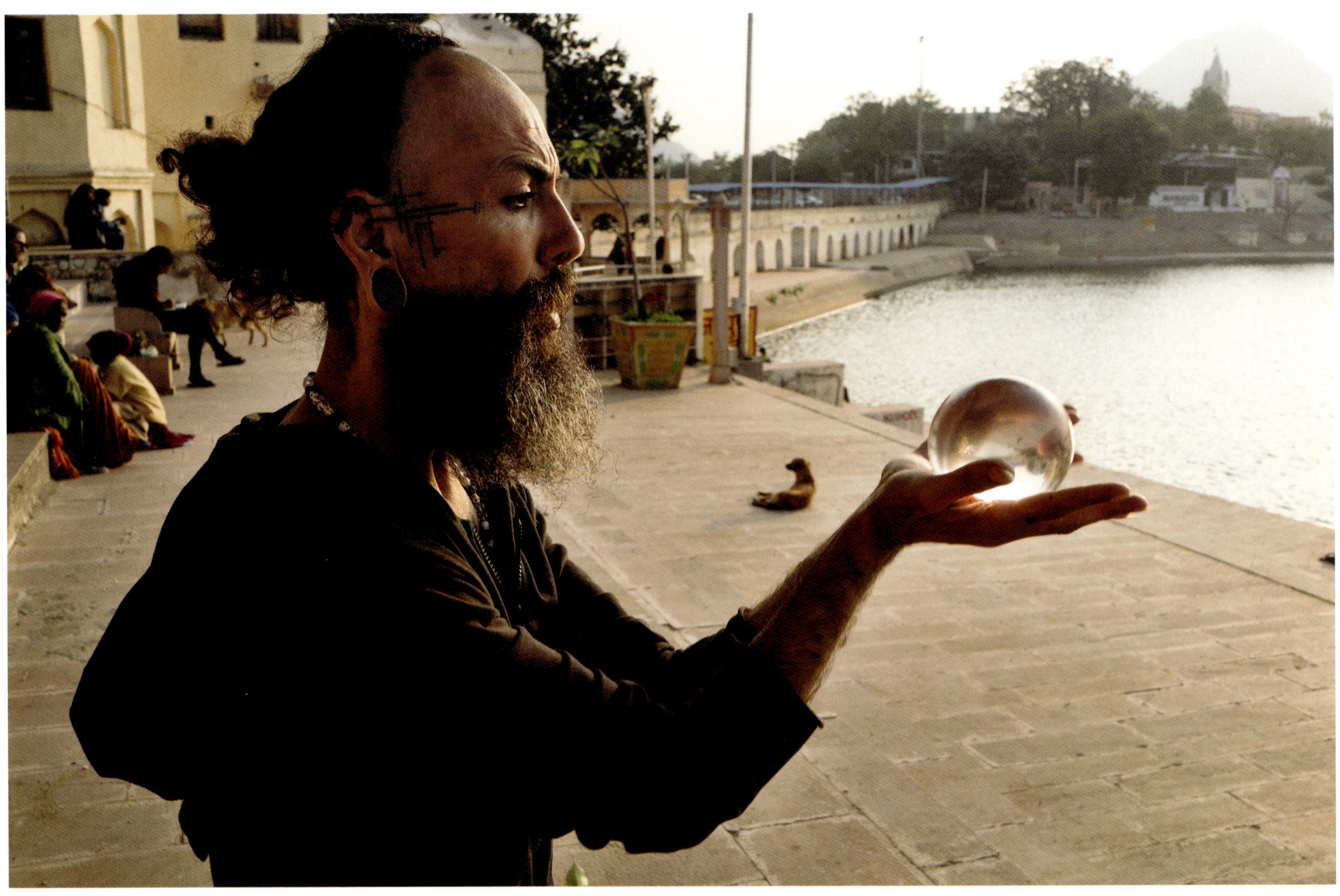

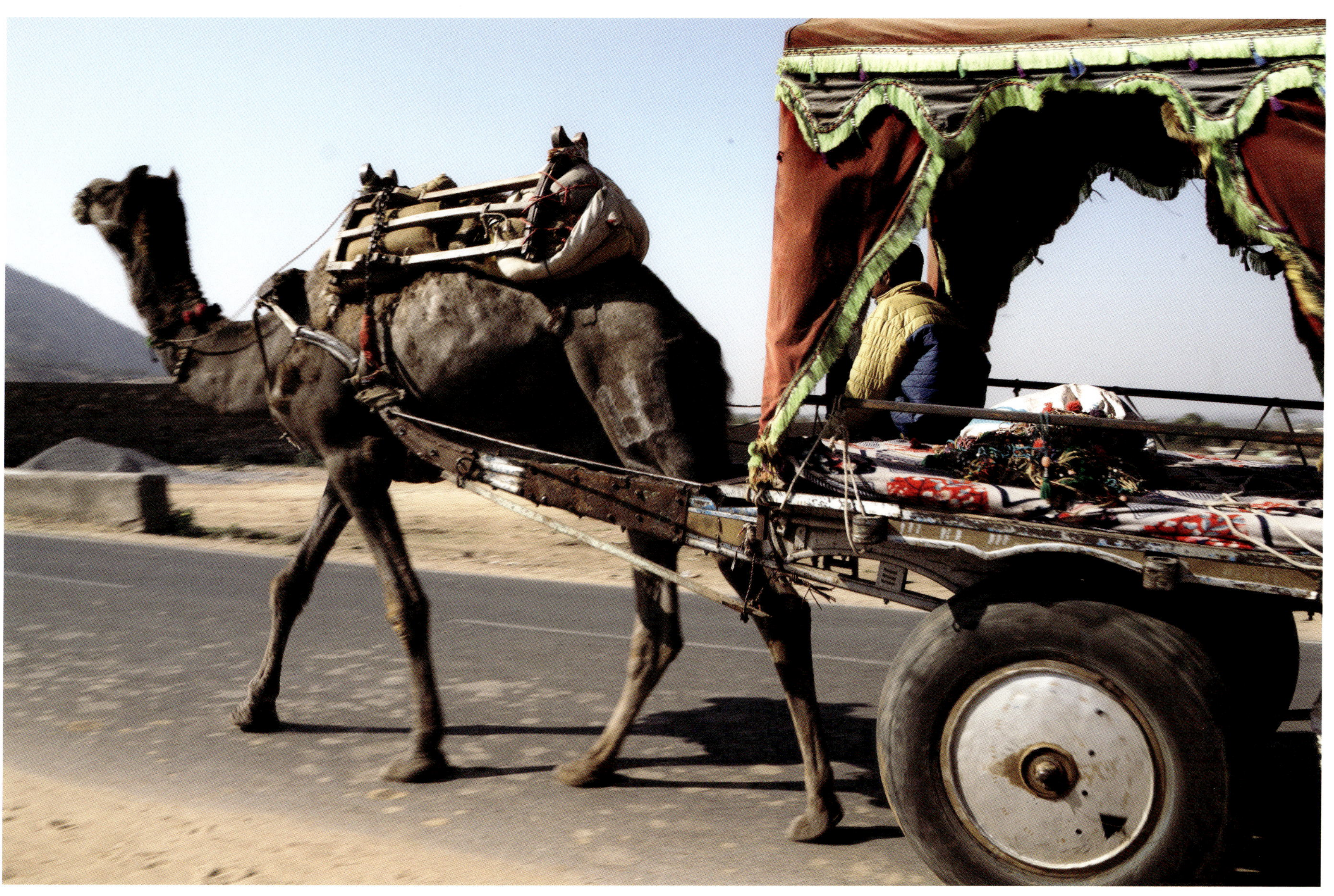

GOA

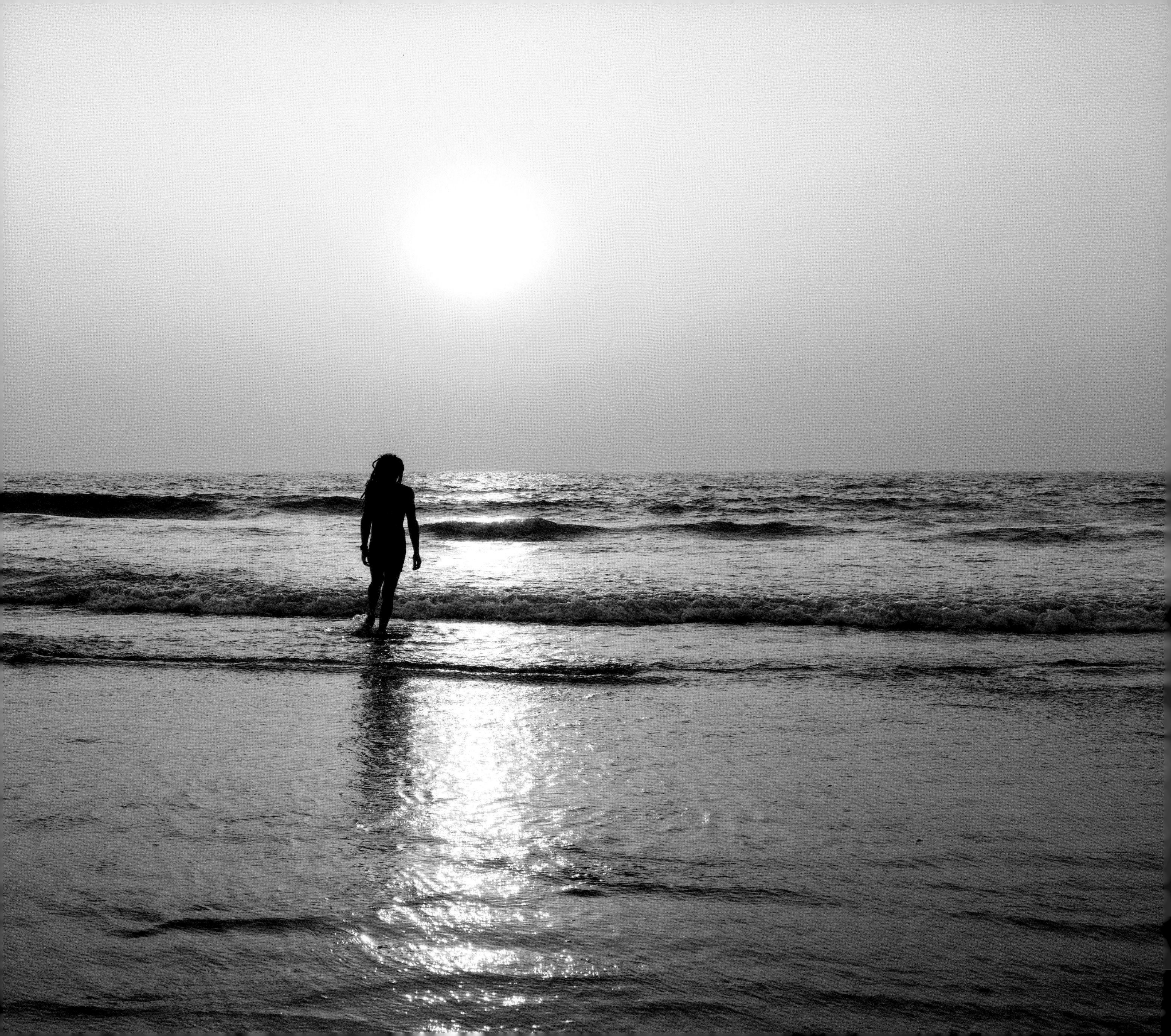

I first heard about Eight Finger Eddie (aka Yertward Mazamanian) in 1980 while I was hanging out in Kathmandu. A large number of western expats living in Nepal at the time fled to India during the winter months and he was the person most responsible for the seasonal exodus to sunny Goa.

An overland journey on the Hippie Trail in the 1960s had taken Eight Finger Eddie to India. He eventually landed in the southern state of Goa and lived there for much of his life, until his death in 2010. In a self-published memoir, he wrote: "I was the first freak in Goa. I turned up and liked it so much, I just wanted to stay." And so he did. Eight Finger Eddie resided in a small bungalow in Goa for 44 years, running a soup kitchen for destitute western travelers, setting up the Anjuna Flea Market where hippies could barter their unwanted possessions, feeding and sheltering flipped-out travelers who had nowhere else to go. His exploits earned him the nickname "King of Hippies" and put Goa prominently on the counterculture travelers' map of India.

A lot has changed in Goa since Eight Finger Eddie's bohemian days. National Geographic recently ranked it number six in its list of top ten nightlife destinations in the world. The hashish and guitars around a beach bonfire days have morphed into full moon rave parties fueled by ecstasy and trance music. Eddie's original flea market is now a bustling retail center. The beach shacks gave way decades ago to holiday resorts where water sports, club-hopping, and selfies dominate tourism activities. Goa's sand, sun, and warm water continue to attract people, but most now arrive as domestic visitors from elsewhere in India.

Certain aspects of Goa still hold appeal for Western counterculture travelers. It is noticeably different from other parts of India. From 1510 until its annexation in 1961, Goa was a Portuguese colony that fused European and Indian cultural influences. The neighborhood where I stayed in old Goa was filled with pastel-colored homes, cafés, and churches that would've looked right at home on any street in Lisbon. Many of the western travelers I met came from colder climes. The tropical weather of south India made them want to linger. And while the coastline no longer harbors the pristine traditional fishing villages of the past, Goa sits on the Arabian Sea and for many travelers that is reason enough to visit.

In keeping with its hippie roots, a new-age spirituality has taken hold in much of Goa. Yoga studios, ayurvedic massage, reiki, and healing resorts abound along the coast. Many of them are chic and stylish affairs, catering to a prosperous clientele, while others, reminiscent of the hippie heyday, may be little more than a thatched yoga shack stuck in the sand. Along the northern coastline, Arambol is among the last of Goa's hippie holdouts. The town remains free of the kind of high-rise developments that populate the beach elsewhere, while its multitude of hostels, cafés, and drum circles manifest the spirit of the counterculture past.

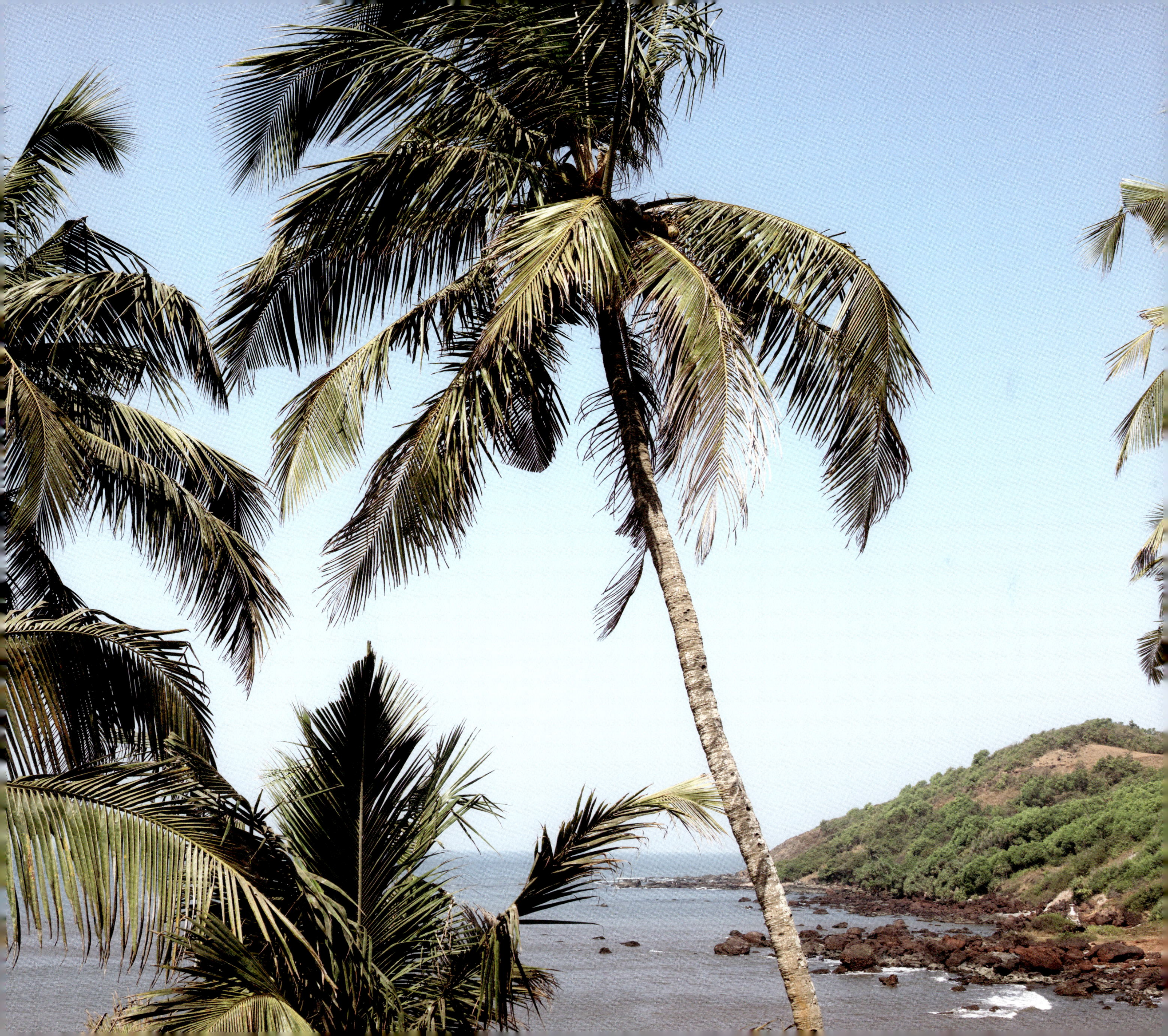

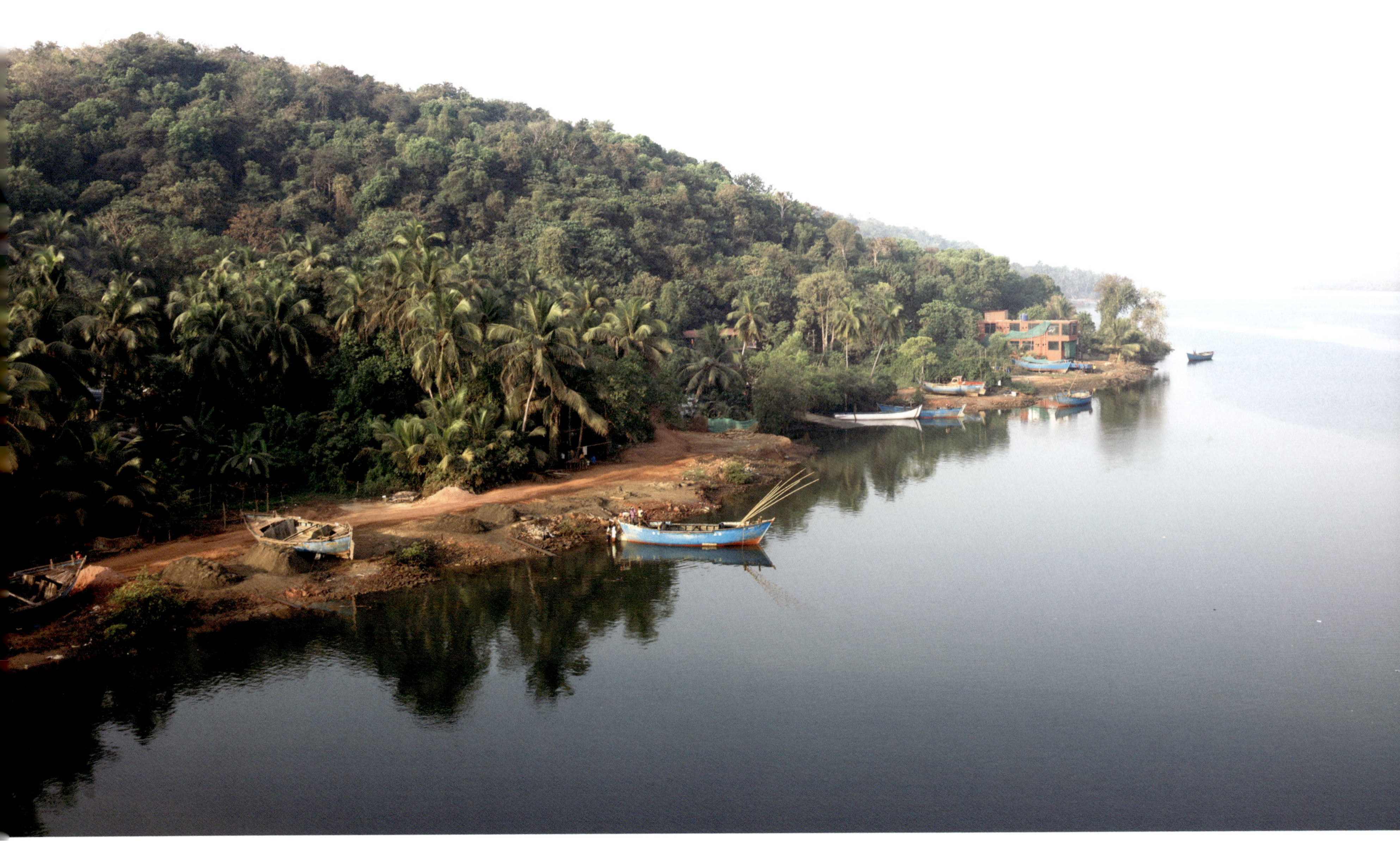

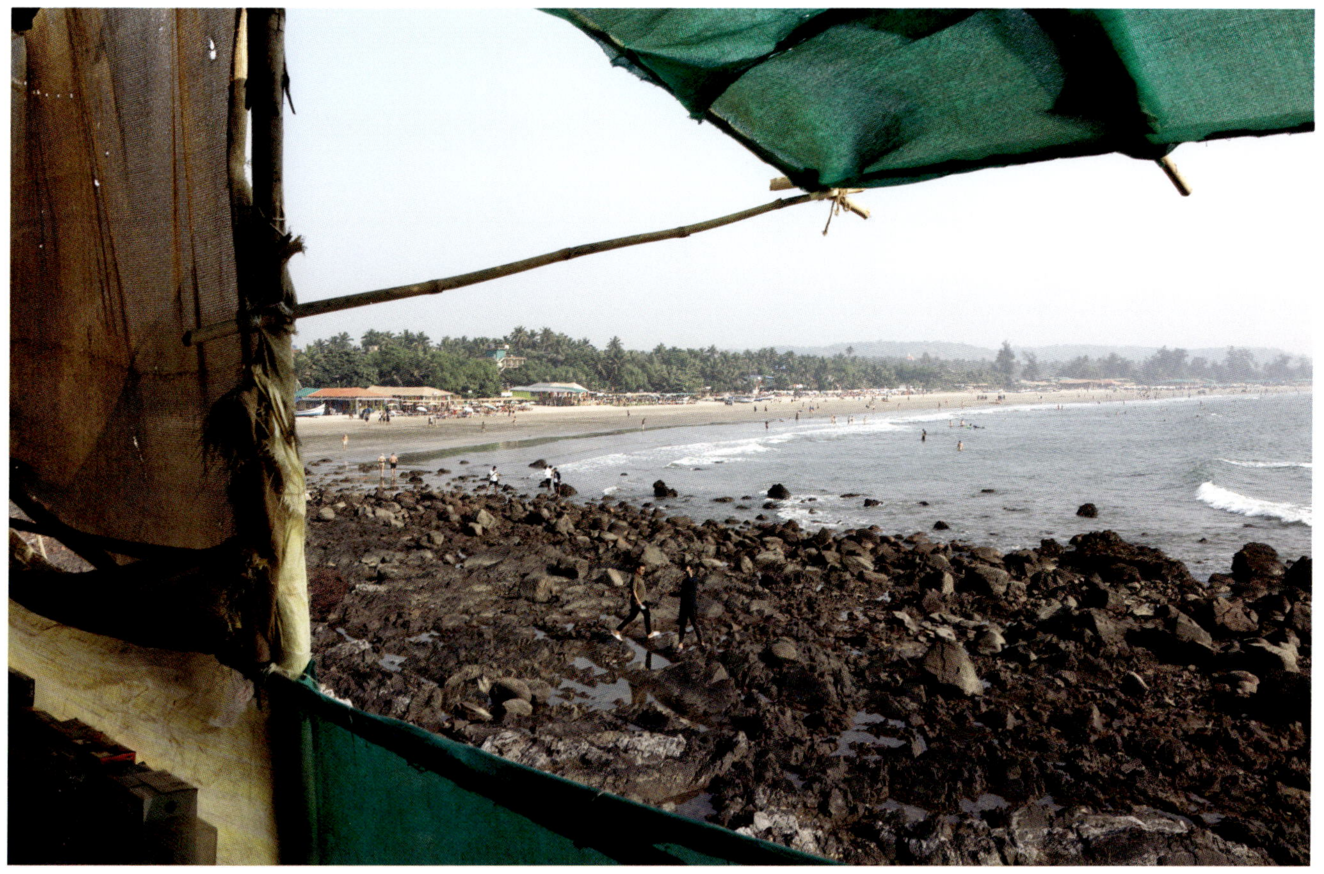

ABOVE: Goa's coastline is marked by a series of coves interrupted by rocky headlands. Most of the sandy stretches have been taken over by tourism infrastructure—hostels, cheap guesthouses, flashy enclave resorts, clubs, restaurants, and watersports. The beaches are no longer pristine. Slow-moving rivers dump clouds of sediments and pollutants into the ocean. While its newly tarnished appearance doesn't deter many domestic Indian tourists from visiting Goa, the Western travelers who frequented the coast in the 1970s and 1980s have all but disappeared. The hippies have moved on to greener pastures.

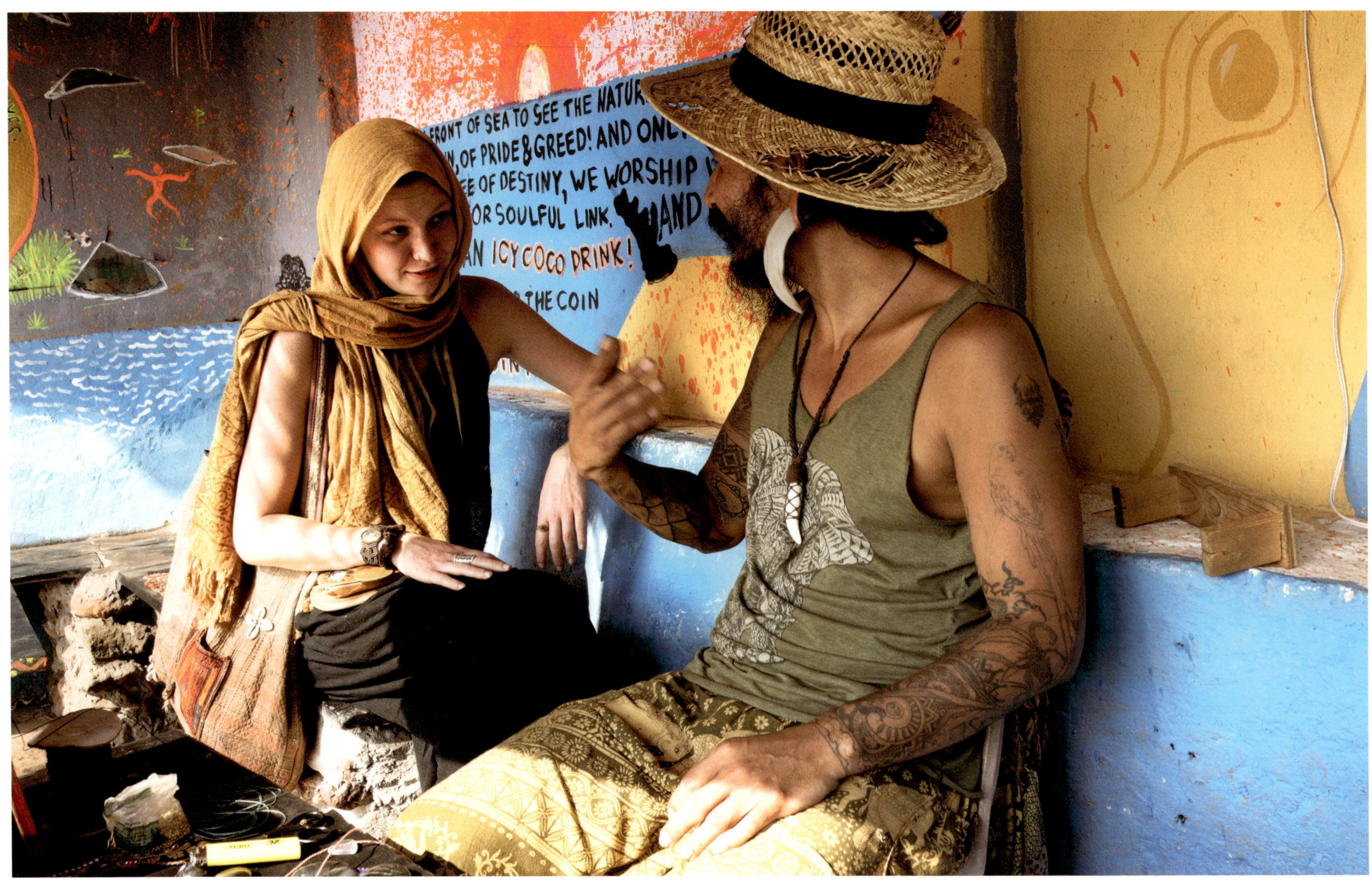

ABOVE: Kira (Germany) and Alex (Peru). I met Kira and Alex when I was strolling along a vendors' pathway next to the ocean. Alex had set up a small handicraft stand in the shade and Kira was sitting there out of the sun. Alex told me he'd been on the road continuously for the last 25 years, supporting himself by making and selling small pieces of jewelry. But it was the first time abroad for Kira. When I asked her what she thought of India, her simple response spoke volumes: "Being in India is like a dream for me."

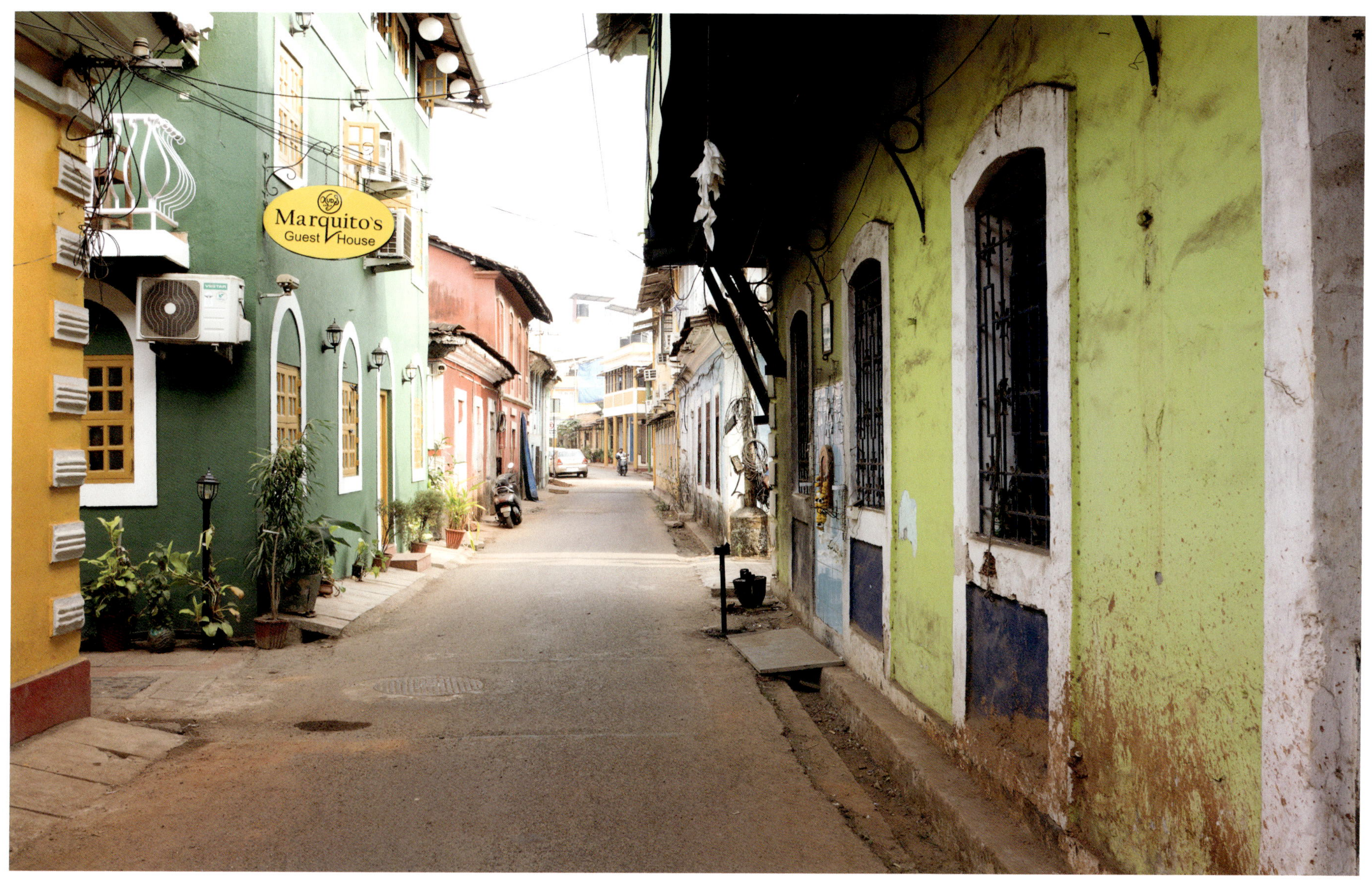

Marquito's
Guest House

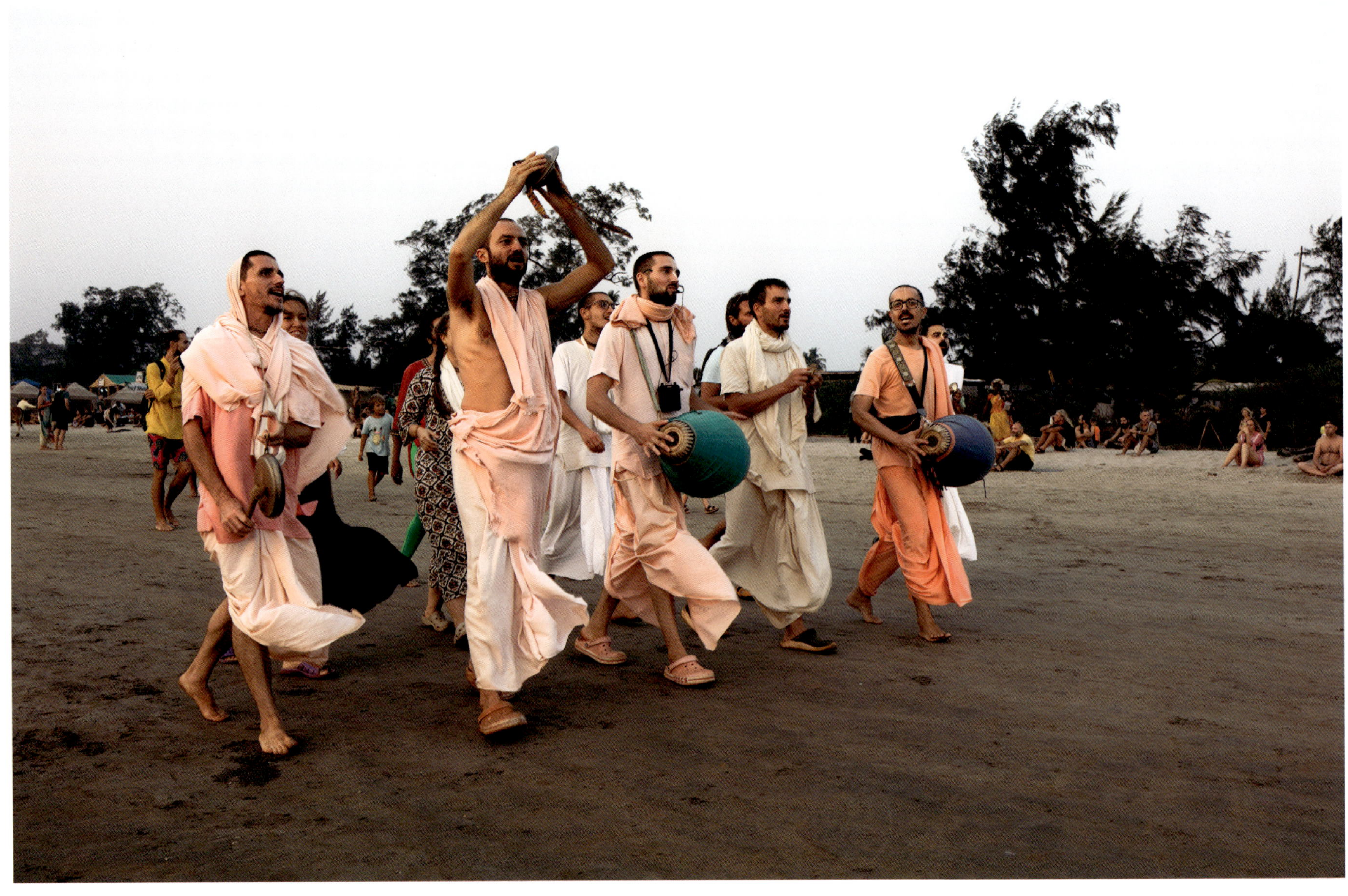

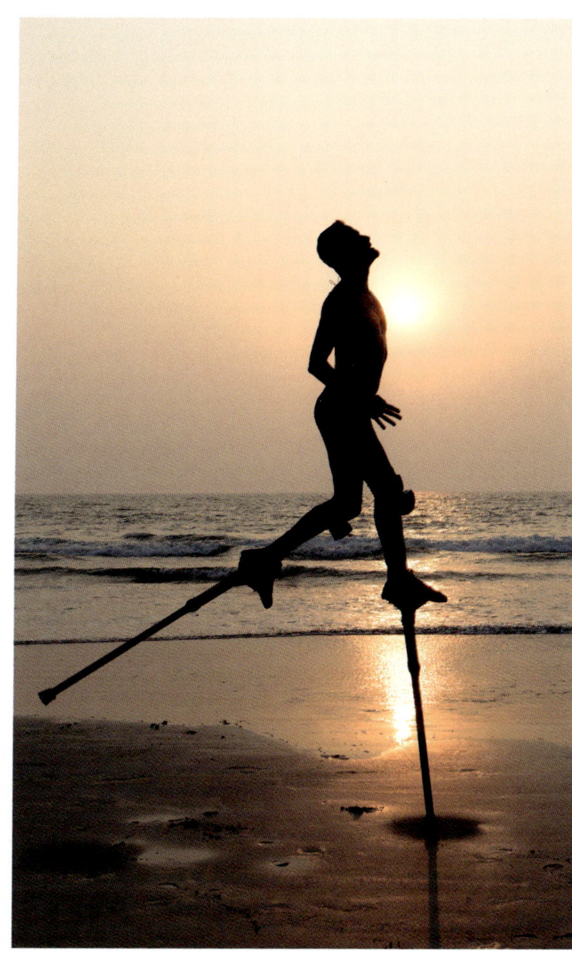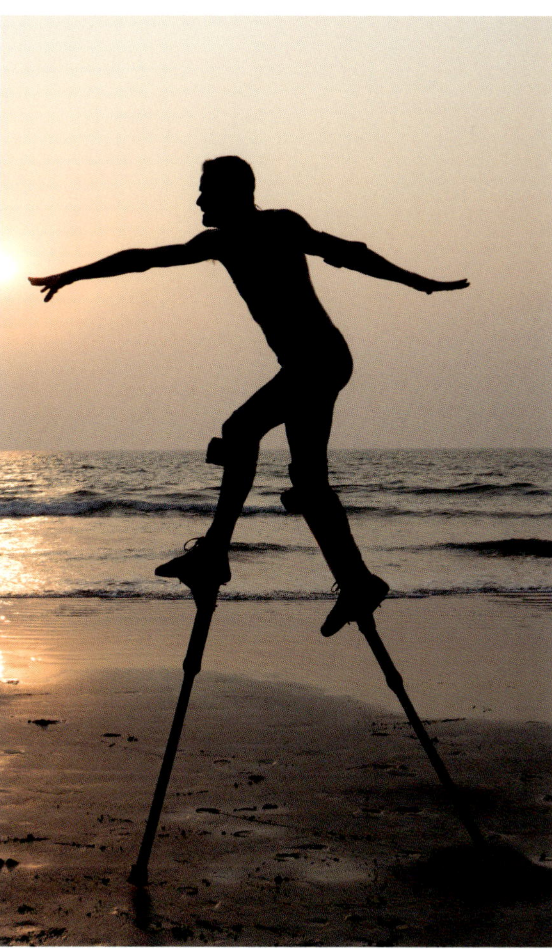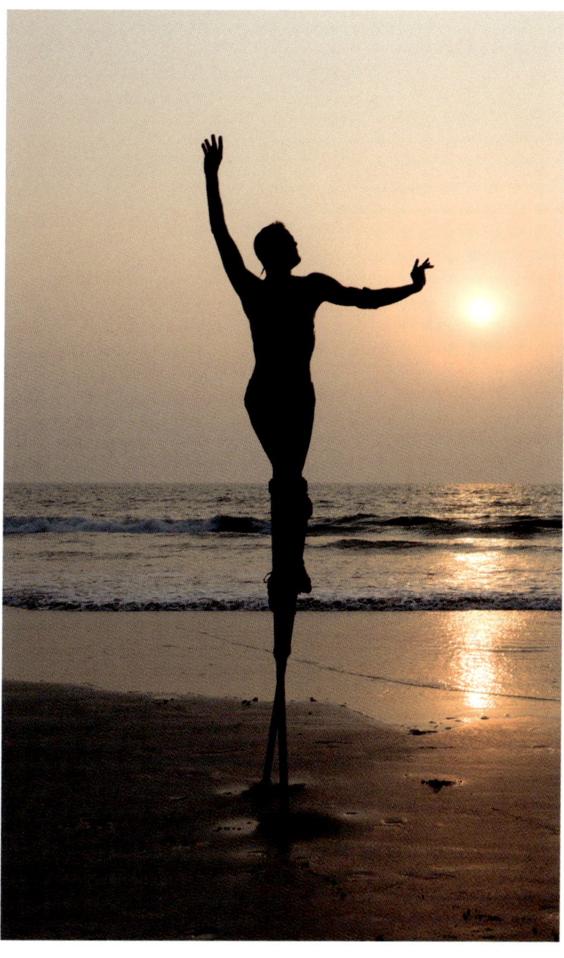

THIS PAGE: Roberto (Italy)

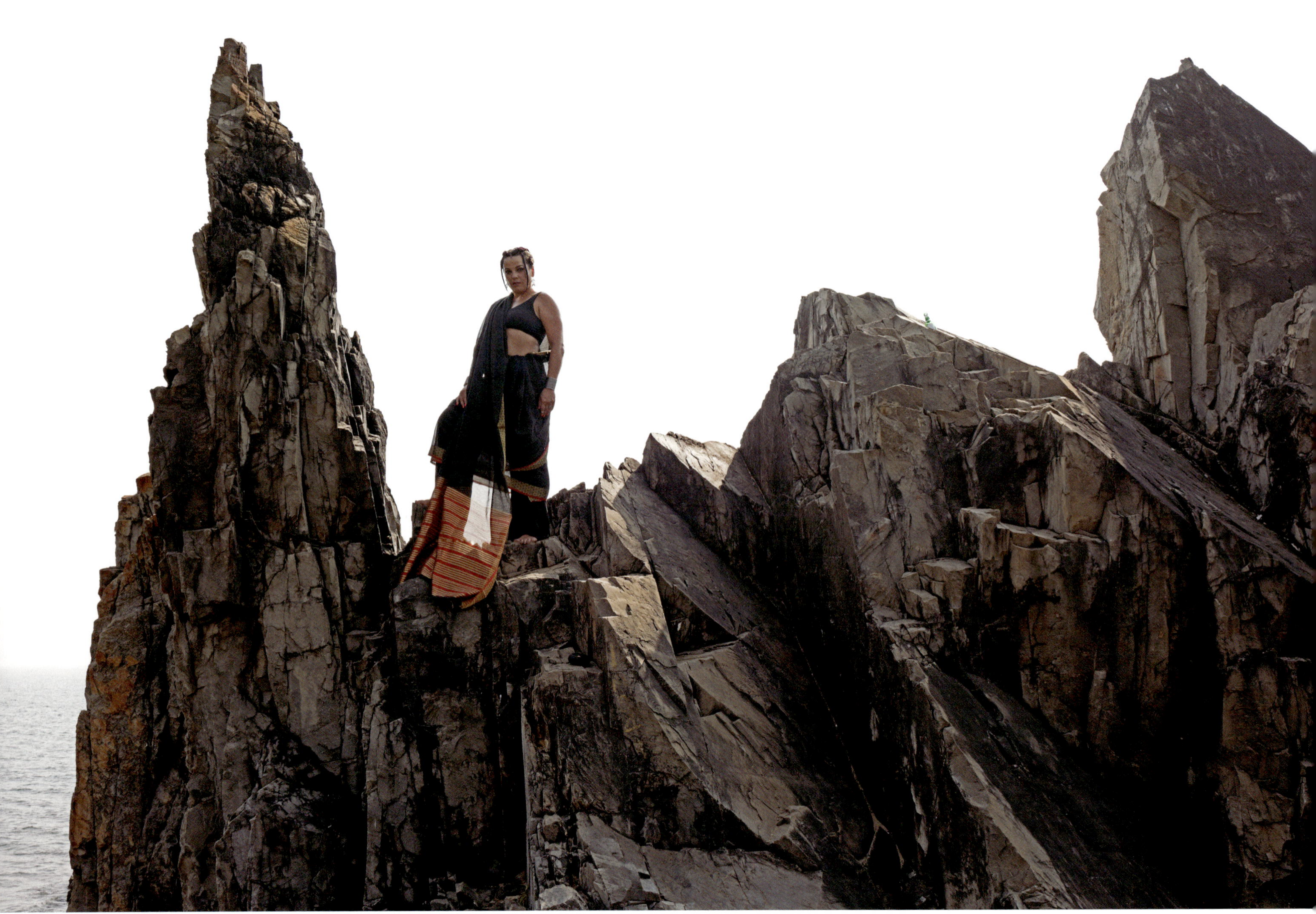

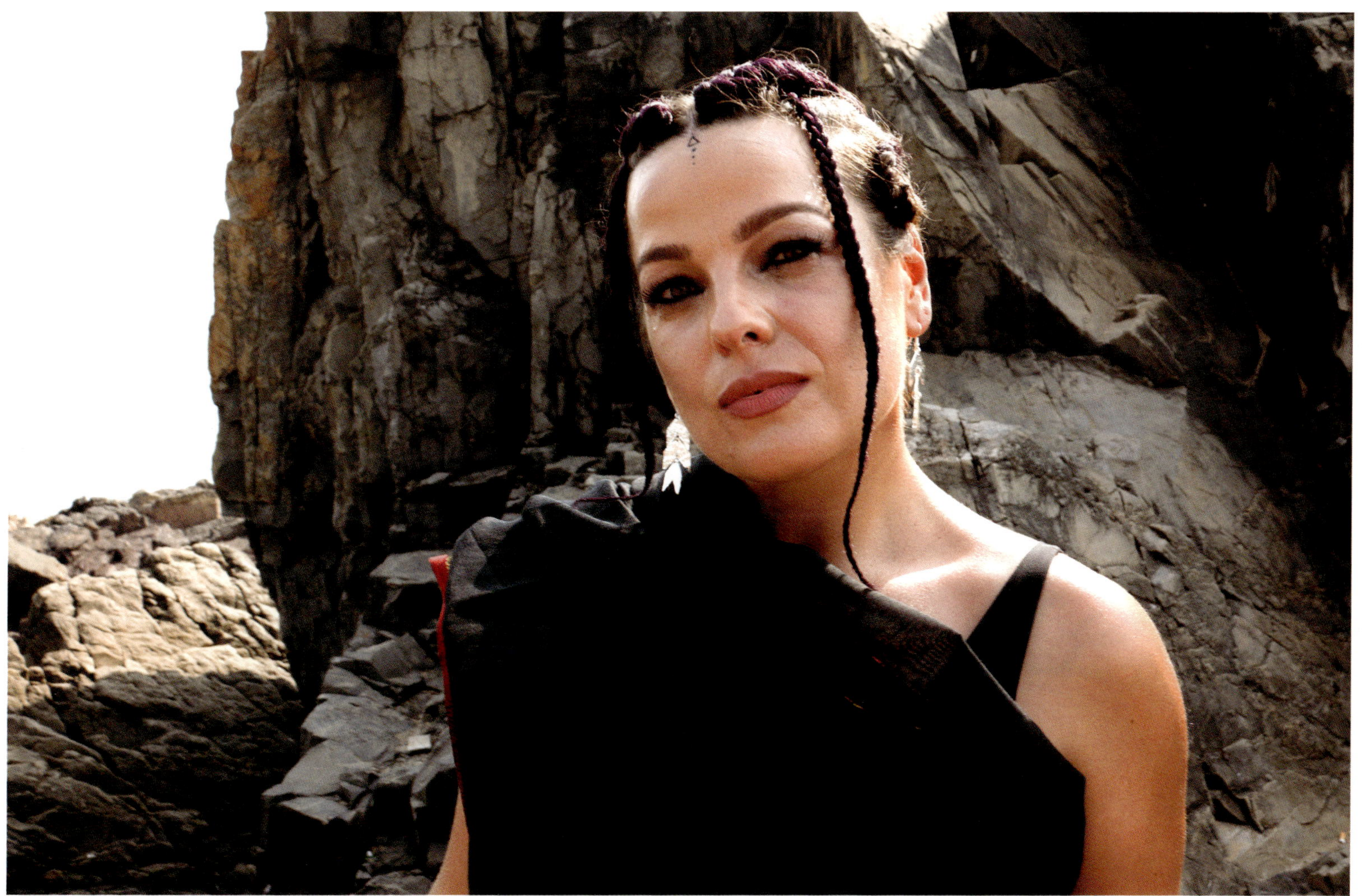

Ksenia (Russia). I observed a woman standing atop an outcrop at the edge of the sea and was drawn to her exotic looks. She clambered down from the rocks and joined me. We talked a while. Ksenia said she'd been in Goa for several months, to enjoy the tropical weather but also because of politics. "I came to Goa to find a place where it is warm and sunny. I also wanted to get out of Russia. It is too crazy there." A desire to escape—from the cold, politics, work, ordinary life—describes many of the travelers I met in India. These "push" factors may be as important to them as any "pull" India might exert on their geographical imaginations.

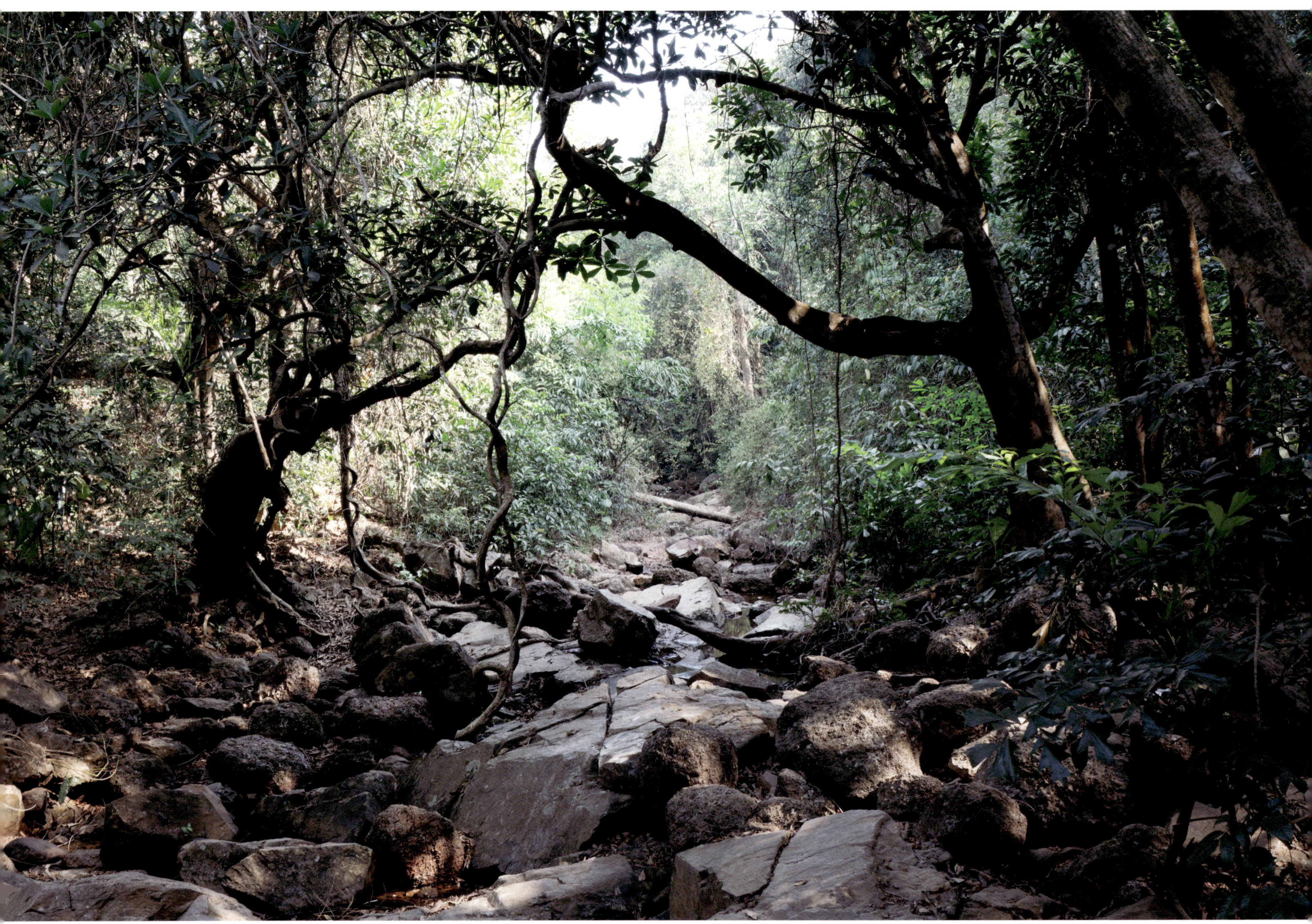

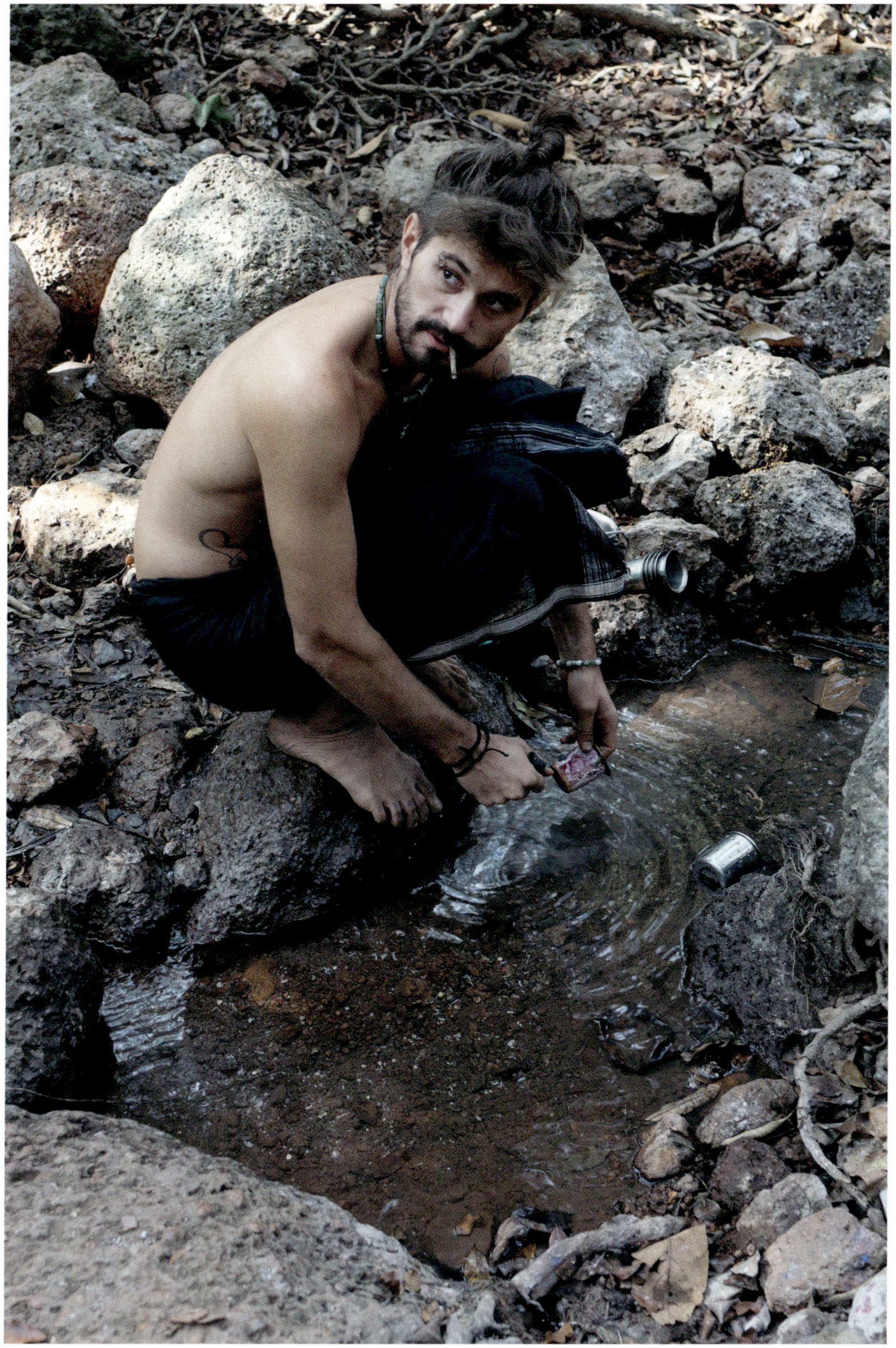

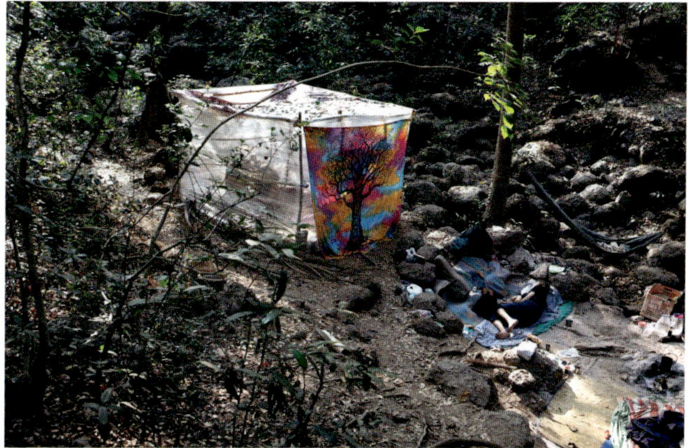

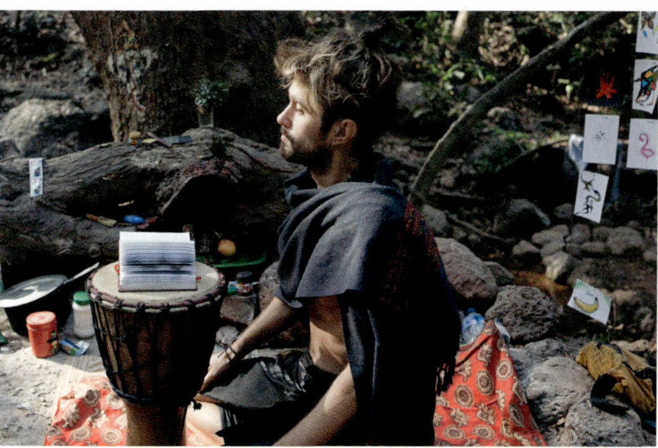

Sergey (Russia). I came upon Sergey's encampment located in a forest near the coast. It had the trappings of an ascetic's retreat. He told me he'd been traveling for four years. "I'm here to escape the madness of Russia and to pursue my spiritual studies." A quietude hung over the place. Nearby were the roots of an enormous banyan tree, which had served as the abode of sadhus and hippies for many decades until a cyclone brought down the tree in 2020. "I am not certain how long I will stay," he continued. "But it will be a while. There is no reason for me to leave."
OPPOSITE: Trail to a sadhu's hermitage

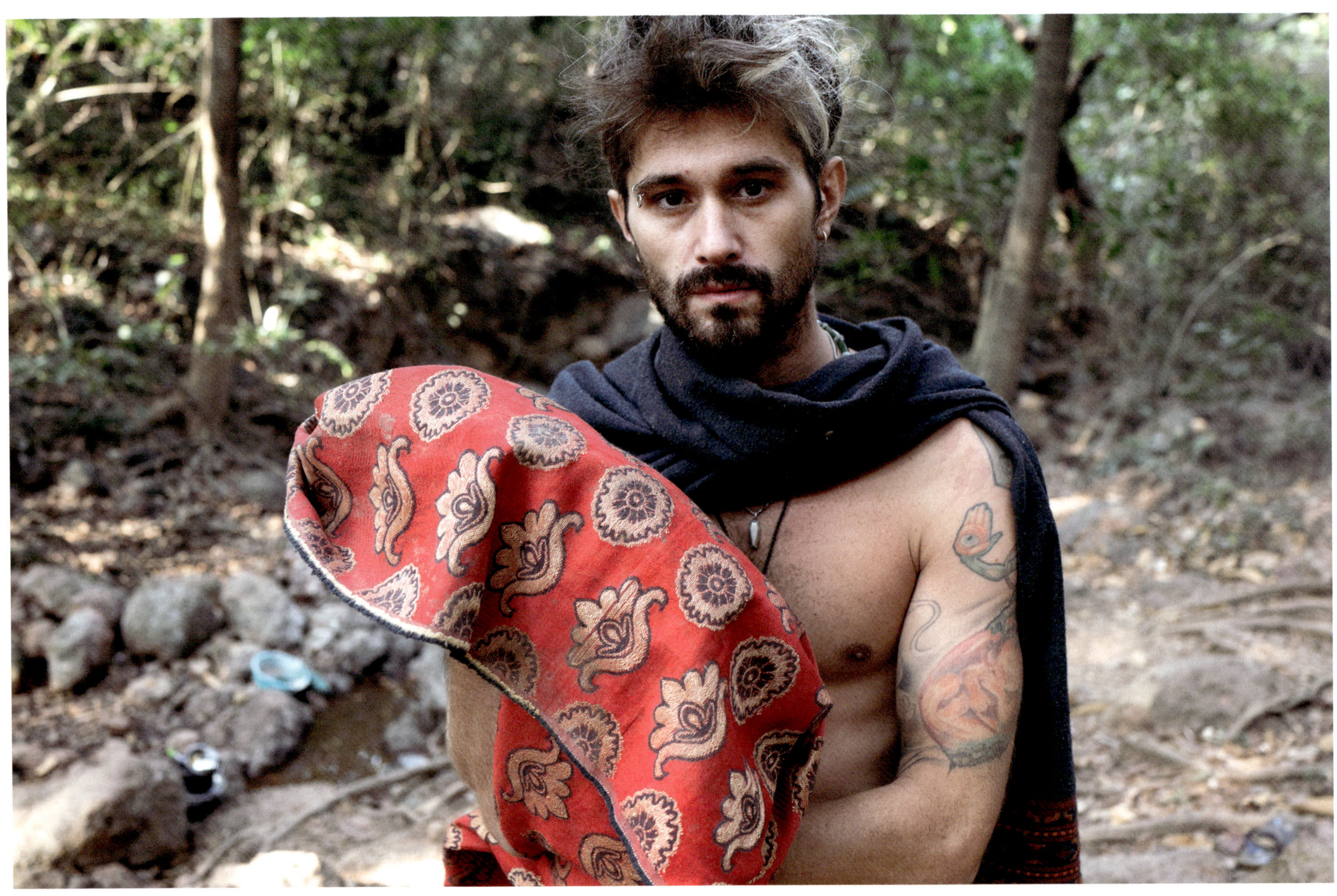

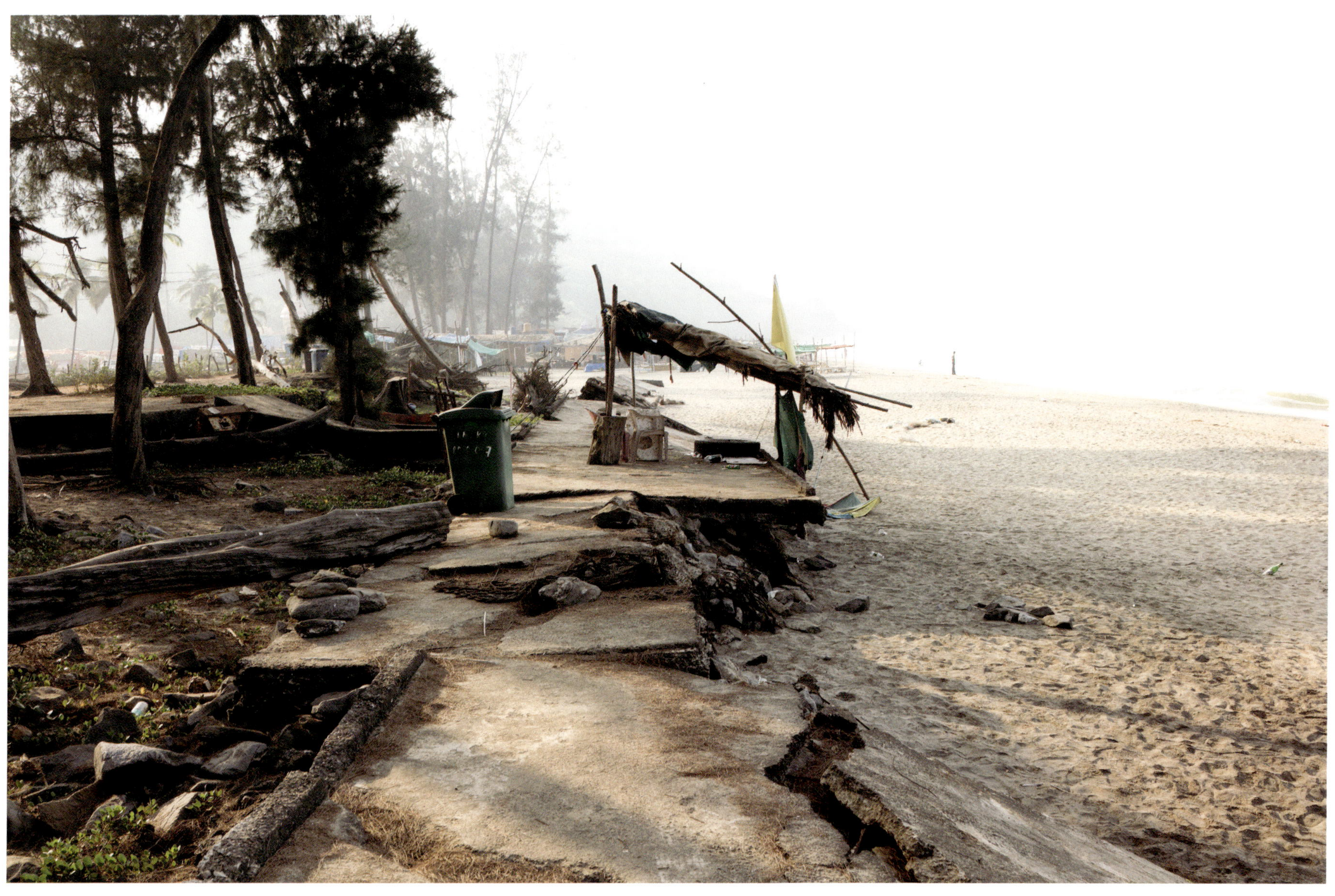

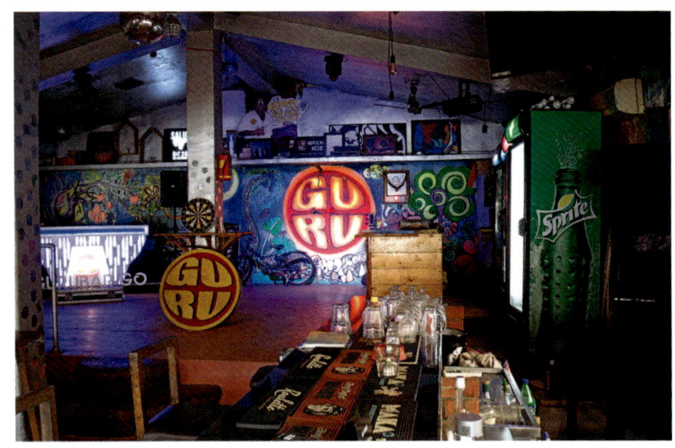

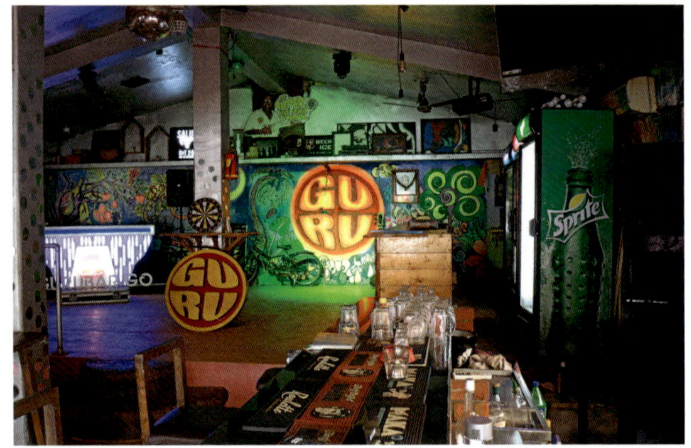

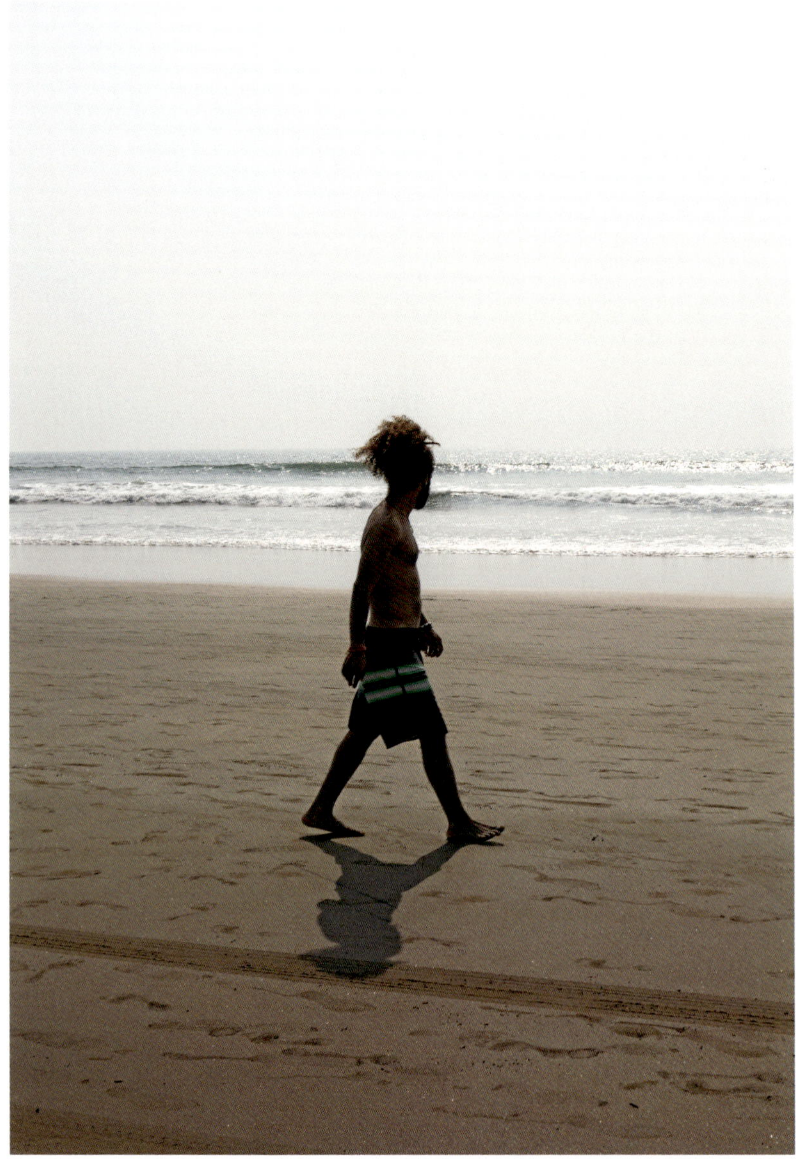

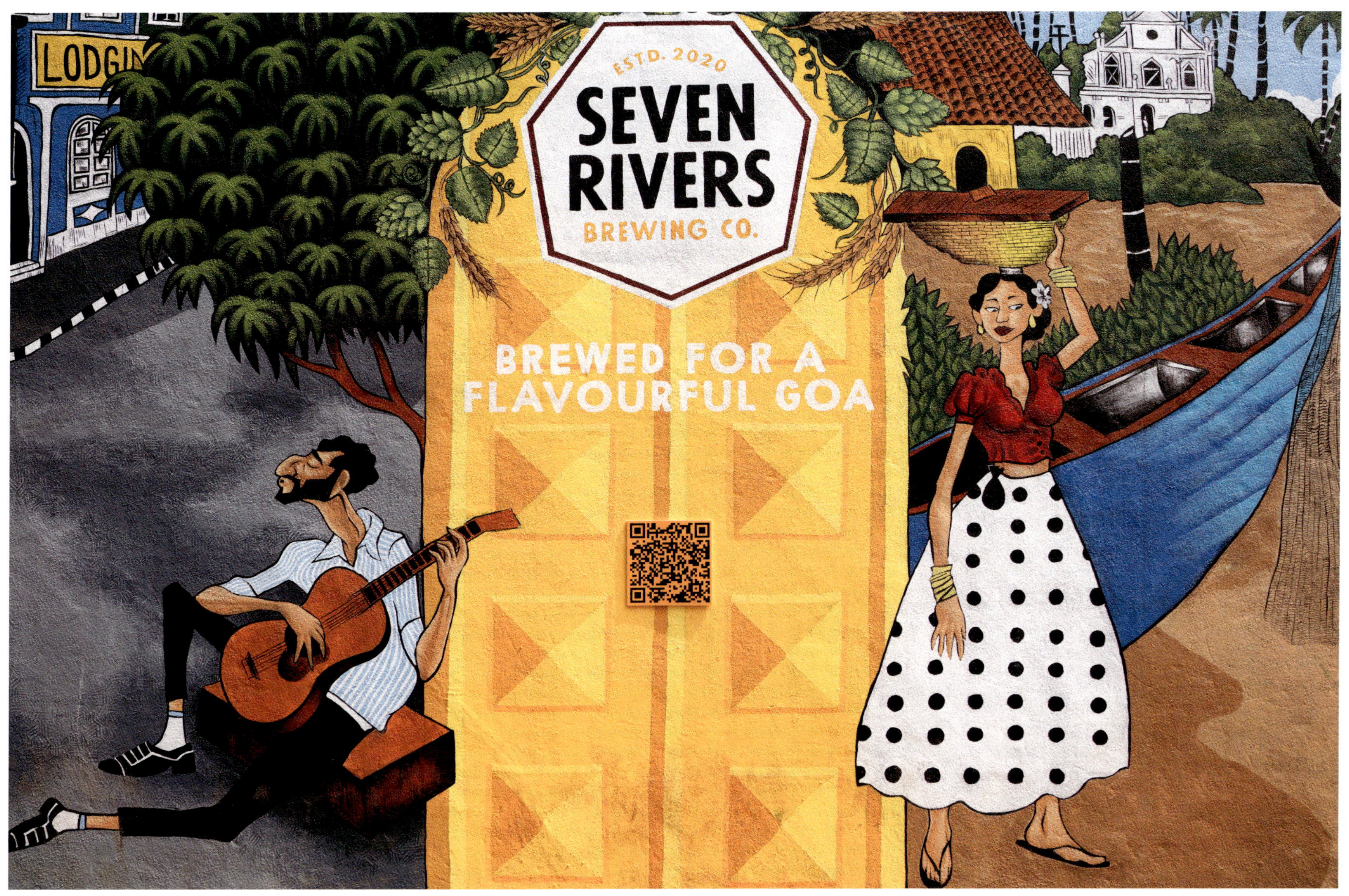

LODGI
ESTD. 2020
SEVEN RIVERS
BREWING CO.
BREWED FOR A FLAVOURFUL GOA

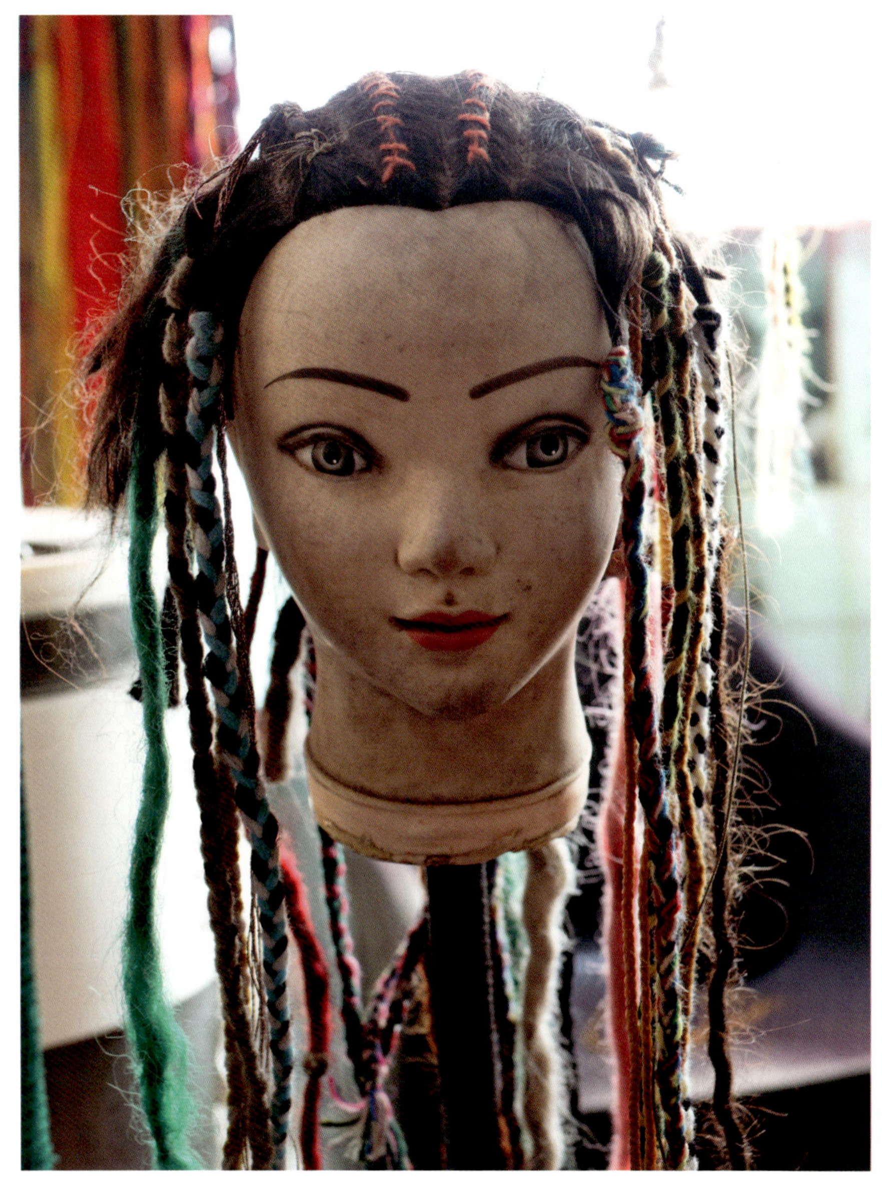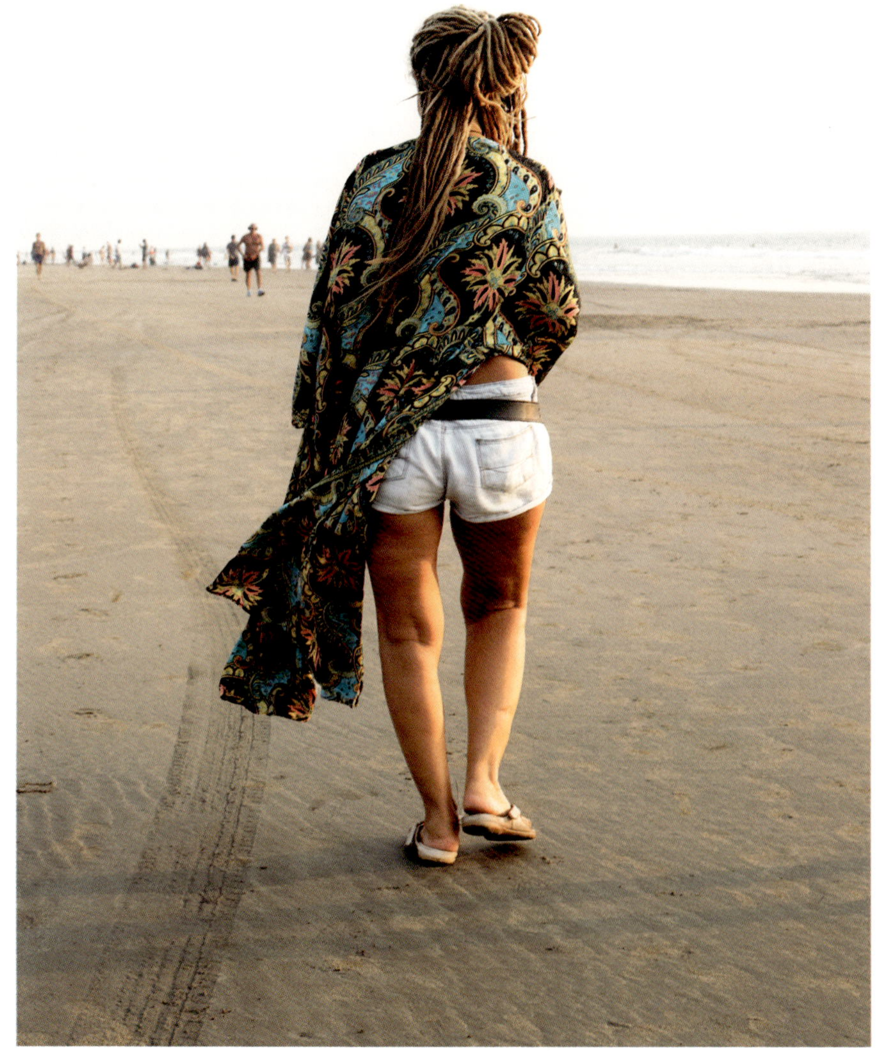

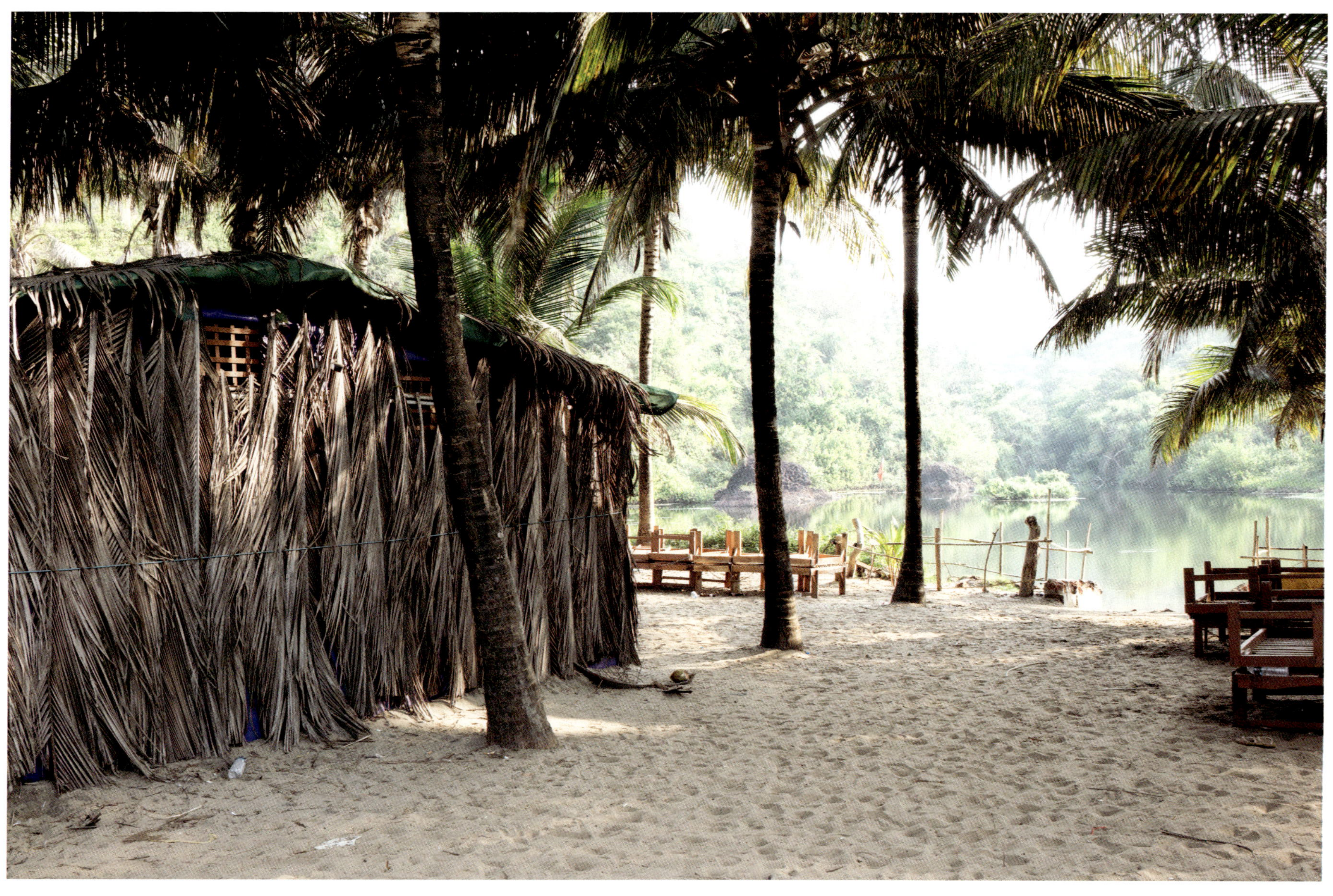

ABOVE: Secret lagoon

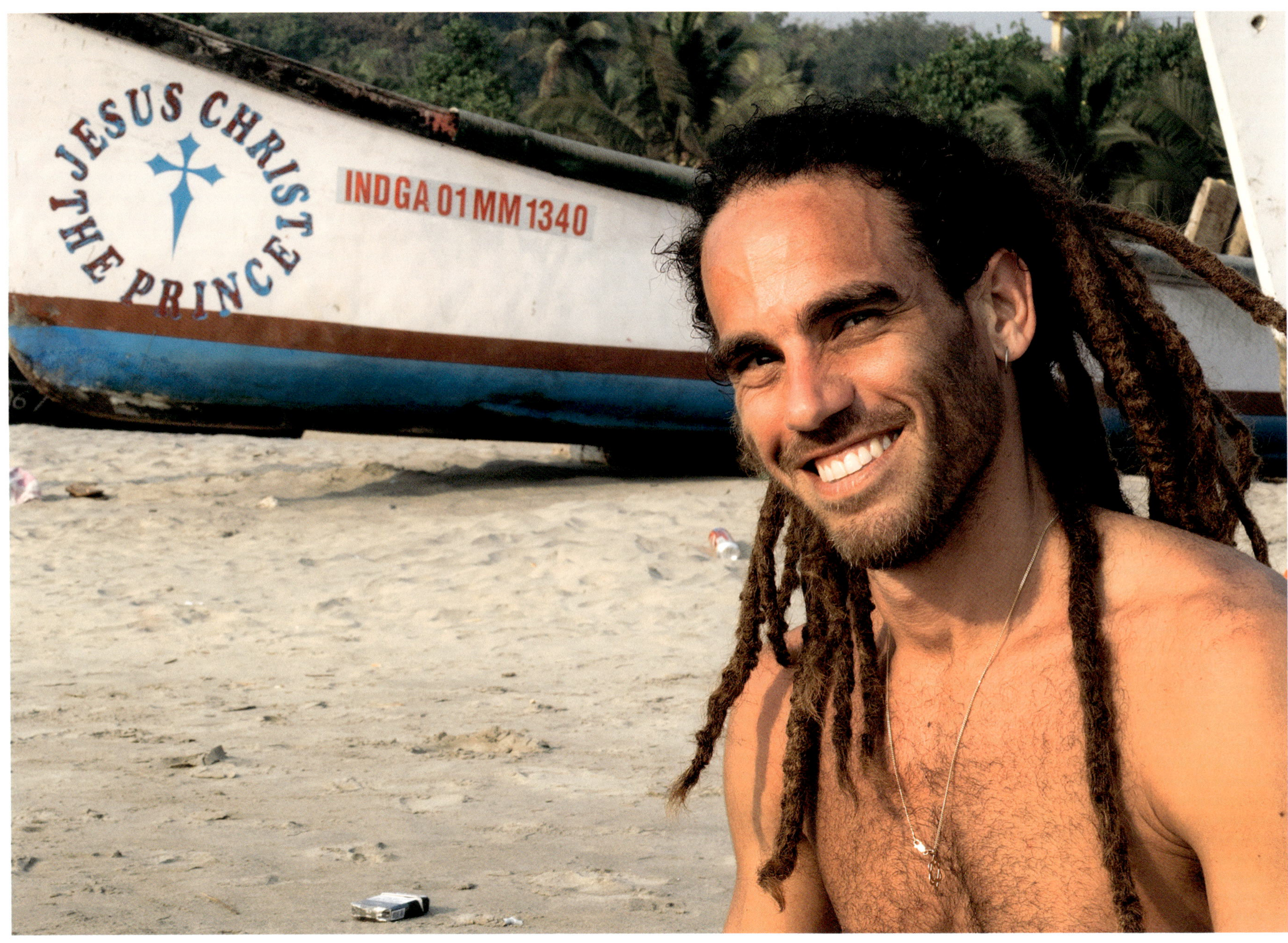

Tabak (Israel)

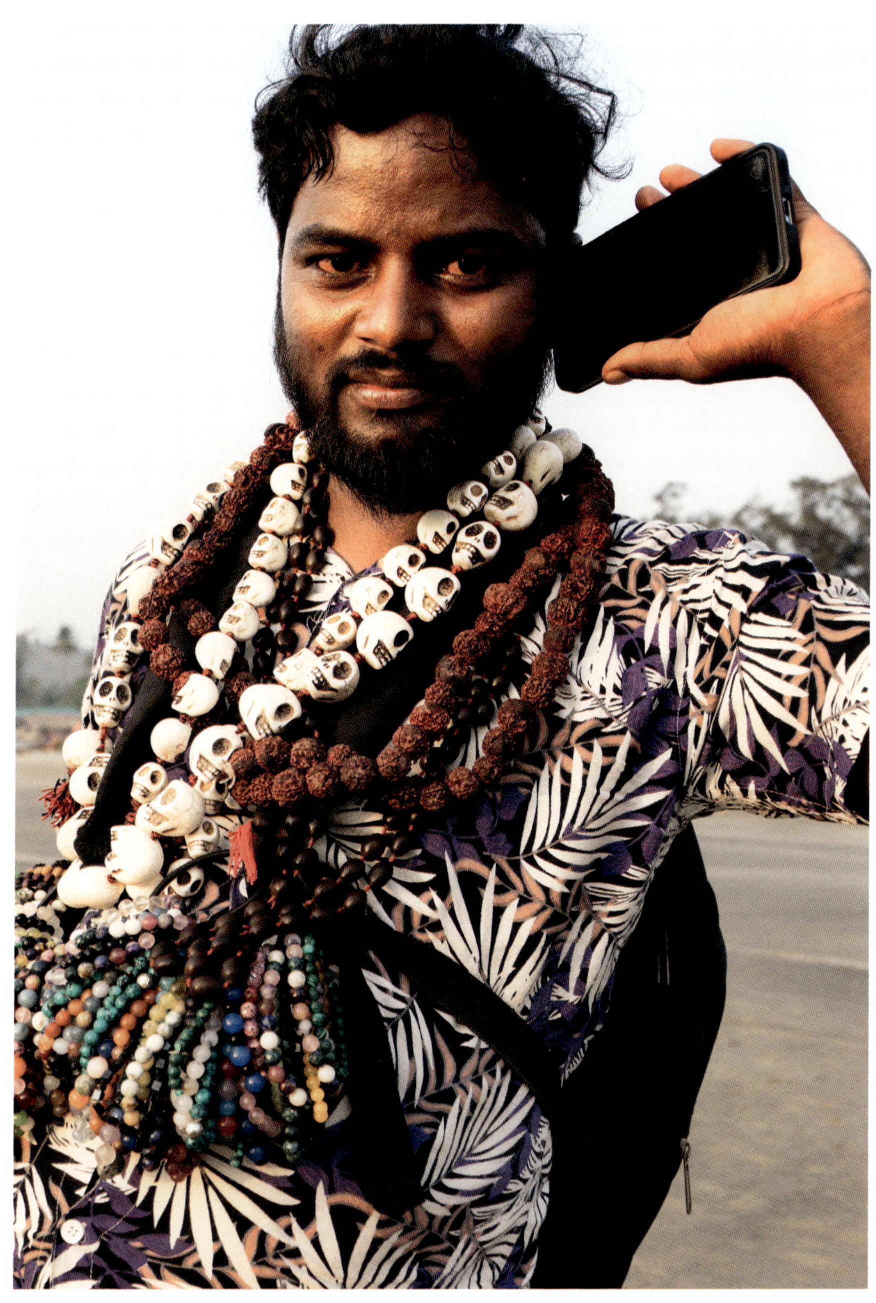

Trinket vendor (India), Anjuna Beach

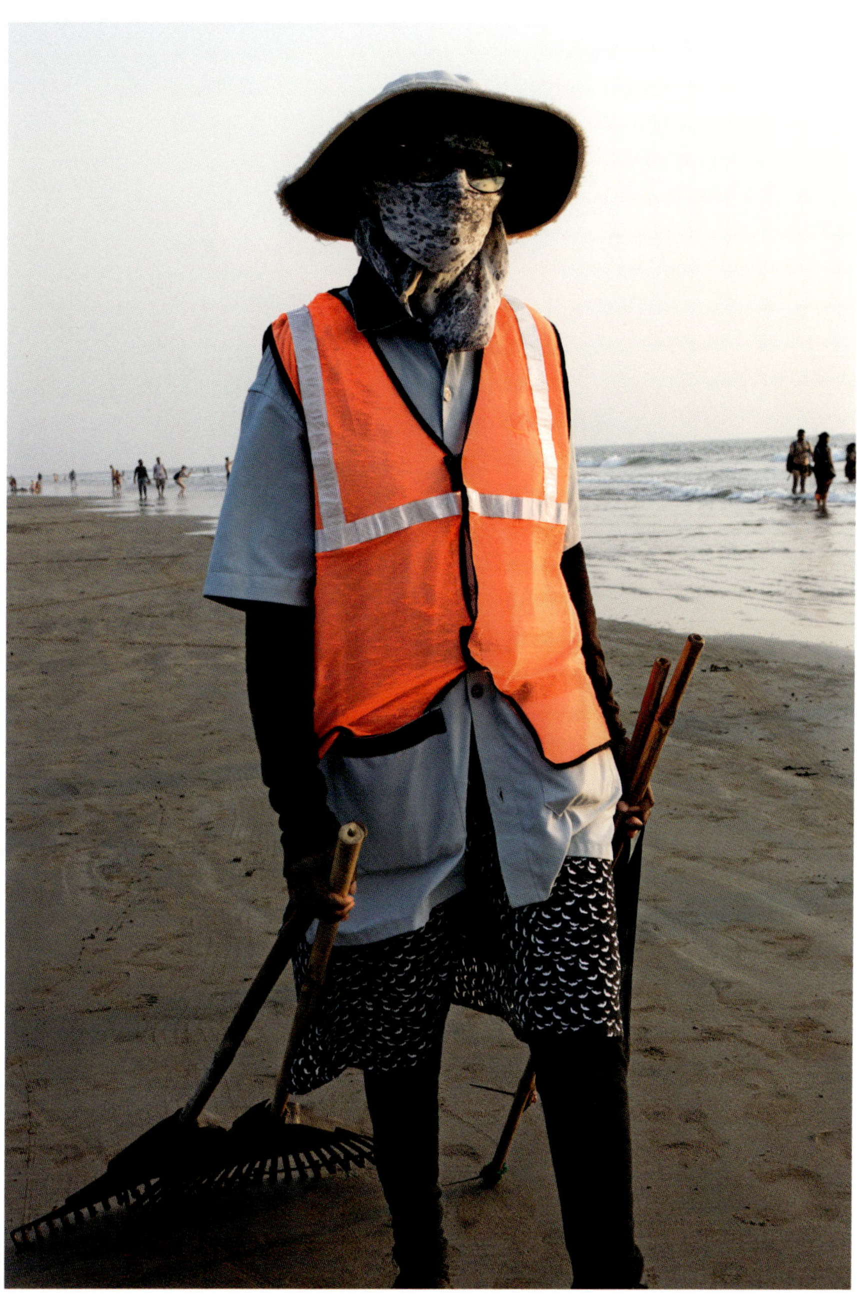

Municipal worker (India), Anjuna Beach

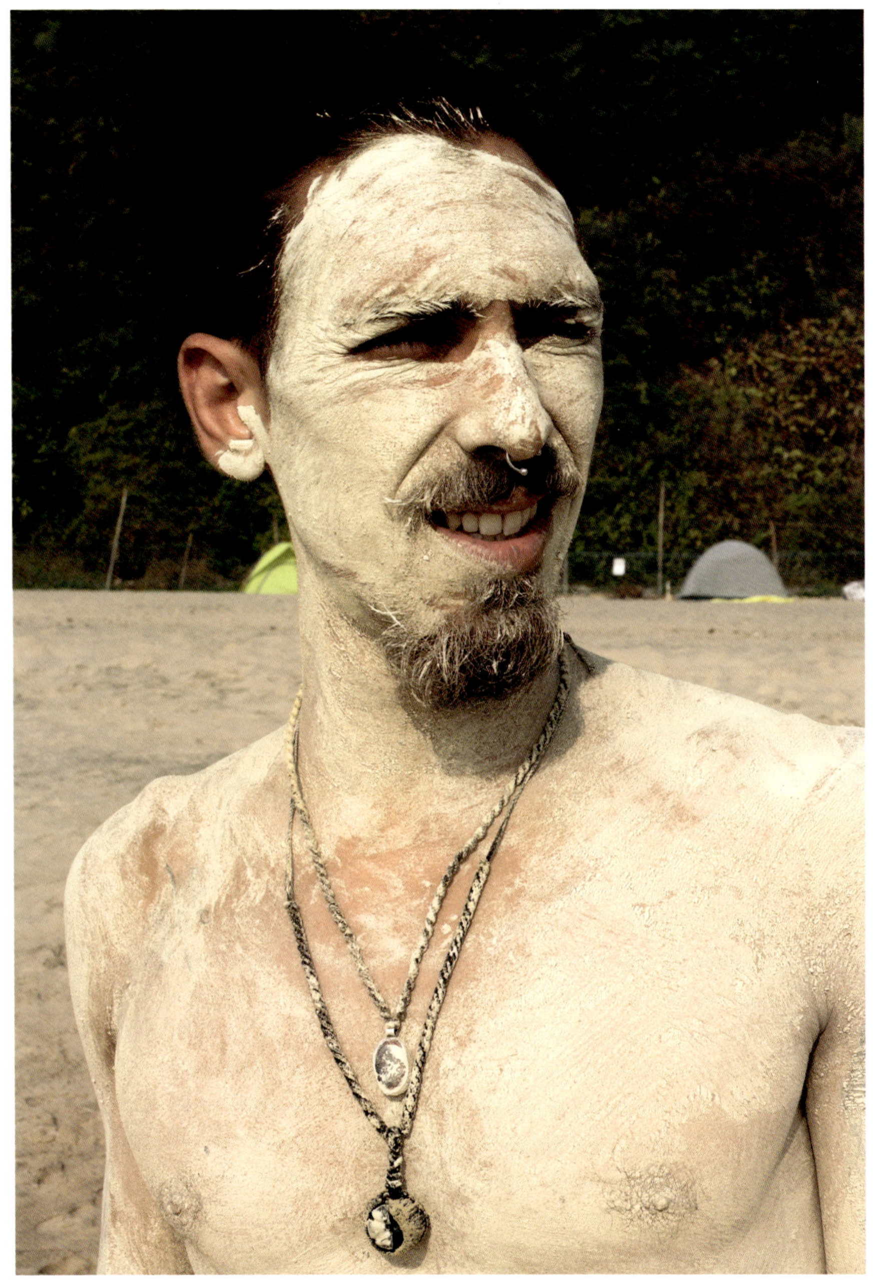

Oreal (Israel)

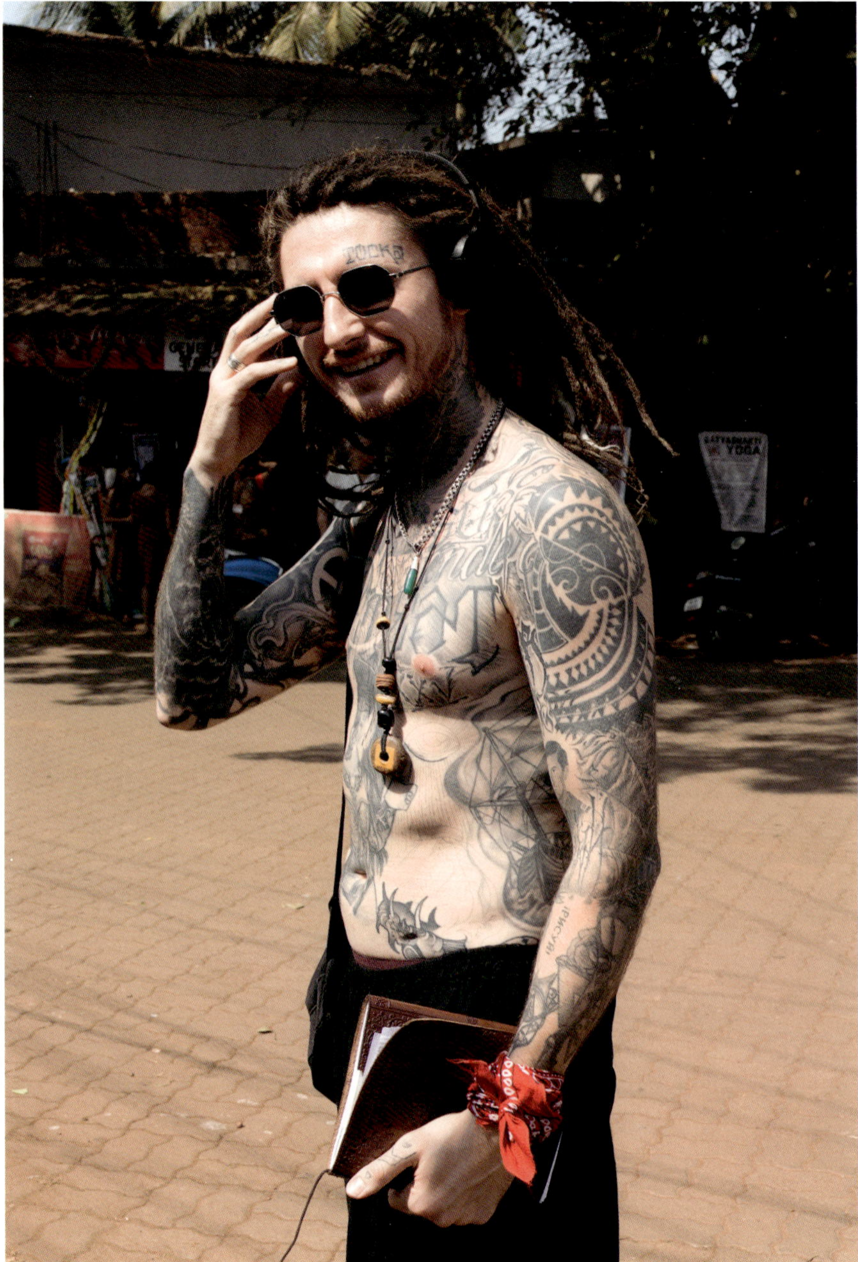

Jinn Tony (Israel)

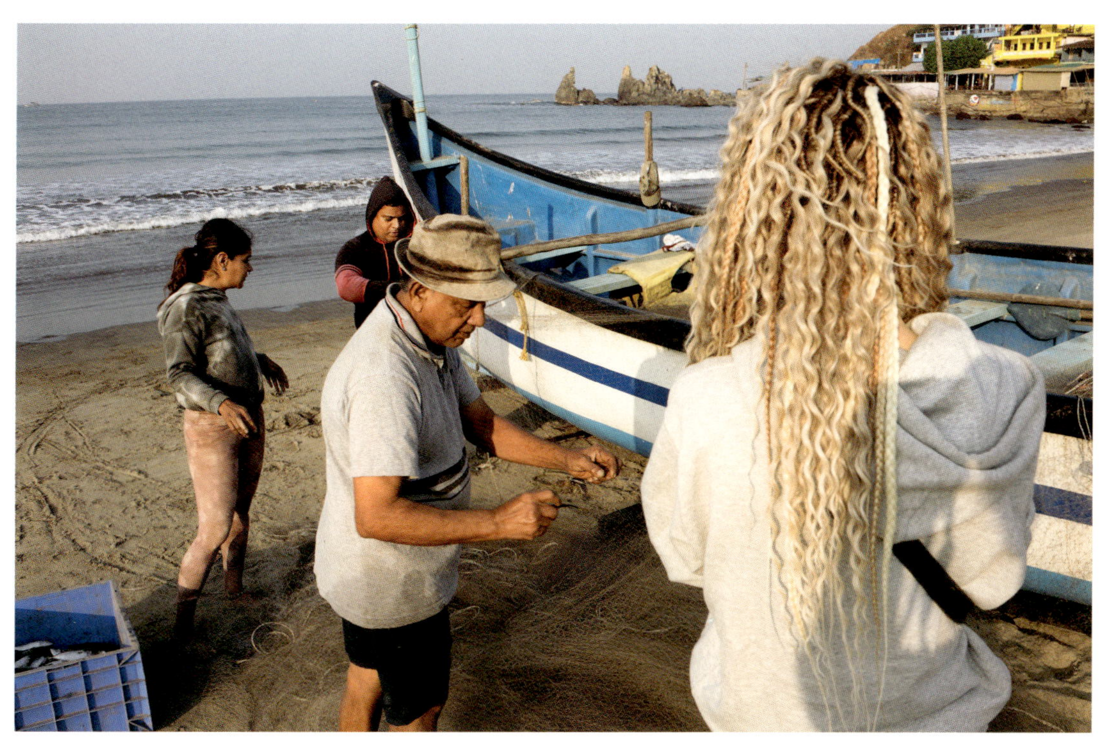

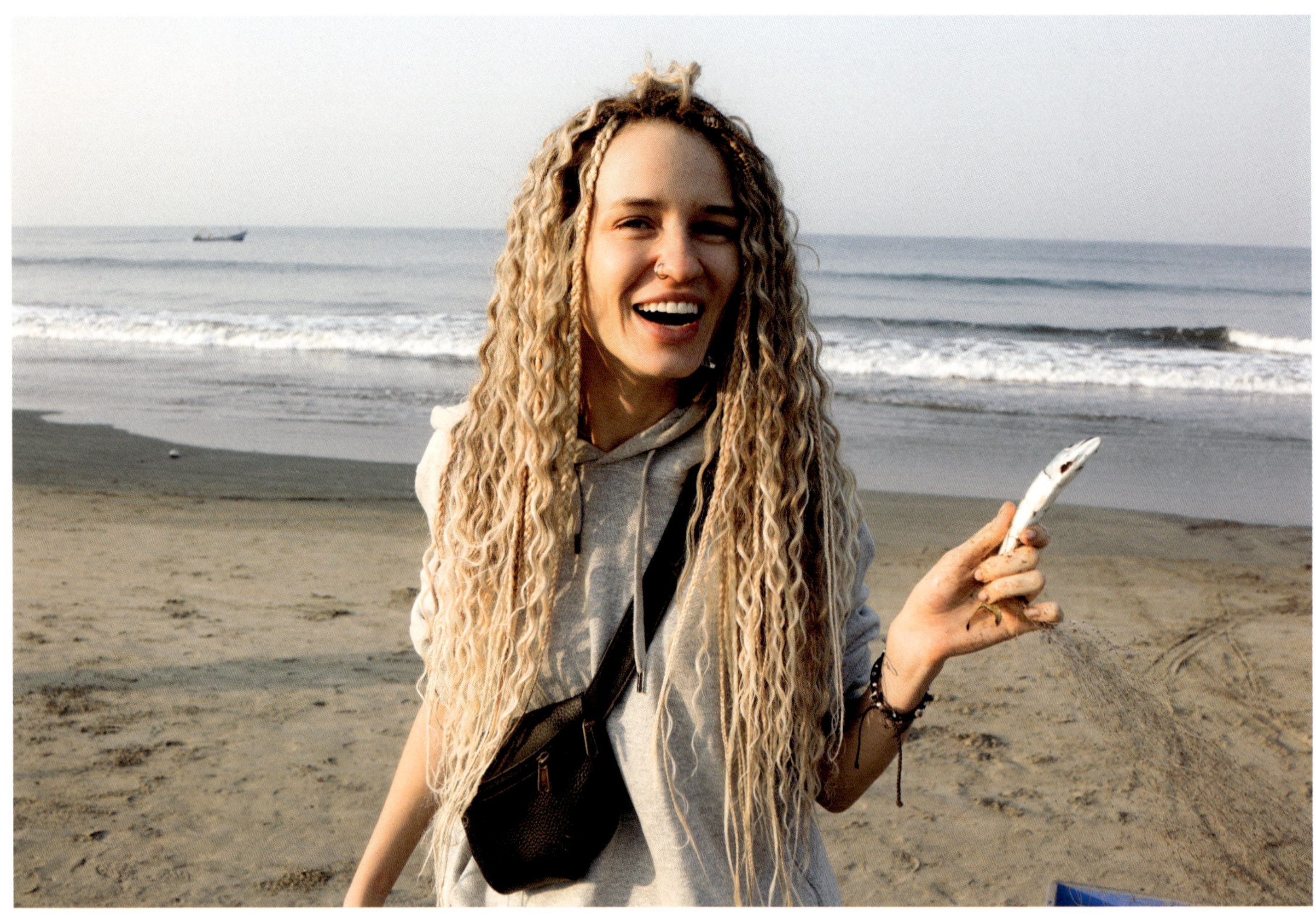

Alona (Russia). I met goldilocks Alona one morning after she'd spent the dawn hours out in the ocean, sardine fishing with her boyfriend Scott and a local fisherfolk family. Scott (Australia) had been living in Goa for the past six years. Alona joined him for a month each winter to, in her words, "chill in a place with spiritual vibes." When I asked Scott how the day was going, he replied, "this morning out on the boat I saw the best sunrise of my life—and I'm from the Australian coast, mate!

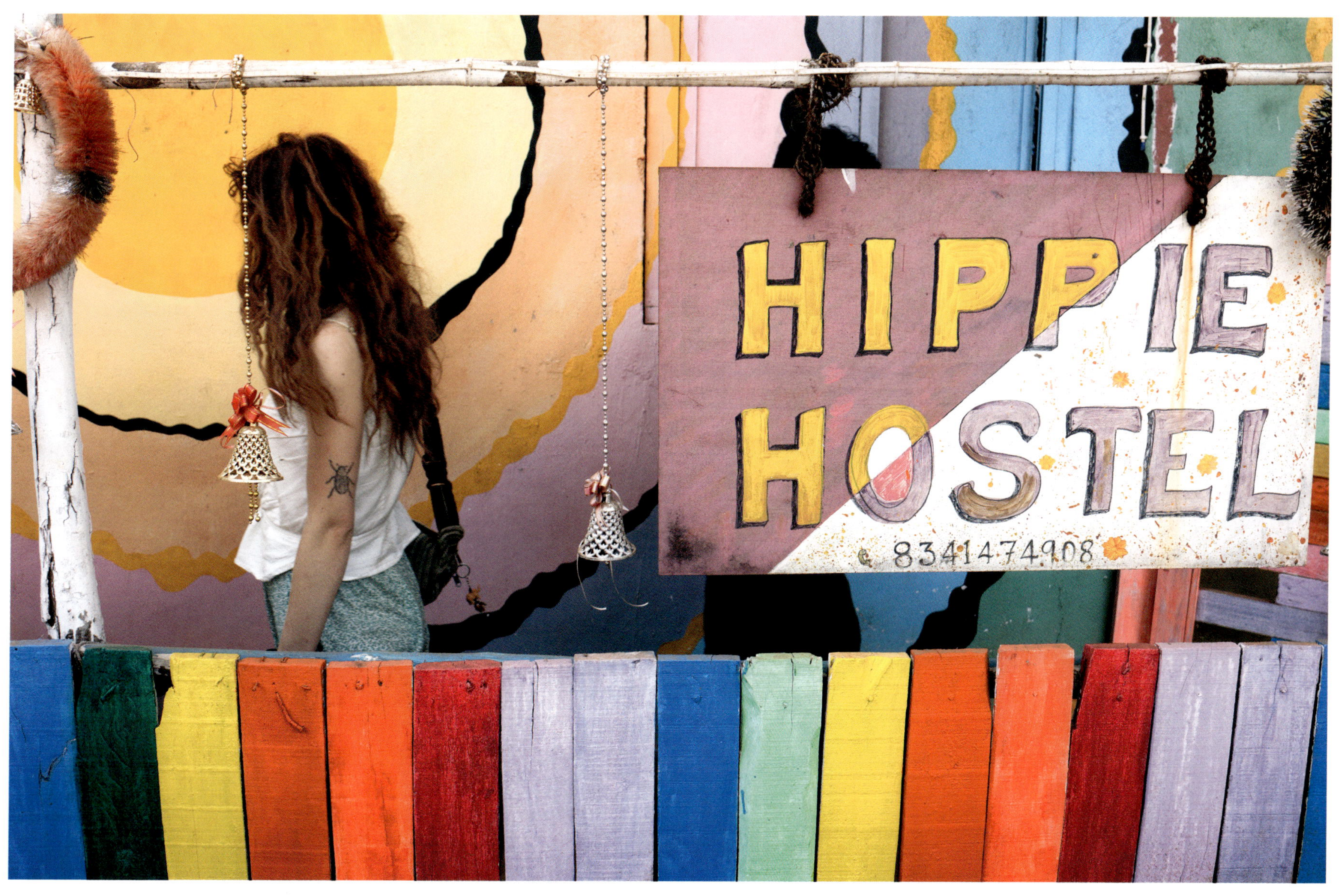
HIPPIE
HOSTEL
8341474908

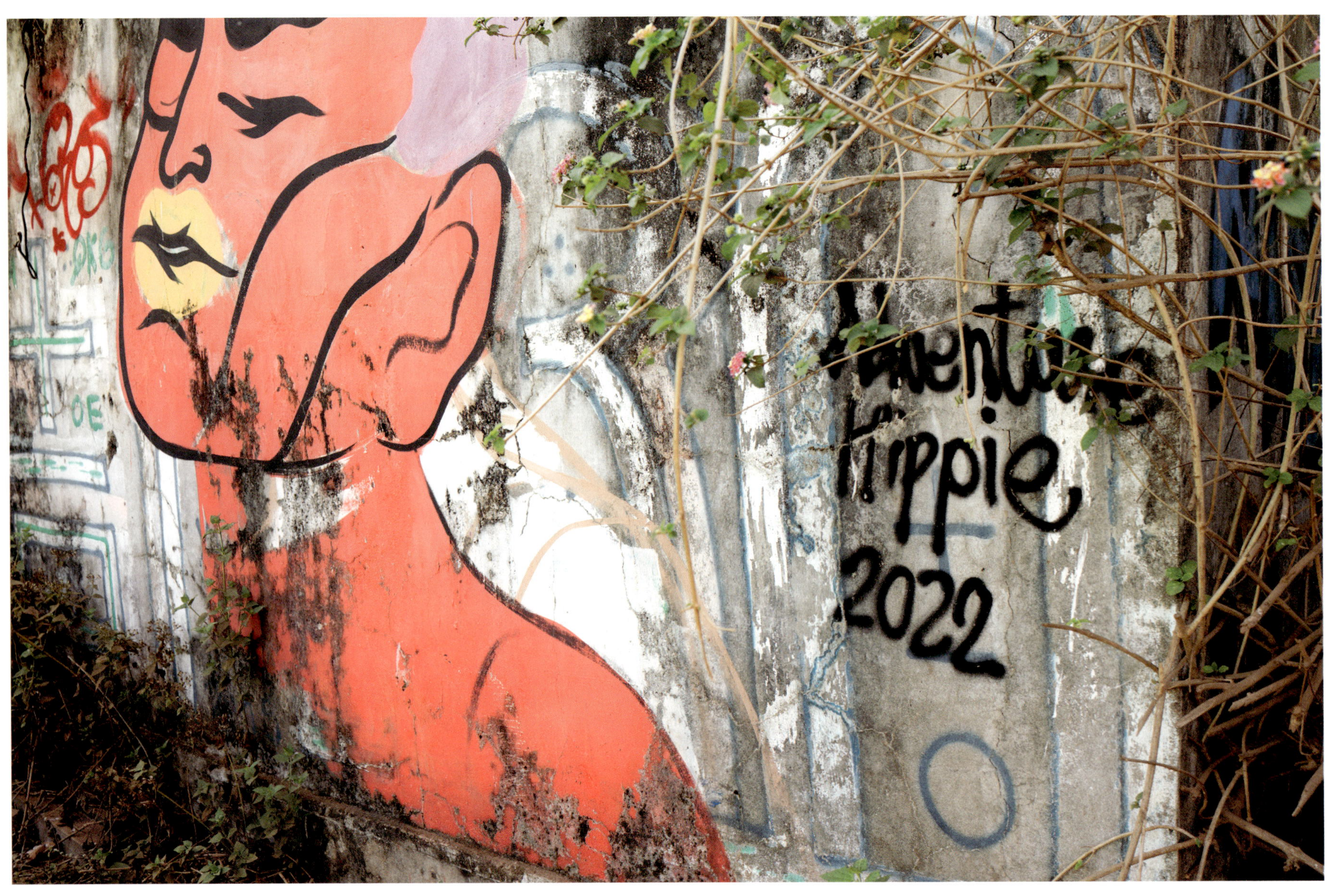
hippie
2022

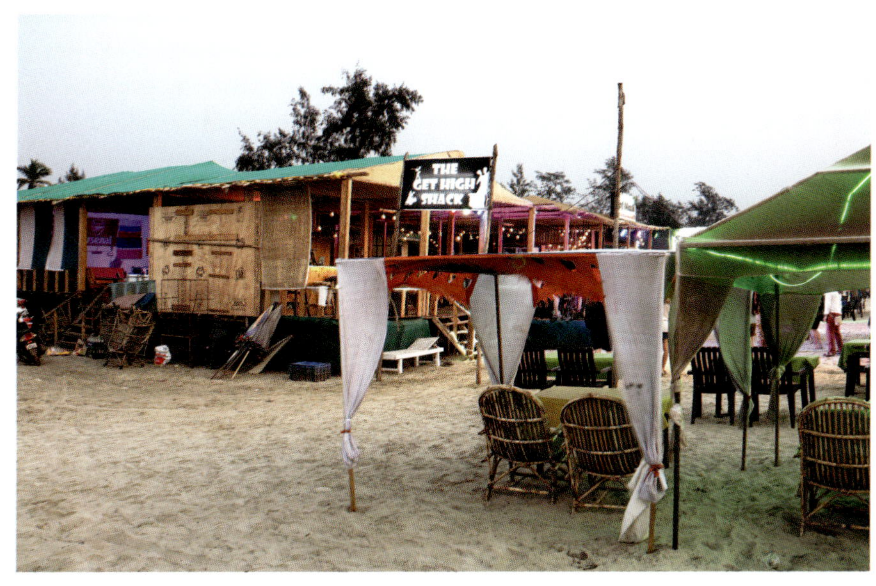

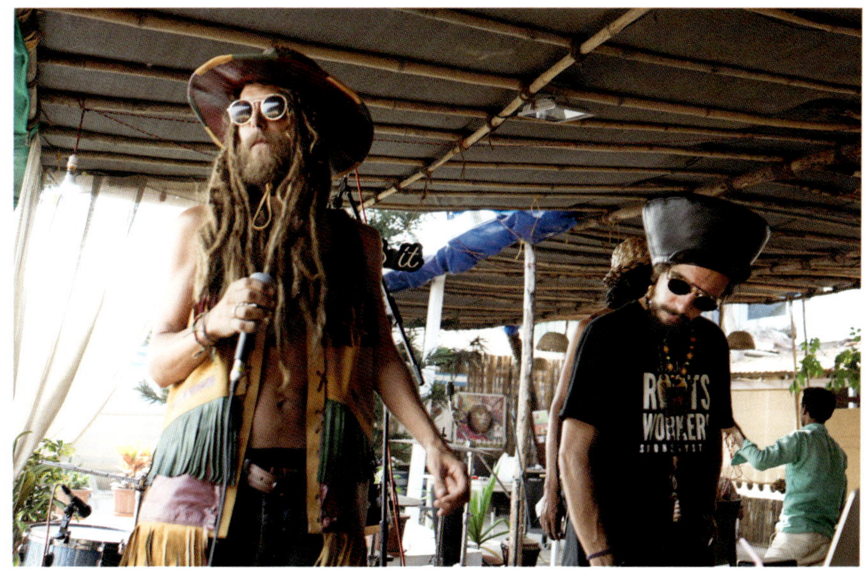

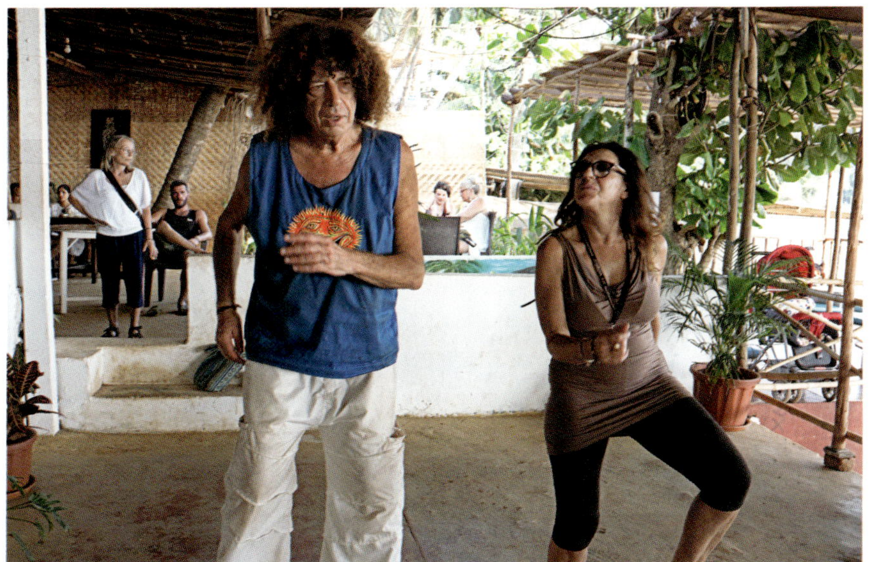

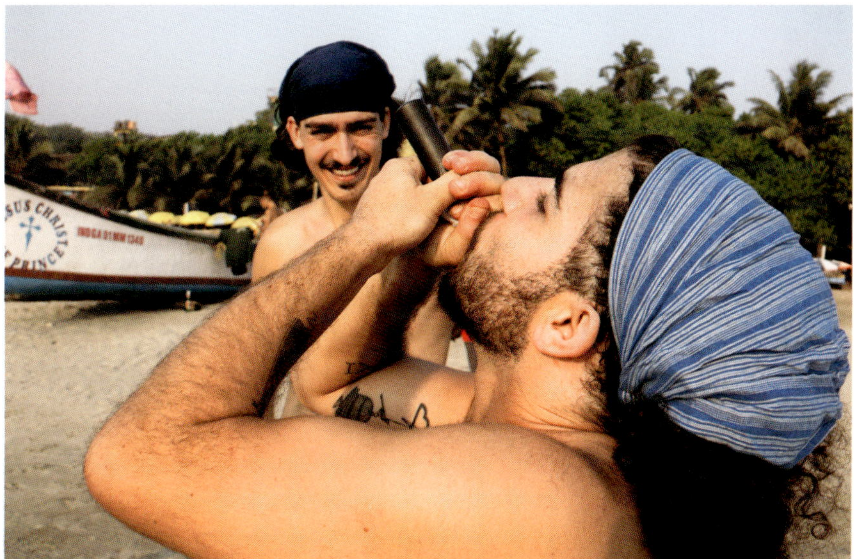

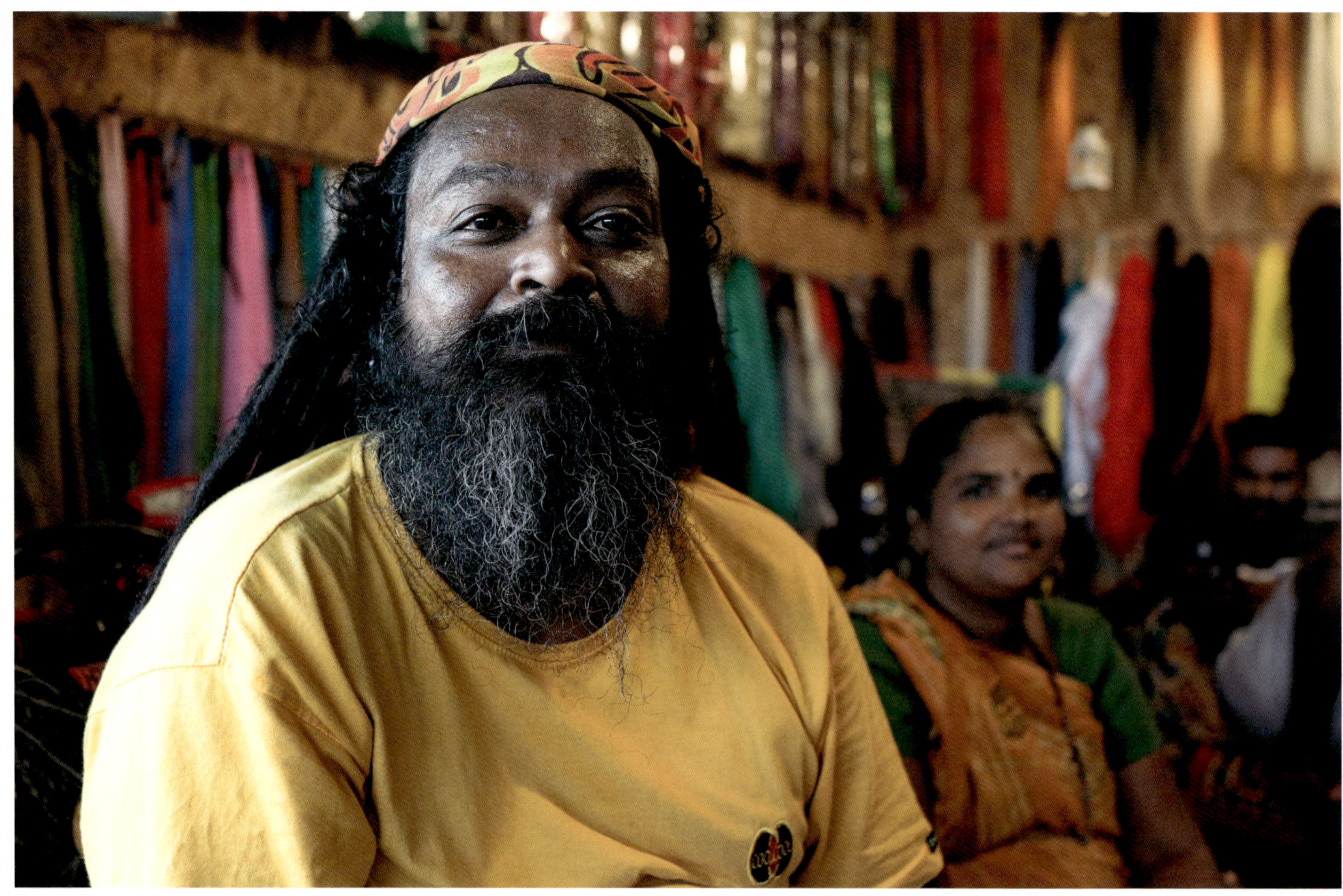

Deej (India). Deej Rasta owns a headshop
in Arambol Beach. I stopped by one day
to examine his wares and we struck up a
conversation. "I set up this shop almost 30
years ago, so I have seen a lot," he related.
"I sell chillums and bongs to the hippies.
A little of this and a little of that. Rolling
papers. A few clothes. Some incense. It's a
pretty good business. And I get to meet a lot
of nice people."

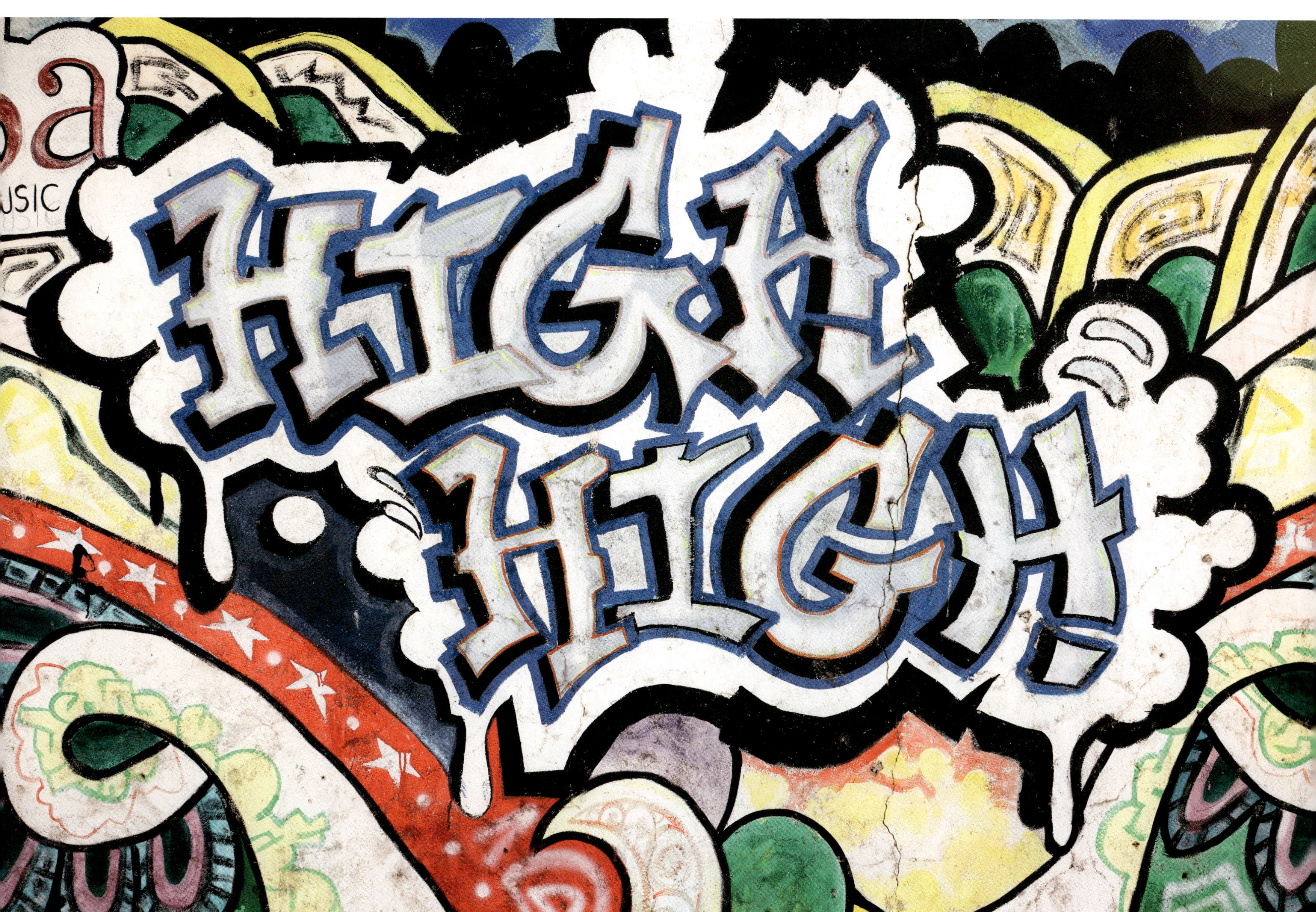

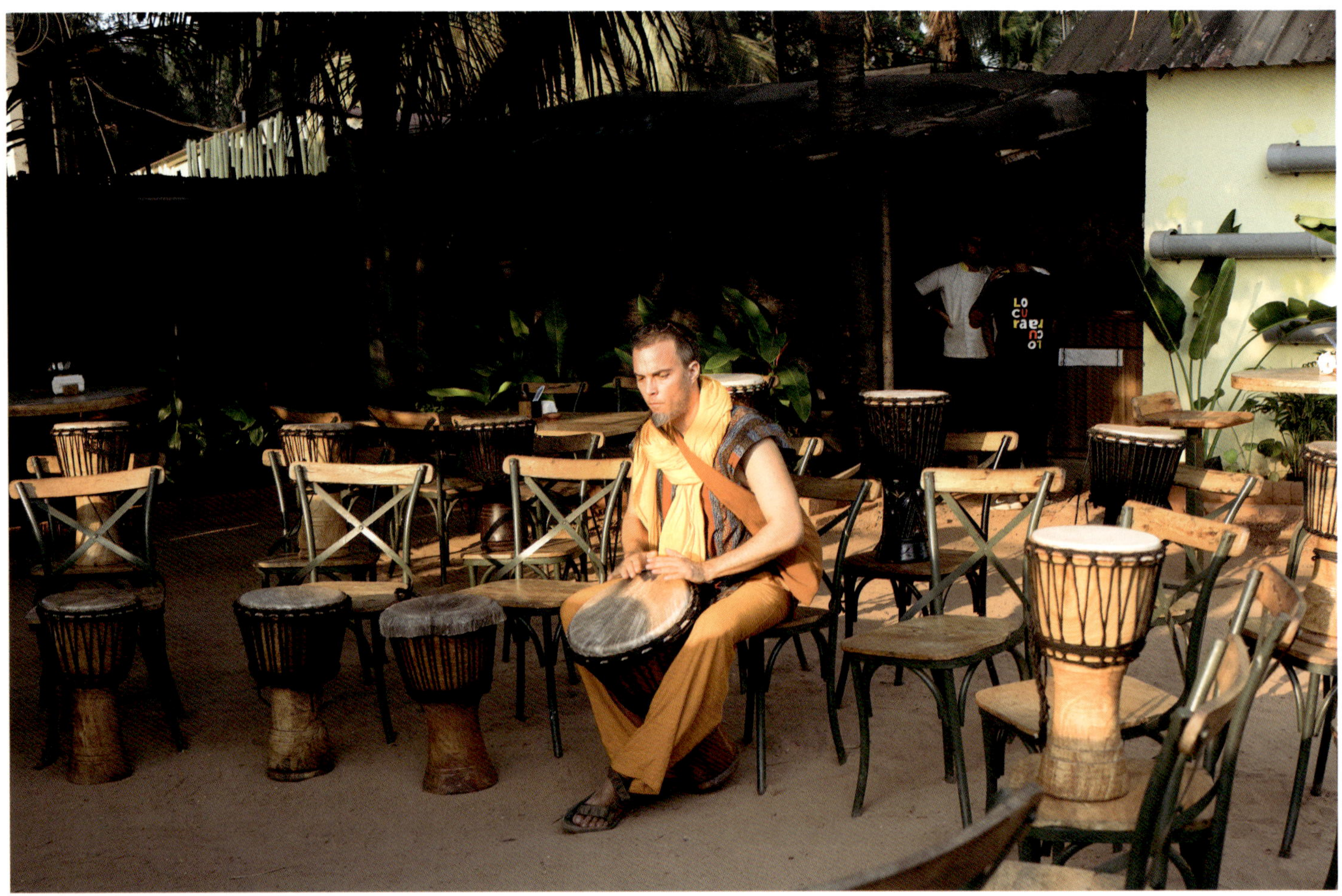

A drum circle has been going steady on the
Anjuna Beach every evening for the past
several decades. It begins slowly, with just
one or two drummers, but picks up steadily
as the sun goes down. Soon the circle
is filled with travelers playing djembes,
bongos, hand cymbals, tambourines,
congas. On the evening I visited, an
international fire dance competition was
being held. Participants from throughout
the world came by the drum circle after the
competition and the party continued well
into the night.

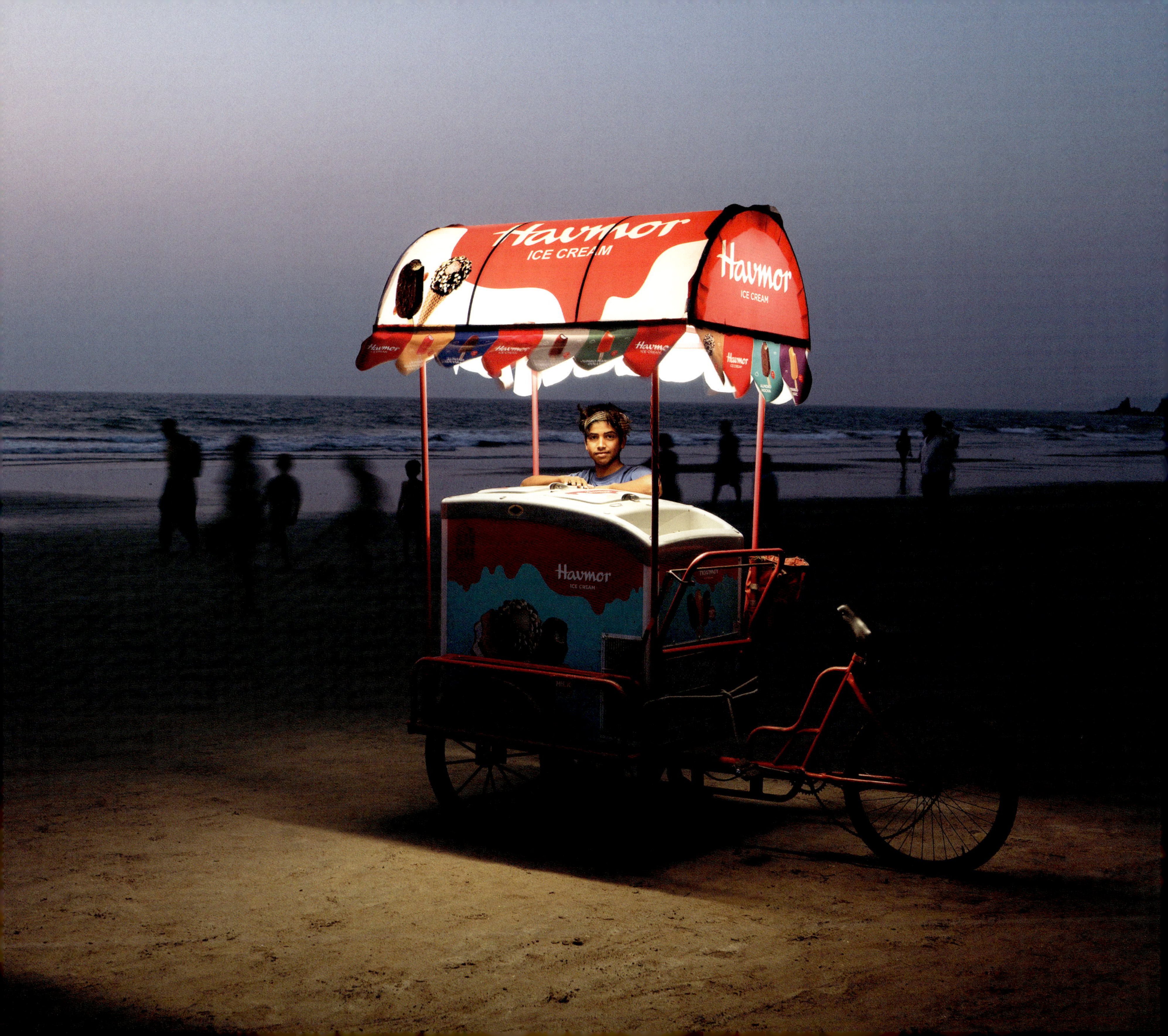

Havmor
ICE CREAM
Havmor
ICE CREAM
Havmor
ICE CREAM

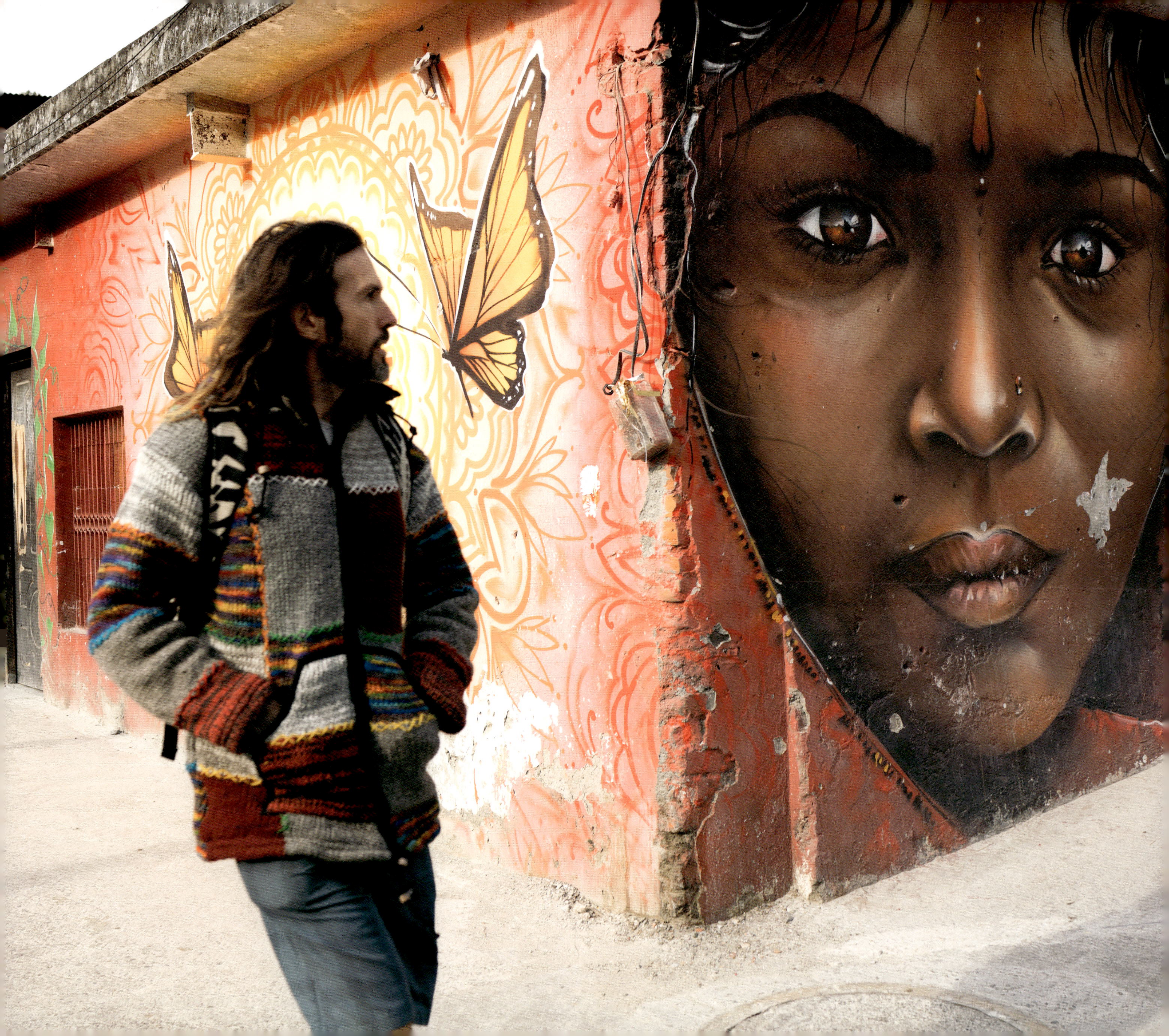

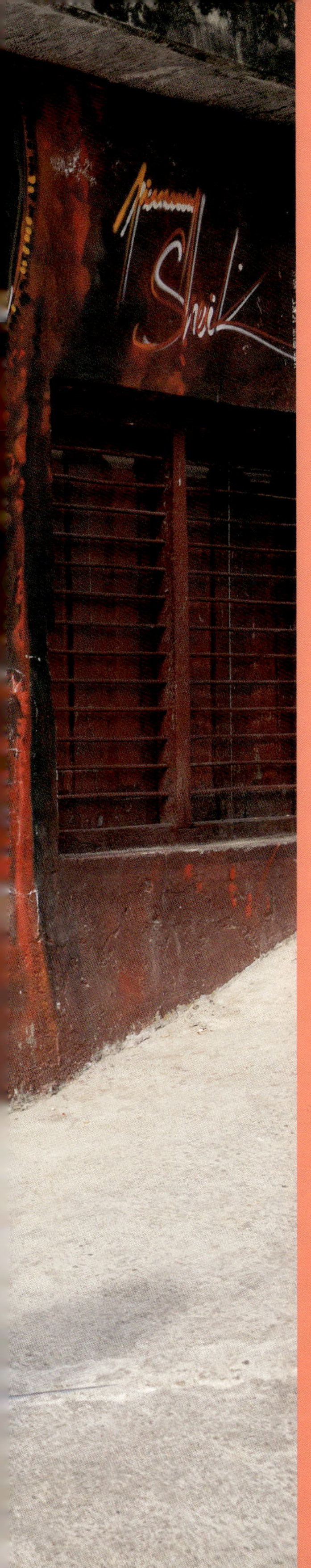

RISHIKESH

I was never a huge Beatles fan. In my early years I leaned more toward Led Zeppelin. In 1975, when I embarked as a teenager on the Hippie Trail to India, their hit song "Kashmir" was climbing the charts. It seemed auspicious at the time, with Robert Plant wailing the lyrics *"Oh, let the sun beat down upon my face and stars fill my dreams, I'm a traveler of both time and space."* As if they were meant specifically for me. It was the Beatles, though, who put Rishikesh on the map. They came in 1968 to study transcendental meditation with Maharishi Mahesh Yogi, and ushered in a hit parade of counterculture travelers visiting from the West that continues today.

Long before the arrival of George Harrison and his bandmates, though, Rishikesh had been a spiritual center of India. Situated on the banks of the Ganges in the foothills of the Himalaya, the town for ages has attracted sages, poets, yogis, and mendicants. Ashrams and temples line the riverbank. Songs of praise fill the air. At dawn, Hindu pilgrims serenely bathe in the Ganges, while the evenings come alive with "Ganga Aarti," a fellowship of psalms and rituals held every sunset on the *ghats* to honor Lord Agni, God of Fire. Intermingling among these timeless practices are the throngs of Westerners who visit

Rishikesh to study its spiritual practices: to practice yoga, to learn to meditate, to seek enlightenment.

At the base of one of the suspension bridges across the Ganges River is Tapovan, a densely packed neighborhood of guesthouses, cafés, and retreat centers. It is hippie central in Rishikesh. The narrow alleyways are filled with people coming from or going to yoga or meditation classes, heading to the river, to a restaurant or back to their lodgings, practicing mindfulness amid a chaotic onrush of pilgrims, Hare Krishna devotees, traders. Through it all a calm prevails. Like the eye of a hurricane, Rishikesh emanates peacefulness while being at the swirling vortex of spiritual and secular energy.

My meetings with Western travelers in Rishikesh were, more often than not, quiet affairs held on the steps of a *ghat* or a street corner, in a temple or an ashram, or over a cup of tea in a café. One day, though, I found myself at a concert featuring Krishna Das (aka Jeff Kagel). Once the frontman for Blue Oyster Cult, a trip to India in 1970 changed his life. He quit the American rock scene and turned to Hindu devotional songs. The New York Times once described him as "the chant master of American yoga." Seated nearby were hundreds of dreadlocked, gypsy-scarved foreigners and Indian devotees, all swaying rapturously to the sonorous music. I felt it was something bigger than a concert. A joyous meeting of cultures. A blending of past, present, and future.

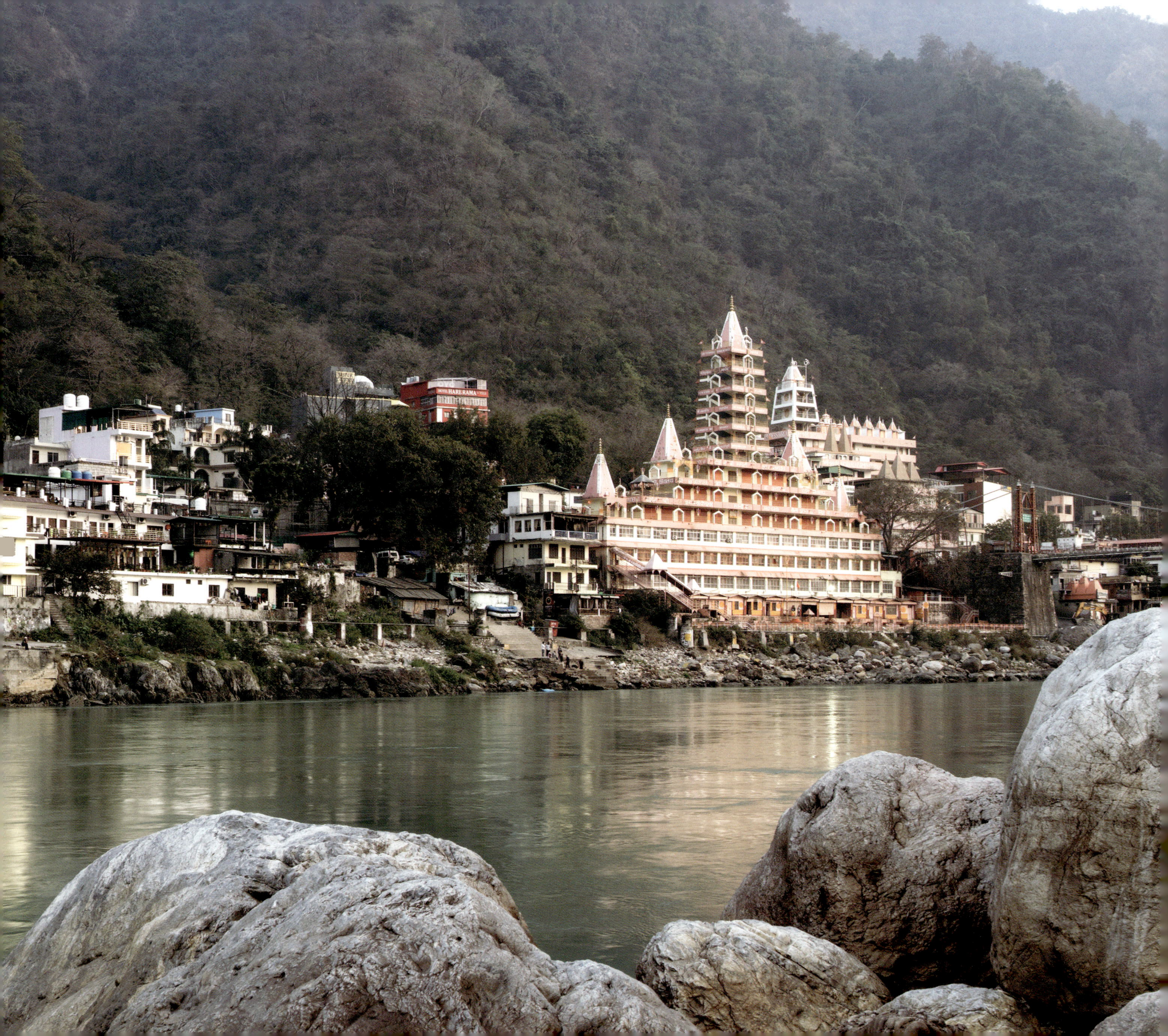

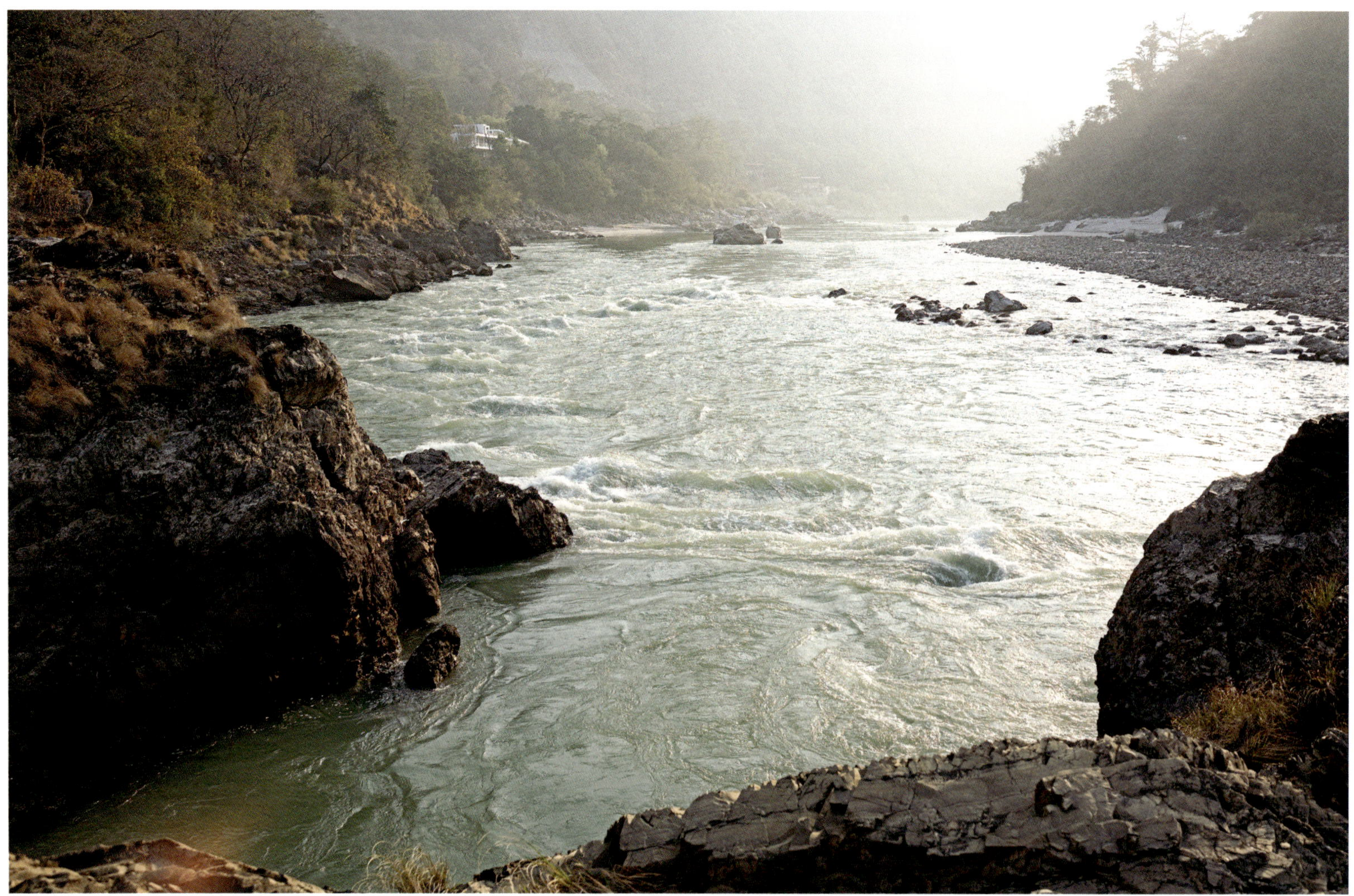

ABOVE: I was seated on a rocky ledge above the Ganges River, a short walk from the tourist hub of Rishikesh. It was early morning, the air was cool, and the sun had just risen over a mountain ridge. The noise of the rushing rapids drowned out other sounds. I was mesmerized by the water and had lost any sense of the passing of time. I thought I was alone when a local man in rags suddenly appeared at my side. I had no idea where he came from. He could've been a pilgrim or a bum. In Hindi, the man asked me: "Are you having a mystical experience?" He turned and walked away without waiting for an answer.

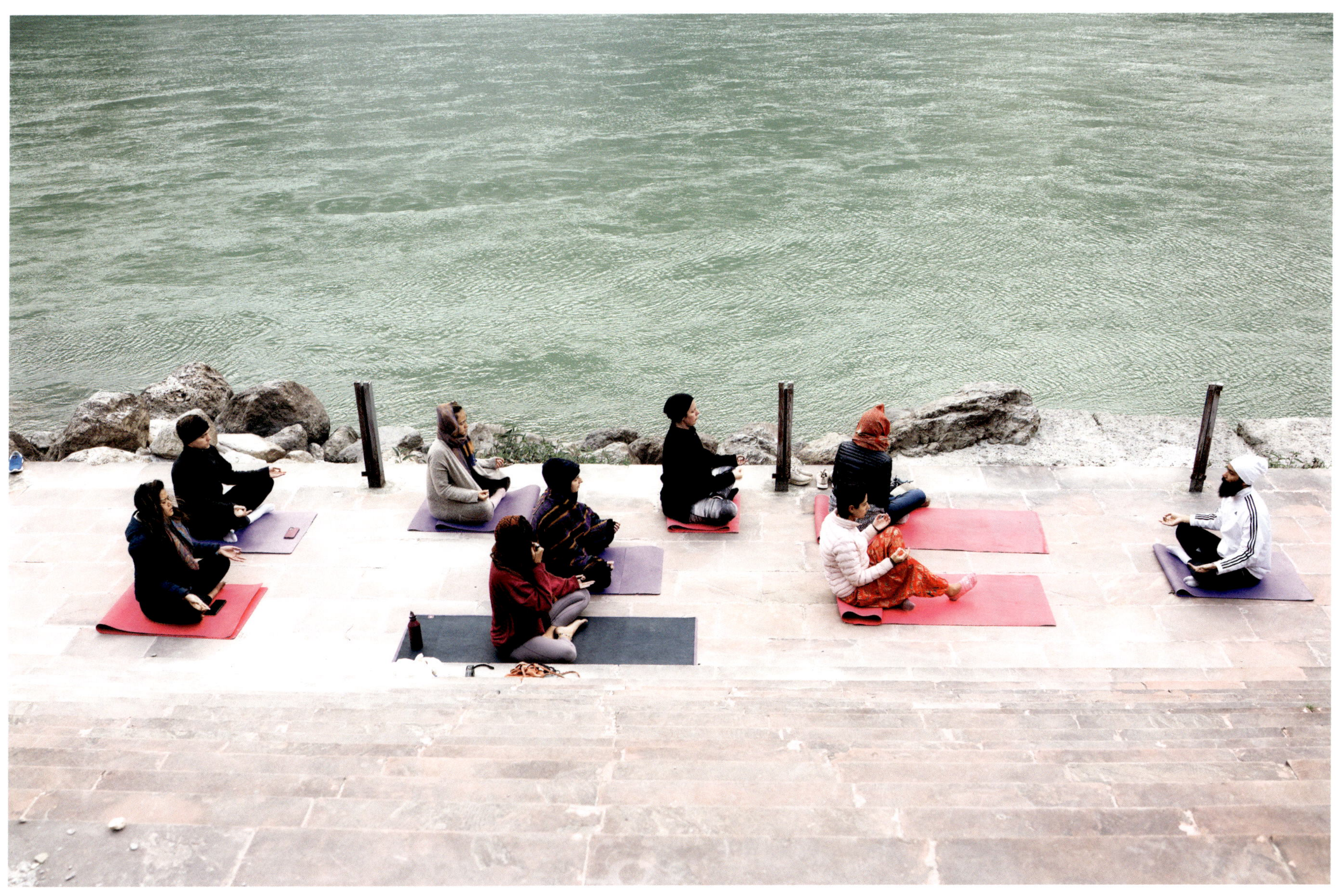

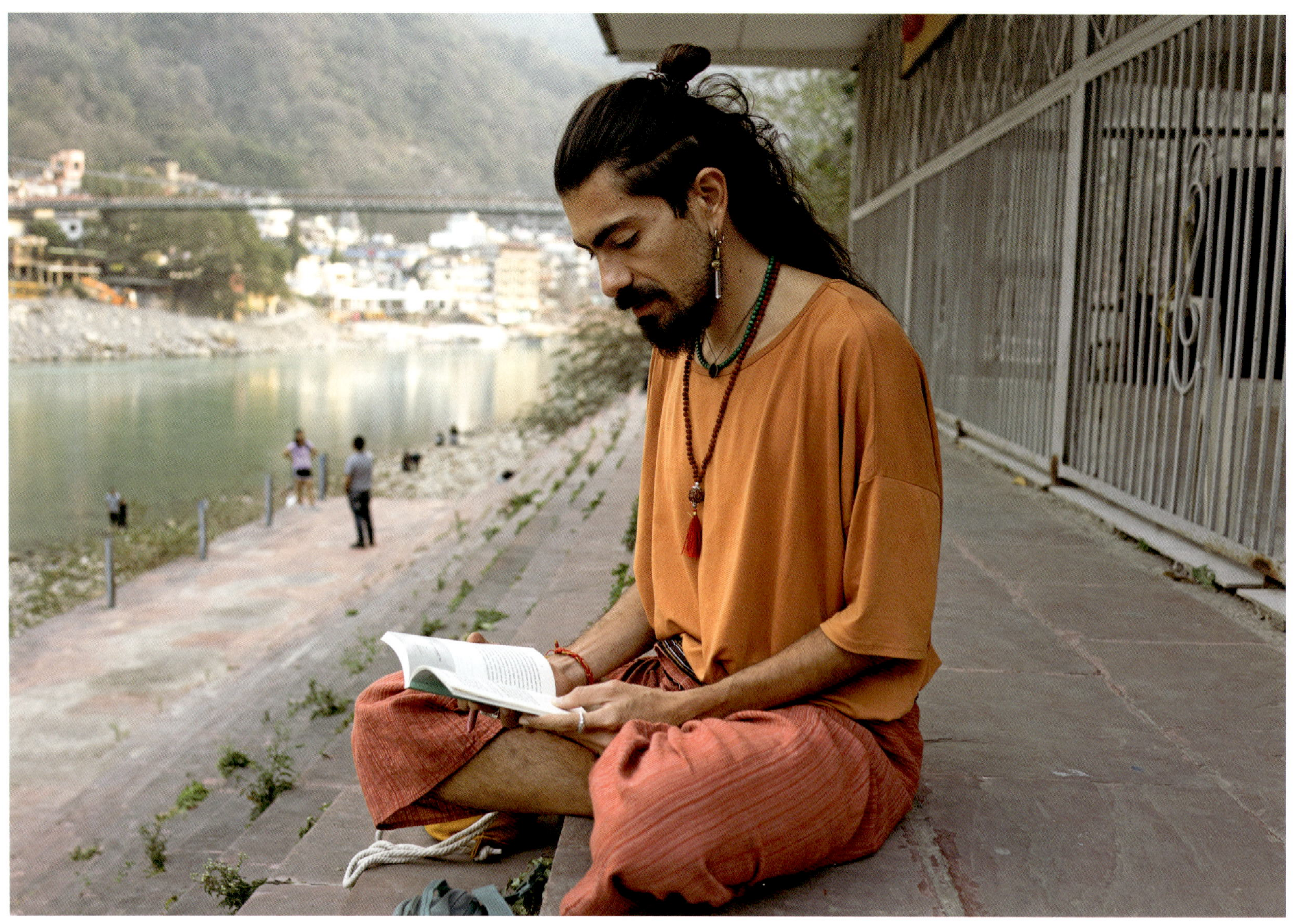

ABOVE: Alejandro (Mexico). I met Alejandro on the steps of Sai ghat. He was reading a book by Eckhart Tolle. Over the course of several days, we met often by the river, or shared a rickshaw, drank tea, and visited temples. We became "road friends." He related to me: "I was traveling in Vietnam and Thailand, and enjoyed those places—the food, the beaches—but it is here in India that I find a kind of spiritual connection. India nourishes my soul. I'm working on expanding my consciousness and Rishikesh is the perfect place for that."

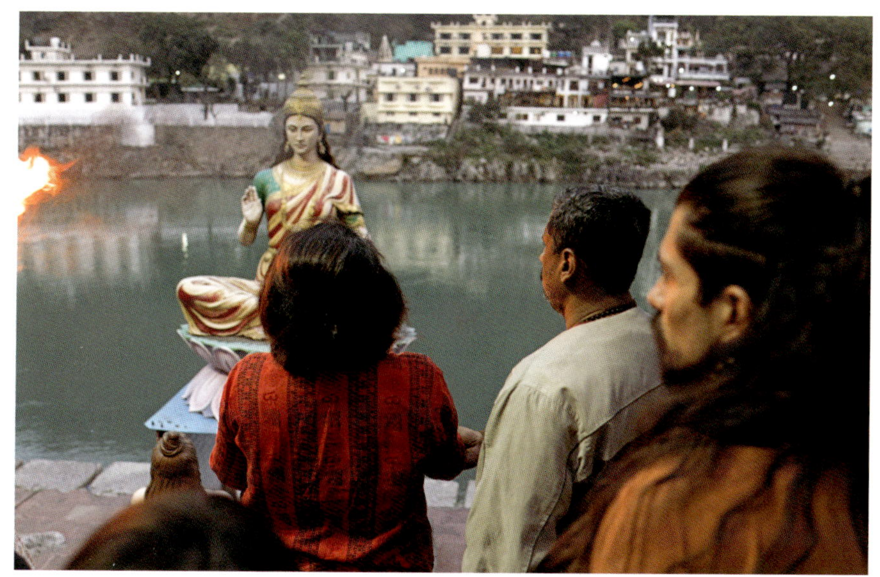

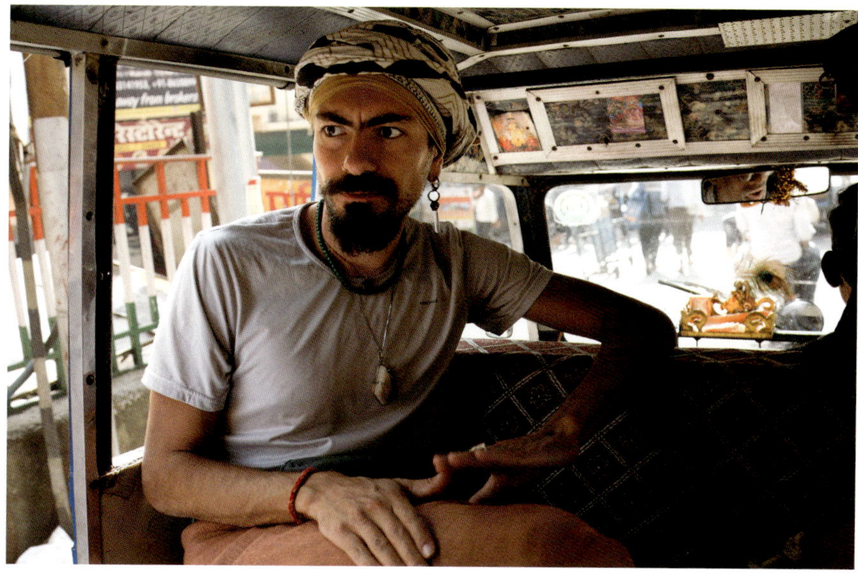

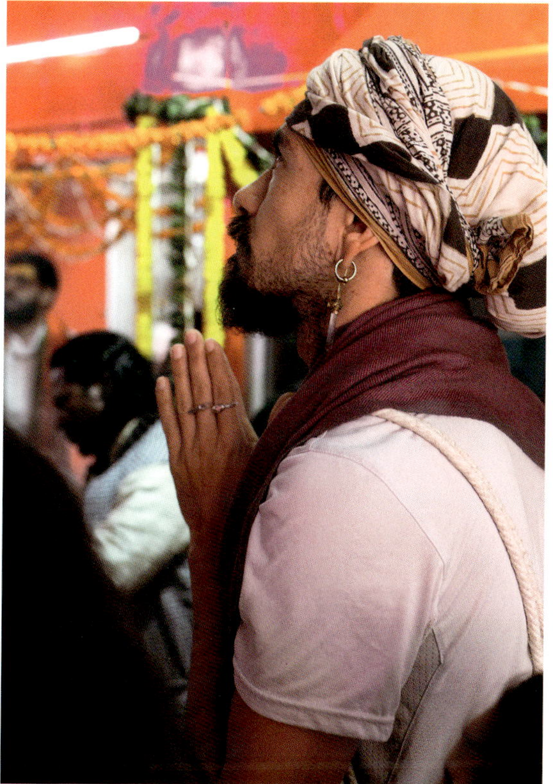

ABOVE LEFT: In a rickshaw heading to Triveni *Ghat*—the confluence of three holy rivers: Ganges, Saraswati, and Yamuna, where they pour out of the Himalayas.

ABOVE RIGHT: Attending the Ganga Aarti evening fire ritual.

LEFT: Alejandro participating in the Shiva Ratri Festival rituals held at the Shiva Mahadev Temple.

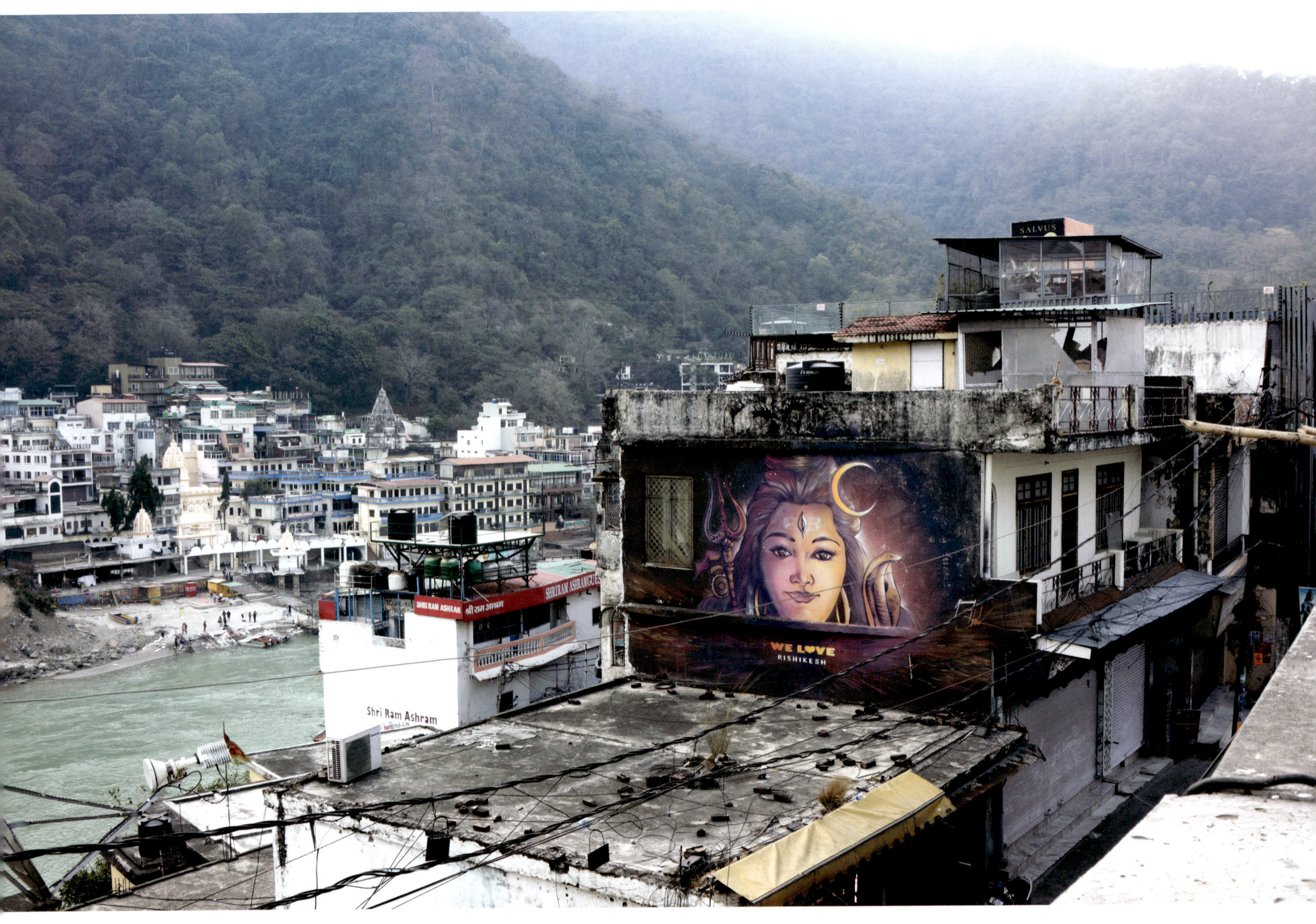
SALVUS
SHRIRAM ASHRAMGUES
SHRI RAM ASHRAM
Shri Ram Ashram
WE LOVE
RISHIKESH

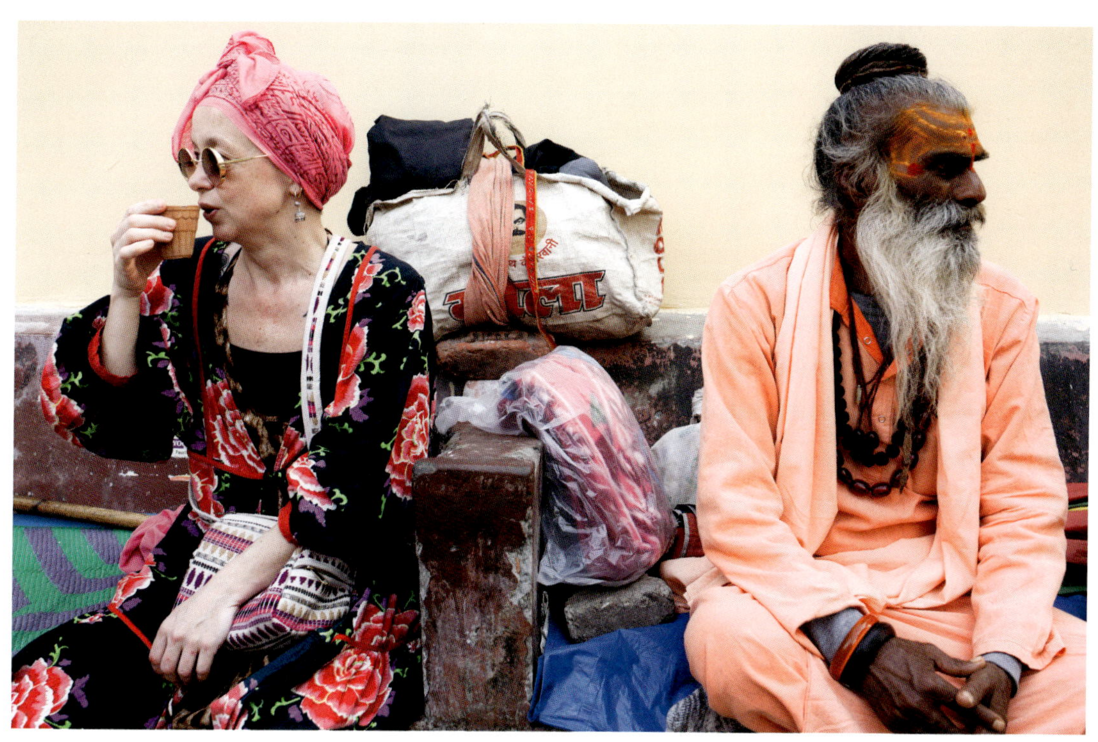

Mary (United Kingdom) and sadhu (India),
Parmath Niketan Ashram

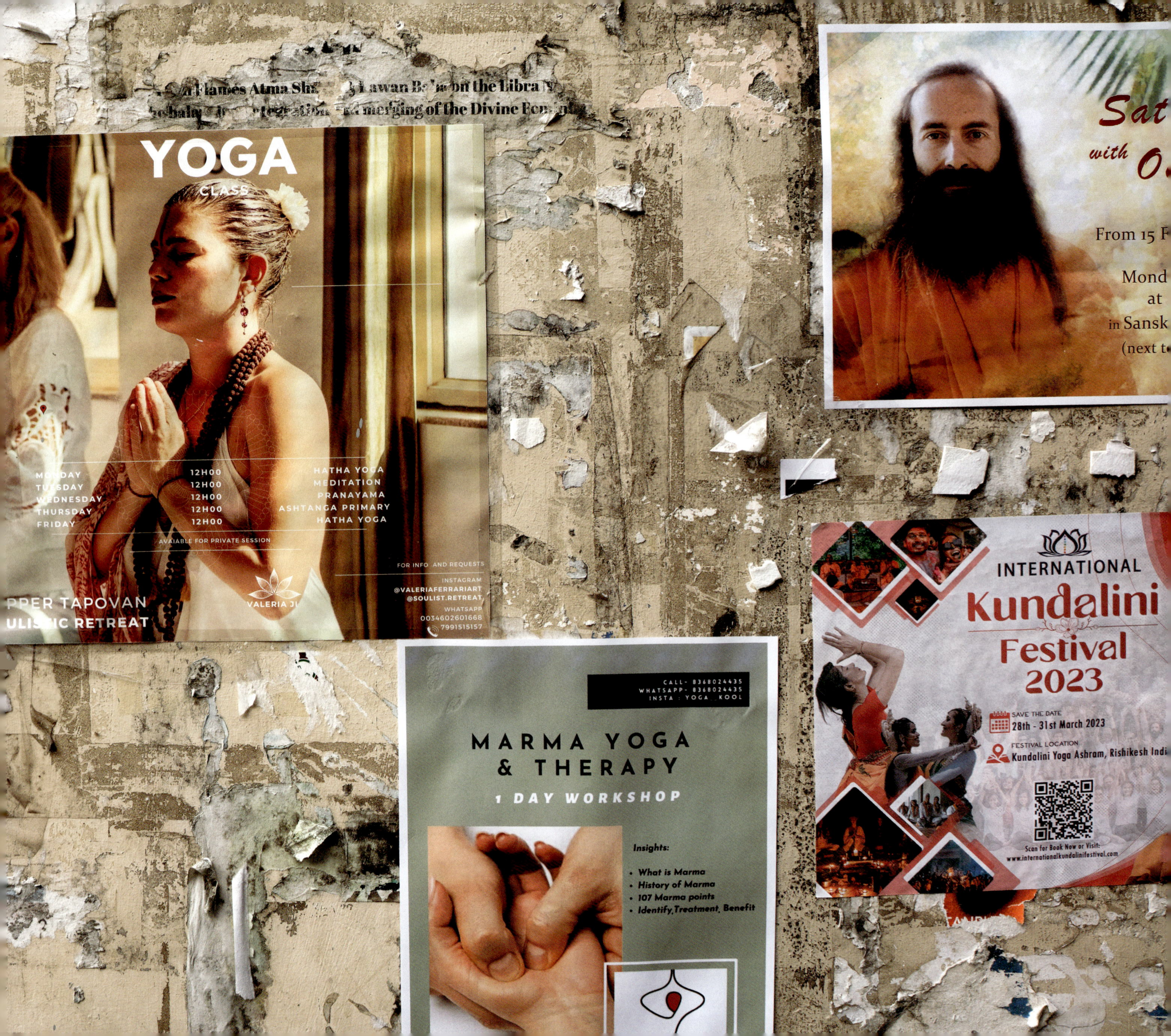
Flames Atma Sha... Lawan Ba... on the Library
...integration...and merging of the Divine Fem...
YOGA
CLASS
MONDAY   12H00   HATHA YOGA
TUESDAY   12H00   MEDITATION
WEDNESDAY   12H00   PRANAYAMA
THURSDAY   12H00   ASHTANGA PRIMARY
FRIDAY   12H00   HATHA YOGA
AVAIABLE FOR PRIVATE SESSION
FOR INFO AND REQUESTS
INSTAGRAM
@VALERIAFERRARIART
@SOULIST.RETREAT
WHATSAPP
003460260166B
799151515B
PPER TAPOVAN
ULISTIC RETREAT
VALERIA J
Sat
with O
From 15 F
Mond
at
in Sansk
(next t
CALL- 836B024435
WHATSAPP- 836B024435
INSTA : YOGA . KOOL
MARMA YOGA
& THERAPY
1 DAY WORKSHOP
Insights:
What is Marma
History of Marma
107 Marma points
Identify, Treatment, Benefit
INTERNATIONAL
Kundalini
Festival
2023
SAVE THE DATE
28th - 31st March 2023
FESTIVAL LOCATION
Kundalini Yoga Ashram, Rishikesh Indi
Scan for Book Now or Visit:
www.internationalkundalinifestival.com

Pierre Reyniers (1948–2019) is one of the unsung heroes of the Hippie Trail. He left France in 1969 on a spiritual journey to India and was so moved by what he found that he spent the next five decades in the Himalayan foothills, dedicating his life to serving local people who had contracted leprosy (Hanson's disease). His efforts were not in vain. He helped establish a number of self-sufficient farms and residential colonies where lepers could live and work without the stigma of society. Many of the children raised and educated in these places have gone on to become professional persons working throughout the world. Mr. Reyniers was cremated in Rishikesh and his ashes strewn into the Ganges River.

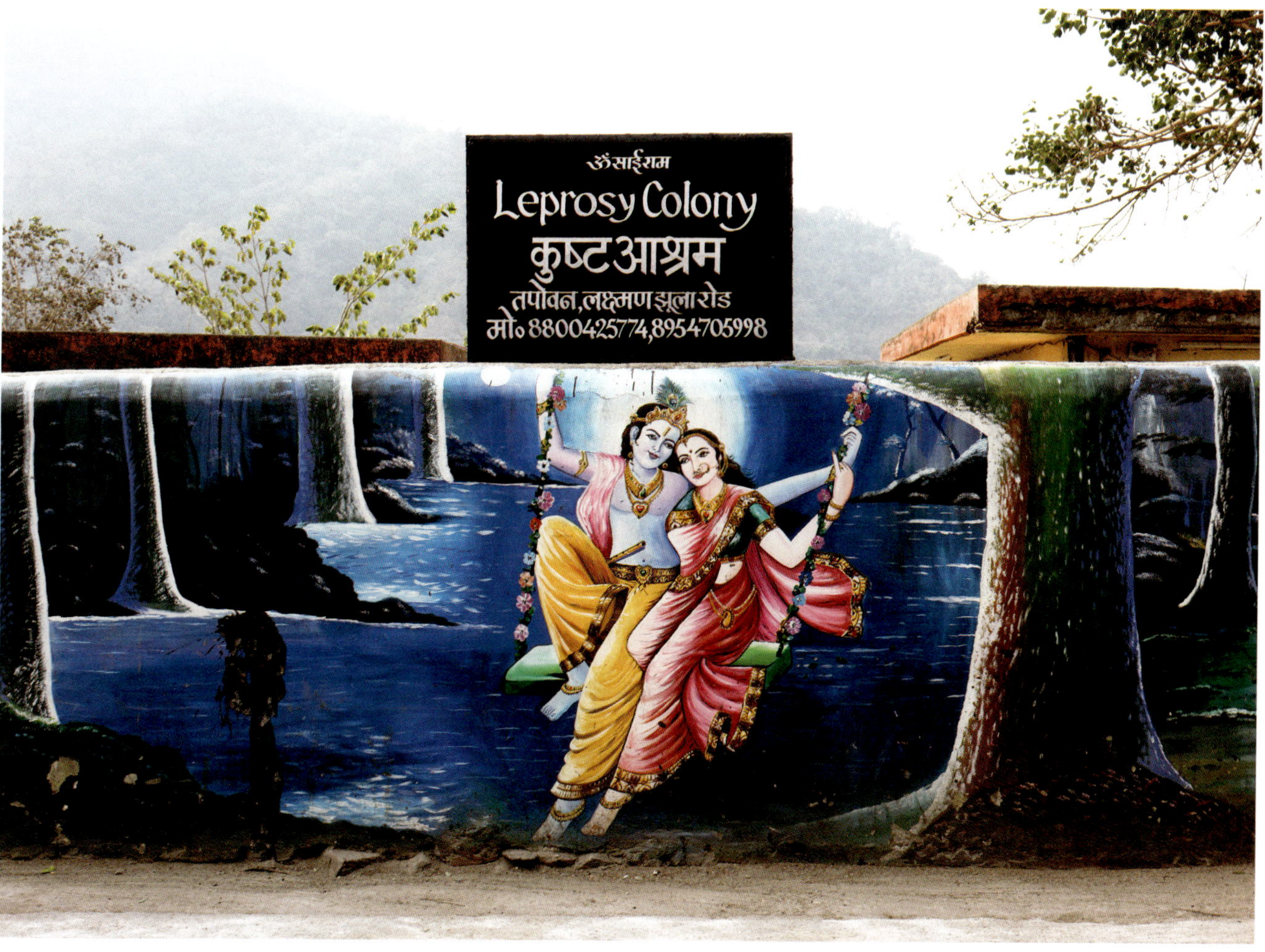

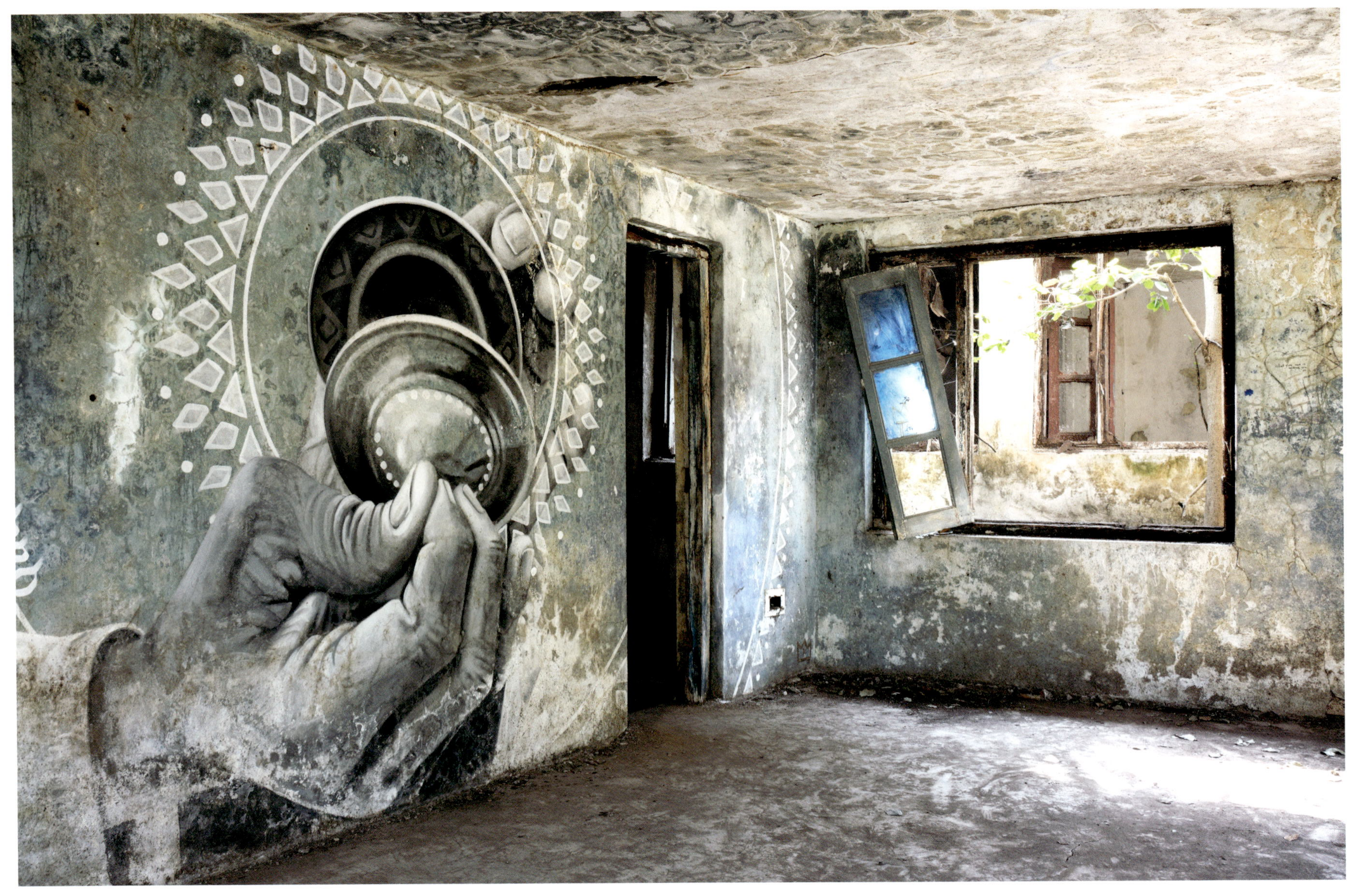

George Harrison's music room, Beatles Ashram

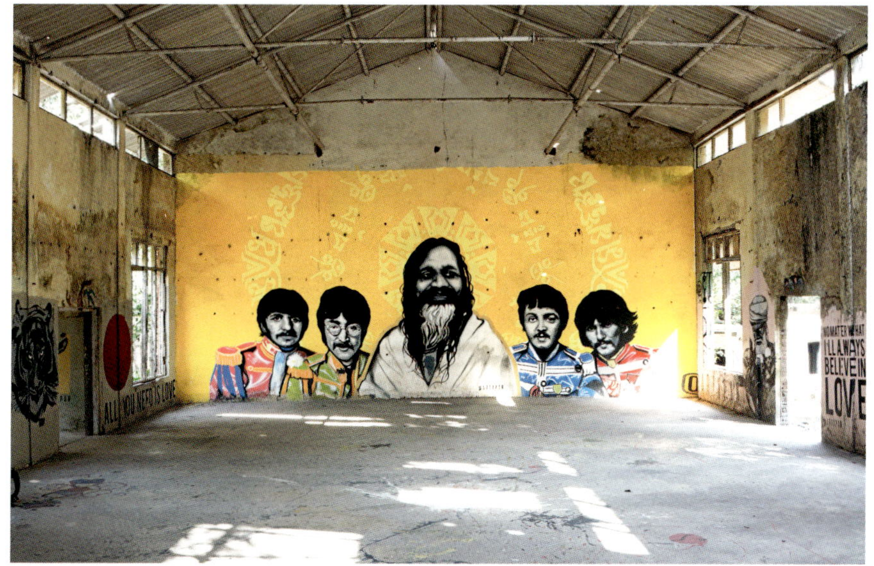

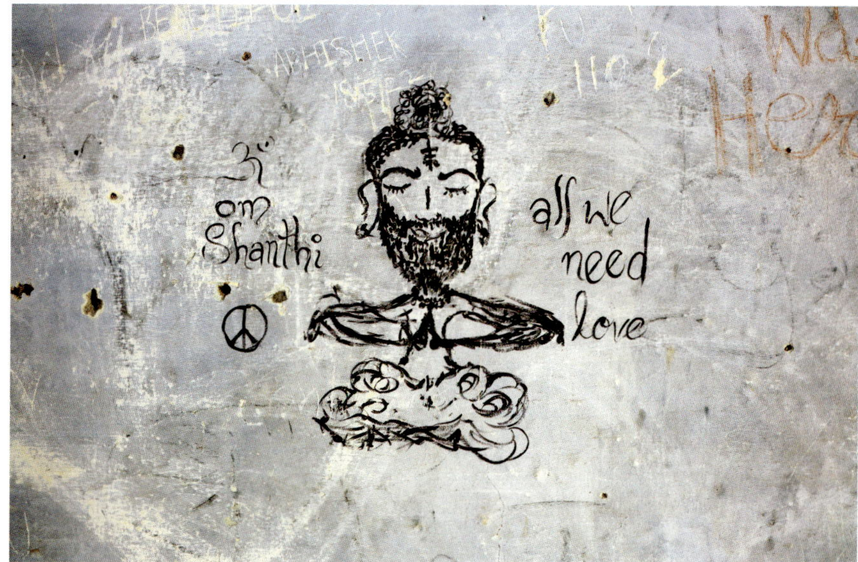

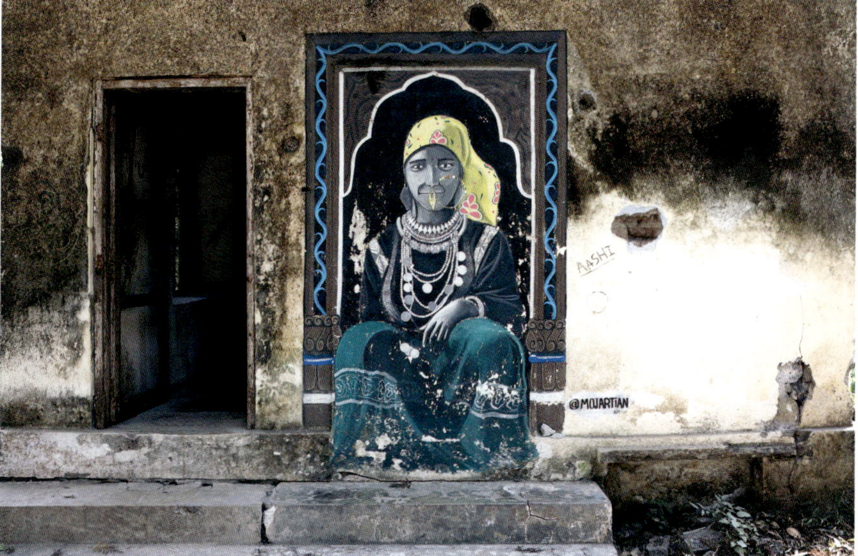

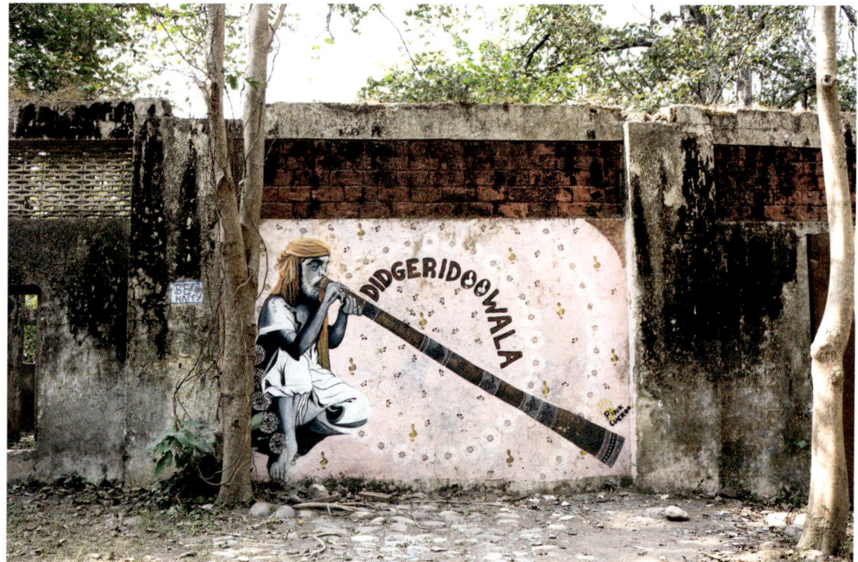

 Wall murals in the abandoned Beatles Ashram

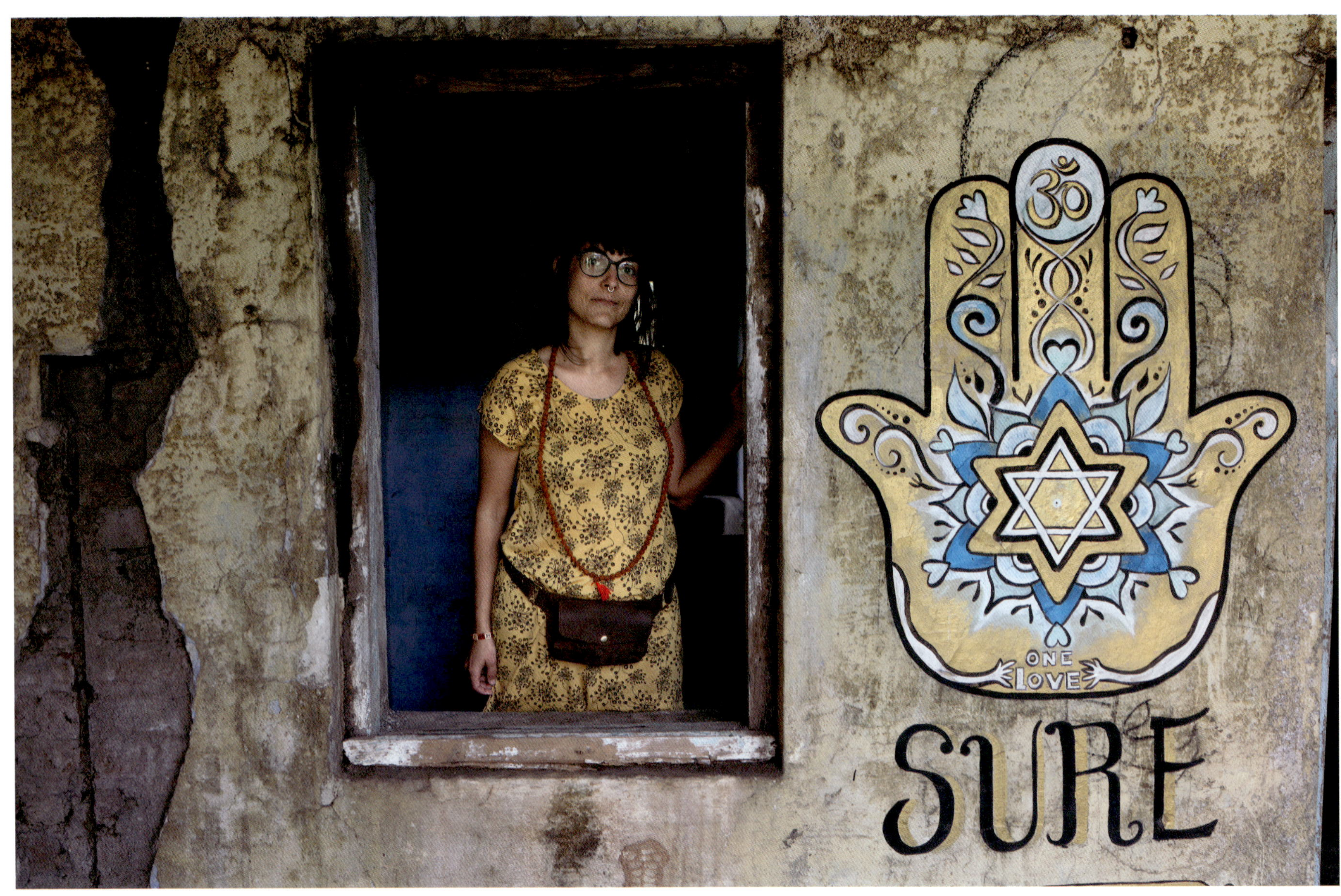

ABOVE: Carolina (Italy), Beatle's Ashram
OPPOSITE RIGHT: Baba (France)

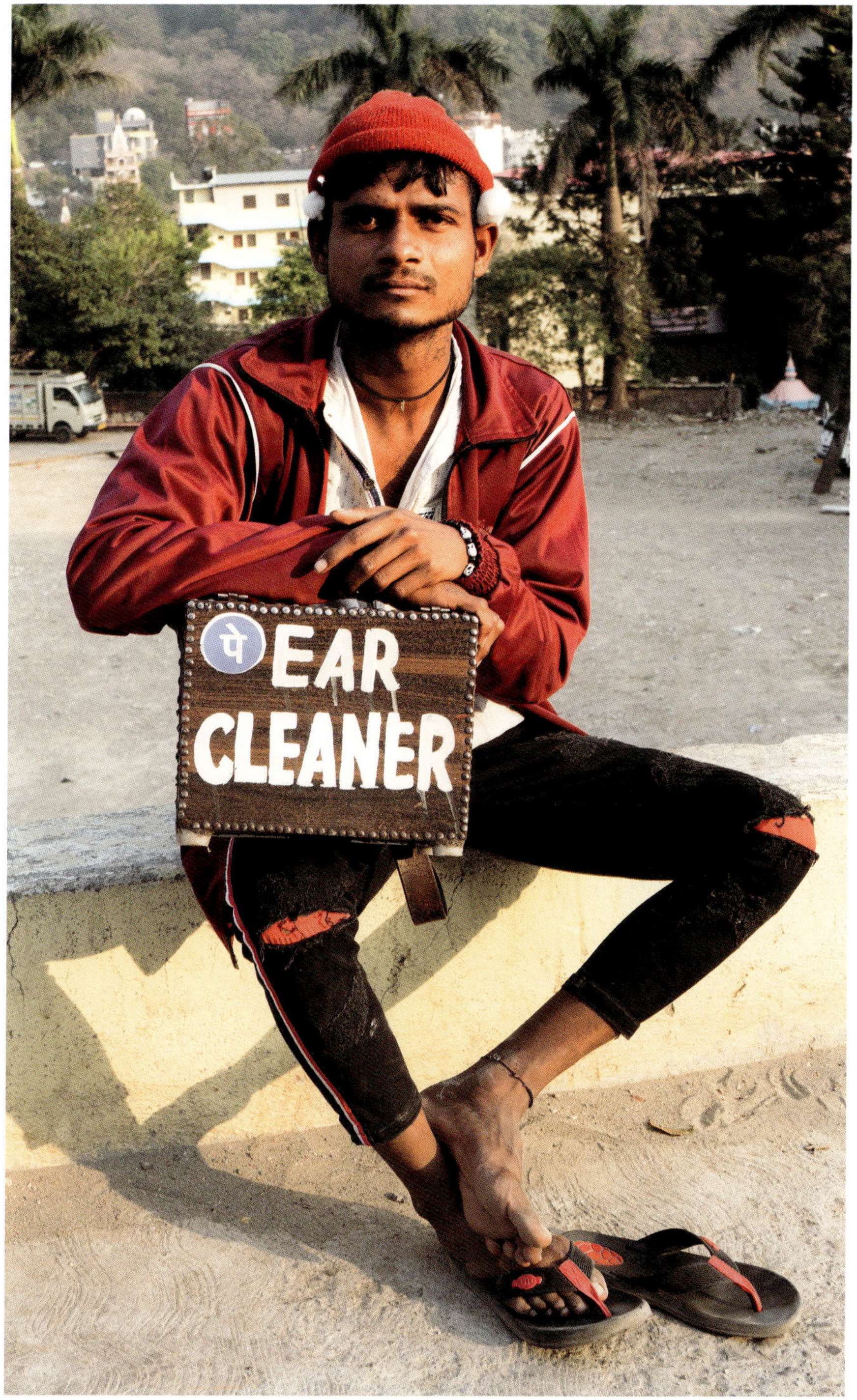

पे EAR
CLEANER

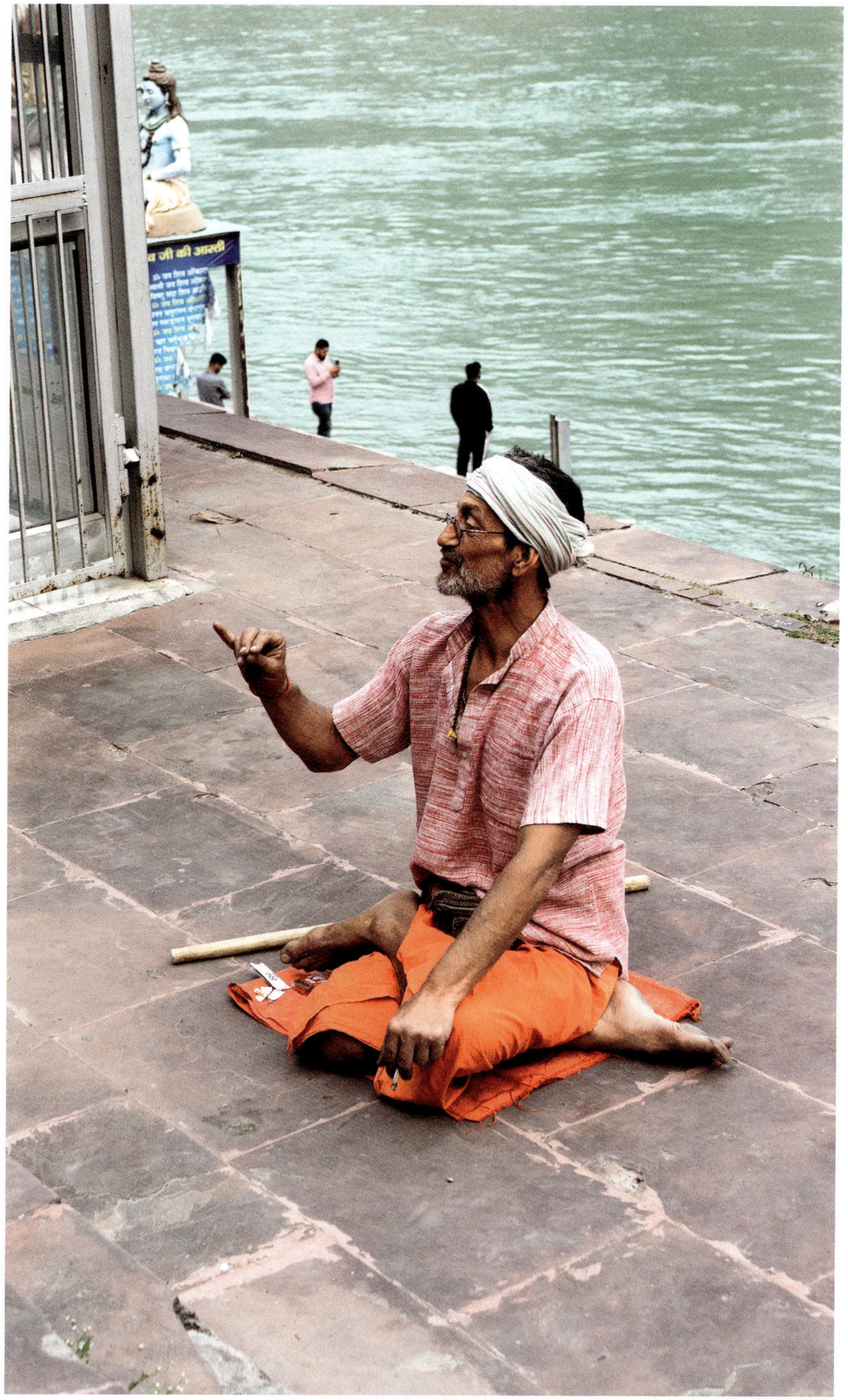

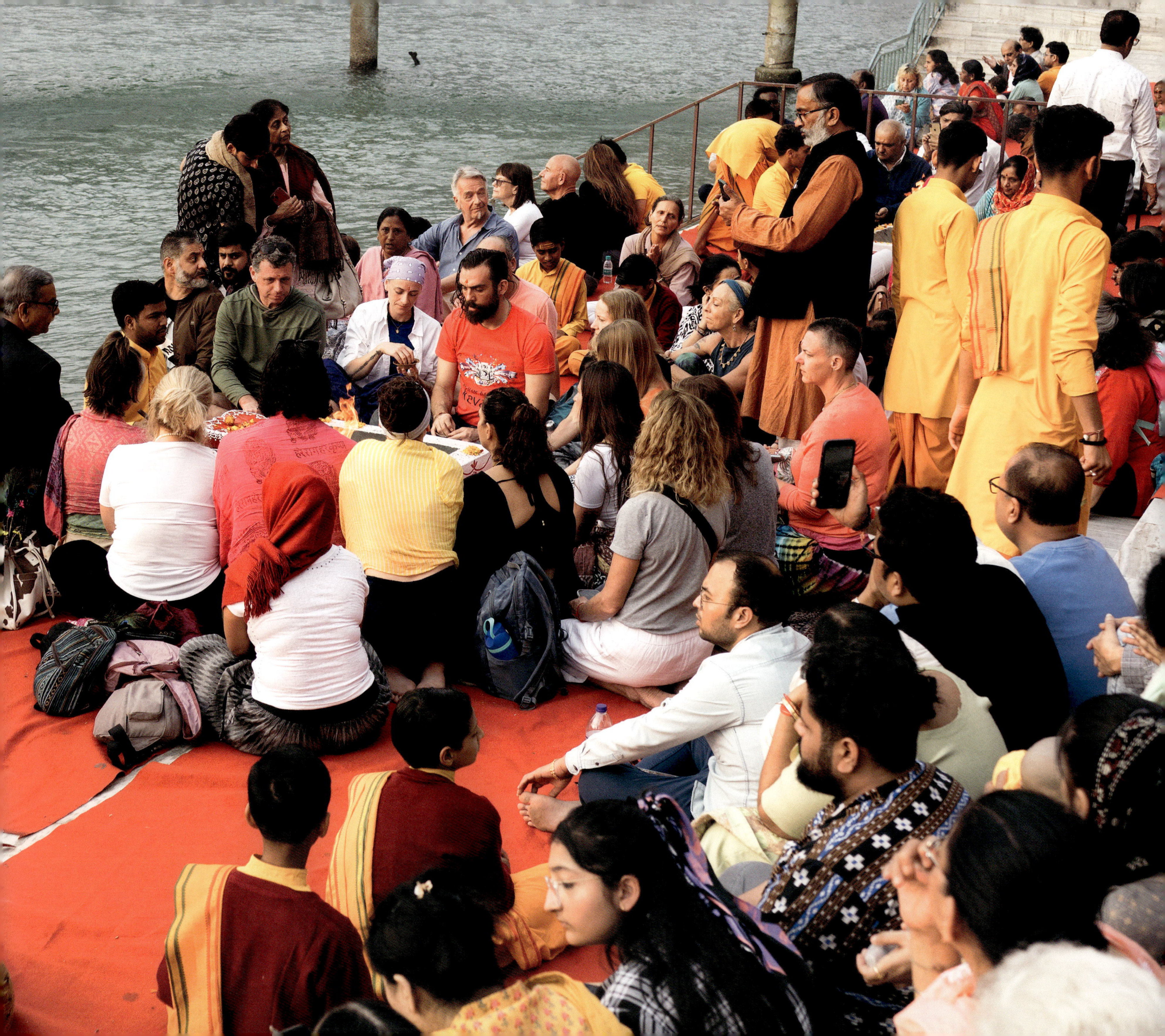

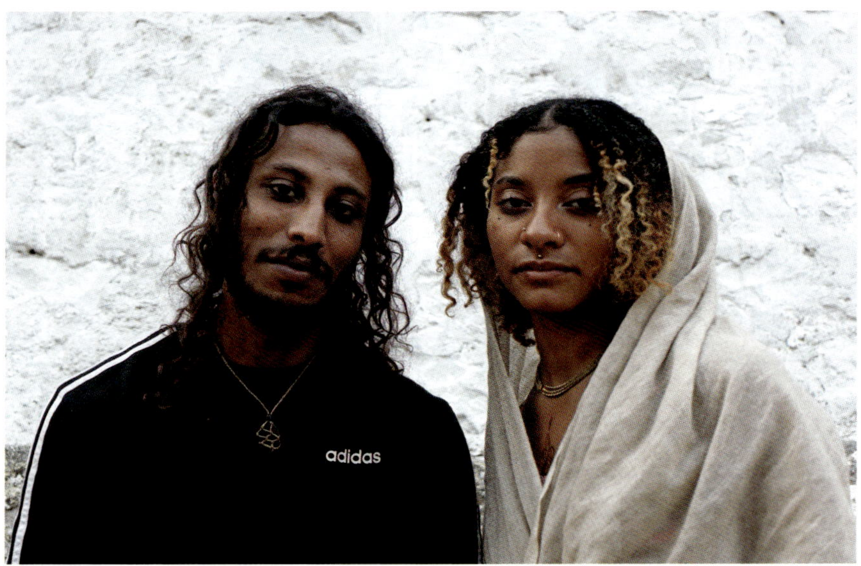

ABOVE: Sahil (India) and Jada (United States). When I came upon Jada and Sahil sitting by the Ganges I was struck by the couple's appearance. Their eyes shared a soulful, mysterious look, like deep pools of spring water coming from a common source. I mistakenly thought they both were from India. While that was true for Sahil, whose ancestral home is in Haryana, Jada hailed from Atlanta in the United States. I asked her the question I asked of so many travelers I met: "What brought you here?" Her reply: "I'd been traveling for several months in India, looking for its spiritual energy. I found it in Rishikesh."

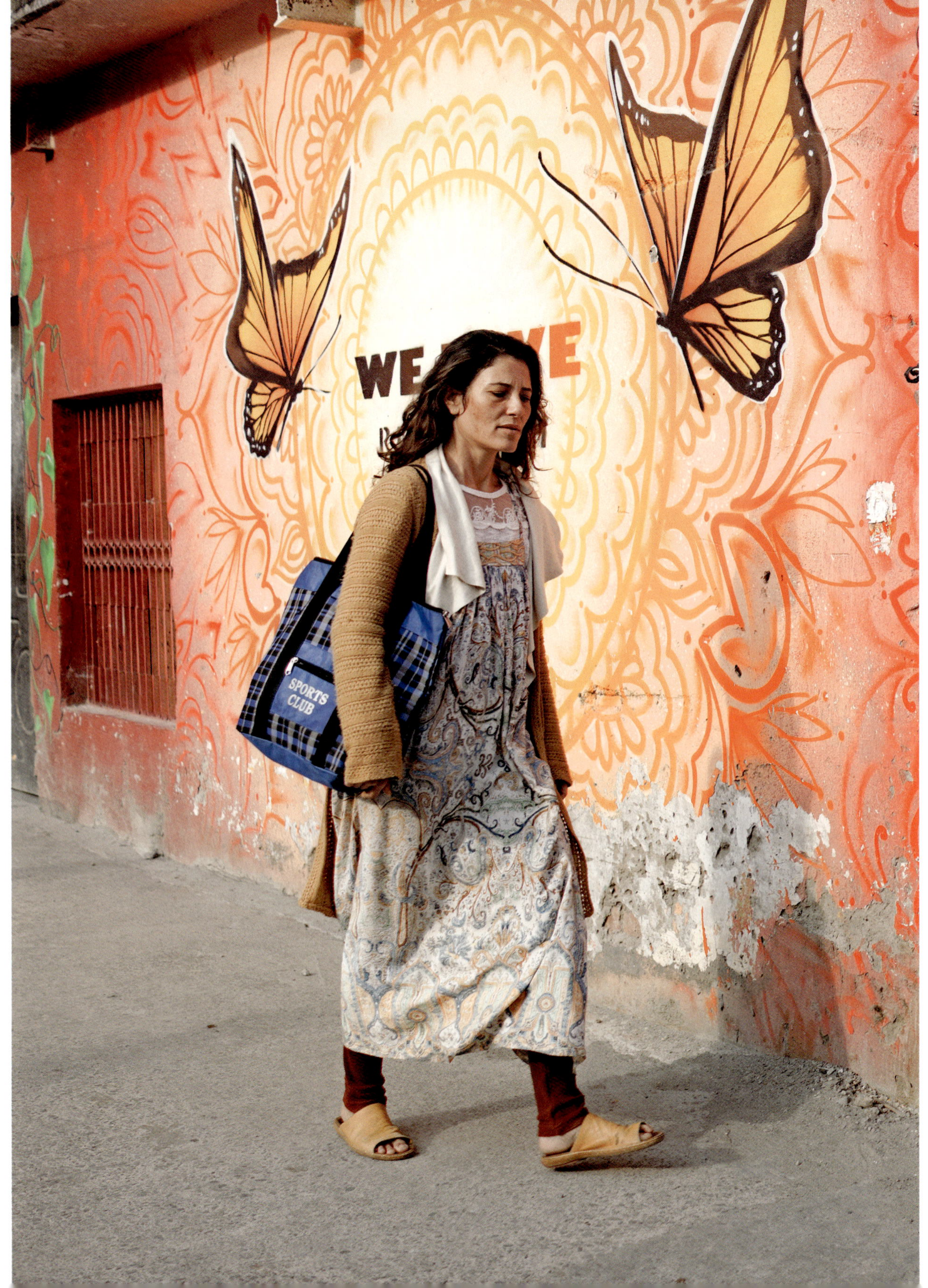

WE LOVE
SPORTS
CLUB

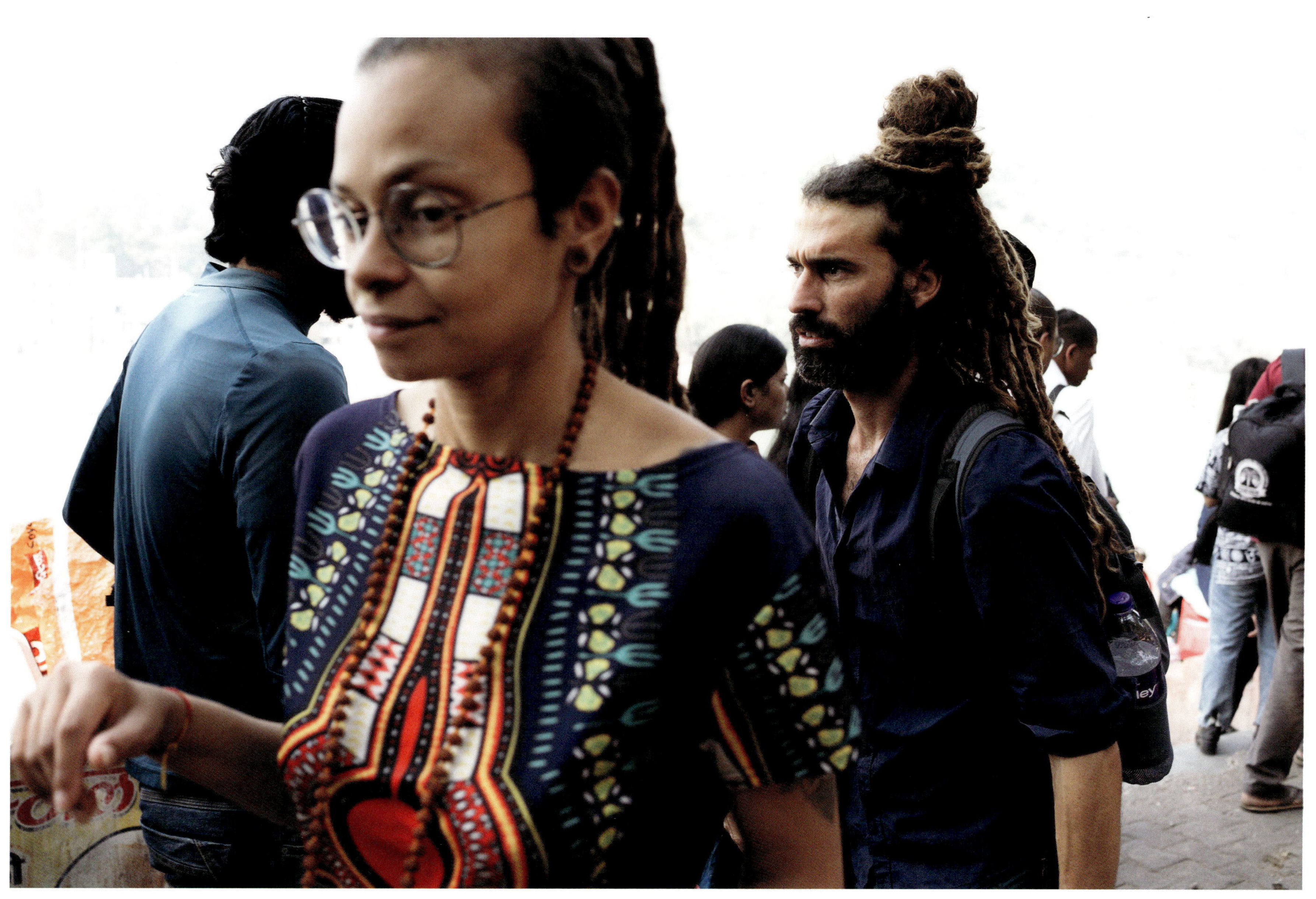

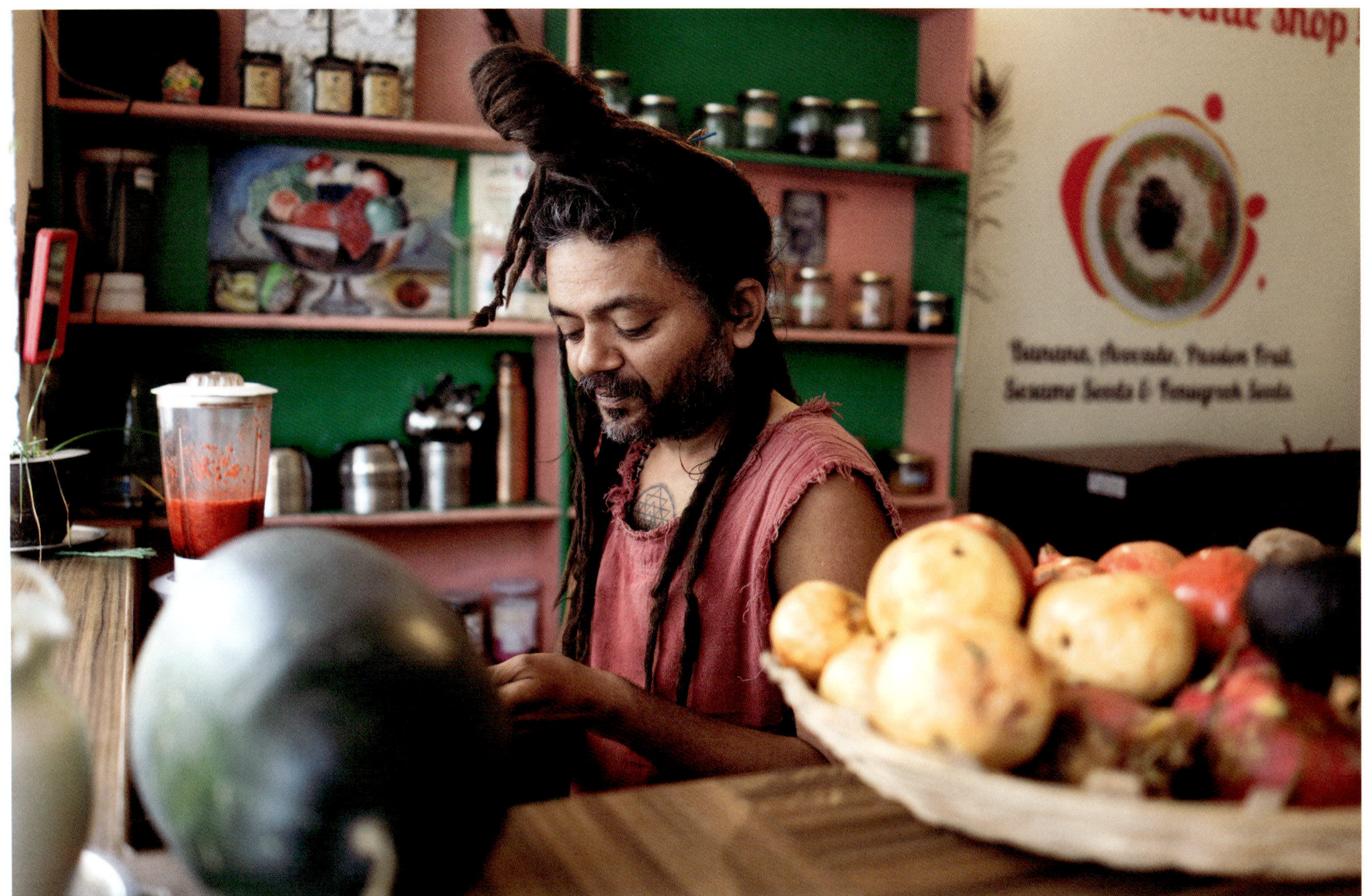

ABOVE: Nipun (India). Located on a small lane not far from my lodgings was the "Love Juice" café. It was open in the mornings and served protein fruit lassis. The café was a popular place. It normally sold out of stock by 10 am. I stopped by one day while Nipun was cleaning a bowl of strawberries. He told me he came to Rishikesh from Gujarat for more than a change of scenery. "I needed to get out of there. My life was spiraling down. I was an addict. I cleaned up here, started meditating, and opened this little café where I sell love juice to western travelers. They love it. I love it. Try some, man!"

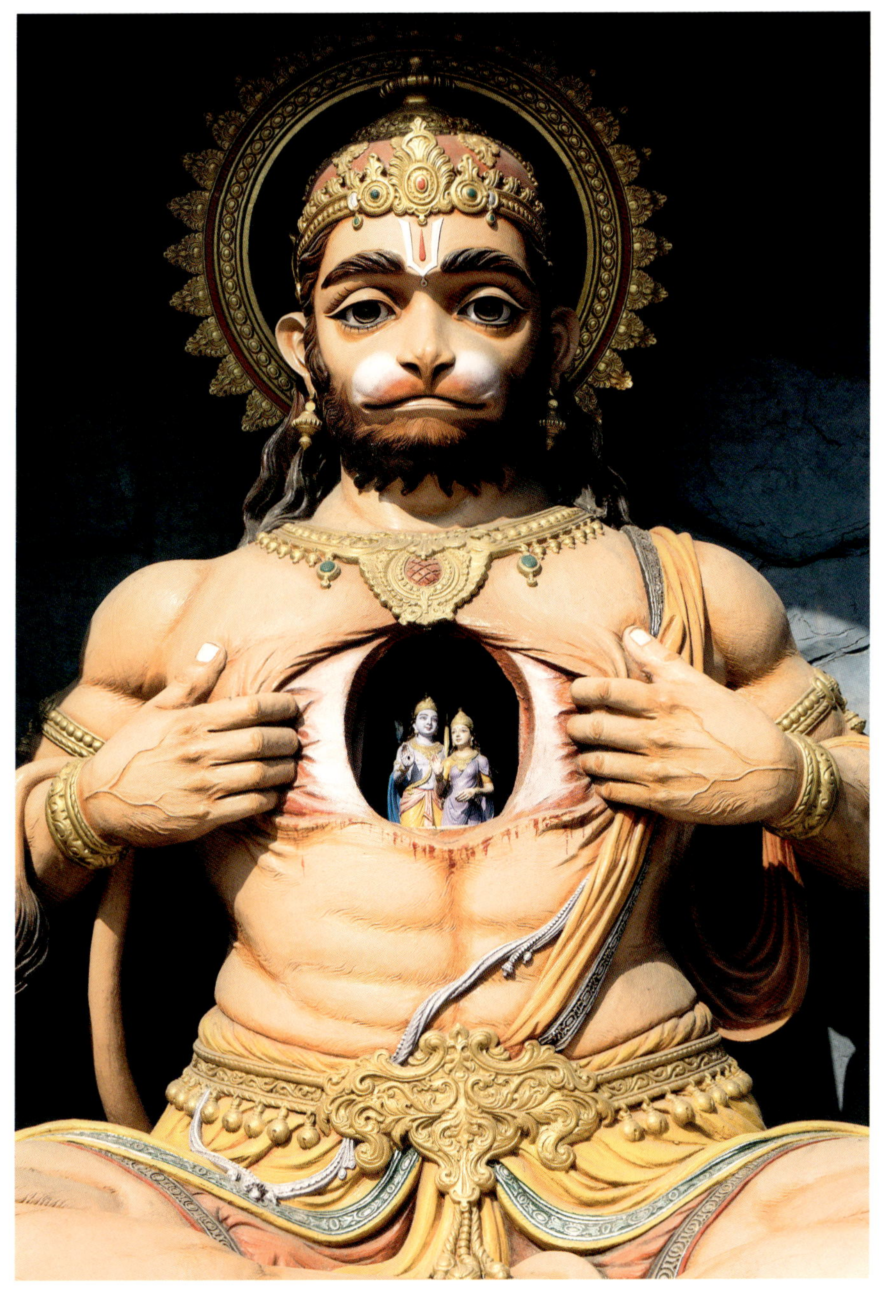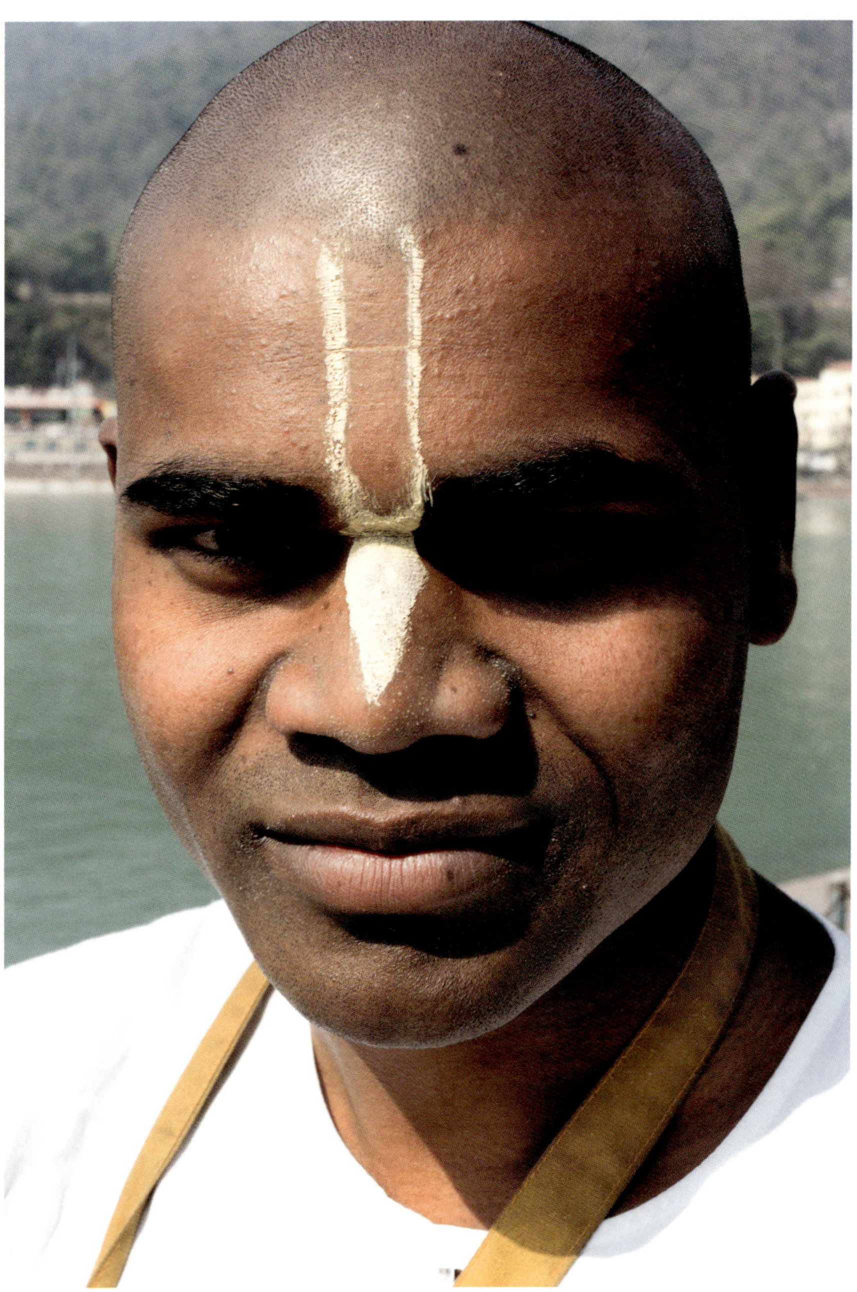

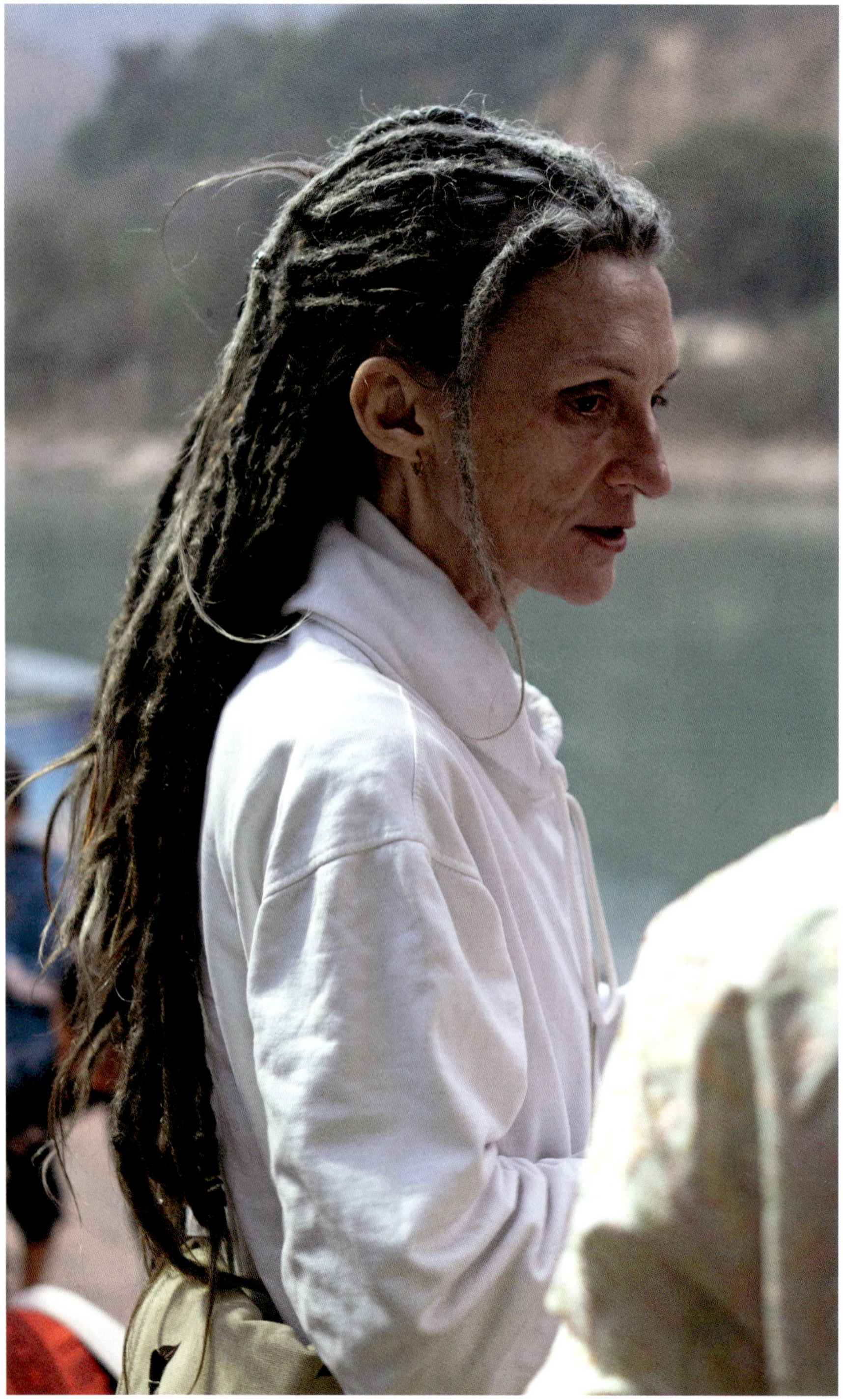

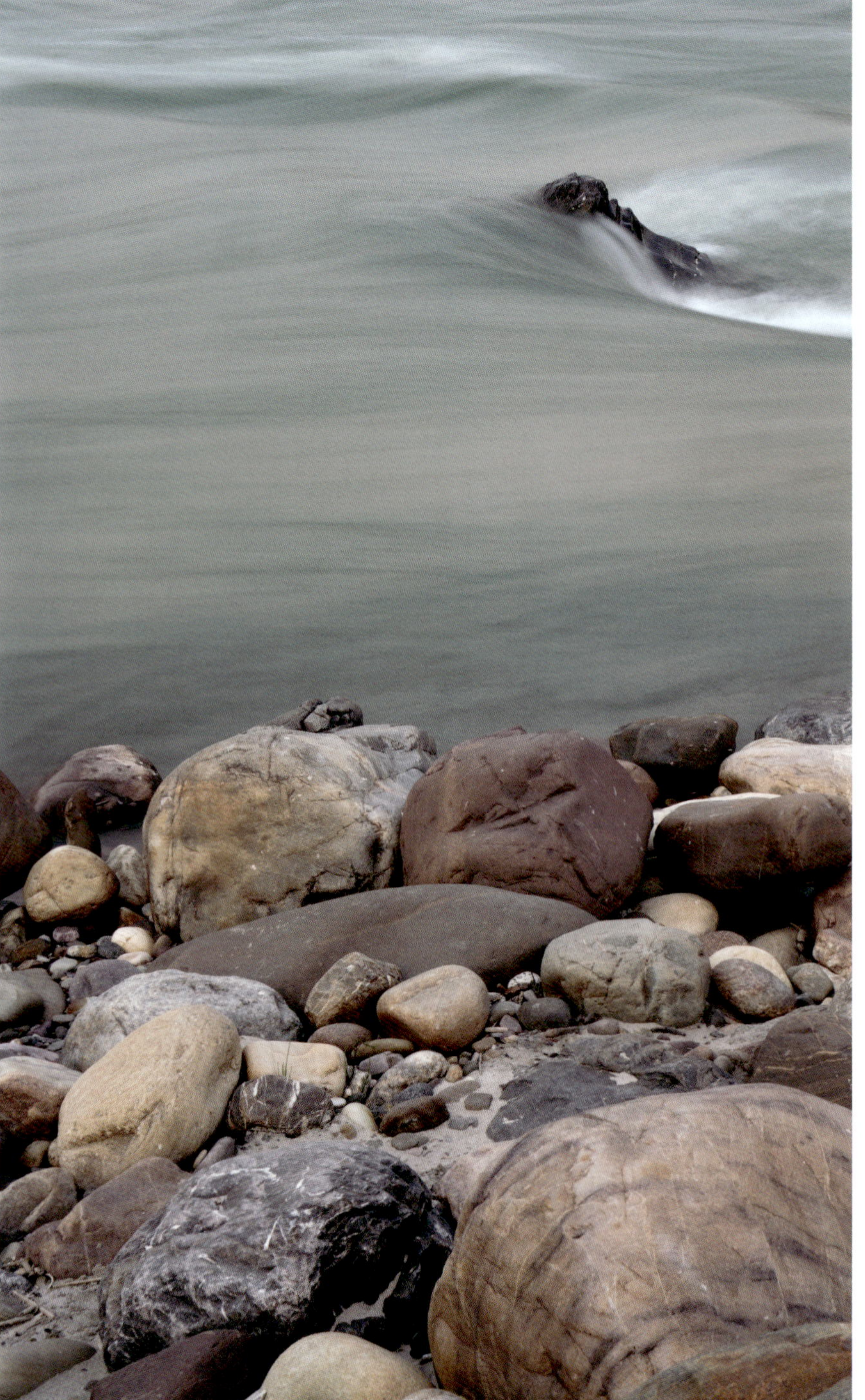

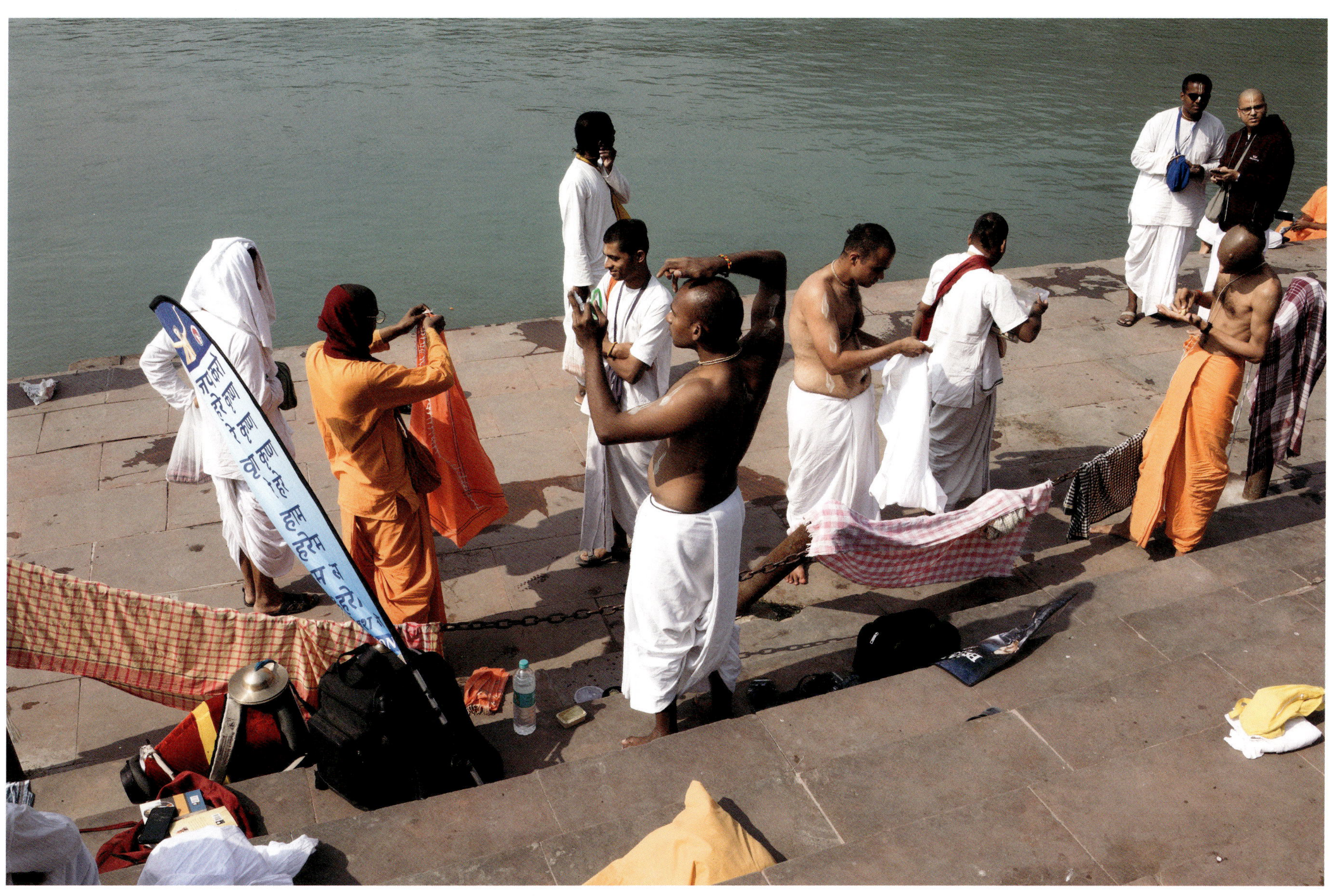

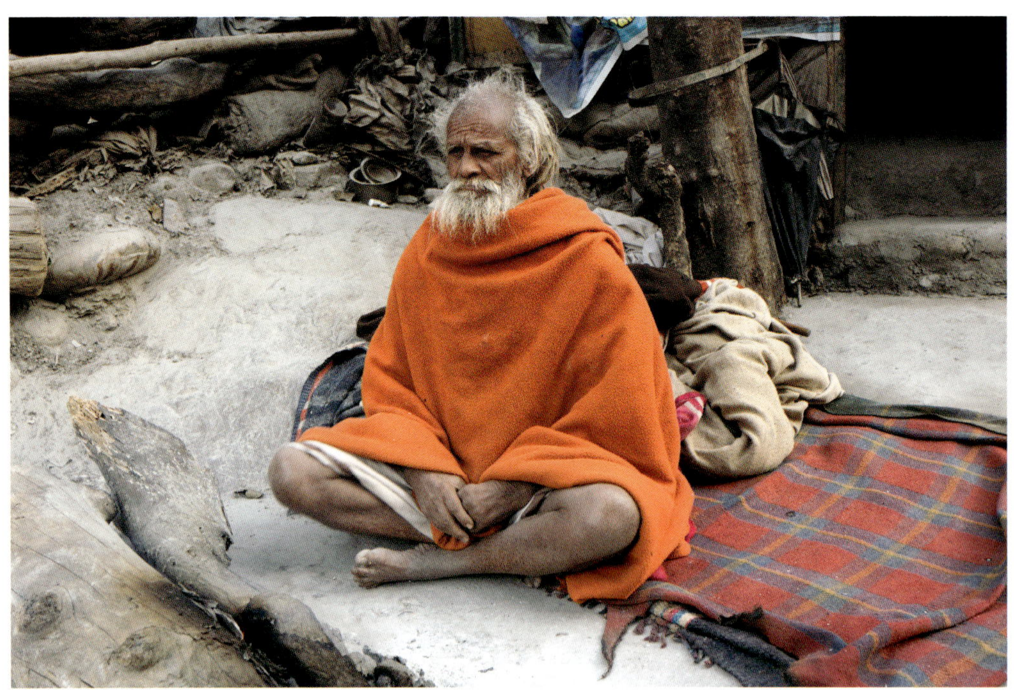

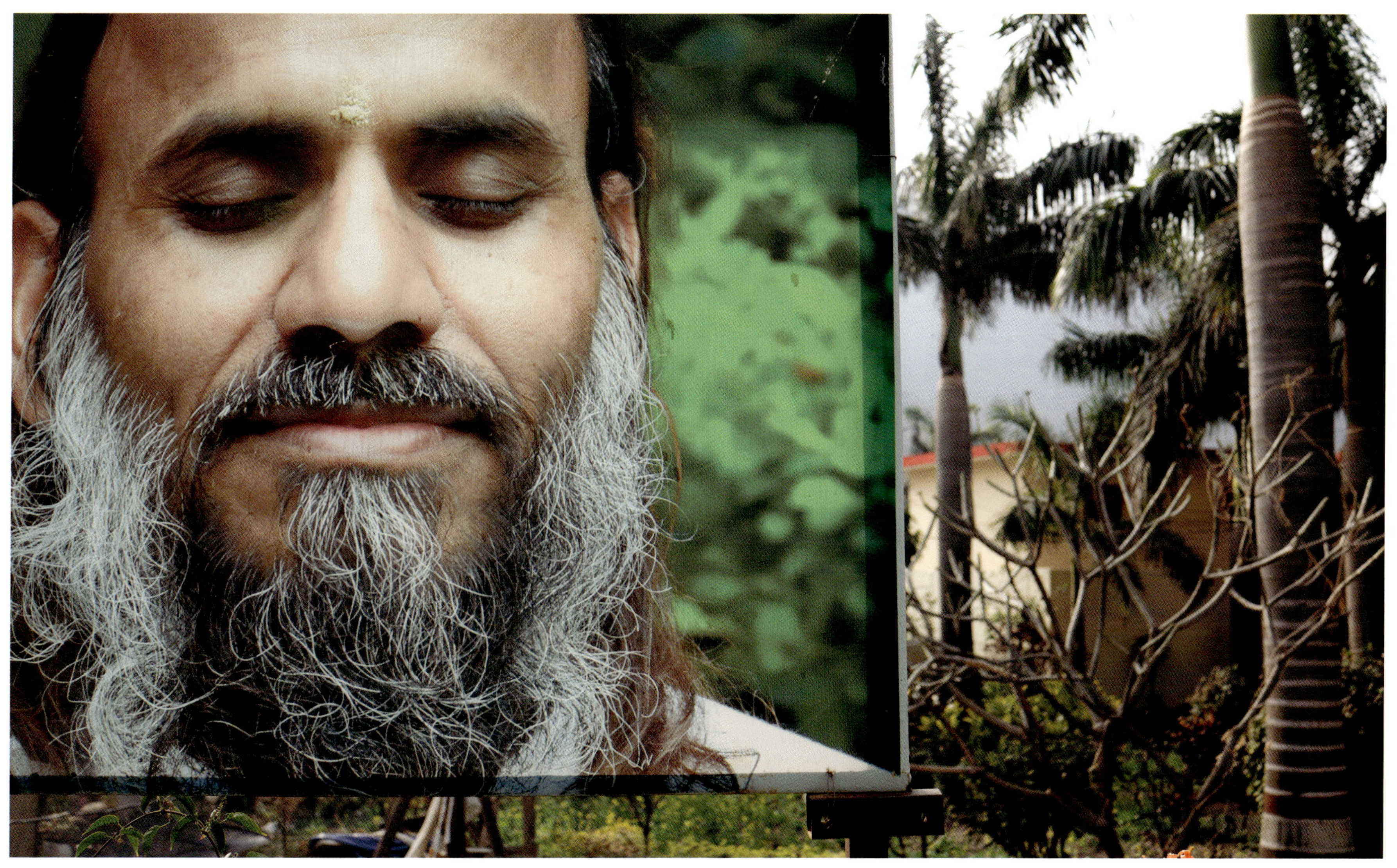

ABOVE: Billboard with photograph of Swami
Anand Boddhisatva, founder of YOGA
ESSENSE, RISHIKESH, advertising his services:
"Spiritual Mentor, Transformational
Life Coach, Meditation and Yoga Nidra
Master, Stress Management and Emotional
Intelligence; also offering workshops on
Inner Wellbeing, Awakening, Mindfulness,
Holistic Living."

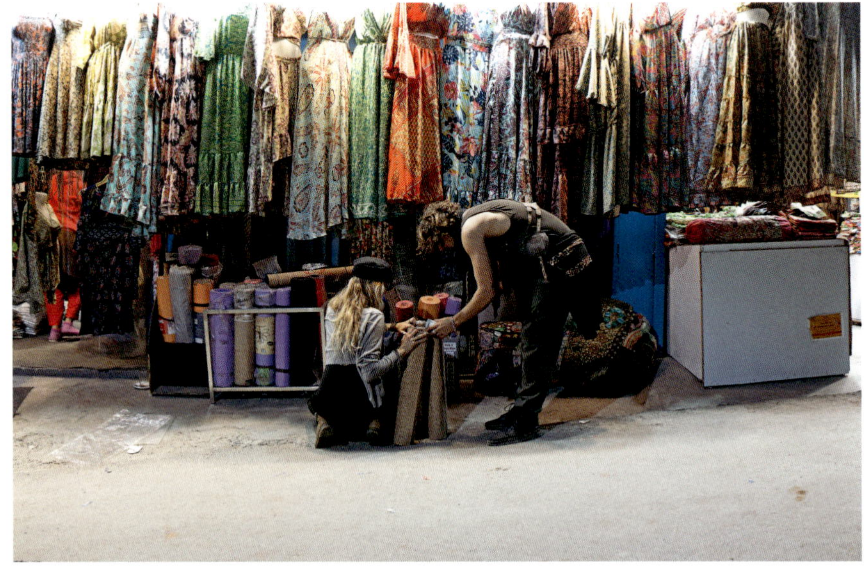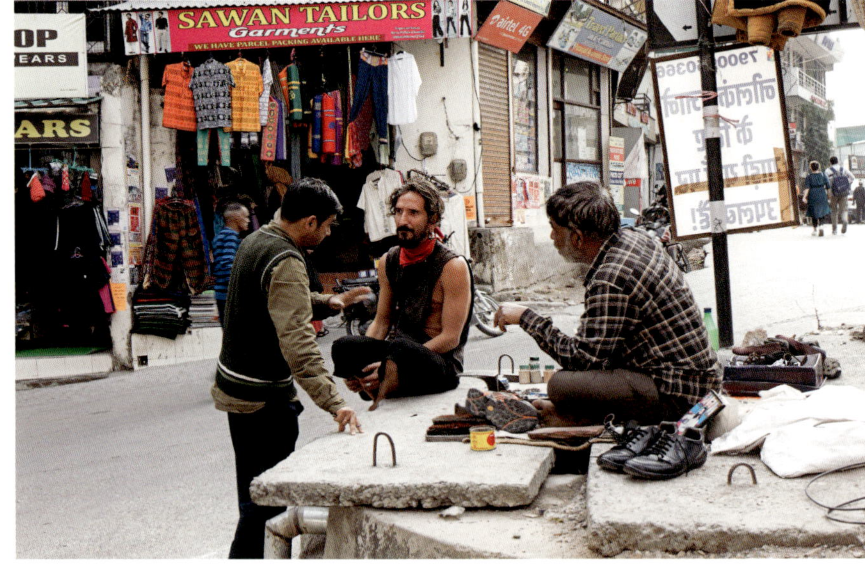

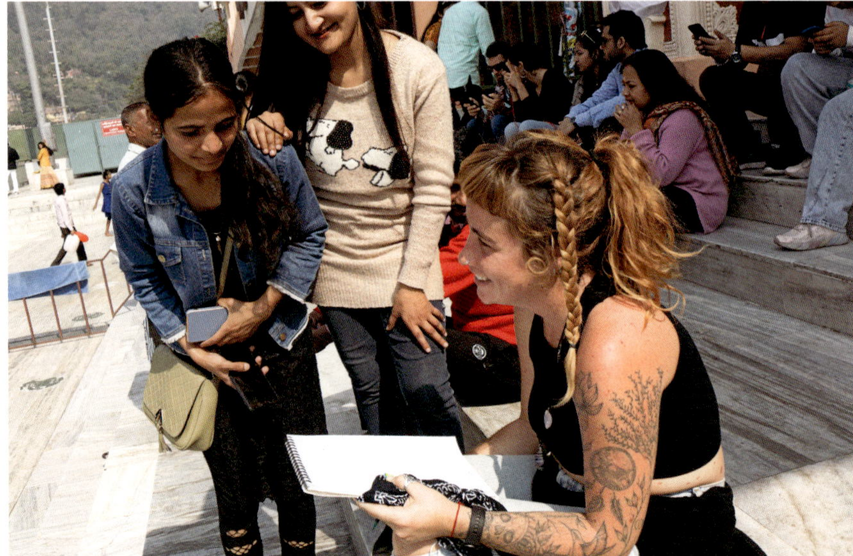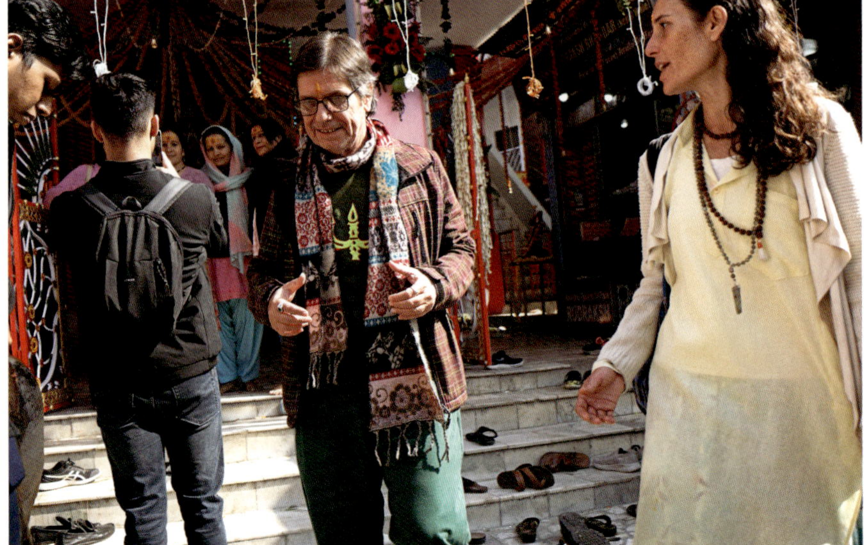

UPPER LEFT: Shopping for a yoga mat
UPPER RIGHT:Street corner conversation
DOWN LEFT: A meeting on the ghat
DOWN RIGHT:Pilgrims from Europe

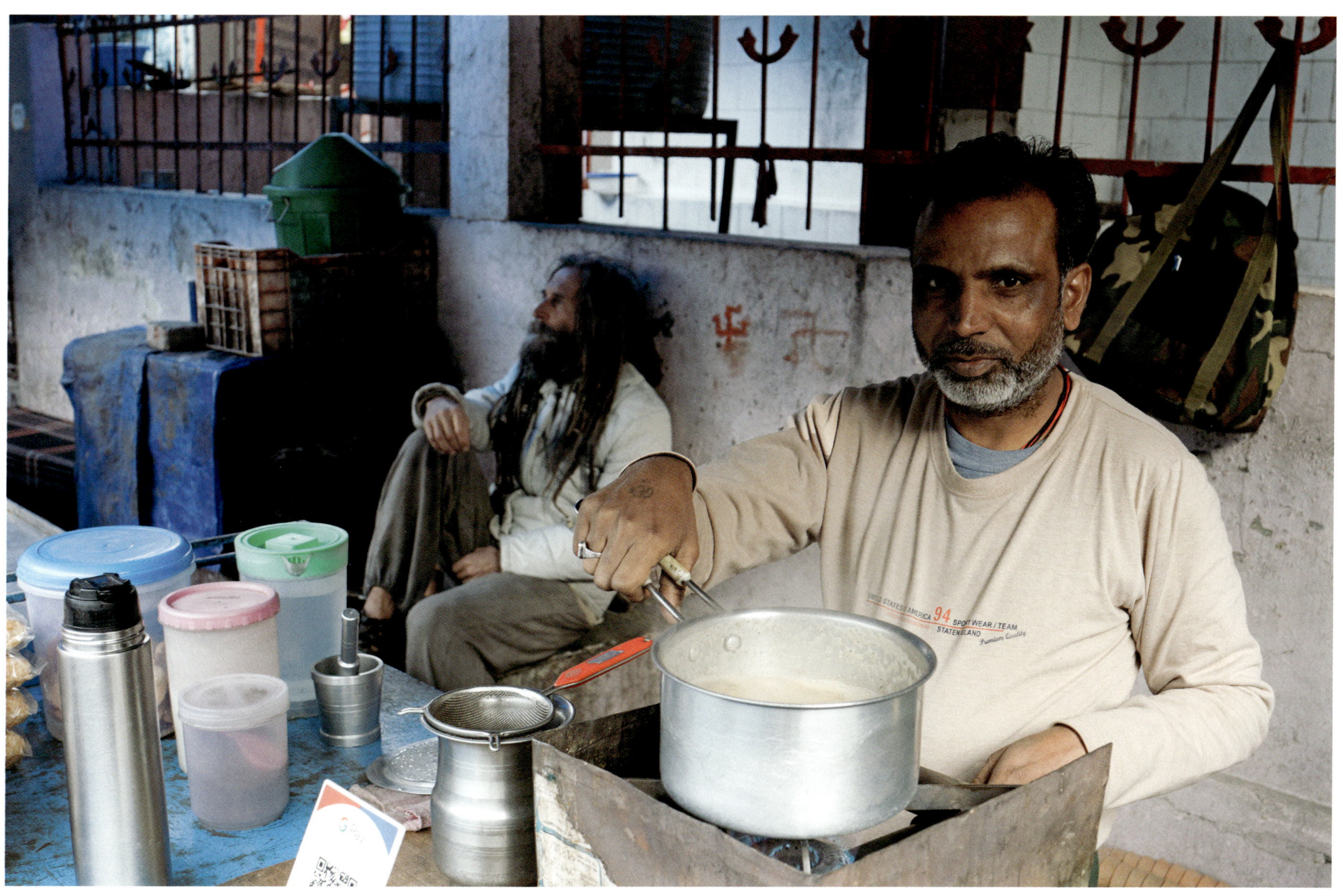

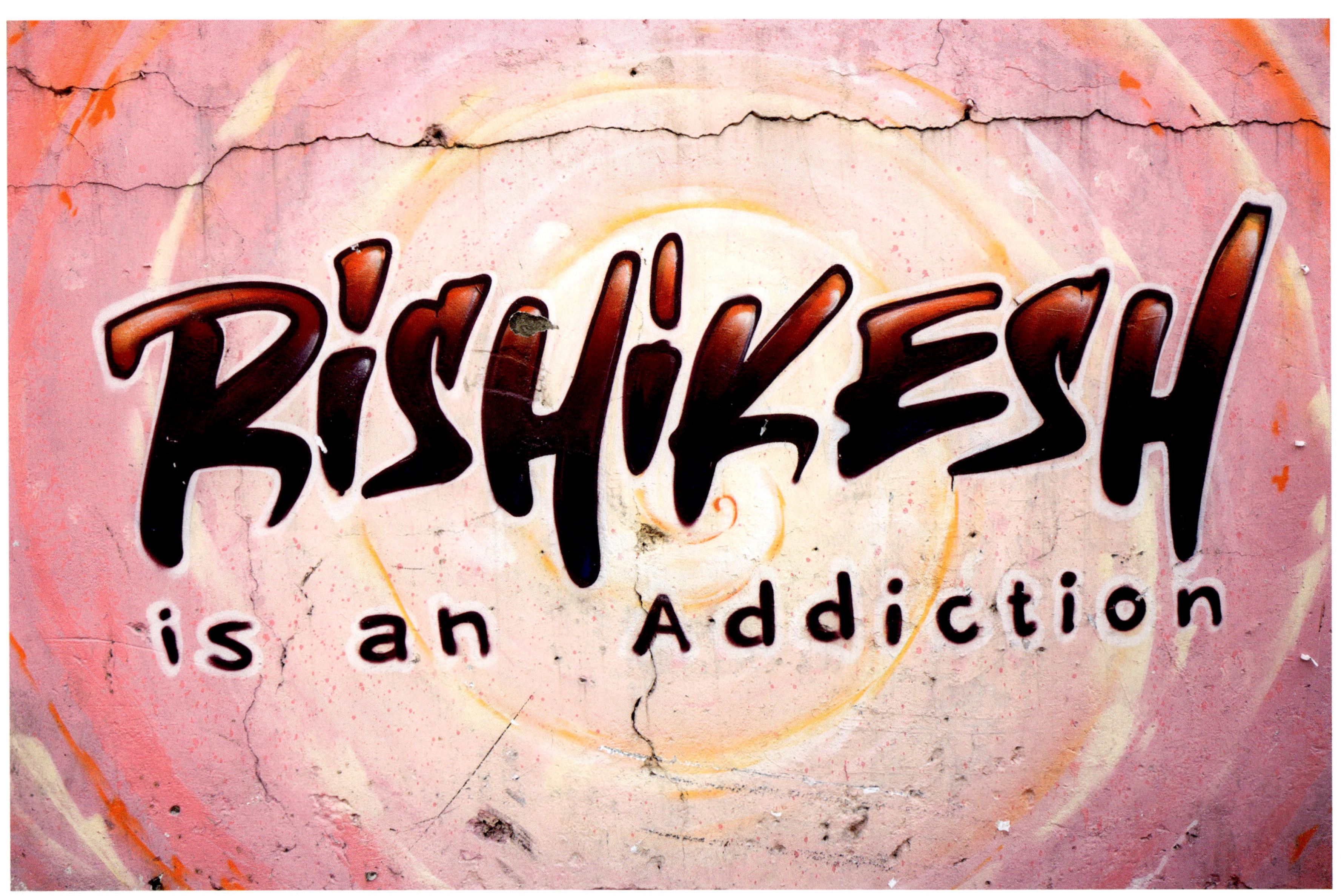

RISHIKESH
is an Addiction

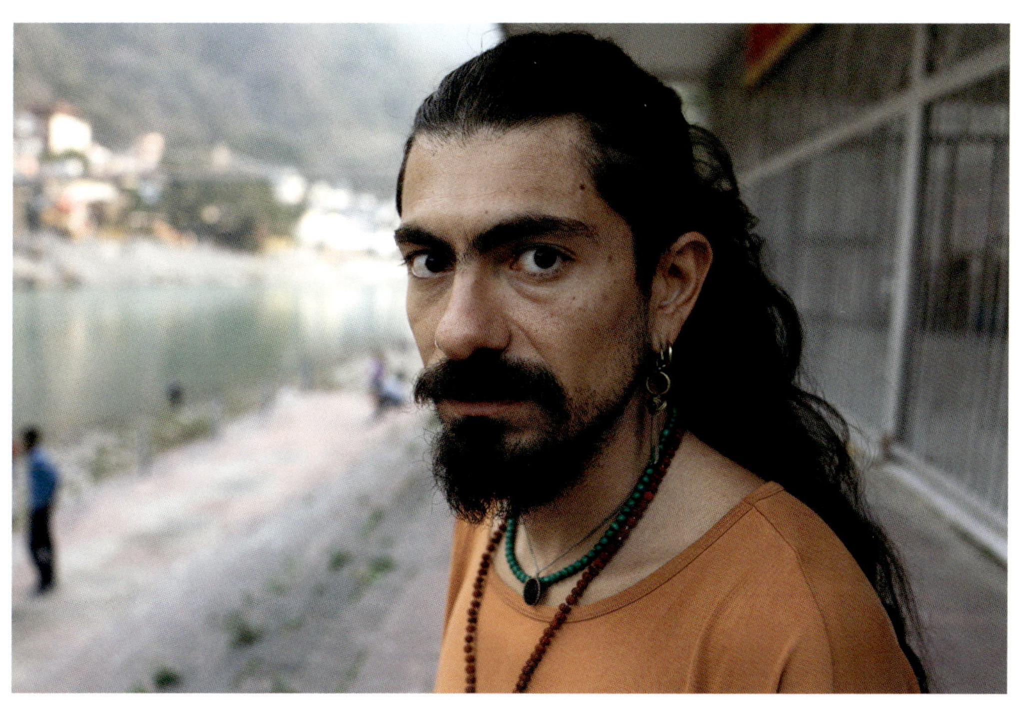

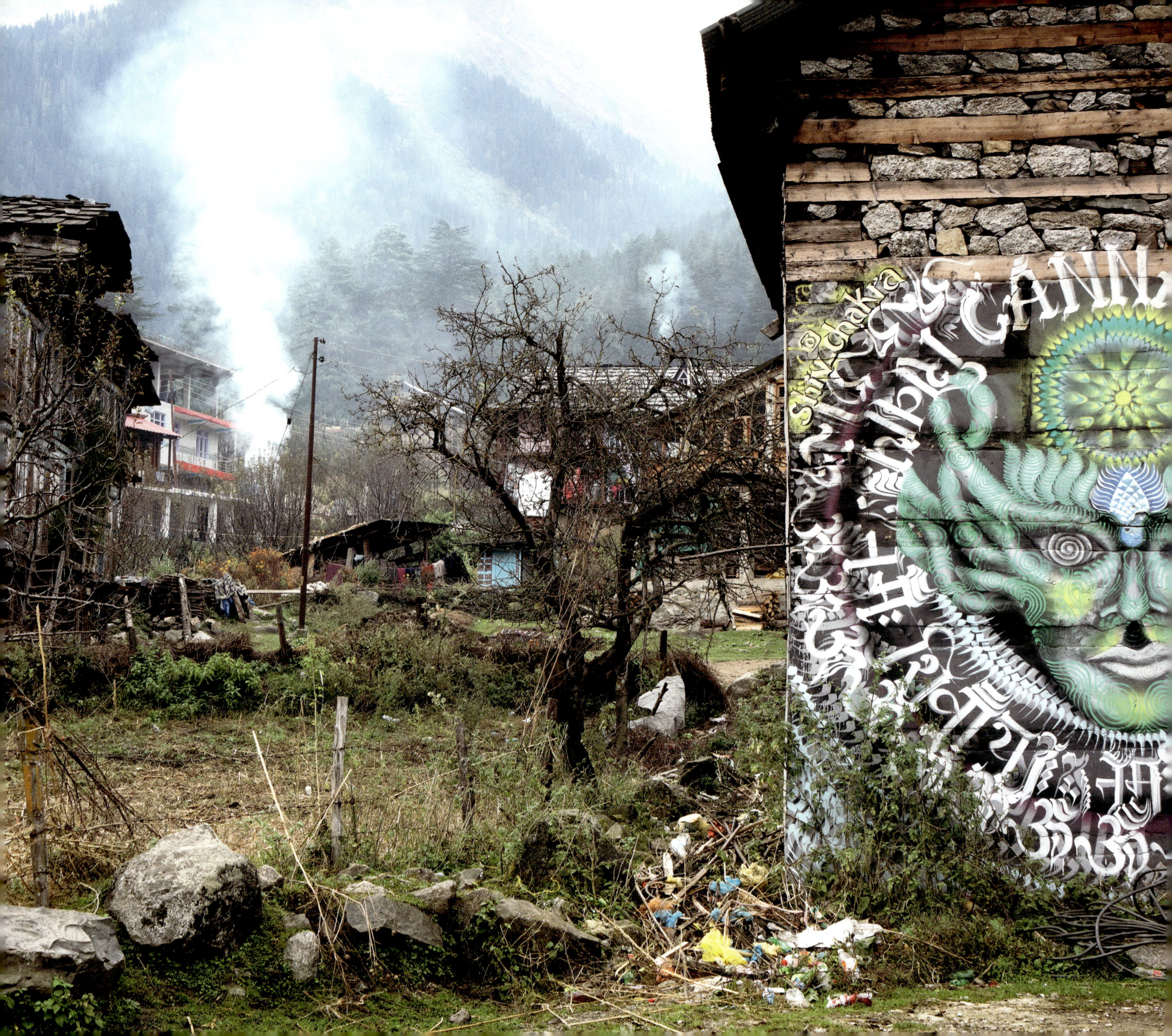
Suya Chakra
CANN

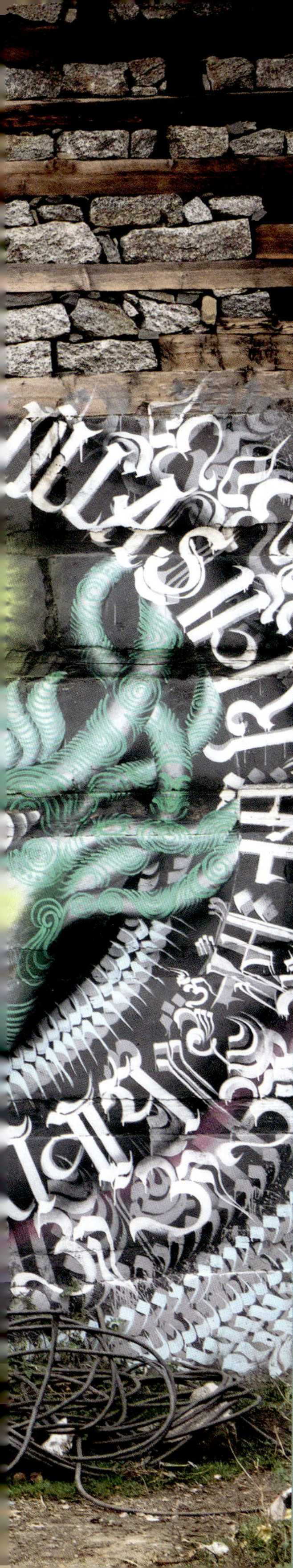

PARVATi VALLEY

I arrived in the Parvati Valley to find it greatly changed from what I'd seen in an earlier era. A cliff-hugging road now reaches highland settlements once accessible only by walking for hours or days on rugged trails. Internet access is available in most places. Power lines snake along the ridgelines, bringing electricity to even the most hard-to-reach hamlets. Many of the villages, long the abode of farmers and herders, are now filled with backpackers, small eateries, and hostels. Traditional architectures have given way to concrete and tin-roofed structures. Litter is beginning to pile up along the roadsides and in makeshift dumps. Such changes are perhaps inevitable, but no longer does the Parvati Valley seem so remote.

However, what hasn't changed is the Himalayan scenery, which is some of the finest in the world and the reason why so many travelers come to the valley. The Parvati Peak (6,632 meters; 21,759 feet) towers over the mountainous landscape. Conifer forests and pastureland drape the slopes in shades of green that constantly change with the moving light. The Parvati River crashes below over boulders the size of small buildings. Rocky glens and free-flowing streams hint at hidden magical places.

The Parvati Valley gained prominence on the Hippie Trail in the early 1970s. Travelers were drawn to the valley's tranquility and natural beauty. Some came for the abundant, locally grown hashish, known as *charas*. Others wanted to see the snow peaks of the Himalayas. The valley's religious mythos also had allure. It was where Lord Shiva is believed to have lived for several thousand years, meditating, cavorting with his consort Parvati—after whom the valley is named—relaxing in the hot springs, sanctifying the mountain landscape by his presence, making it a holy place where spiritual revelation might be had around every bend in a trail.

The valley's mystique continues to attract people from throughout the world, including, most recently, large numbers of backpackers hailing from Delhi or Bangalore and any number of other Indian cities. From my conversations with them, I came away with the impression that the primary motivations for the young Indian travelers visiting the Parvati Valley were to escape the confines of their traditional societies and to spend time in a place where they could be their free-spirited selves. In this way, they do not differ at all from their Western counterparts.

Despite its reputation as a hippie haven, there is an edge to the Parvati Valley. Beautiful yes, but it is no Shangri La. The vertiginous trails can be dangerous and not everyone a person meets on them is friendly. Drug gangs roam the marijuana fields. Theft has become more commonplace. The road into the valley is in terrible shape, causing loss of lives by the busloads. Electronic music blasts from all-day rave parties, drowning out the songbirds and river rapids. More ominous, though, is the fact that each year for the past several decades a backpacker or two has gone mysteriously missing in the Parvati Valley. They simply vanish, leaving behind only rumors, earning the place the moniker "Valley of Death."

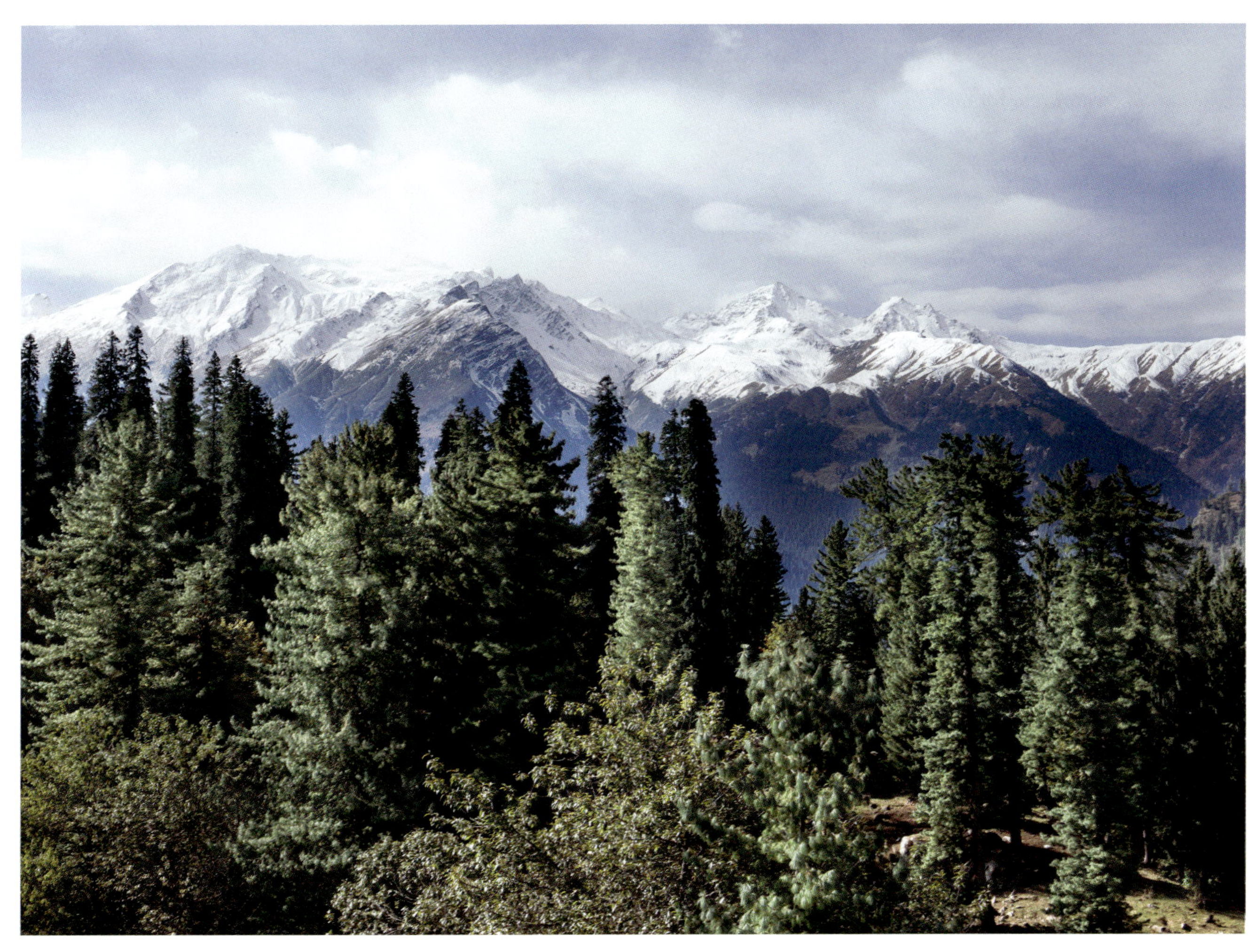

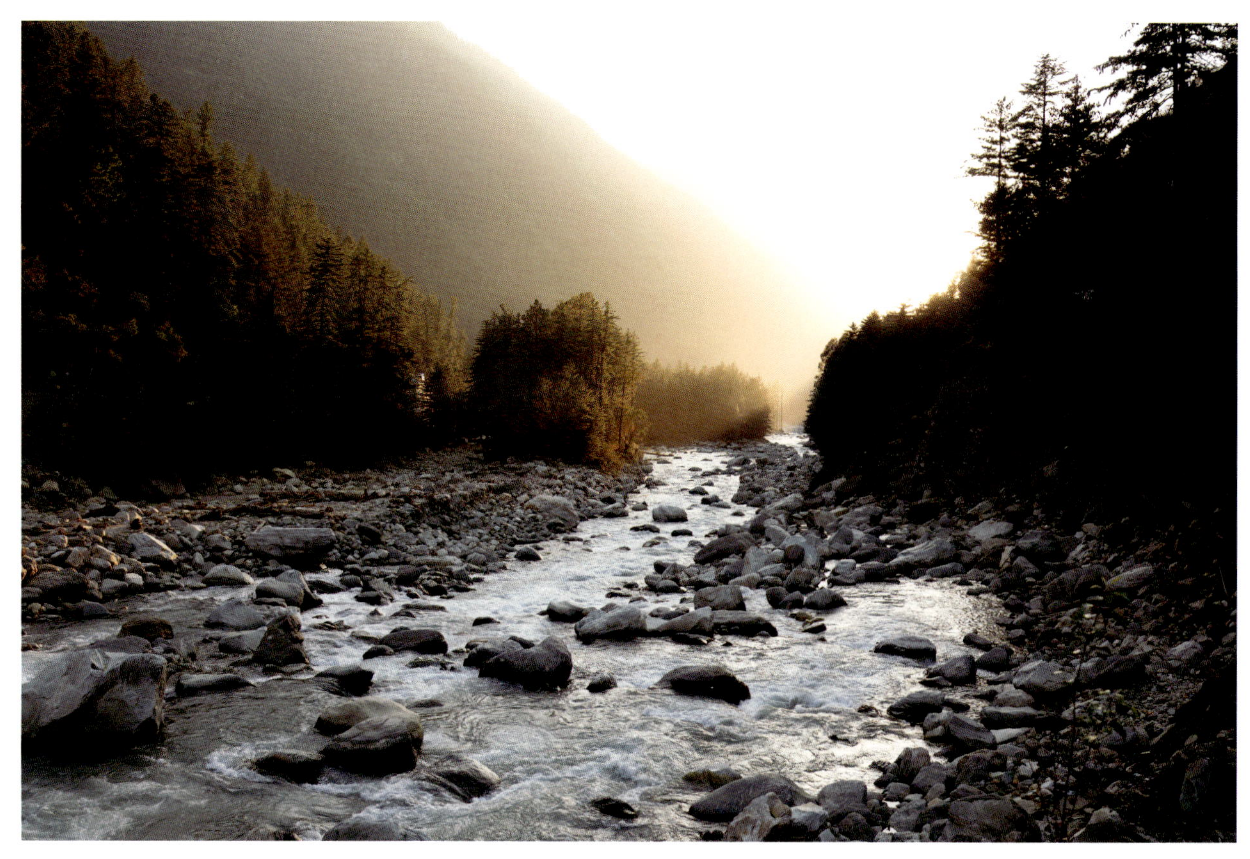

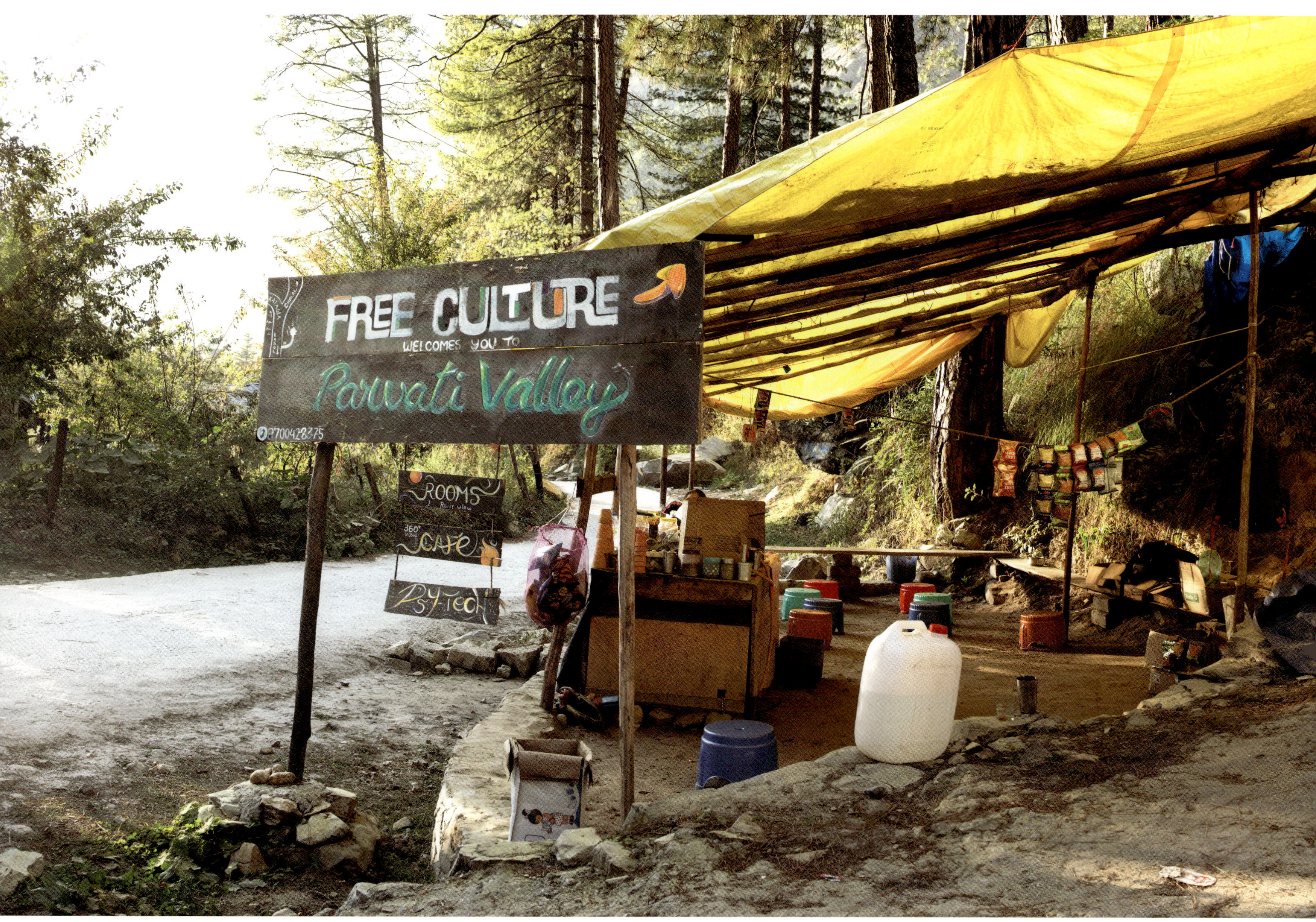
FREE CULTURE
WELCOMES YOU TO
Parvati Valley
7700428375
ROOMS
360°
CAFE
PSY-TECH

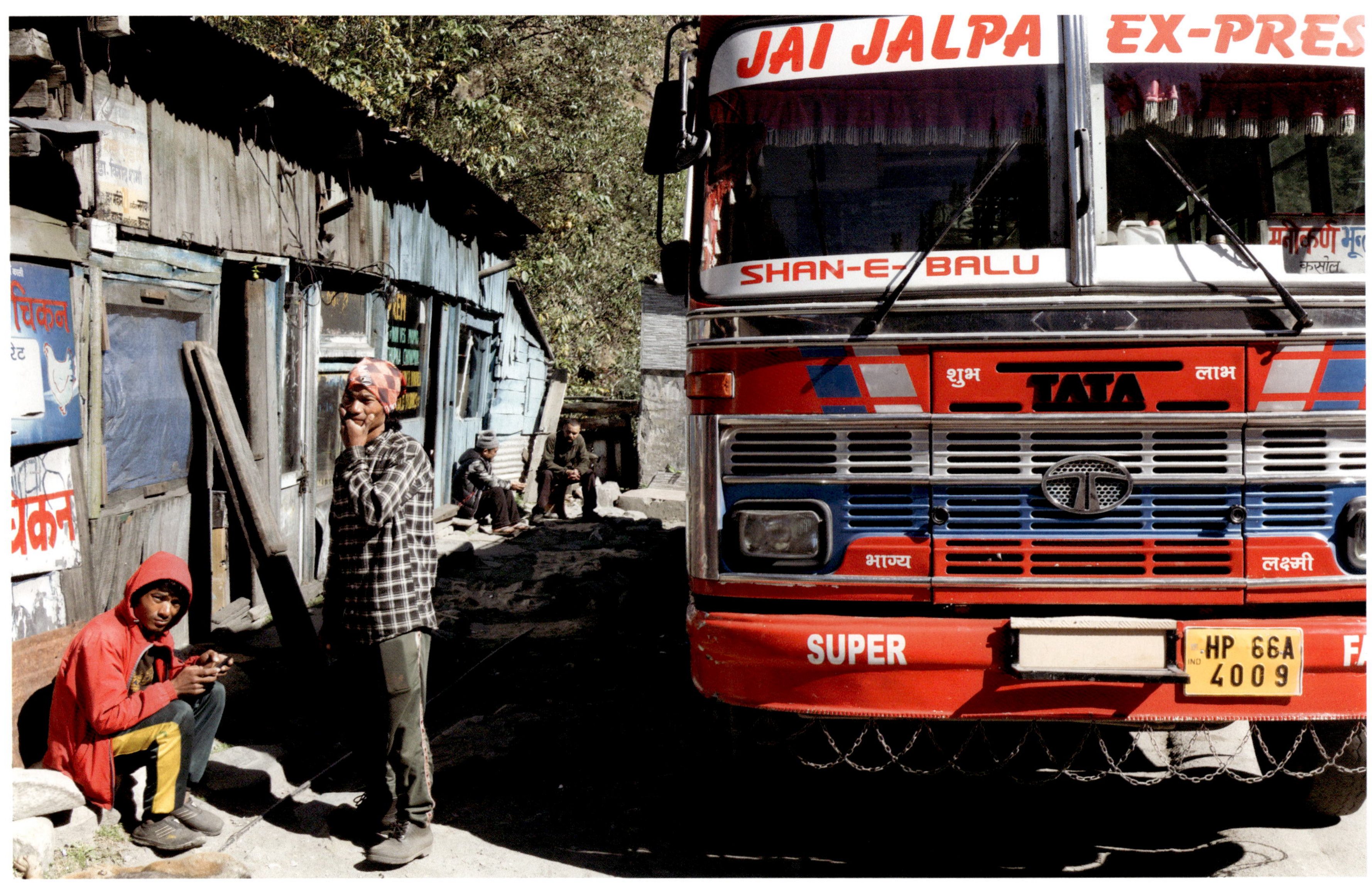

JAI JALPA EX-PRES
SHAN-E-BALU
शुभ TATA लाभ
भाग्य लक्ष्मी
SUPER
HP 66A 4009

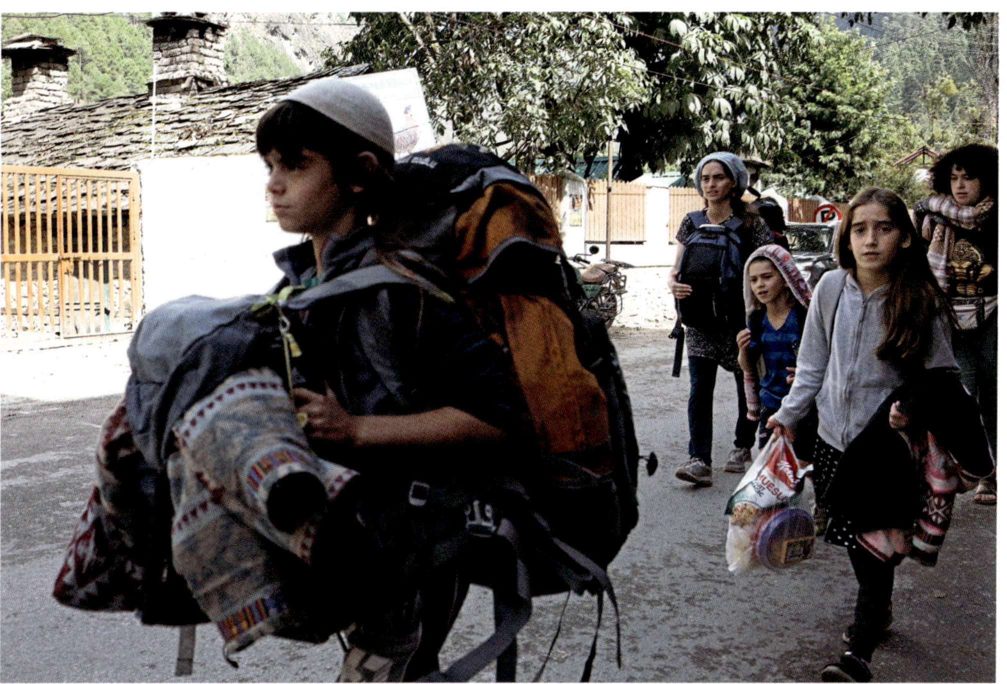

ABOVE: The Parvati Valley is known as "Little Israel" due to the large number of Israeli travelers who visit it. I arrived on the day the Israelis were all leaving. War had broken out in their homeland. Some explained they were returning to their country out of concern for their loved ones. Others said they felt the call of duty. Most had no choice in the matter. I met a few Israelis who had been traveling in India for many months and flew under the radar—no phone, no GPS tracker, no credit card. They planned to stay put in the Parvati Valley and wait things out. But many of them faced a prospect expressed to me by one distraught traveler: "I have to go back to Israel, get my dreadlocks cut, pick up a rifle. It's shit man."

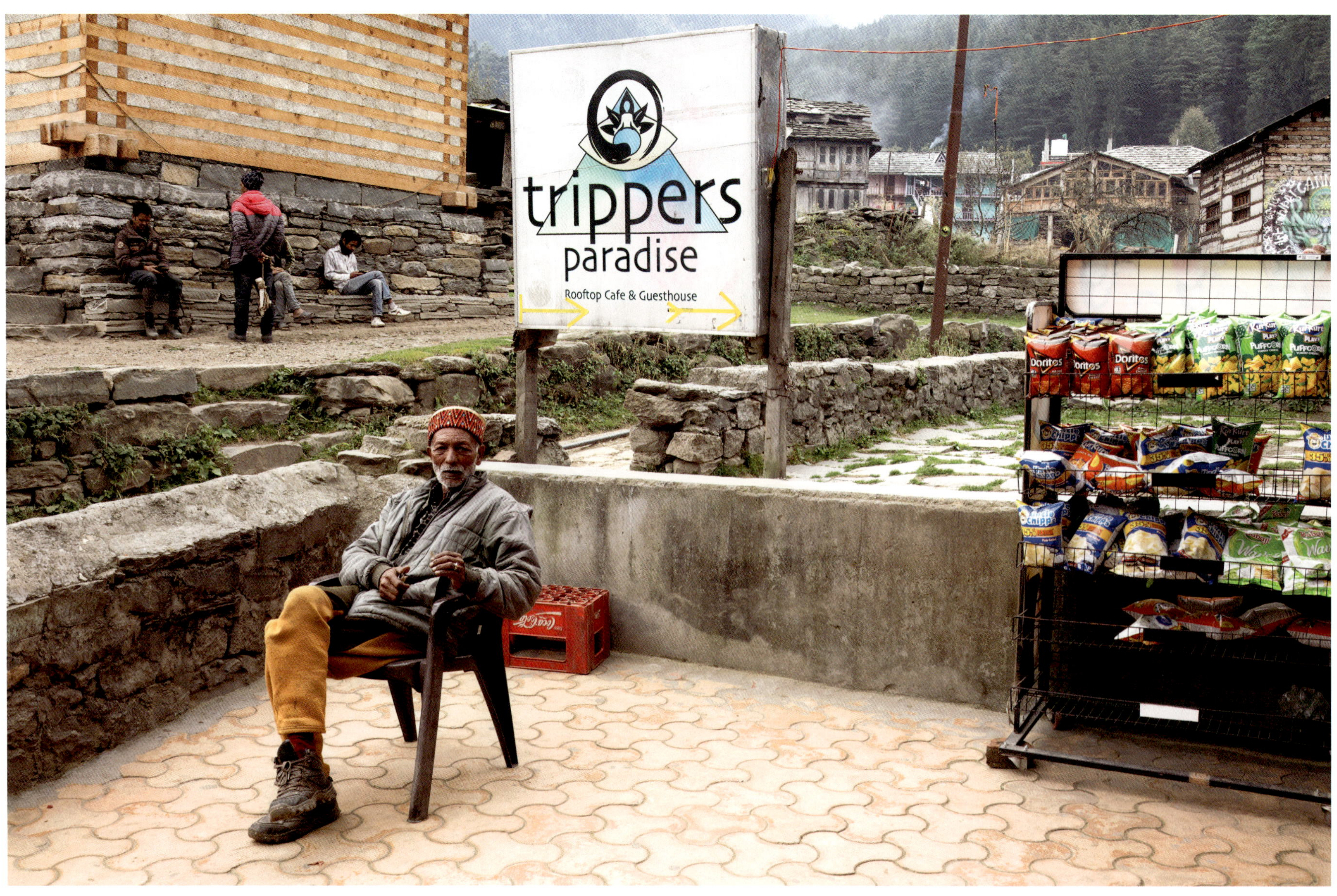

ABOVE: Pulga village
OPPOSITE: Djane Cosmodelica (Russia)
and Majid (Iran), Choj

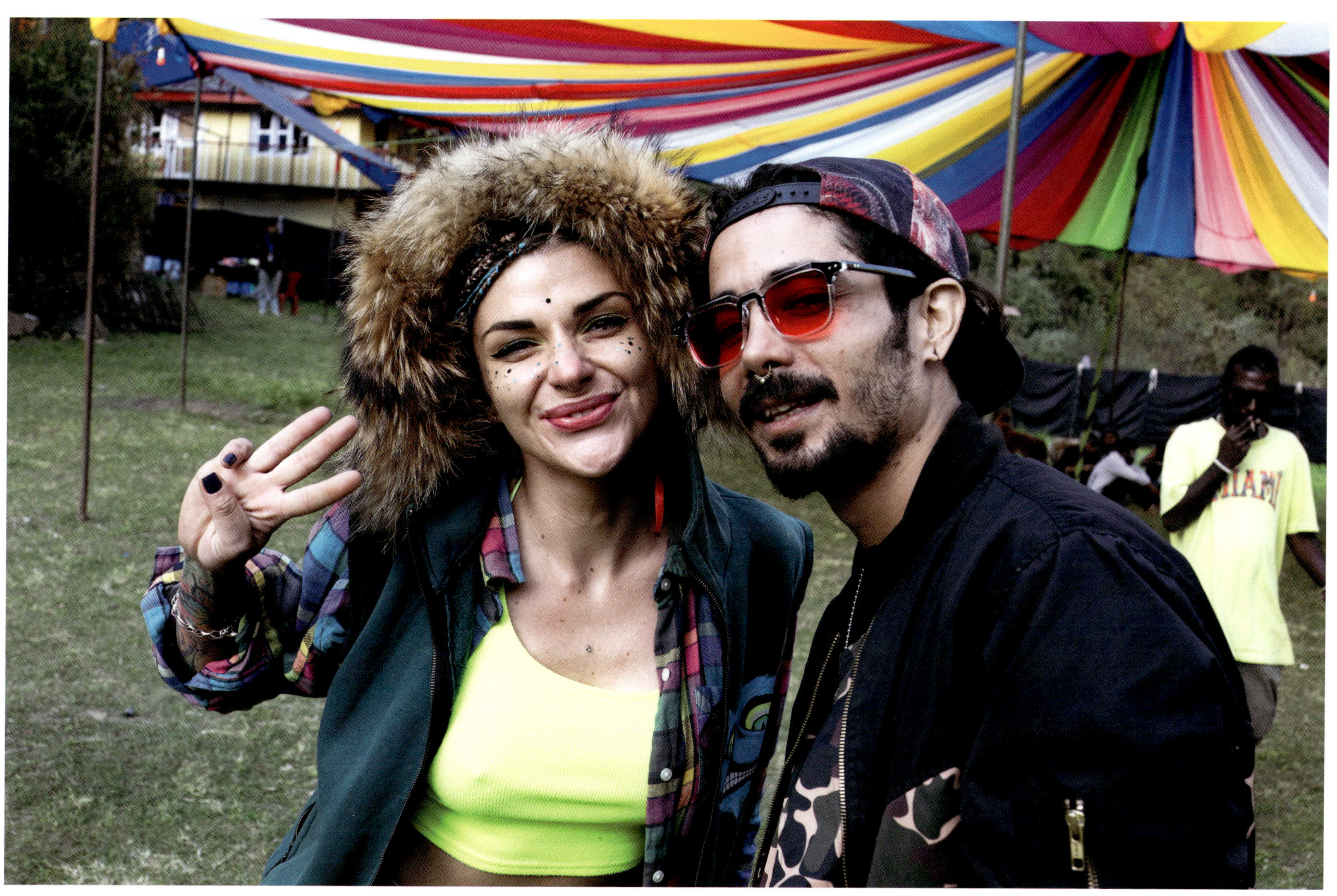

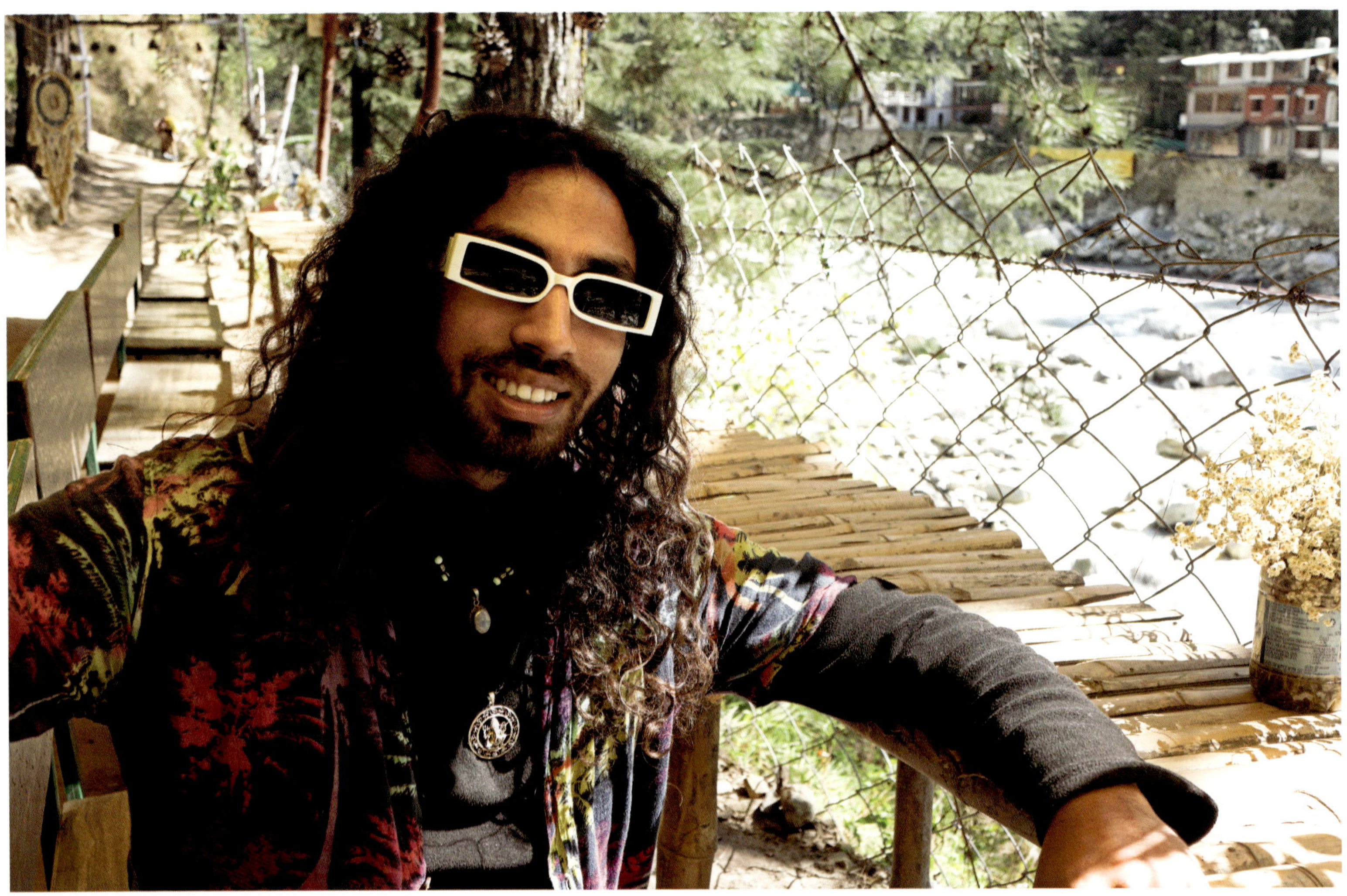

ABOVE: Elee (India), Chalal village. Elee runs a small café and hostel popular with travelers. "I own this place, but really I'm a musician, man," he told me. I asked what instrument he plays. "The computer," he replied. "I make electronic music on my computer and take it to the rave parties."

Elee grew up in the Parvati Valley and has been around Western travelers his entire life. He identifies with the hippies who come to the valley. "We're members of the same tribe. Just living free. Spreading love around the world."

OPPOSITE: Shambu (India) and David (Spain), Chalal trail

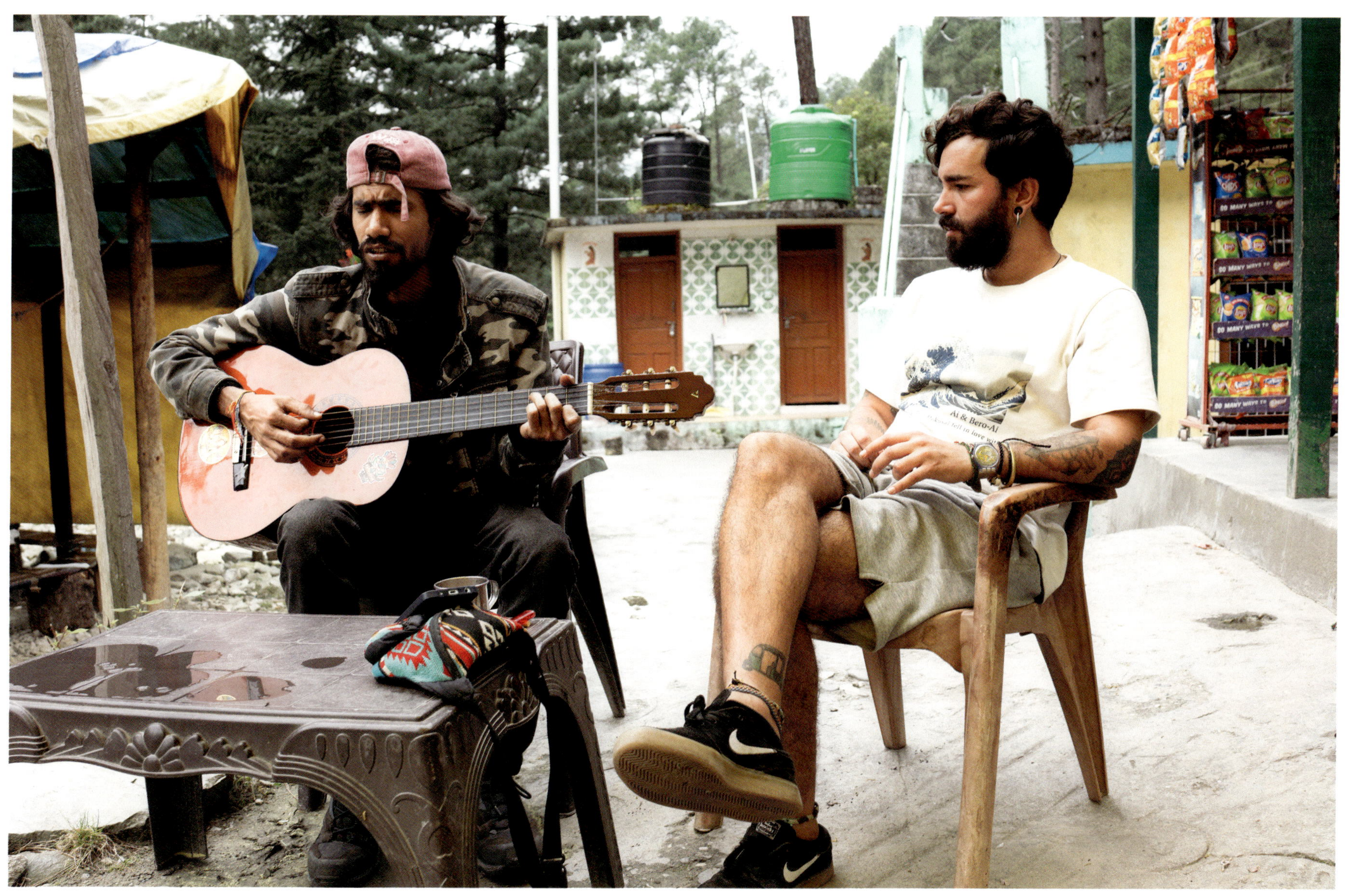

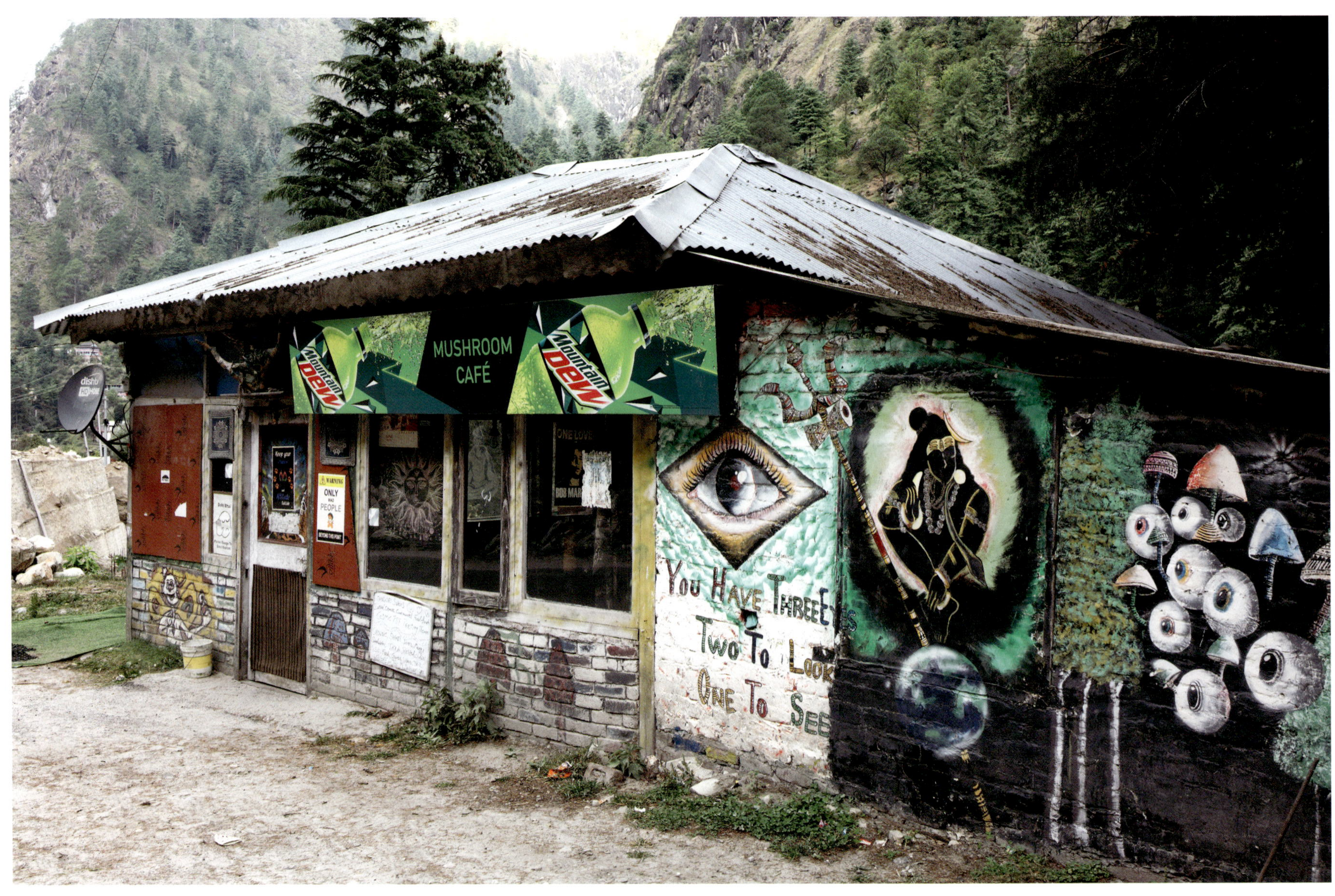

Mountain Dew
MUSHROOM CAFÉ
Mountain Dew
ONE LOVE
BOB MARLEY
WARNING
ONLY
PEOPLE
BEYOND THIS POINT
YOU HAVE THREE EYES
TWO TO LOOK
ONE TO SEE

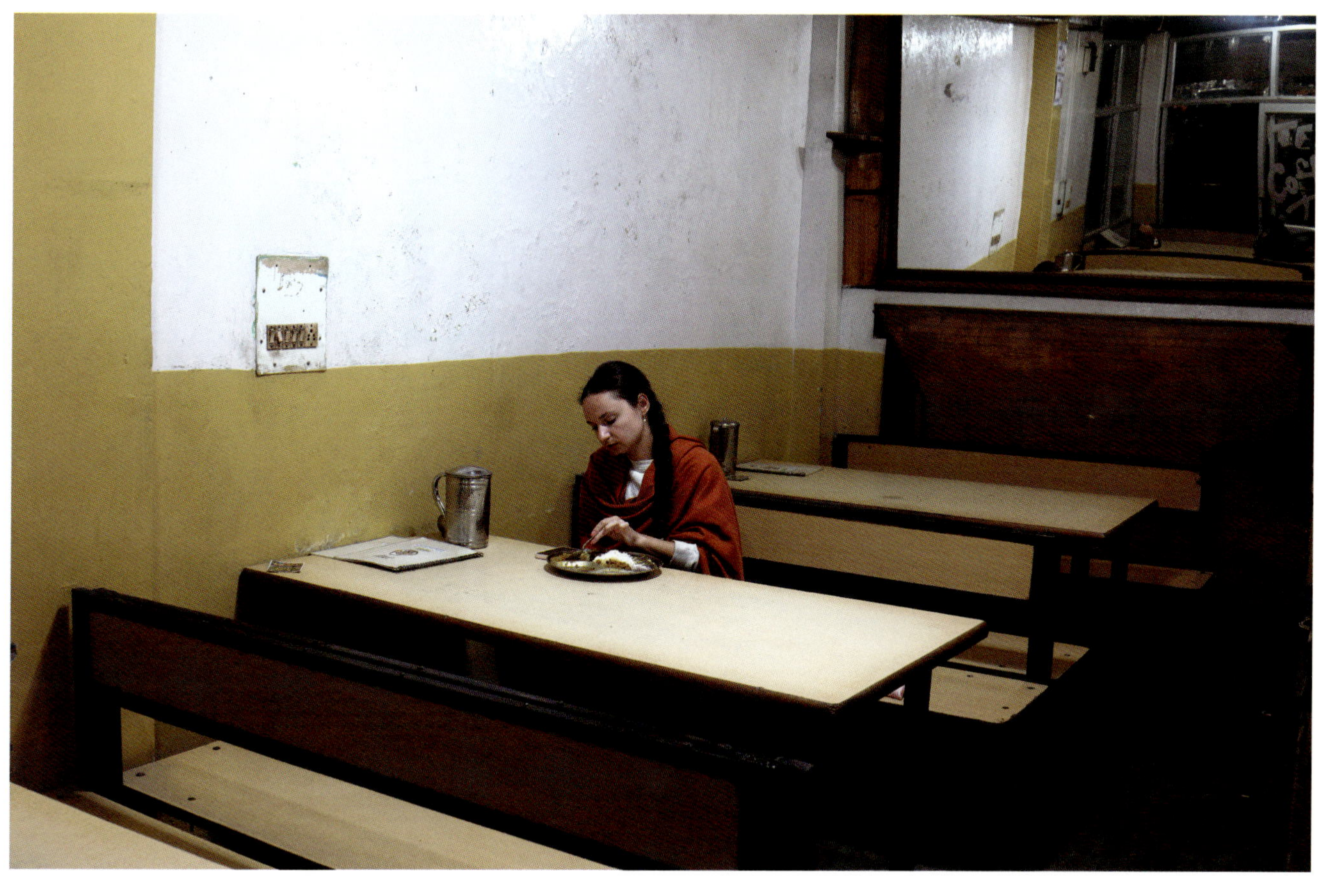

ABOVE: Anna (Ukraine and Israel), Kasol. I popped into a little café for lunch and met Anna inside. She was alone and looked a little lost. We struck up a conversation. "I am of Ukrainian descent living in Israel. Now, both my countries are at war. I have no place to return to. I guess I will travel in India until my visa runs out, and then go to Nepal. I heard it is beautiful there."

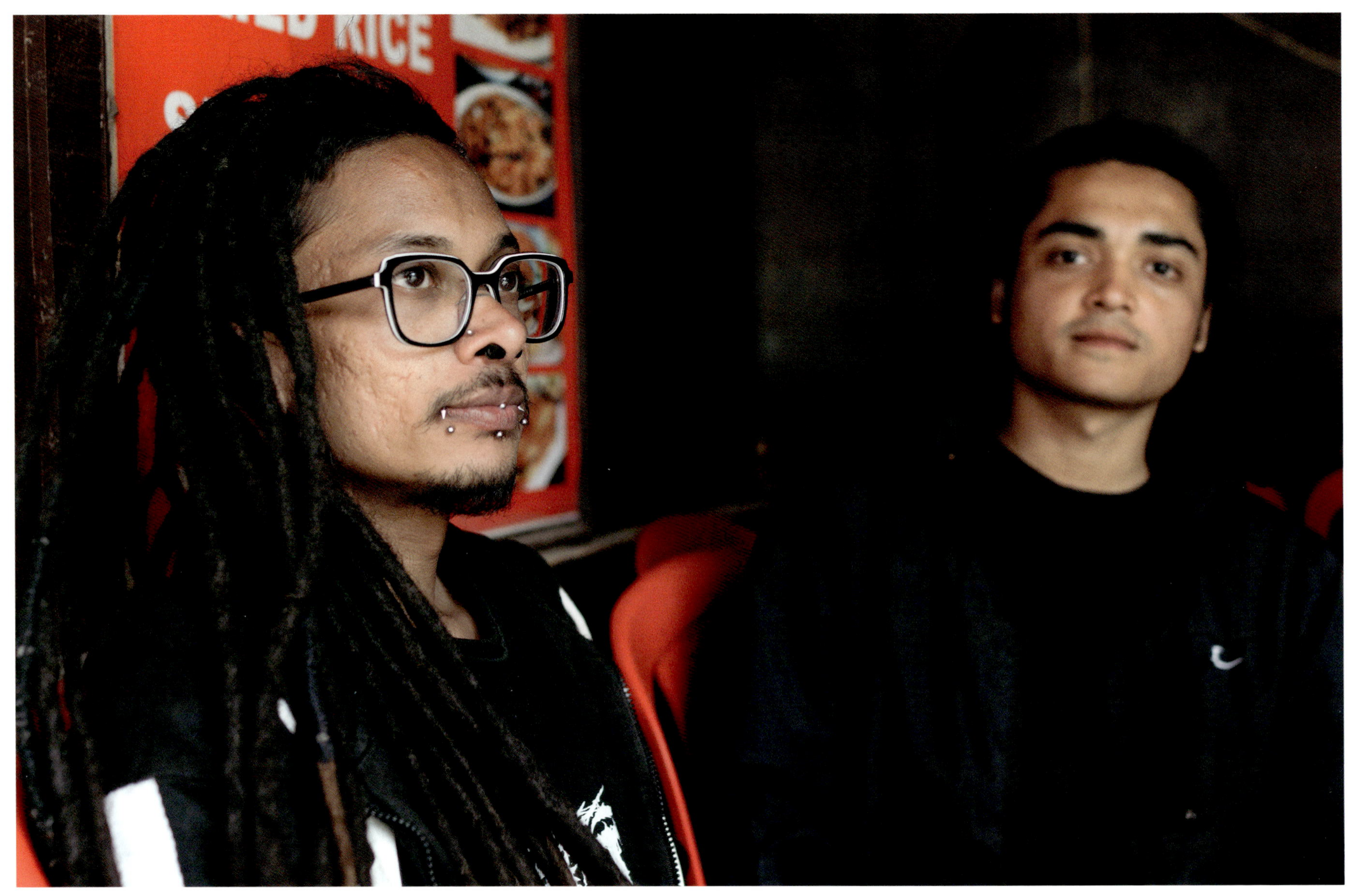

Nik (India) and Sac (India), Kasol

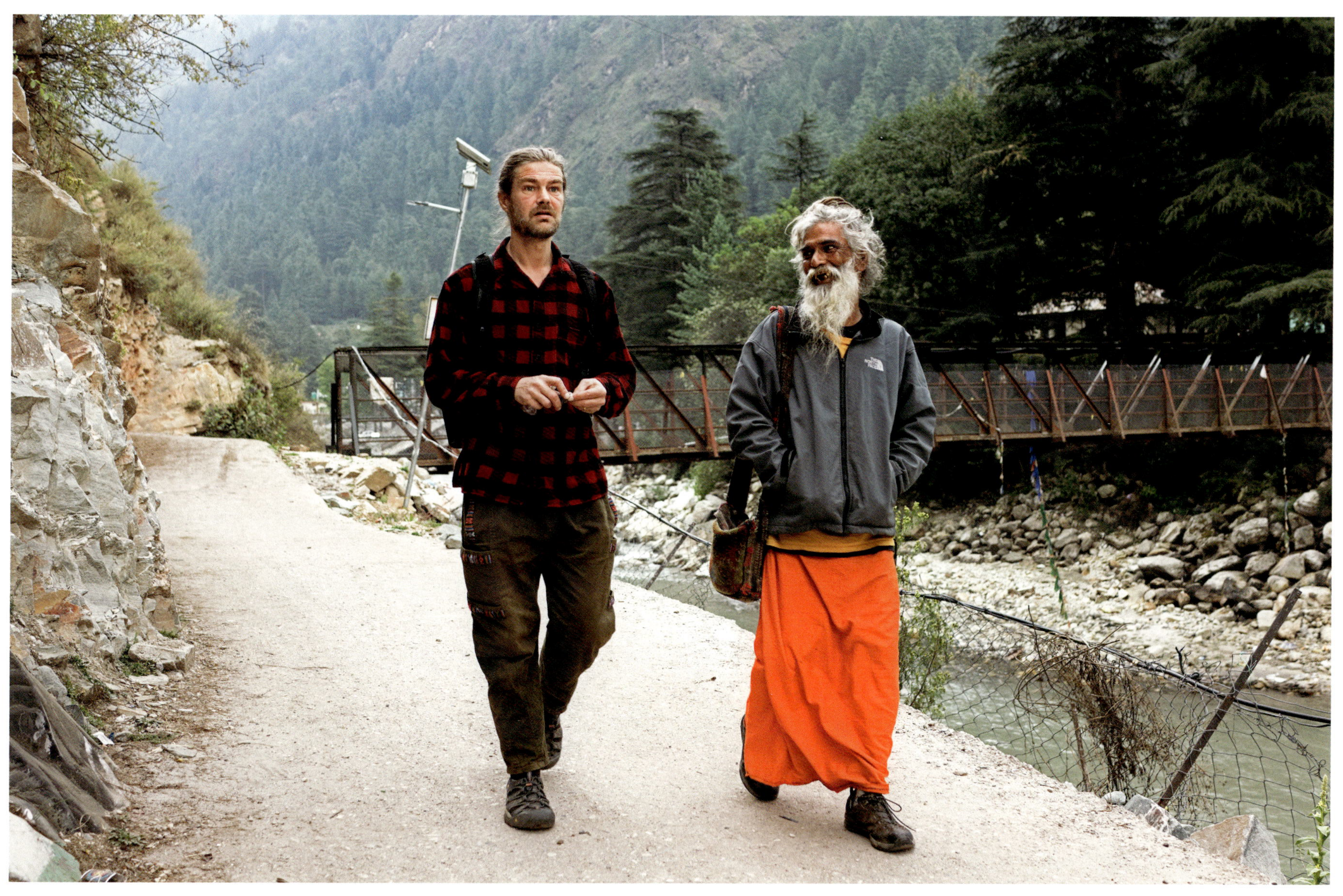

Robert (Netherlands) and Baba (India), Chalal trail

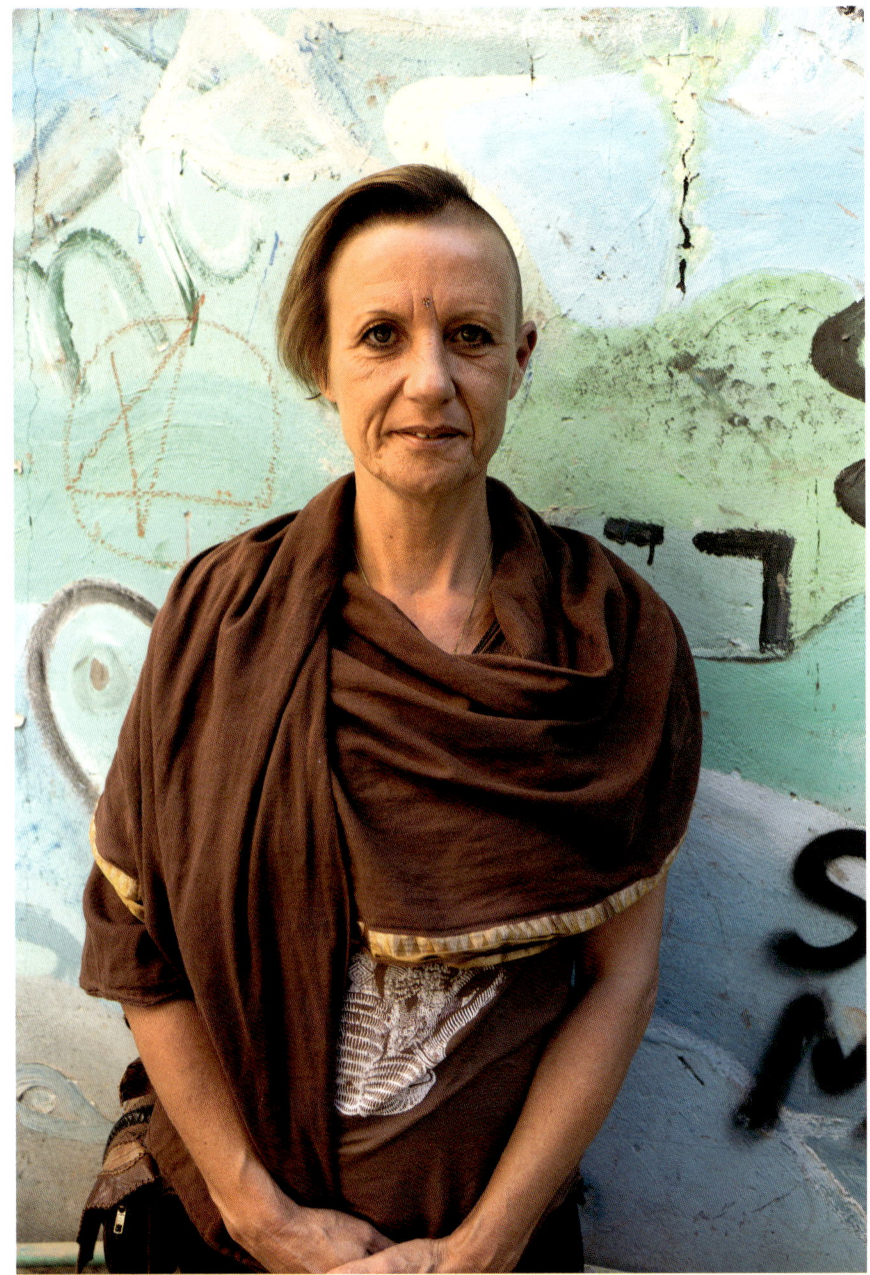

Melanie (Germany), Kasol

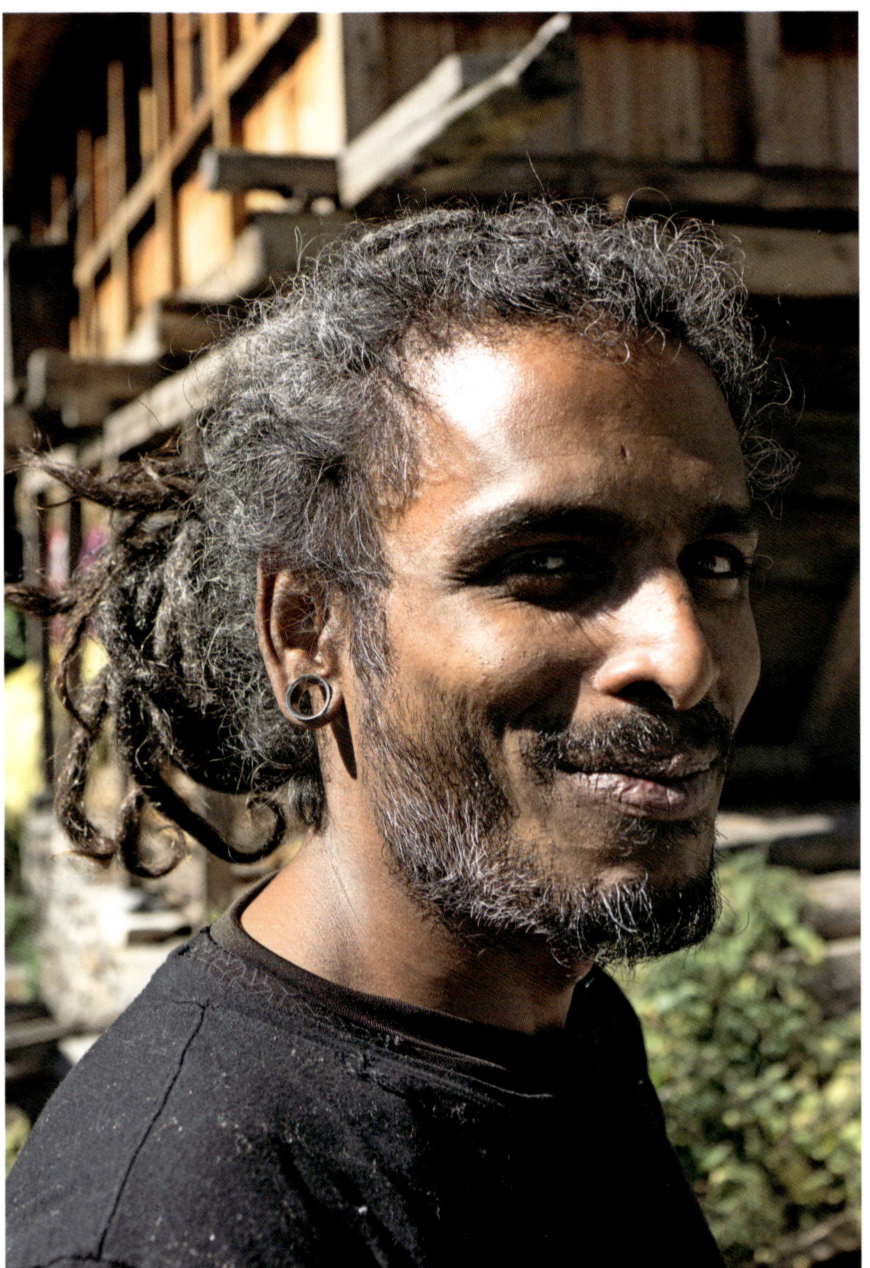

Raj (India), Grahan village

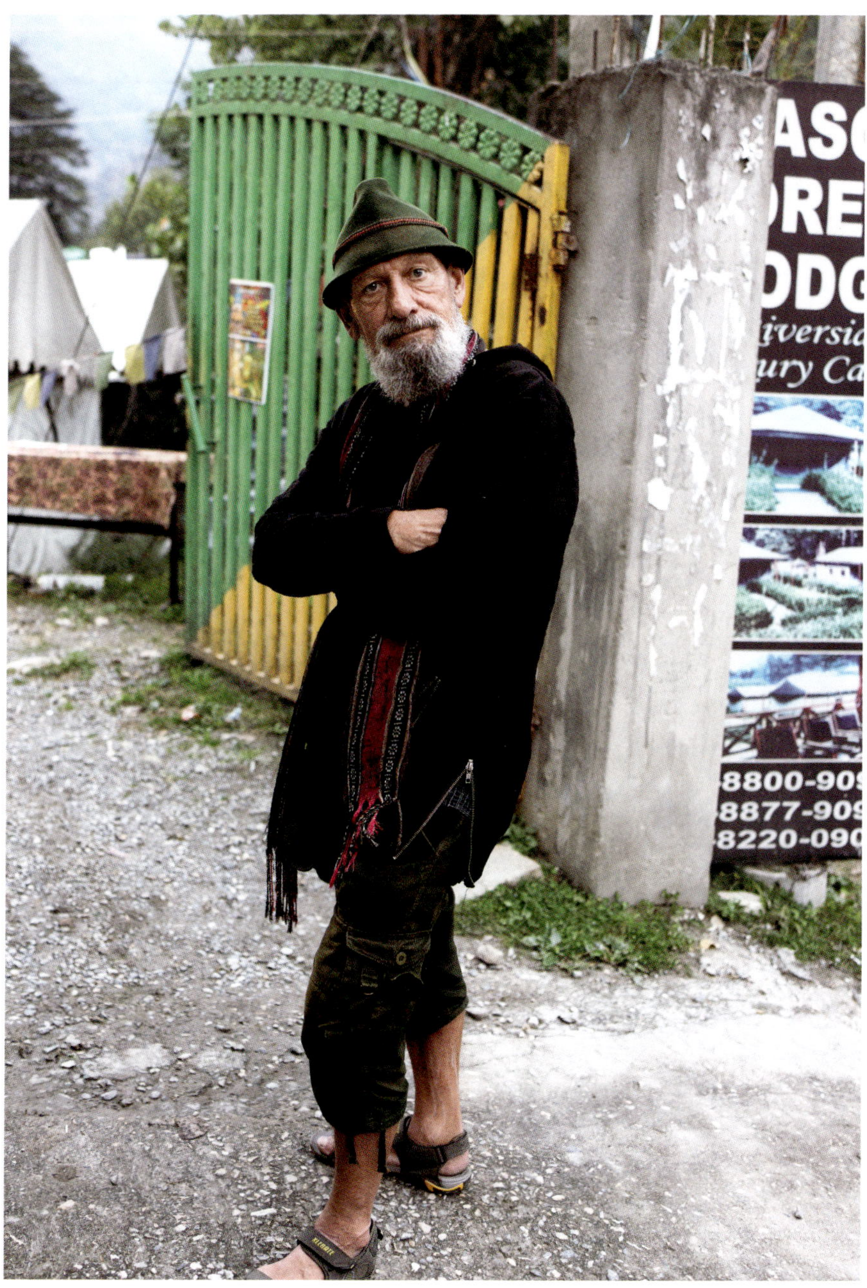

Paul (Wales), Kasol

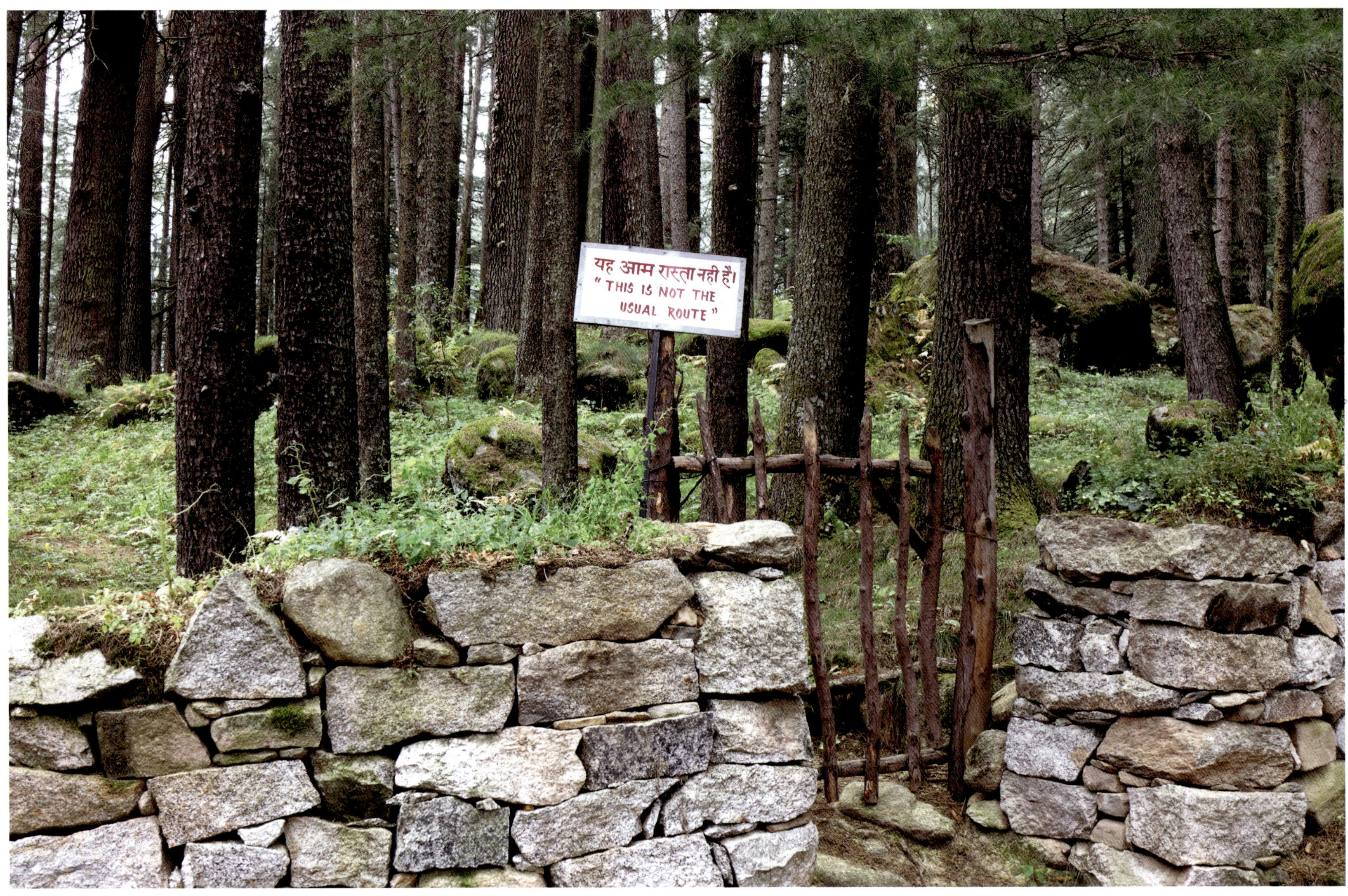यह आम रास्ता नहीं है।
" THIS IS NOT THE
USUAL ROUTE "

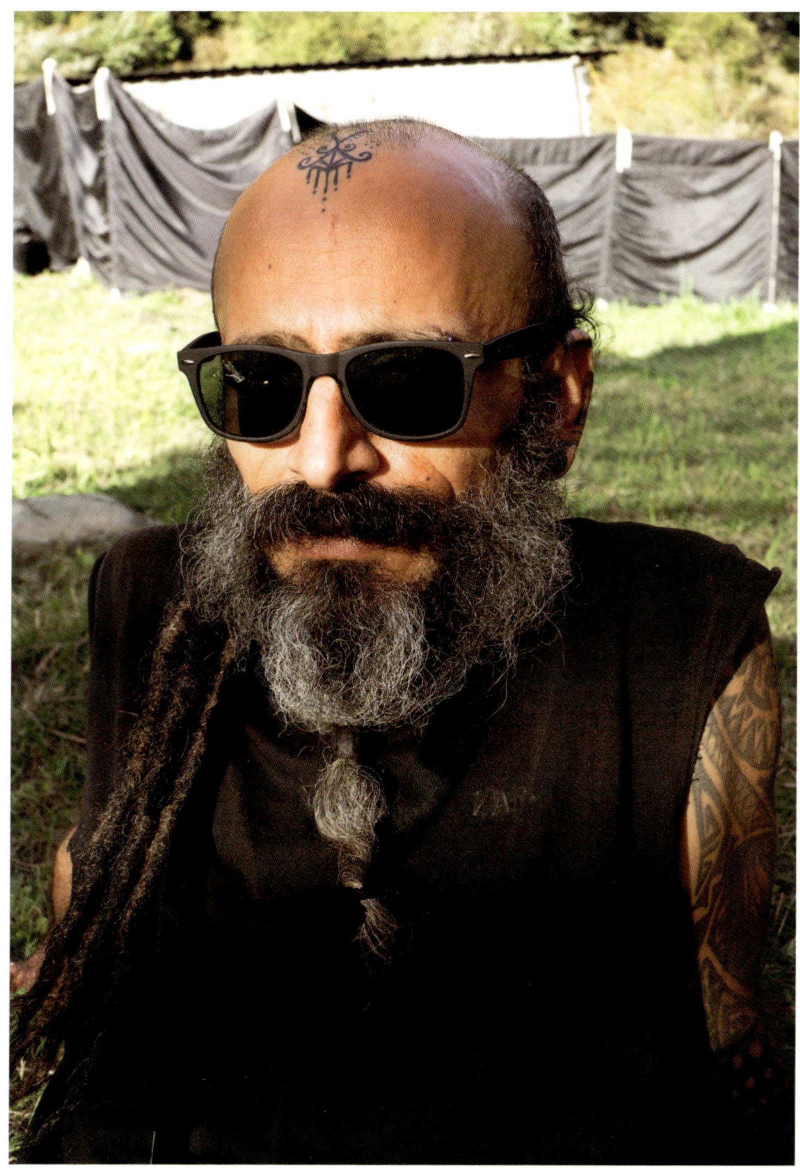

Herculis (Jordan), Choj village

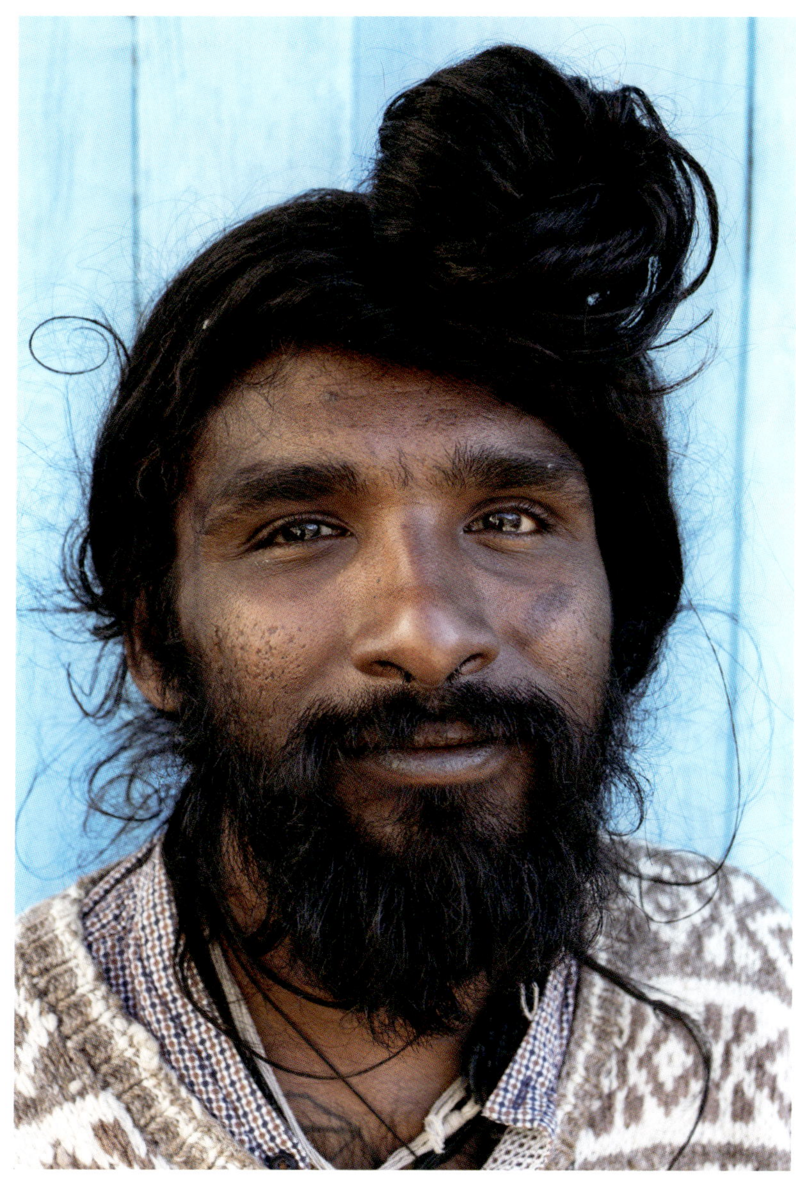

Dev (India), Tosh village

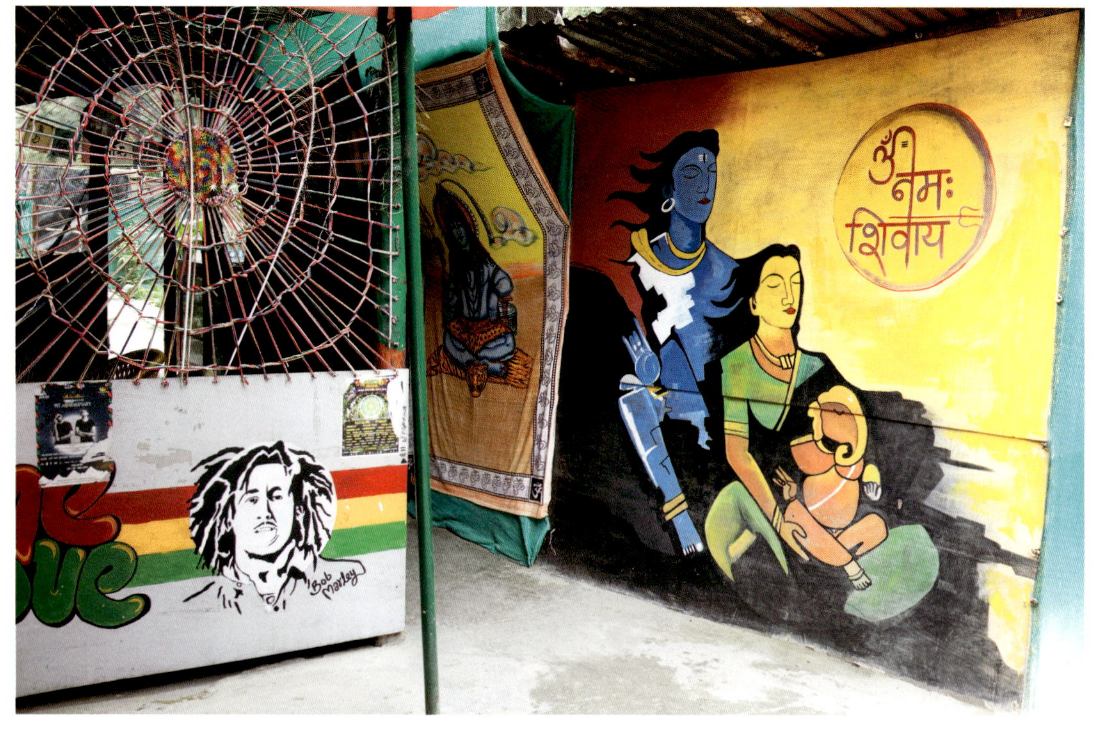

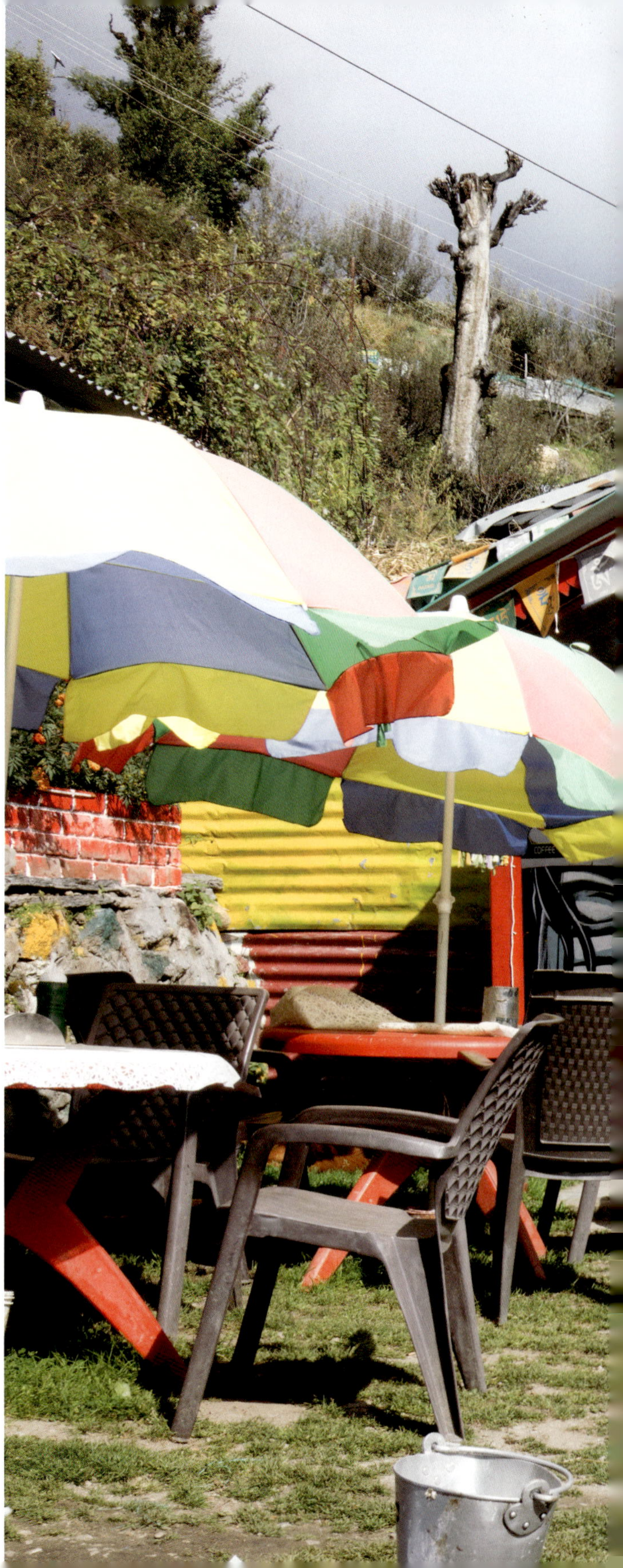

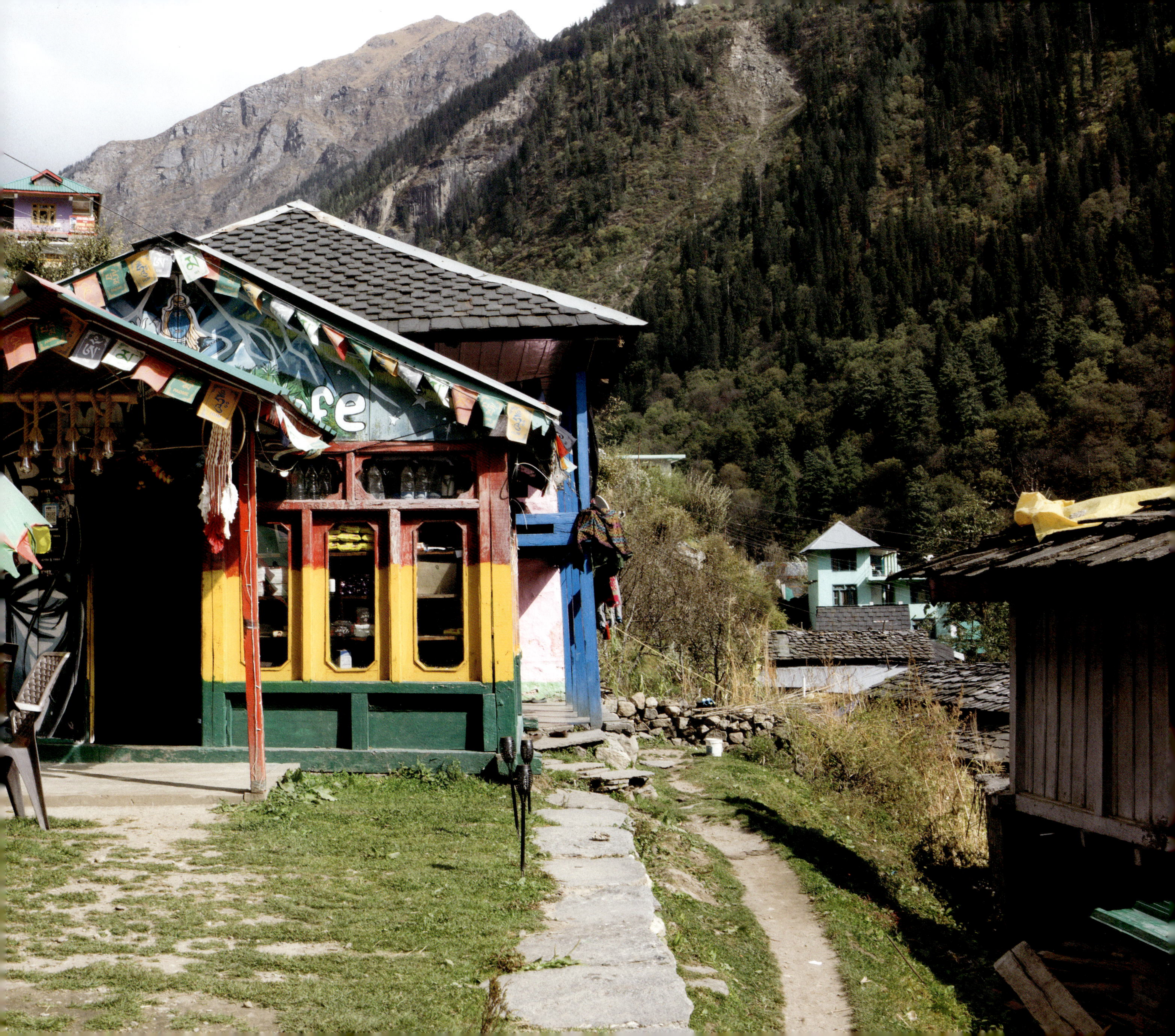

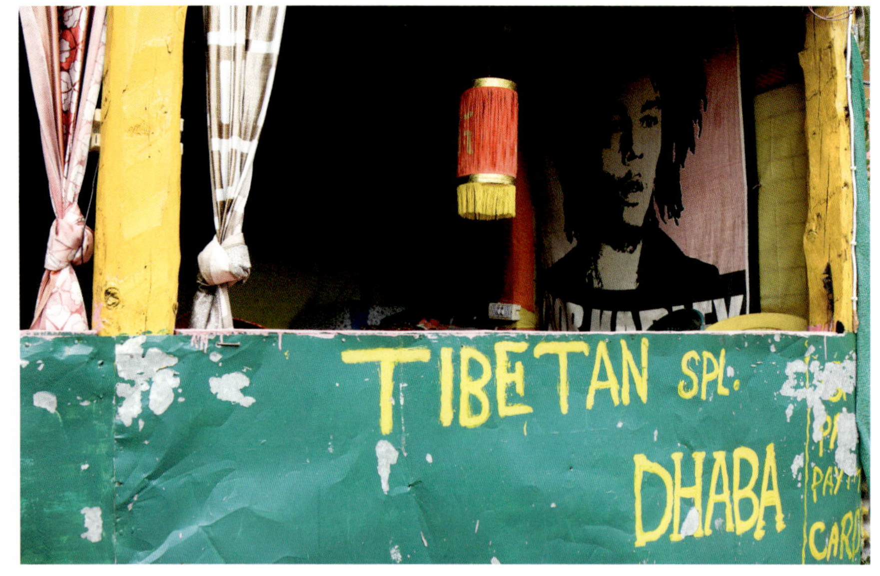

TIBETAN SPL.
DHABA

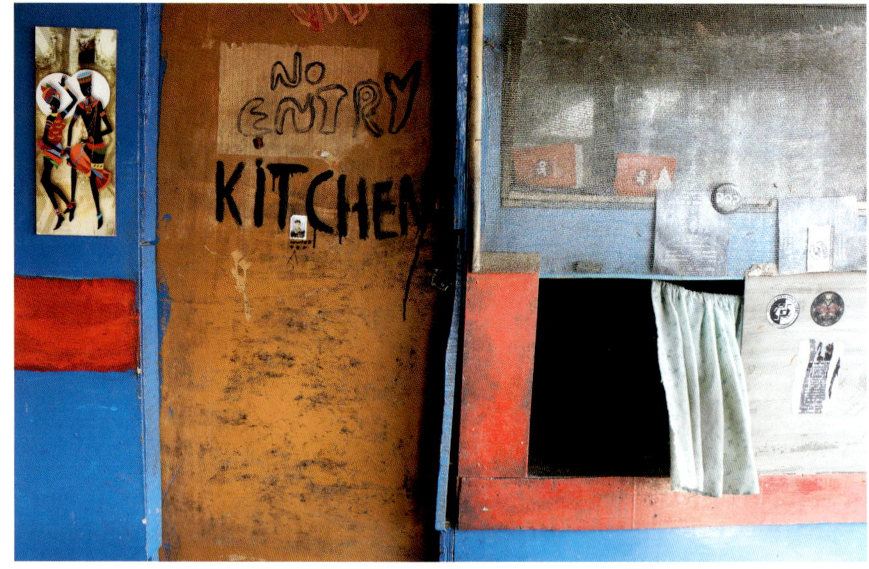

NO ENTRY
KITCHEN

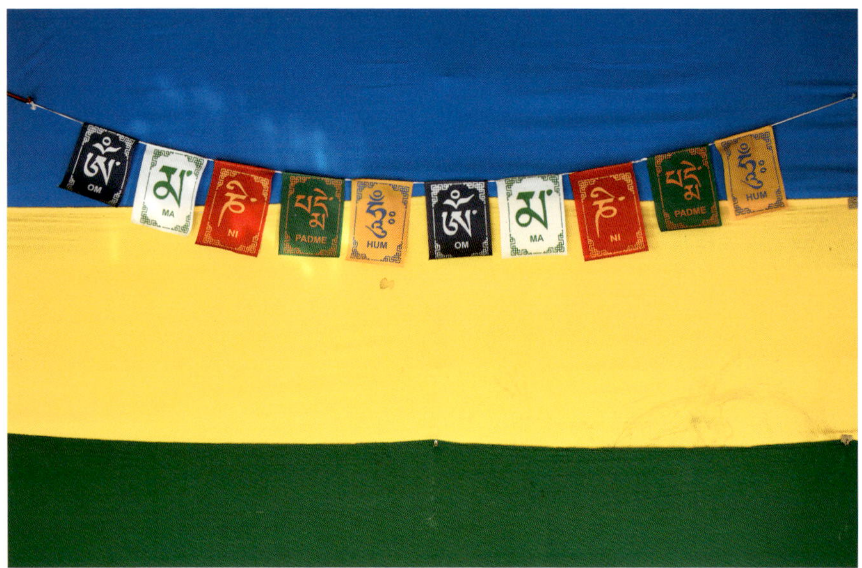

OM
MA
NI
PADME
HUM
OM
MA
NI
PADME
HUM

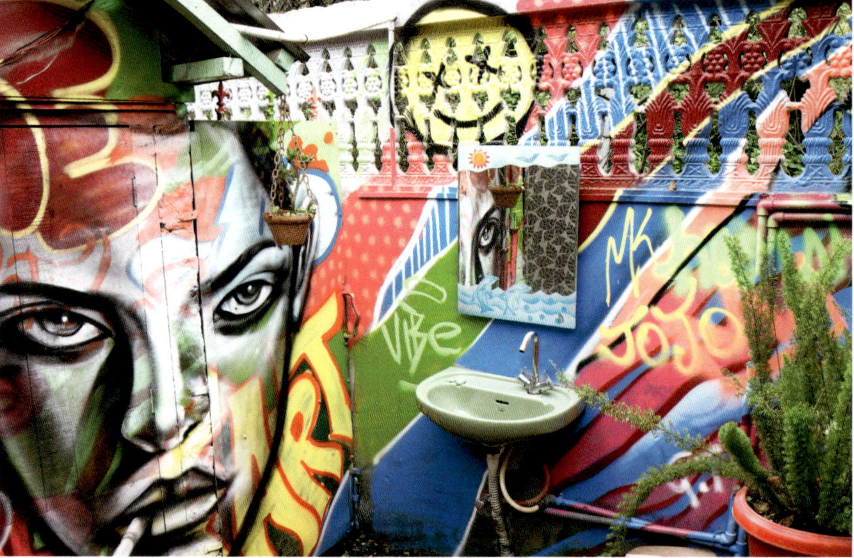

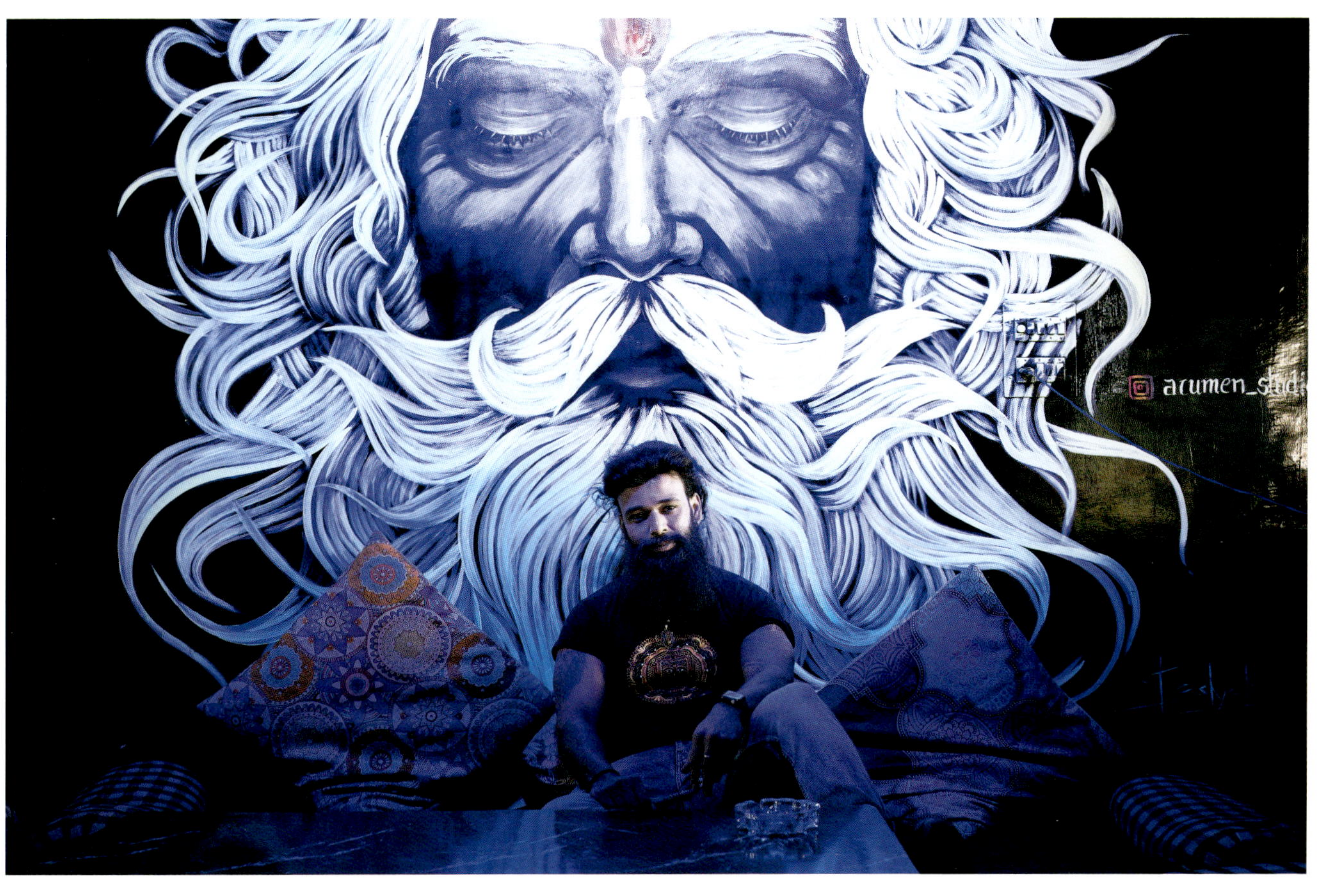

Rudra (India), Kasol. Rudra runs a small psychedelic café in the Kasol bazaar. Sporting a chest-length beard, metal piercings, and a tattoo sleeve on his muscular arms, he comes across as someone you wouldn't want to mess with. He lived a roughneck past life, however, I found Rudra to be kind-hearted, genuine, and an extremely thoughtful person—introspective in nature. He also makes the finest cup of hot chocolate to be found in the Parvati Valley. "I dropped out of mainstream India when I realized it was spiraling me down," he told me. "I was angry a lot of the time. Kasol is my home now. I can live peacefully here with my dogs, close to nature, among like-minded friends."

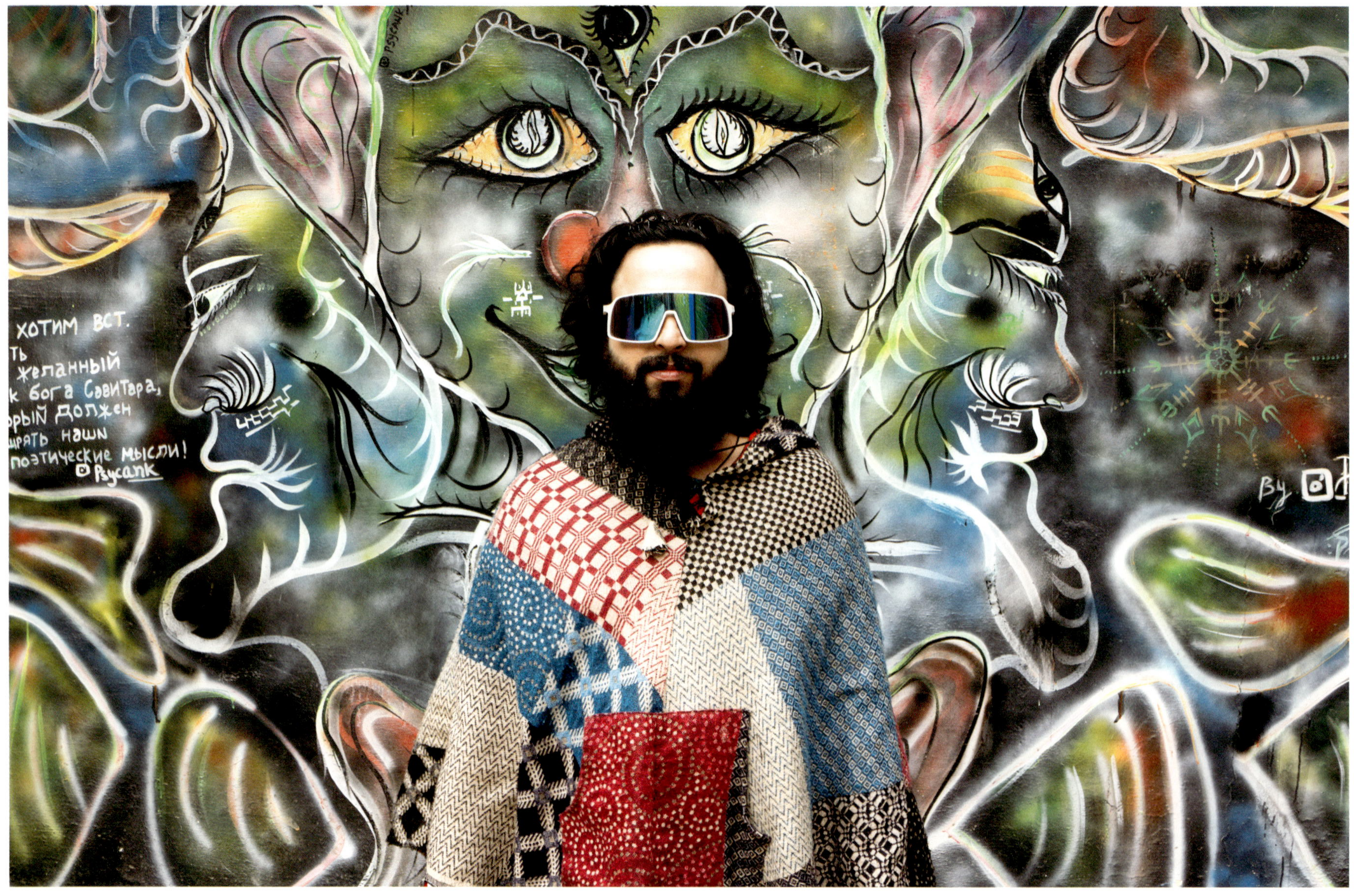

Thakur (India), Kasol

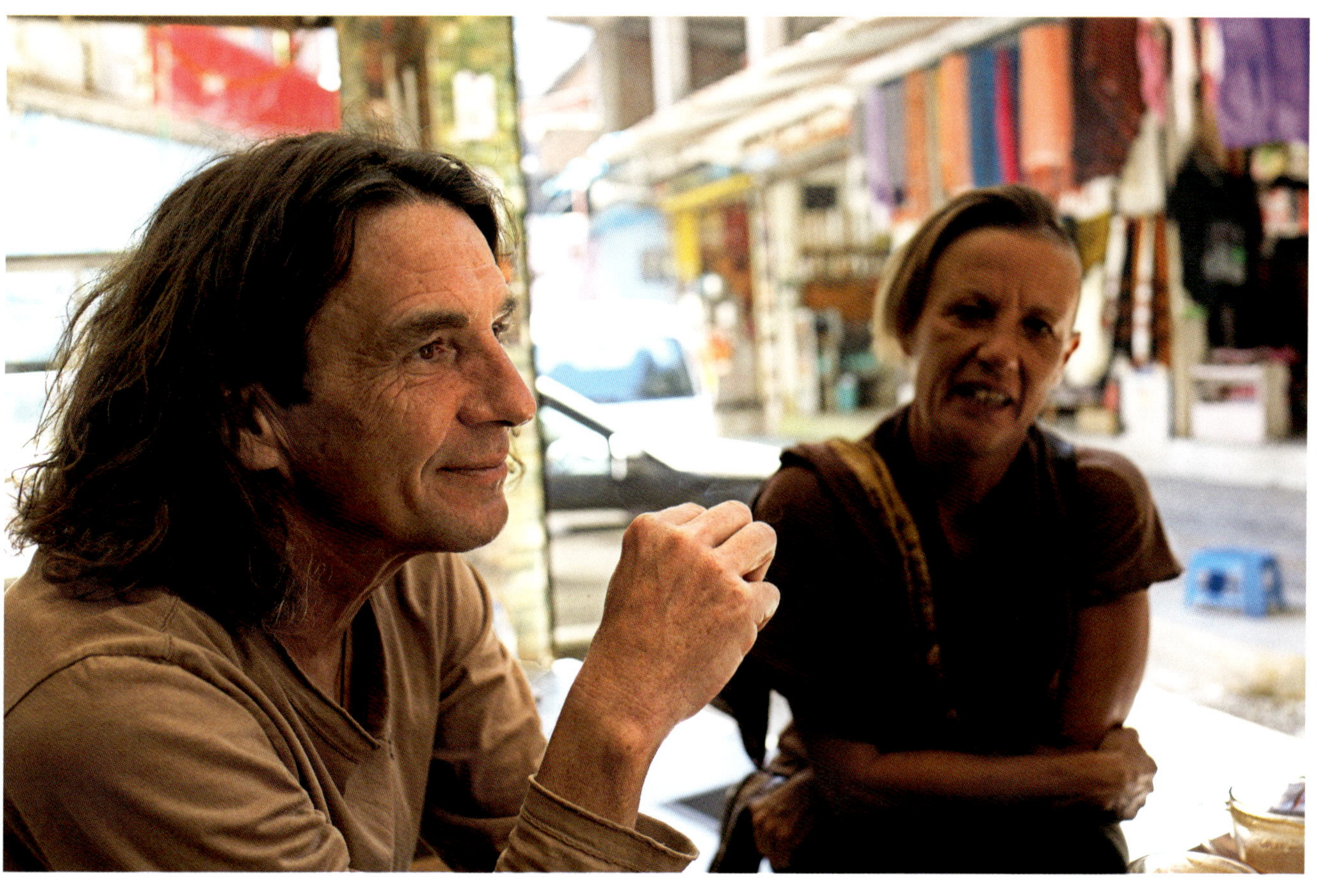

Andreas and Melanie (Germany), Kasol. A German couple told me their story over morning coffee. "We had a house and a nice garden. But we felt we no longer fit into German society, so we sold the house and everything else. During COVID we lived in a camper van in the forest in the southern part of Germany until we found some countries that would allow people to visit during the pandemic—Tanzania and Mexico. So, we went there. We've been traveling continuously now for three and half years. We like it in the Parvati Valley. It's quiet here. The mountains are beautiful. We can live like we want. We meet a lot of nice people."

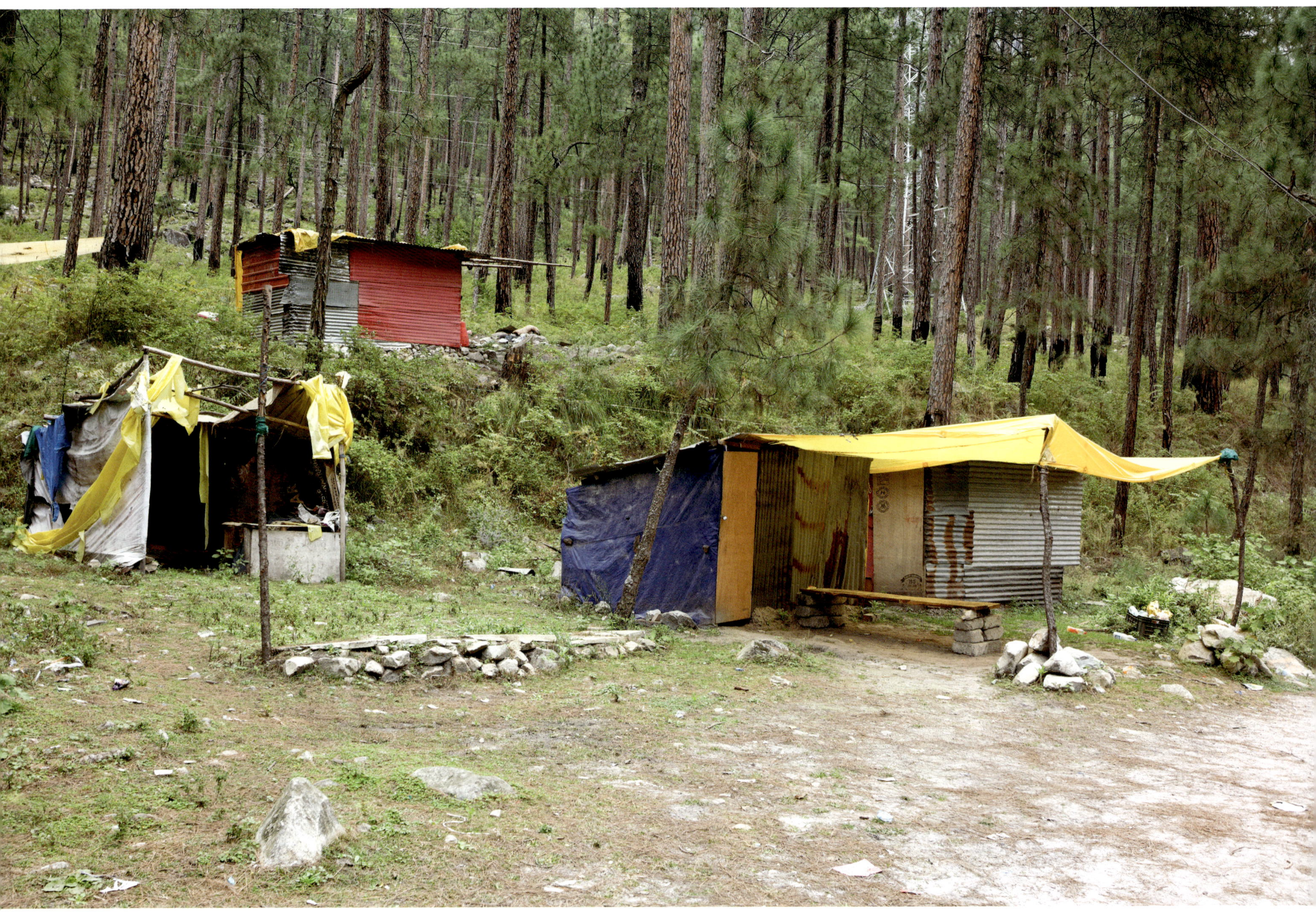

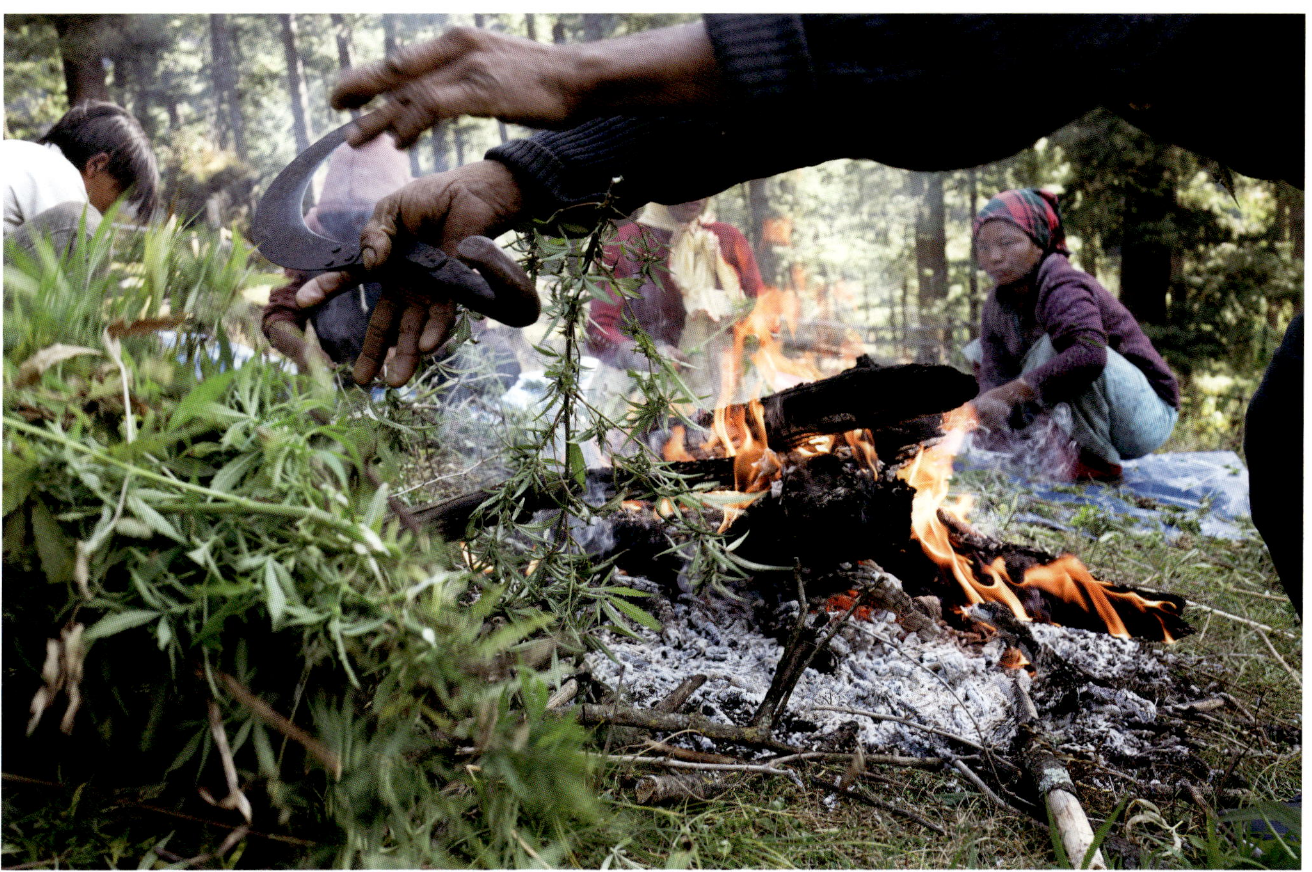

October is a busy time in the marijuana fields located in the high meadows of the Parvati Valley. It is when the crop is harvested and the flower buds are rubbed to make hashish. A local variety, known as Malana Crème, is considered by connoisseurs to be among the best in the world. Hashish cultivation has a long history in the valley, going back to mythological times when Shiva first offered it to humankind, and the local people have been using it for many centuries. Although illegal in India, cannabis use in the remote mountains is largely ignored by the authorities; it is freely smoked among travelers throughout the Parvati Valley.

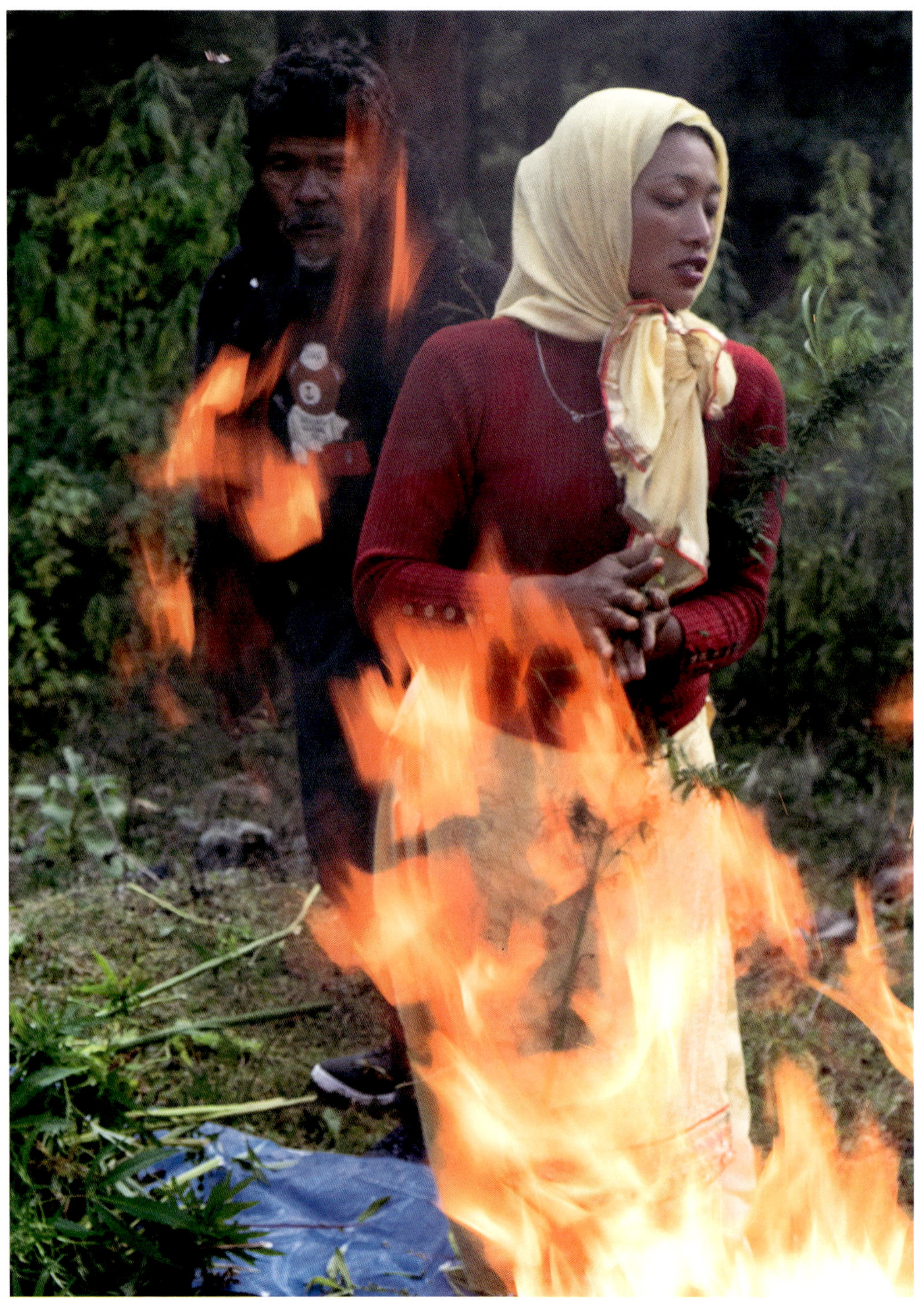

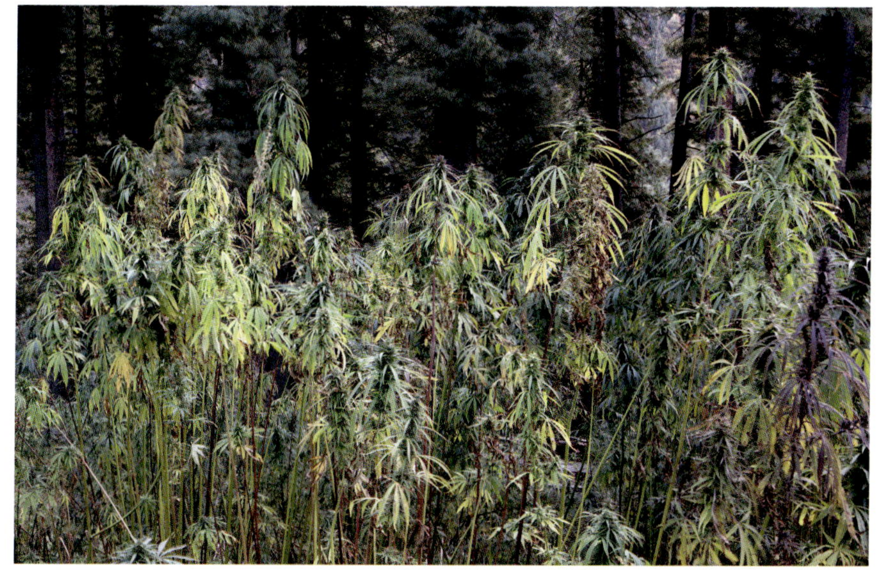
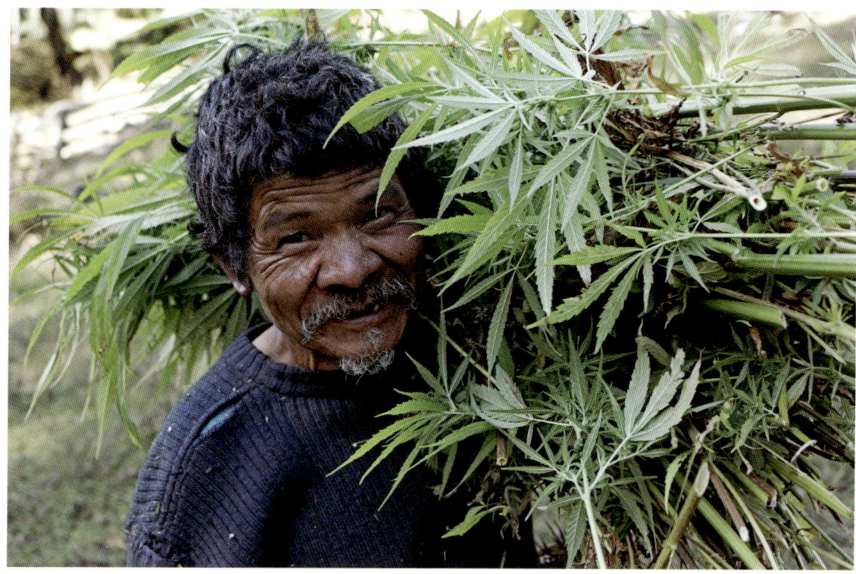
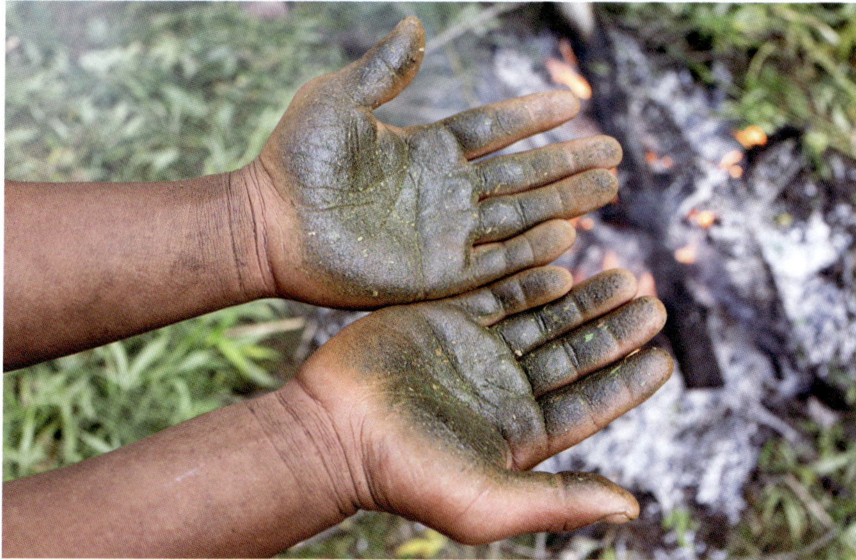
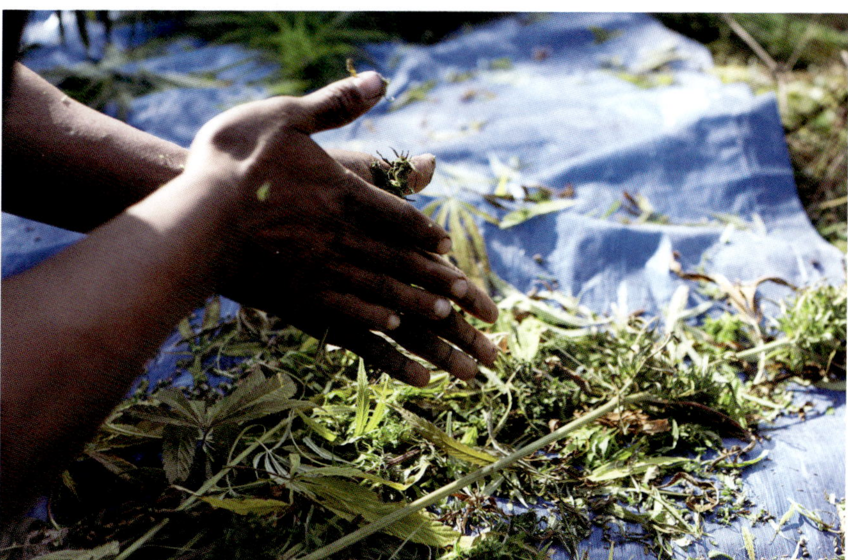

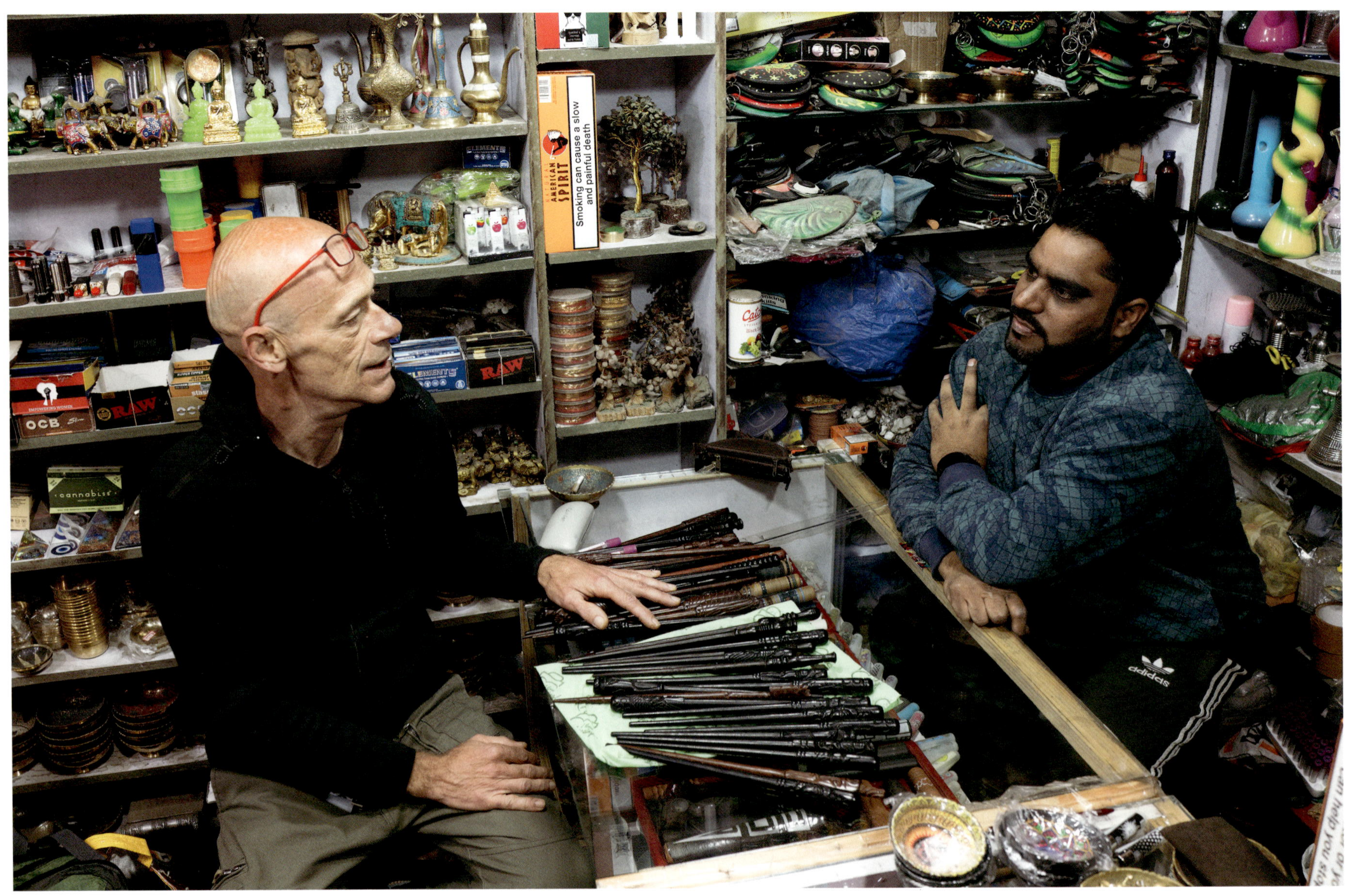

Daniel (Italy), chillum maker and Rahul
(India), smoke shop trader, Kasol

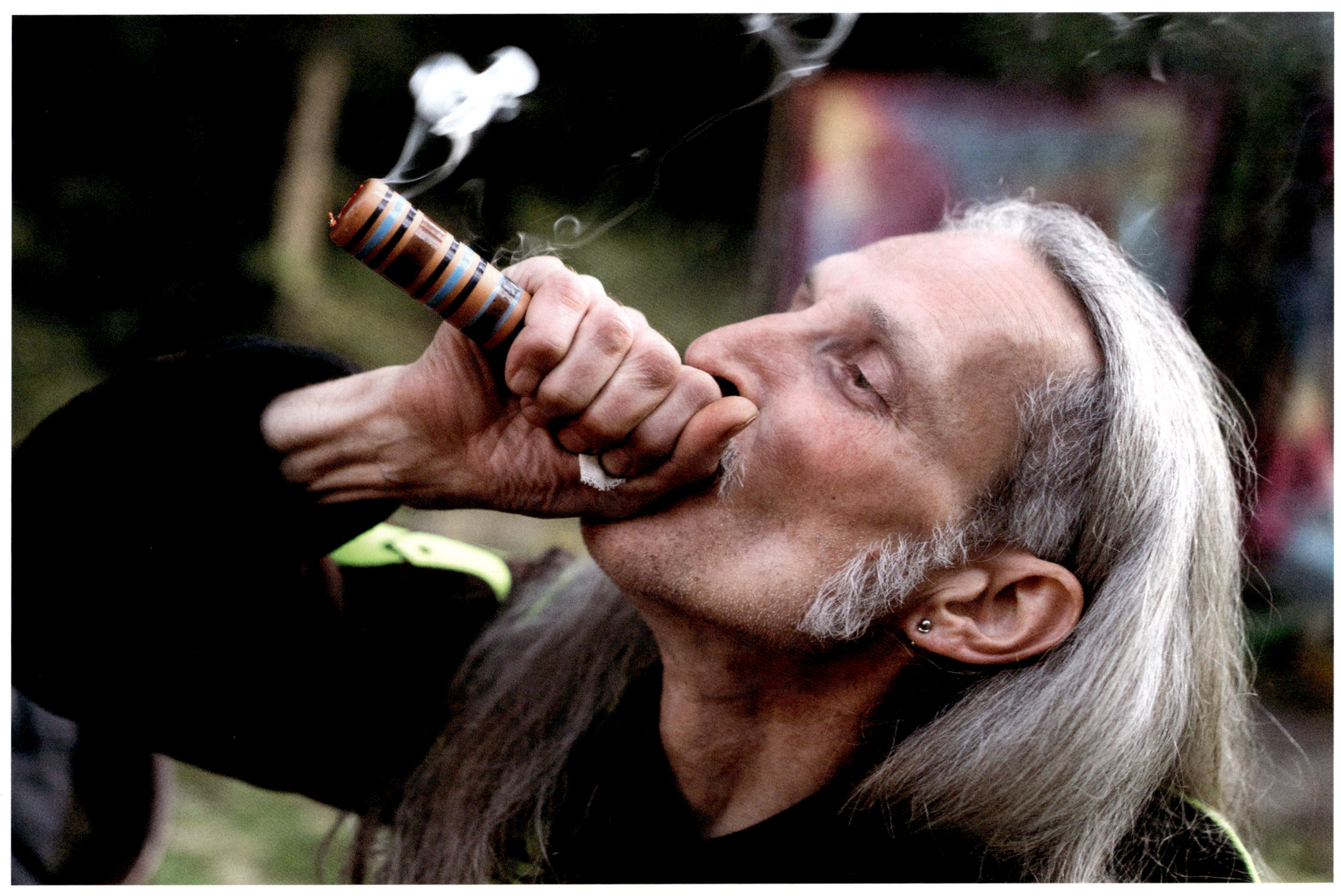

Pierre (Italy), Chalal

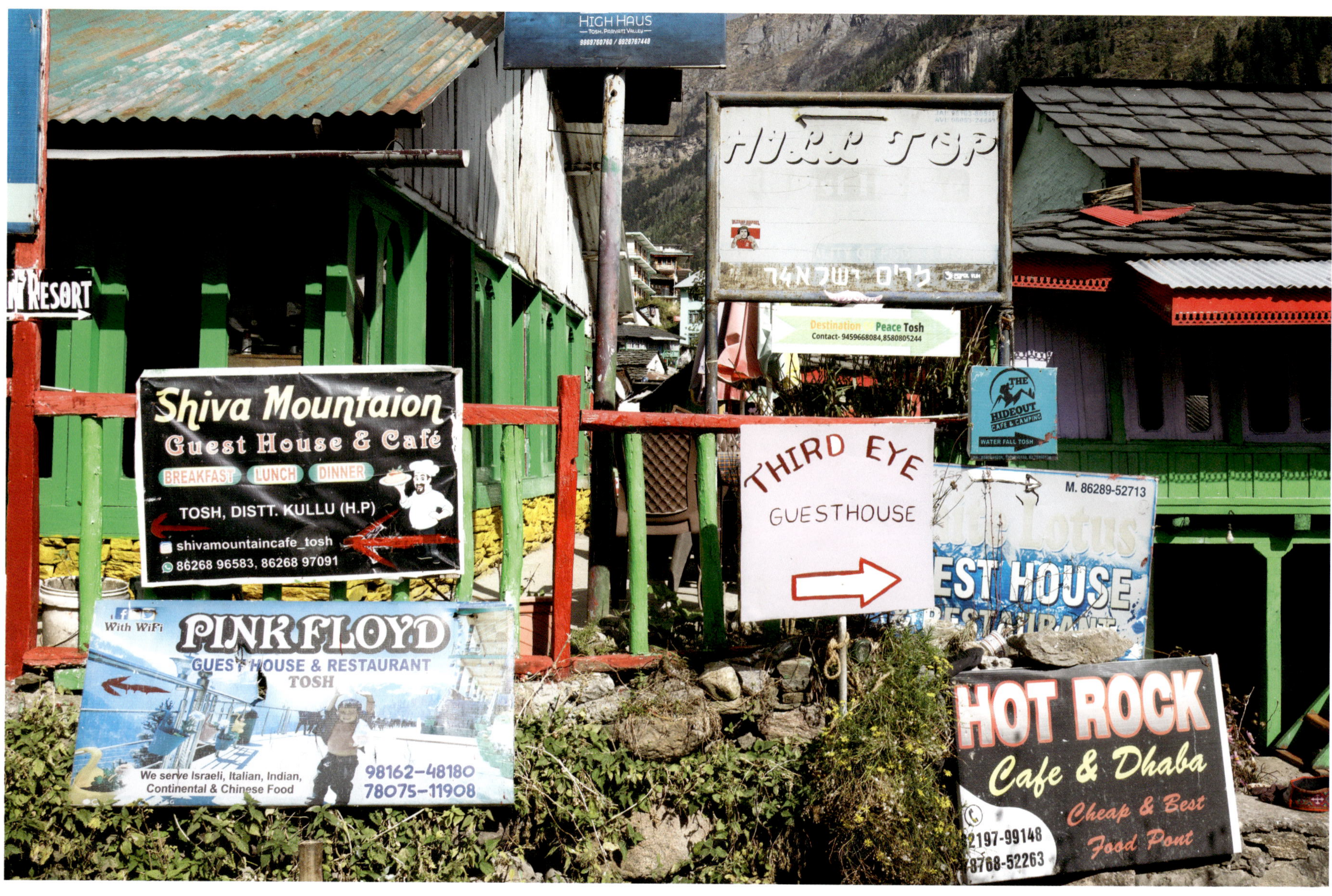

HIGH HAUS
TOSH, PARVATI VALLEY
HILL TOP
Destination Peace Tosh
Contact- 9459668084, 8580805244
THE HIDEOUT
CAFE & CAMPING
WATER FALL TOSH
RESORT
Shiva Mountaion
Guest House & Café
BREAKFAST LUNCH DINNER
TOSH, DISTT. KULLU (H.P)
shivamountaincafe_tosh
86268 96583, 86268 97091
THIRD EYE
GUESTHOUSE
M. 86289-52713
Lotus
EST HOUSE
With WiFi
PINK FLOYD
GUEST HOUSE & RESTAURANT
TOSH
We serve Israeli, Italian, Indian,
Continental & Chinese Food
98162-48180
78075-11908
HOT ROCK
Cafe & Dhaba
Cheap & Best
Food Pont
2197-99148
8768-52263

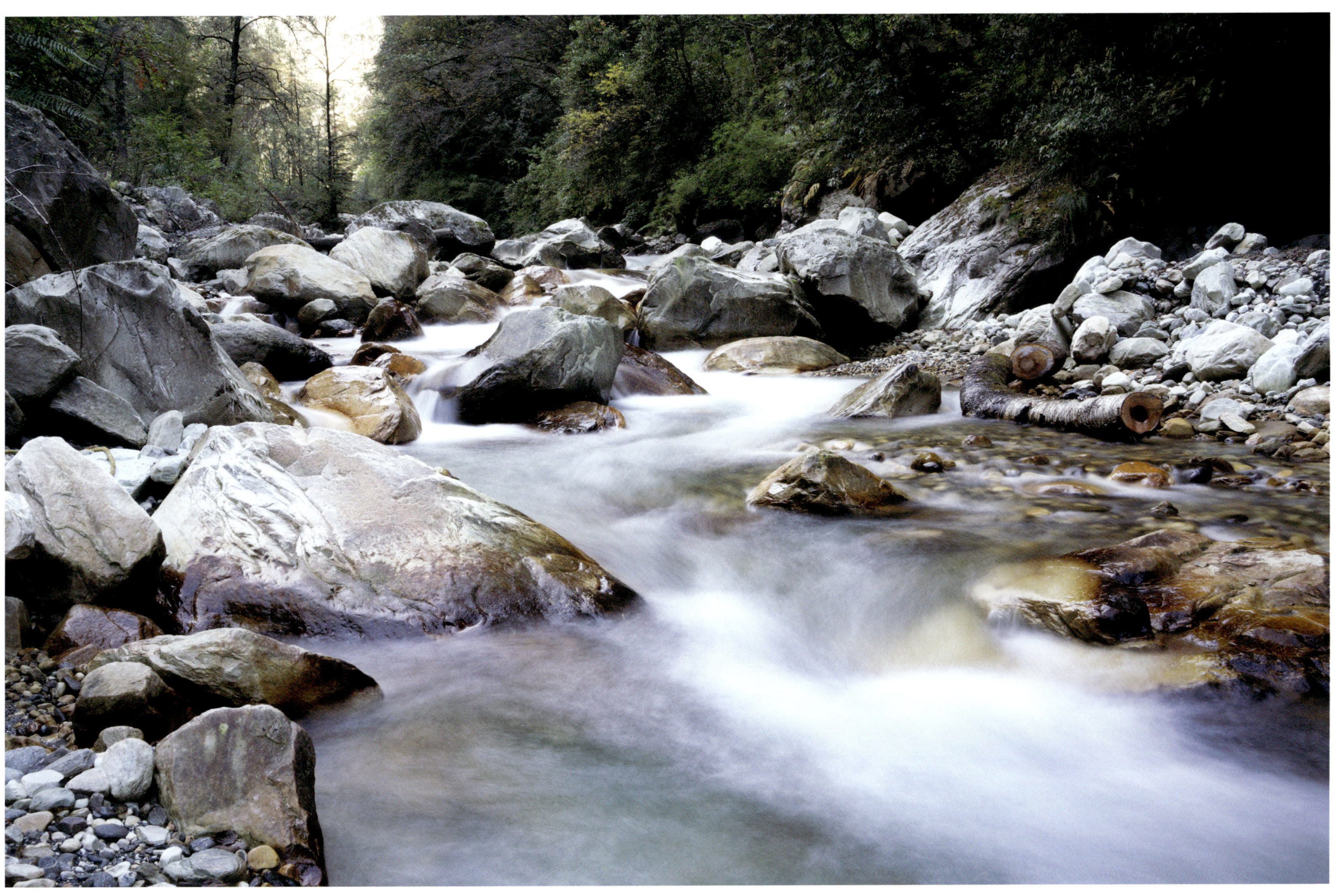

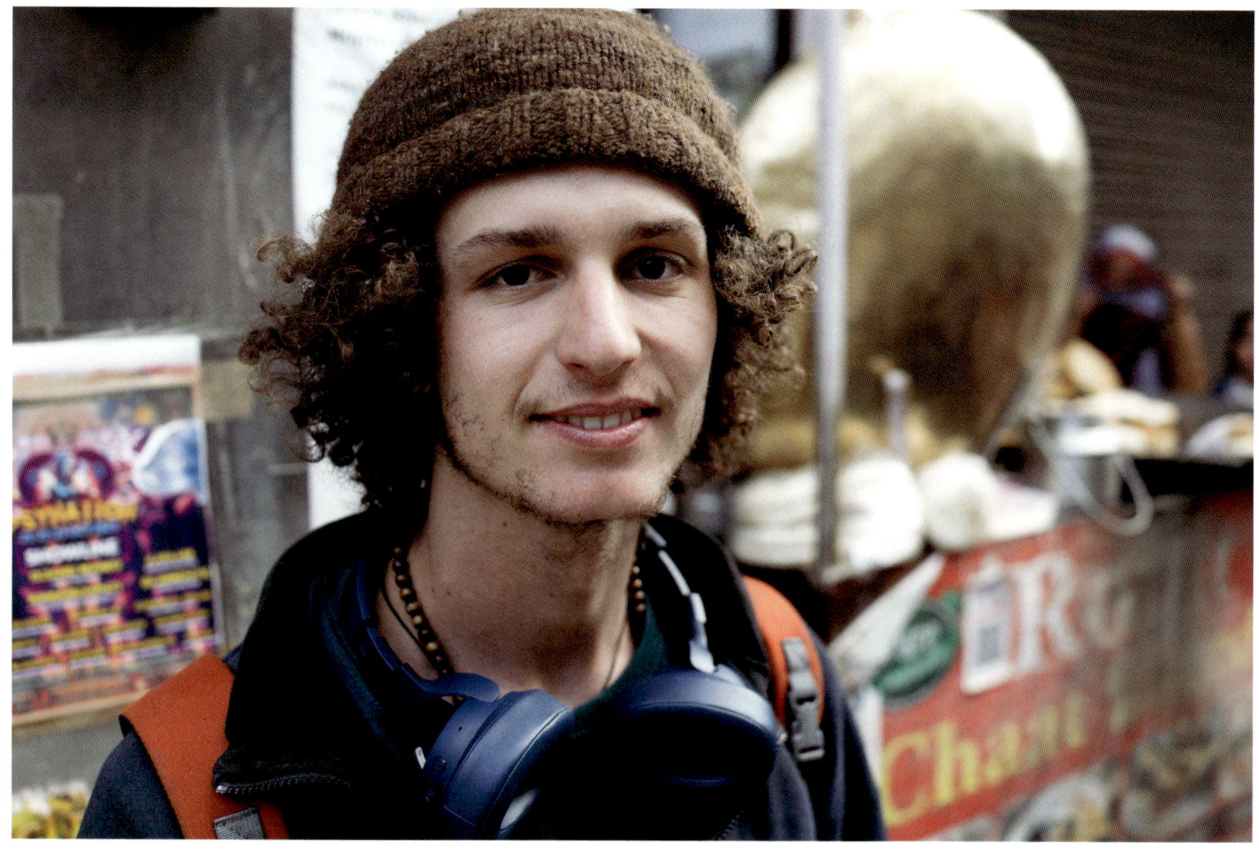

RIGHT: Satya (New Zealand), Kasol. I was waiting in line at a street food stand when I met Satya. He told me he is a second-generation India traveler. His parents gave him his Hindi name, which means Truth, after traveling in India. "I came to India because of my parents. They traveled here many years ago when they were my age, and they've been telling me stories about India my entire life. So, I had to come to see it for myself. I've been visiting a lot of temples, experiencing the culture, and learning about the religion. Visiting some of the hippie places my parents had told me about. Rishikesh. Pushkar. Now, I am in the Parvati Valley."

OPPOSITE: Forest sadhu, Manikaran

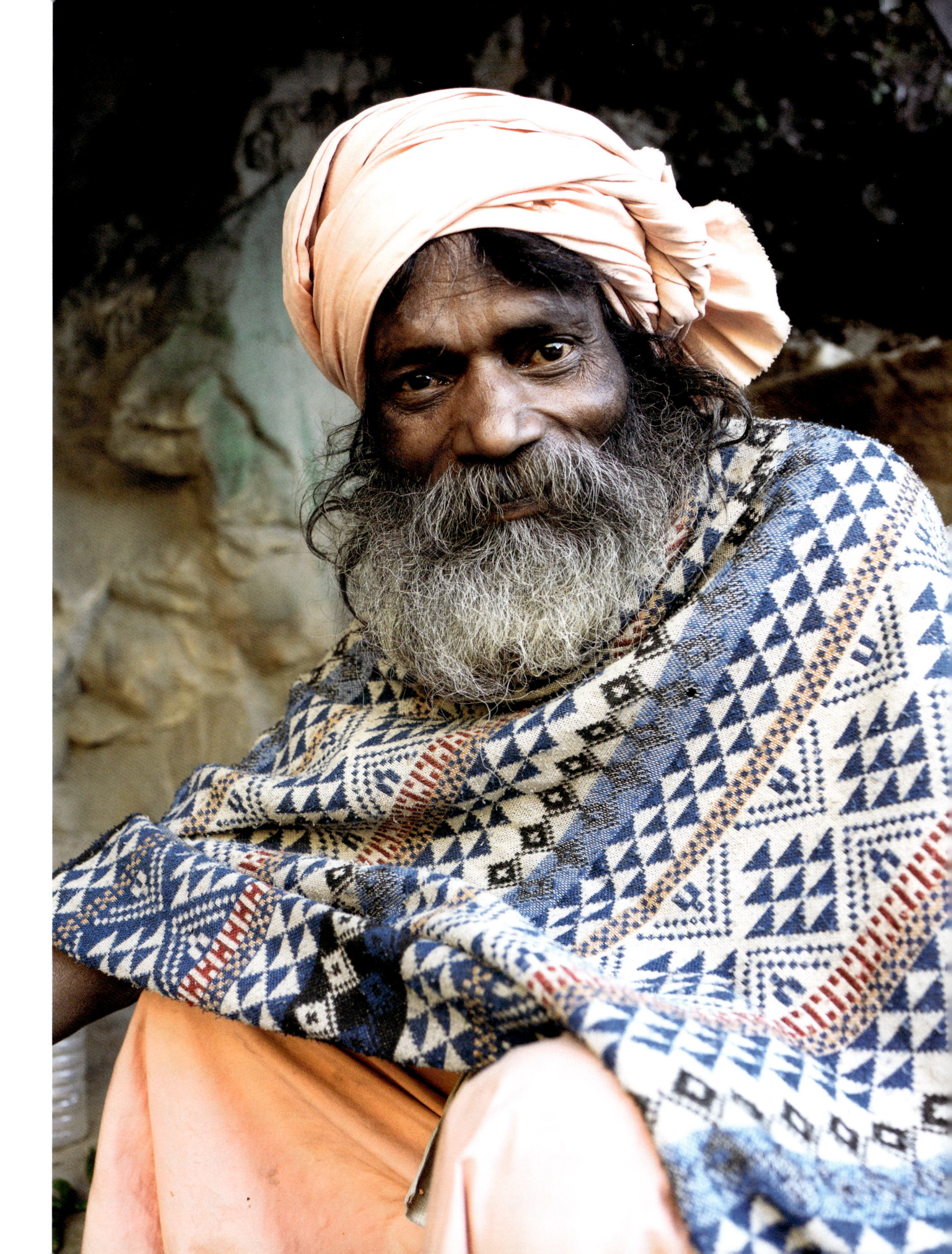

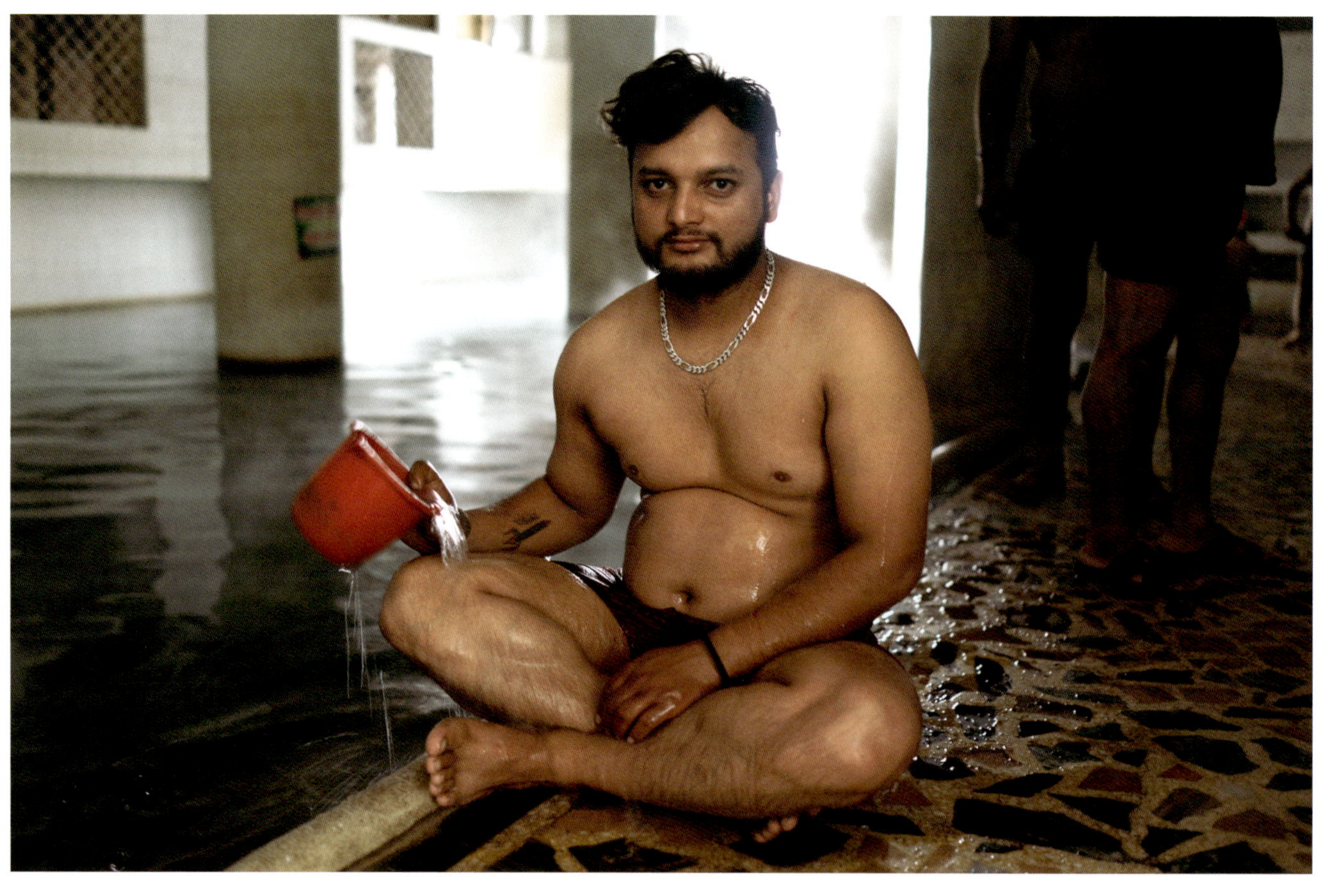

Pilgrim bather (India),
Manikaran Temple hot springs

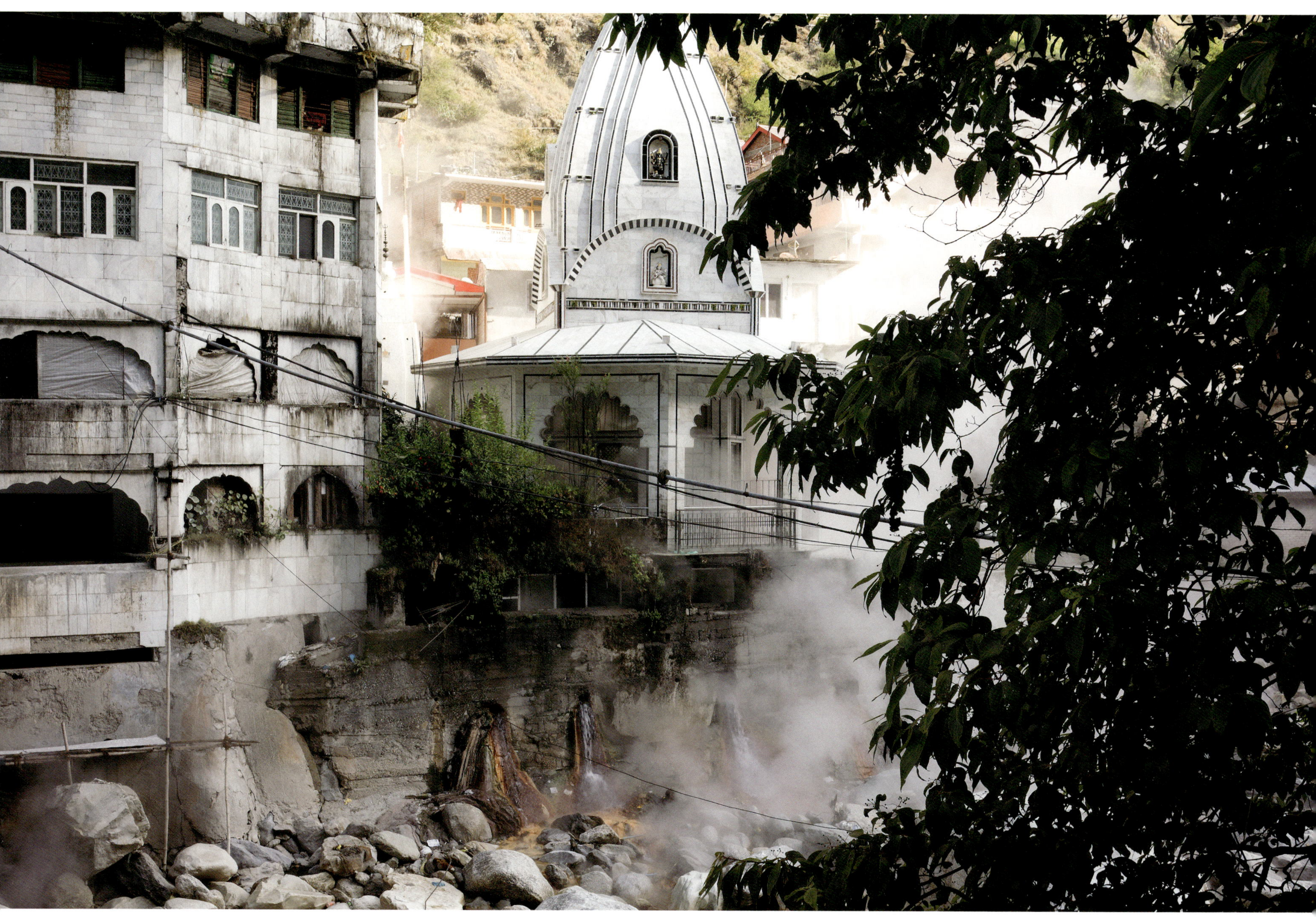

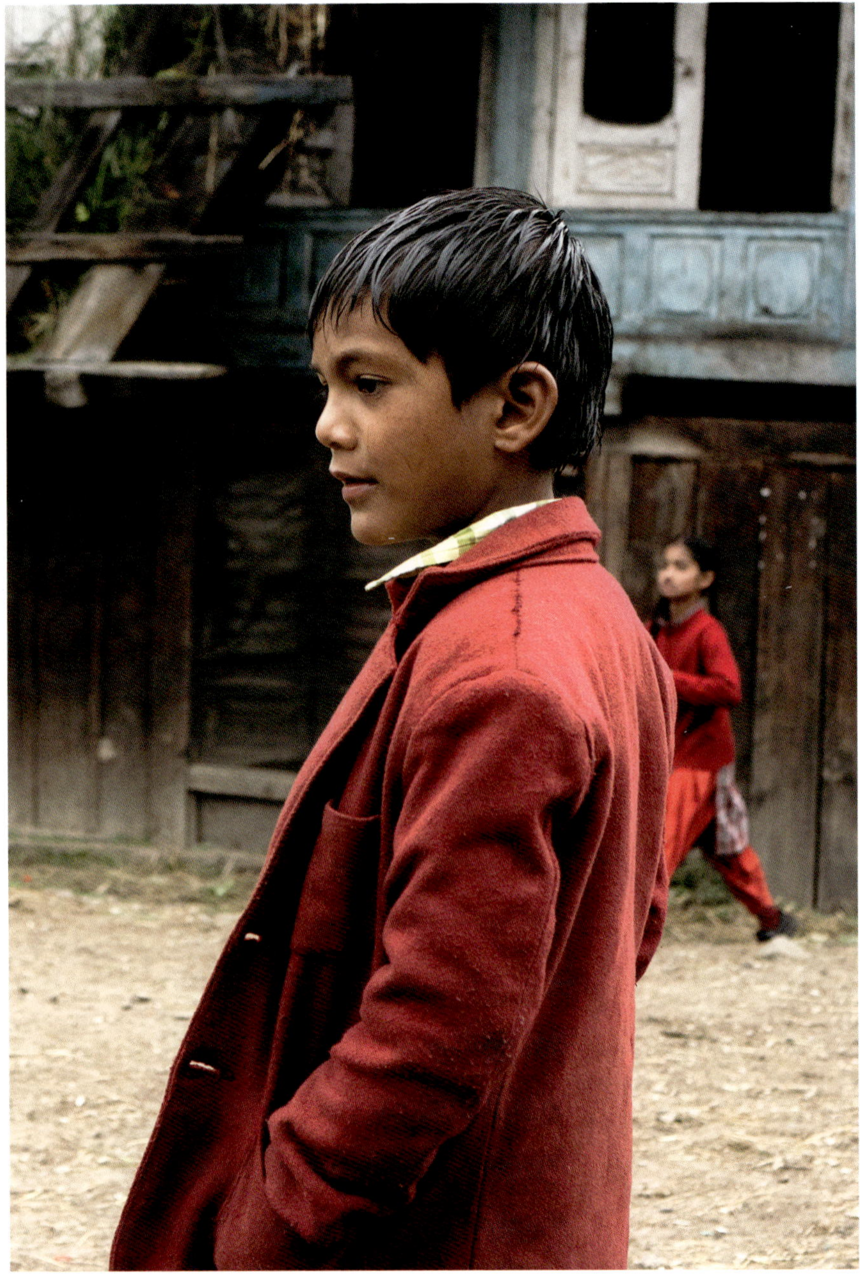

Pulga village

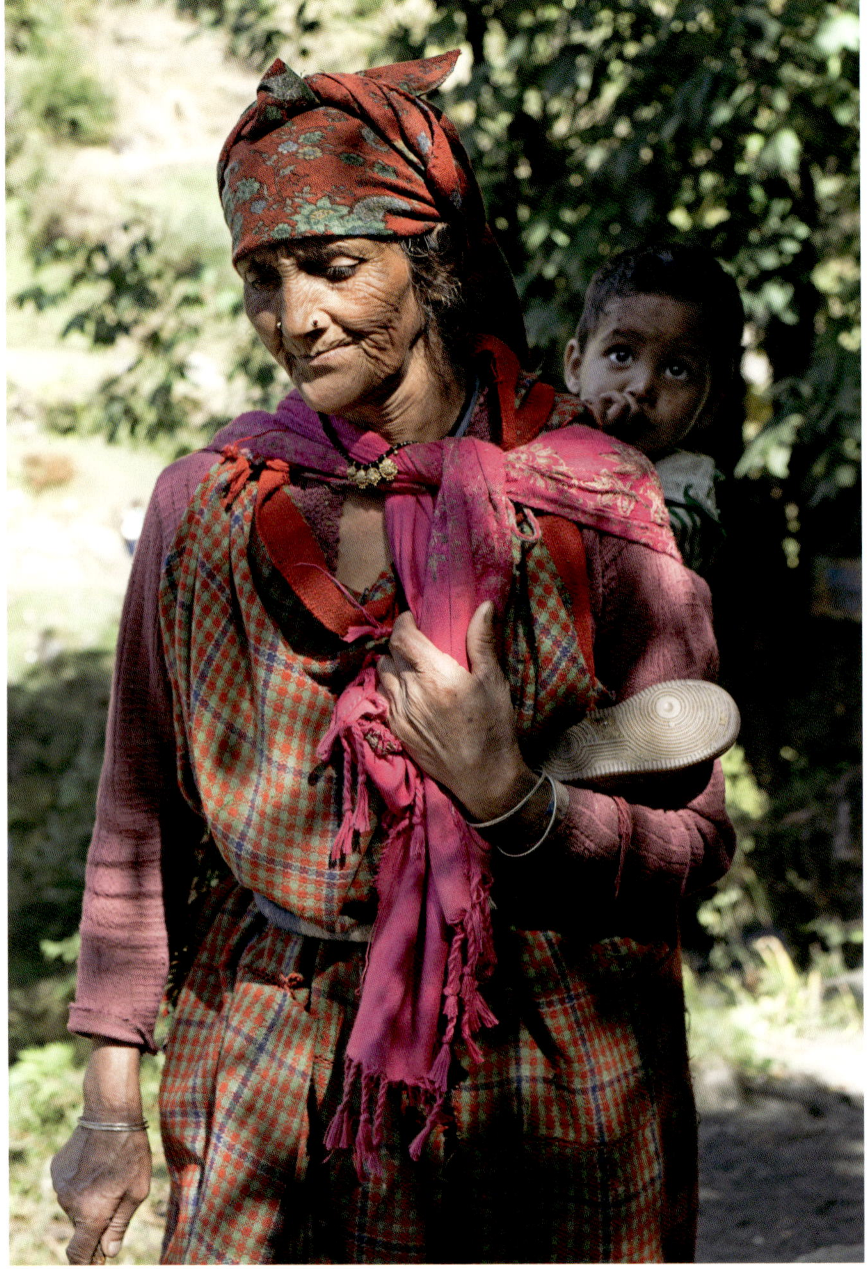

Grahan village

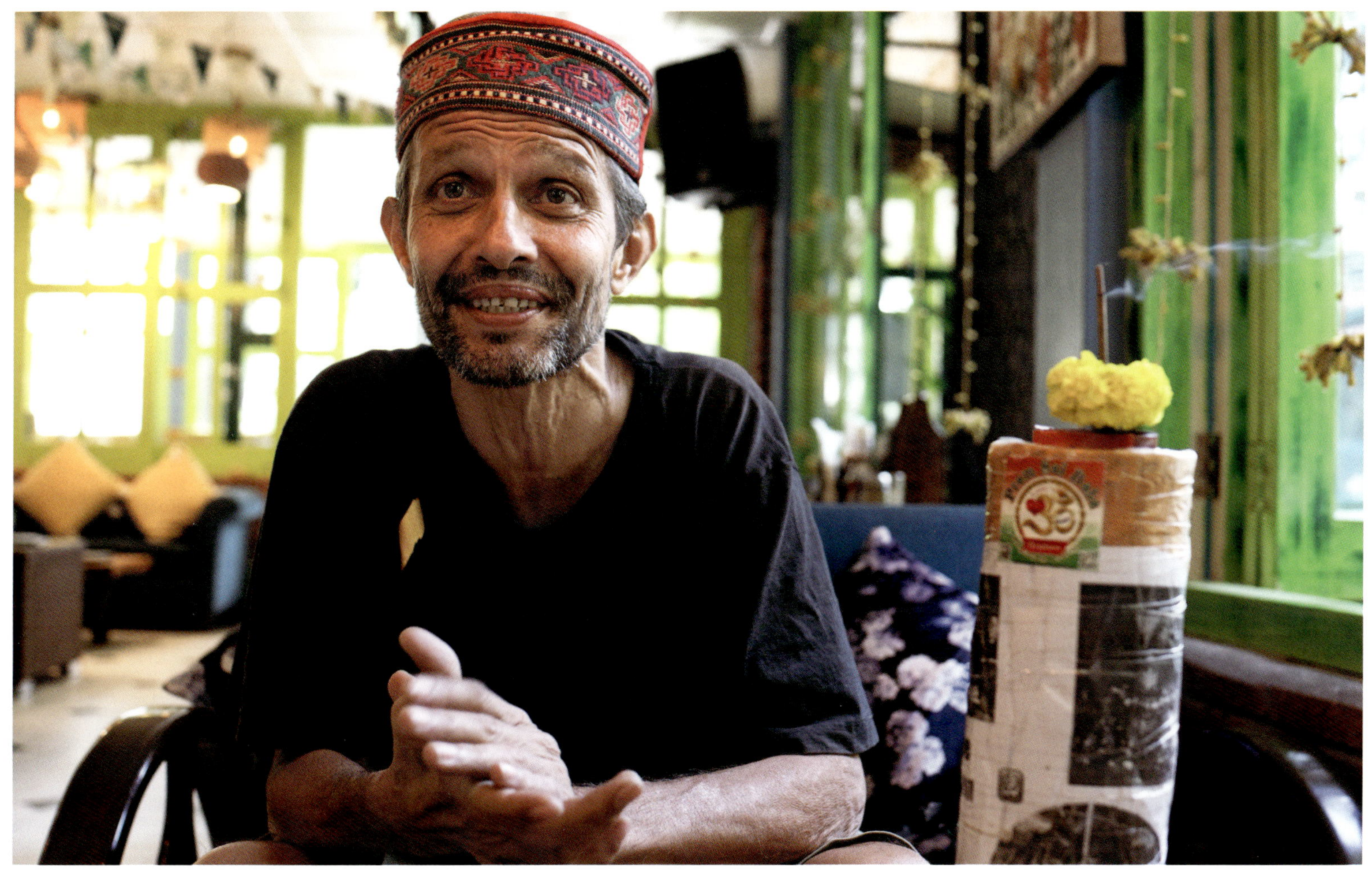

Raheem (Scotland), Kasol. Wearing the traditional embroidered cap of village men in the Parvati Valley, Raheem could easily be mistaken for a local person. Yet, as we talked and his background came up in a rapid-fire account, it was clear the valley was just the most recent stop in a whirlwind life of almost nonstop travel. He bicycled the length of Africa, studied with Shaolin monks in China, practiced martial arts in Kerala, and built dome houses in Nigeria. Raheem showed me a memoir he'd self-published entitled *Dance of the Zebra: Let Freedom Reign*. When I asked if he sold very many copies, he replied, "No. It's not for sale. I don't want to feed the monster."

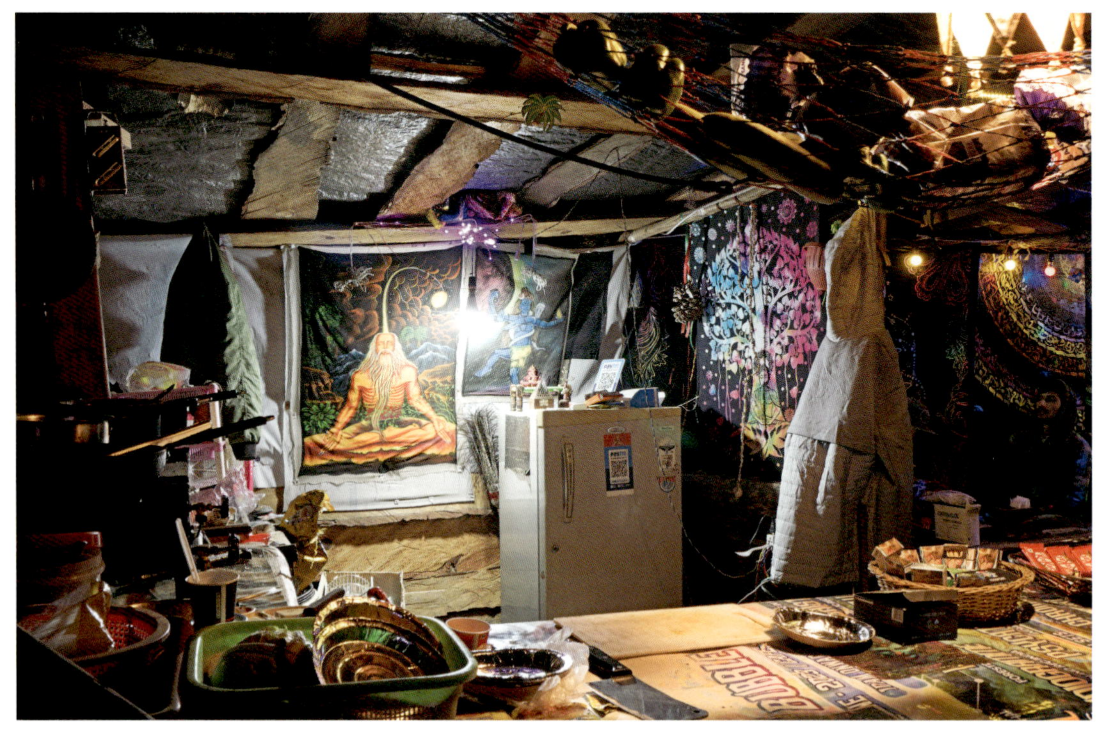

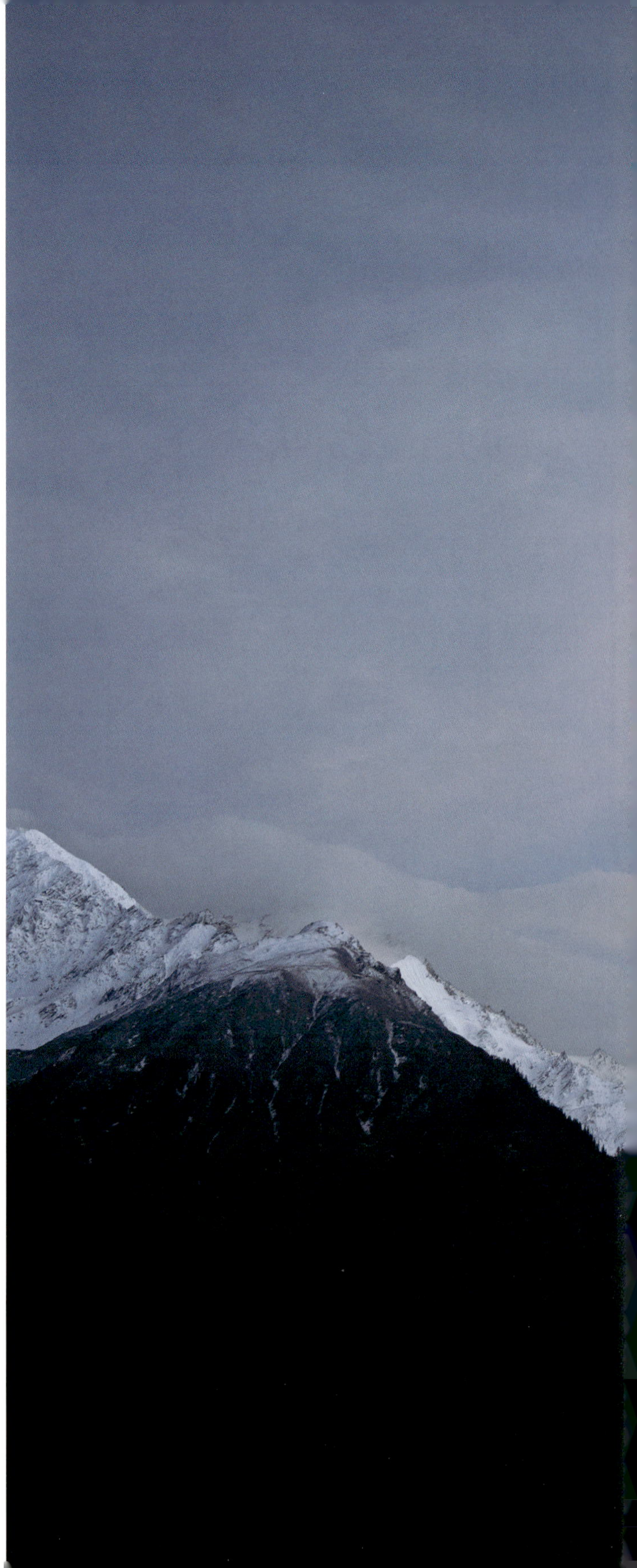

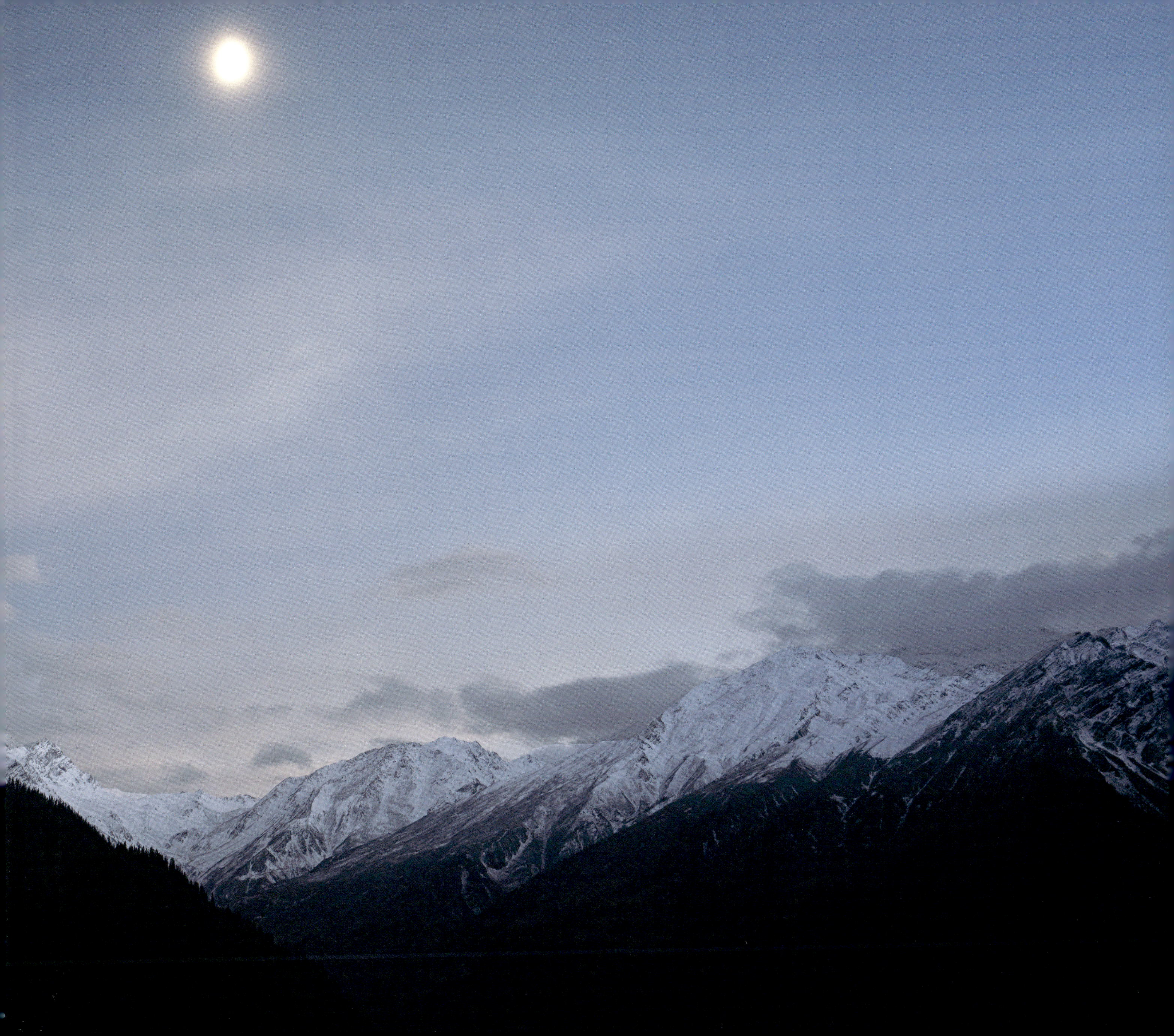

RECOMMENDED READINGS

A few recommended books for persons interested in reading more about the quest for spiritual enlightenment in India and adjoining regions:

Ian Baker, *The Heart of the World*
(Penguin Books, 2006).

Mick Brown, *The Nirvana Express*
(C. Hurst and Company, 2023).

Paul Brunton, *In Search of Secret India*
(Rider & Co., 1934).

Joseph Campbell, *The Power of Myth*
(Anchor, 1991).

Paolo Coelho, *Hippie*
(Knopf, 2018).

William Dalrymple, *Nine Lives*
(Vintage, 2011).

Ram Dass, *Be Here Now*
(Harmony, 1978).

Allen Ginsberg, *Indian Journals*
(Grove Press, 1996).

Hermann Hesse, *Sidhhartha*
(Simon and Brown, 2017).

Pico Iyer, *Video Nights in Kathmandu*
(Vintage, 1989).

Richard Jaffe, *Seeking Sakyumani*
(University of Chicago Press, 2019).

Rory MacLean, *Magic Bus*
(Penguin Books, 2007).

Somerset Maugham, *The Razor's Edge*
(Vintage, 2003).

Peter Matthiessen, *The Snow Leopard*
(Penguin Classics, 2008).

Gita Mehta, *Karma Cola*
(Vintage, 1994).

Matteo Pistono, *In the Shadow of the Buddha*
(Plume, 2012).

Harley Rustad, *Lost in the Valley of Death*
(Harper, 2022).

Colin Thubron, *To a Mountain in Tibet*
(Harper Perennial, 2012).

Paramahansa Yogananda, *Autobiography of a Yogi*
(Self Realization Fellowship, 1998).

ACKNOWLEDGEMENTS

One of the great joys of this project was the opportunity to meet so many fine young travelers from throughout the world. I'm grateful to them for offering their time with kindness and in a shared spirit of fun and discovery, and also for giving me permission to make and use the photographs that appear in this book. I came to see in them not just a past way of travel—the old Hippie Trail, a younger me, and so forth, but a way forward for all those persons who cherish the idea of having thoughtful and free-spirited adventures in the world.

Special thanks to David for sharing trails and meals of *dal-bhat* in the Himalayas; to Patrick, with whom I found communion among the rocks and boulders in Hampi; to Alejandro for his spirited companionship on the Ganges ghats; to Melanie and Andreas for inspiring conversations over coffee in the Parvati Valley; to Pinka (Spain) and Ato (Argentina) and their lovely children for sharing sunset views in Pushkar. I also want to thank (not in any particular order): Ben, Beth, Pamir, Ran, Thibault, Vinciane, Ganesh, Stine, Caroline, Davide, Molly, Tiago, Chandra, Romi, Migu, Luca, Ricarda, Sheru, Veronica, Costa, Siri, Kira, Alex, Ksenia, Sergey, Tabak, Jinn Tony, Scott, Alona, Deej Rasta, Ilai, Oreal, Mary, Giulia, Carolina, Sahil, Jada, Nipun, Djane, Majid, Elee, Anna, Nik, Sac, Robert, Alan, Raj, Paul, Herculis, Dev, Rudra, Thakur, Shahar, Pierre, Daniel, Silvina, Satya, and Raheem.

For logistical support, thanks to Rajesh (a fine driver on many awful roads); the staff at the Alfonso Guesthouse, Dr. Francesca (who fixed my broken tooth); Prakash; Kardar; Sharma, Gautam, and Shaitan. For geographic insights and travel advice: Robbie and Kapil. The genesis for this project goes back to 1975 and my initial journey on the Hippie Trail, and so a special thanks to Craig for his companionship on that very first international adventure.

Great gratitude goes to Pico Iyer for writing the foreword. His insightful words have always been warm companions during various travels; I'm honored that he wrote a few new ones for this book. Special thanks goes to Gordon Goff for taking on the project, and to my editor Jake Anderson for ushering it through to completion. As ever, my greatest gratitude goes to my wife Jennifer, who accompanies me on some of my travels and tends the home fire when I go off on my own.